CHINA'S THRILLING SAGA *of* NEGOTIABLE INSTRUMENTS

www.royalcollins.com

CHINA'S THRILLING SAGA *of* NEGOTIABLE INSTRUMENTS

Editor in Chief: XIAO XIAOHE
Deputy Editor in Chief: ZHAO WEIZHE
Translator: LUO ZHONGWU

Books Beyond Boundaries
ROYAL COLLINS

China's Thrilling Saga of Negotiable Instruments

Editor in Chief: Xiao Xiaohe
Deputy Editor in Chief: Zhao Weizhe
Translator: Luo Zhongwu

First published in 2025 by Royal Collins Publishing Group Inc.
Groupe Publication Royal Collins Inc.
550-555 boul. René-Lévesque O Montréal (Québec) H2Z1B1 Canada

10 9 8 7 6 5 4 3 2 1

ISBN: 978-1-4878-1334-5

To find out more about our publications, please visit www.royalcollins.com.

Editorial Board

Contents

Part Three

BILLS SINCE THE FOUNDING OF THE PEOPLE'S REPUBLIC OF CHINA

Preface

After more than four decades of reform and opening up, China's bill market has undergone dramatic changes. Bills have evolved into sophisticated financial credit instruments with multiple functions—exchange, payment, settlement, financing, regulation, investment, and trading. They play a vital role in promoting the development of the real economy, especially small and medium-sized enterprises (SMEs), as well as advancing green finance and enterprise credit. Moreover, bills are crucial in driving the supply-side structural reform of finance and transmitting monetary policies.

China's bill market has evolved significantly over the past four decades. First, the market size has expanded remarkably. Amid swift economic development following the start of the reform and opening up in 1978, China's bill market has gone through three stages: initial exploration, rapid growth, and standardized development, with consistent expansion throughout. According to data, the national bill acceptance amount in 1995 was 242.4 billion yuan, with a discount amount of 141.2 billion yuan and a national rediscount balance of just 32 billion yuan at the end of that year. Fast forward to 2021, the figures are staggering—the national bill acceptance amount reached 24.16 trillion yuan (22.2% of GDP), the endorsement amount hit 56.56 trillion yuan, and the discount amount rose to 15.02 trillion yuan (13% of GDP). Perhaps most impressively, the rediscount balance surged to 590.3 billion yuan. These numbers unequivocally demonstrate the bill market's remarkable growth.

Second, market participant diversity has increased significantly. During the 1980s and 1990s, the fledgling bill market was dominated by the People's Bank of China (PBC), state-owned banks, and a handful of large state-owned enterprises. To enhance bill management expertise, specialized institutions were gradually established. Post-2010, the market underwent a surge of innovation, driven by abundant funds, comprehensive operations, and the rise of internet finance. This led to an influx of financial enterprises and urban commercial banks. Trust companies, securities firms, and even individual investors gained indirect access to the market. Private bill intermediaries also became increasingly active. In response to growing market complexity and the need for regulation, Shanghai Commercial Paper Exchange Company Ltd. was established in 2016.

Third, the institutional system has undergone gradual improvements. A series of laws, regulations, and departmental rules have been introduced, clarifying the development path for China's bill market and promoting its systematic enhancement. These include the *Interim Measures for the Acceptance and Discount of Commercial Bills*, *Trial Measures for Rediscounting of the People's Bank of China*, *Measures for Bank Settlement*, and *The Negotiable Instrument Law of the People's Republic of China* (hereafter referred to as *The Negotiable Instrument Law of the PRC*). Equally significant are *Implementing Measures for the Administration of Negotiable Instruments*, *Measures for Payment and Settlement*, and *Measures for the Administration of Acceptance, Discount, and Rediscount of Commercial Drafts*. *General Provisions on Lending*, *Measures for the Administration of Electronic Commercial Bill Business*, *A Notice on Regulating and Promoting the Development of Electronic Commercial Bill Business*, and *Measures for the Administration of Bill Trading* have also been integral to this progress.

Fourth, technological advancements have revolutionized the bill market. The introduction of bill IT systems and electronic bills has fundamentally altered market operations. Cutting-edge technologies—big data, cloud computing, AI, and blockchain—now serve as powerful catalysts for innovation in this sector. In a significant move to boost efficiency and user experience, Shanghai Commercial Paper Exchange Company Ltd. overhauled the Electronic Commercial Draft System (ECDS) and Commercial Paper Exchange System (CPES) in May 2021. They unveiled a next-generation bill business system capable of managing the entire life cycle of bill functions. This sophisticated system is set to drive future innovations and significantly enhance risk management in the bill market.

Fifth, bill innovations are constantly emerging. In the early 2000s, these innovations focused on enhancing and combining traditional practices. The acceptance business spawned services like commercial bill guarantees, pledge invoicing, bill splitting, and bill exchange. Discount-based operations introduced commercial bill guarantee discounts, bill package purchases, on-demand discount credit, third-party guarantee discounts, and repurchase discounts. The interbank discount business developed models such as bill asset management bridging, bank agency repurchase bridging, and bill agency holding. Concurrently, value-added services emerged, including bill consulting, brokerage, authentication, and bill pooling.

After 2009, ample funding, financial institutions' comprehensive development, the ECDS launch, and the surge of internet finance created fertile ground for bill innovation. This period saw the introduction of bill wealth management, bill asset management, and bill asset-backed securities (ABS). Trading models like maturity mismatch, buying back for sale, and sale and repurchase became widespread in bill operations. Since 2016, the Shanghai Commercial Paper Exchange Company Ltd. has spearheaded bill innovation, introducing products such as the Bill Payment Pass, the Discount Pass, standardized bills, and supply chain bills. The exchange's release of bill yield curves, coupled with the Shanghai Clearing House's standardized bill indices, has continually improved the bill user experience and deepened the multifaceted functionality of bills.

Sixth, the marketization of bill interest rates has made significant strides. Over the past four decades, interest rates in the bill market have gradually shed administrative controls. They've evolved through four distinct pricing stages: first based on loan rates, then rediscount rates, followed by Shibor, and now bill yield curves. Today, these rates stand as one of China's most market-driven interest rate mechanisms.

Seventh, bill risks are effectively managed. Regulatory authorities have issued numerous documents based on market trends and risk control experience to prevent and control these risks. They've strengthened risk prevention systems, ensuring quality control at the top level. The Shanghai Commercial Paper Exchange Company Ltd.'s establishment promotes the creation of a unified national bill trading market. This exchange allows for more extensive market information collection, enabling unified supervision of all market entities, products, and businesses. This helps establish a risk quantification management model that identifies, measures, and monitors bill risks in real-time. The promotion of electronic bills has guided the development of IT systems for bills, managing operational and ethical risks such as counterfeit or altered bills, theft of inventory bills, and substituting genuine bills with counterfeit ones. By leveraging financial technology—including big data, cloud computing, AI, and blockchain—more precise judgments can be made on market interest rate and situational changes, ensuring more effective market risk control.

Last, applied theoretical research has yielded significant results. The establishment of the Shanghai Commercial Paper Exchange Company Ltd. in 2016 marked a turning point, bringing fundamental changes to China's bill market and system. This period saw the emergence of key research institutions, including Joint Institute for Commercial Paper of JUFE and BOJJ, the Bill Professional Committee of Jiangxi Financial Society, the China Bill Research Center, and the Cloud Bill Research Center at Central University of Finance and Economics. These institutions have been instrumental in advancing bill theory in China. Through their diverse activities—research projects, essay competitions, seminars, and high-level forums—they have created a vibrant research environment, offering ongoing intellectual support for the development of the bill market.

In line with the country's push for structural reform in the financial sector, embracing new development concepts, accelerating the establishment of a dual-circulation development pattern, and promoting high-quality economic growth, the Chinese bill market will hasten its reform and opening up. The focus will be on enhancing legal frameworks and infrastructure, fostering innovation in institutional mechanisms, harnessing financial technology, and creating cutting-edge platforms. The market will also prioritize the growth of commercial acceptance bills, implement risk prevention measures, and advance bill digitization, standardization, trading, internationalization, and popularization. These efforts aim to bolster the real economy, particularly benefiting SMEs.

To chart a successful course for the future, understanding the historical development of bills is crucial. In 2020, Joint Institute for Commercial Paper of JUFE and BOJJ published

A History of Negotiable Instruments—China's pioneering comprehensive work on bill history. This groundbreaking book paved the way for systematic research in the field. It explores bills in their narrow sense, covering promissory notes, checks, and bills of exchange. Organized chronologically, each chapter of the book is structured into four parts: historical context, bill market development, evolution of bill systems, and the functional role of bills. Through this approach, the book offers a systematic narrative of how Chinese bills have evolved over time.

In December 2020, the book earned recognition as one of the top 12 economic history books by the China Economic Education and Research Network, underscoring its significance in bill history research. However, due to time constraints, limited resources, and inexperience, the book faced challenges such as inadequate focus on bill development, incomplete historical narratives, weak overall continuity, unclear organization, and a lack of engaging storytelling. To address these issues, Joint Institute for Commercial Paper of JUFE and BOJJ dedicated over a year to planning improvements. The institute collaborated with some original team members, experts in bill historical materials, and new master's students specializing in the field. Together, they refined the writing approach, gathered additional materials, sharpened the focus on Chinese bill development history, and linked it with current market trends. This concerted effort culminated in the revised edition, *China's Thrilling Saga of Negotiable Instruments*.

The revised edition distinguishes itself from its predecessor through its laser focus on bills, coherent narrative structure, engaging storytelling, and robust summarization. The book meticulously traces the historical evolution of Chinese bills, omitting foreign bills. It follows a chronological order of dynasties, with slight modifications to the developmental phases of bills in ancient China, the late Qing era, the Republic of China period, and post-1949 China. Each section spotlights crucial bills, events, institutions, and documents, emphasizing bill-related content while briefly touching on peripheral information. This approach equips readers with a comprehensive understanding of bills.

The book's logical structure shines through its chapter-opening overviews, which encapsulate the bill development process against the backdrop of historical context, market dynamics, and institutional evolution. It elucidates the developmental logic of bills and pivotal events. Every section begins with a bridging passage that links to both preceding and subsequent chapters, summarizing content and highlighting developmental patterns. These summaries deftly sketch the historical trajectory of Chinese bills, illustrating their gradual evolution through significant milestones.

This book boasts a meticulously structured format, with each section progressing from historical context to main content and subsequent impact, maintaining a laser focus on bills throughout. The sections are tightly interconnected, with each chapter concluding with a summary that illuminates the role of bills in social, economic, credit, and financial spheres across different eras. Embracing a narrative approach, the book weaves in a richer tapestry of historical materials, bill samples, and anecdotes compared to its predecessor. It's further enriched with a wealth of rare bill images, offering history buffs a more immersive reading experience. The book doesn't just recount the history of Chinese bills; it caps off with a thought-provoking final chapter. This chapter not only traces the evolution of bill functions but also distills centuries of lessons from bill development. It then casts an eye to the future, pondering the trajectory of China's bill market and proposing potential avenues for growth.

In terms of structure, this book is divided into three parts: bills from ancient China and the late Qing Dynasty, bills from the Republic of China period, and bills since the founding of the People's Republic of China (PRC). The first part follows a chronological order, while the second and third parts are organized into stages, reflecting the developmental characteristics of the bill market. The book concludes with a dedicated chapter for reflection.

The first part, focusing on bills in ancient China and the late Qing Dynasty, is structured chronologically, dedicating each chapter to a historical dynasty. These chapters explore the evolution of ancient bills, introducing key bills, institutions, and systems of each era. The second and third parts, focusing on the Republic of China period and the era since the founding of the PRC, respectively, are organized around significant events. In these latter parts, each chapter is titled after crucial events, institutions, or documents that shaped the development of the bill market.

The contributors to this work were as follows: Cai Zhenxiang authored the first part, and Li Ziwei penned the second part. For the third part, Peng Jing wrote the sixth chapter, while Zhao Siyan and Gan Dejian collaborated on the seventh chapter. Chen Chen authored both the eighth and ninth chapters. The tenth chapter was split between Cai Zhenxiang (first section) and Li Ziwei (second section). Guo Kai supplied sample bills and their accompanying text. During the writing process, Pan Yu, Chen Yueming, and Huang Shenhui also provided valuable materials.

This book primarily targets bill regulators, bill line managers of financial institutions, practitioners, corporate finance personnel, professional researchers, college educators, and students. It's also a valuable resource for anyone curious about bills. Due to time constraints, limited resources, and our own inexperience, this book may have shortcomings. We warmly invite readers to offer constructive criticism and corrections. We also welcome fellow enthusiasts of bill history to join us in further research and discussion.

In compiling this book, we drew upon a wealth of literature from numerous experts and scholars. Zhao Weizhe oversaw the reprinting and English publication process. We extend our heartfelt gratitude to the Bank of Jiujiang, Jiangxi University of Finance and Economics, and China Financial Publishing House for their substantial support. Their contributions have been invaluable to this project.

THE EDITORIAL BOARD

PART ONE

BILLS IN ANCIENT CHINA AND THE LATE QING DYNASTY

CHAPTER ONE

Bills from the Zhou Dynasty to the Ming Dynasty

For thousands of years, the evolution of history has seen the continuous development of the commercial economy and credit, laying the groundwork for the growth of bills. These elements have mutually fostered each other's progress. From the Zhou Dynasty (1046–256 BCE) onward, the commercial economy under the enfeoffment system began to develop, and borrowing and lending practices emerged, sparking the need for proof of commercial transactions and loans. The precursors of bills, including *zhiji* (质剂),[1] *fubie* (傅别),[2] and *shuqi* (书契),[3] were created and utilized in a binary system. These documents could serve as proof of debt, gifting, buying, and selling, and could also be used in official rulings. This marked the beginning of using documents as transaction and loan vouchers, paving the way for the emergence of bills.

During the Tang Dynasty (618–907), following the eras of prosperity like the "Prosperity of Zhenguan" era and "Kaiyuan Heyday Period," the commercial economy saw unprecedented development. Markets thrived, cross-regional trade boomed, and commercial credit advanced. Deposits emerged, and large cross-regional businesses sprouted. The rise of Buddhism, implementation of the two-tax law, and the "policy prohibiting private minting, use, or circulation of currency" led to a copper coin shortage and restricted circulation. This sparked the creation of China's first bill—*feiqian* (飞钱),[4] akin to modern bills of exchange, leading to the birth of bill exchange functions. Its business model split into official and private operations. Used for cross-regional remittances, *feiqian* was the public's response to the "currency prohibition" policy. Though swiftly banned by the government, the prohibition proved ineffective. The government then attempted to monopolize *feiqian* operations to maintain full control over currency issuance. Yet, private *feiqian* persisted covertly, defying complete suppression. Additionally, the Tang Dynasty witnessed the emergence of *shutie* (书帖)—the precursor to checks—used for withdrawals and transfers.

During the Song Dynasty (960–1279), the commercial economy experienced further growth, reaching its zenith in ancient Chinese history. The surge in cross-border trade, prolonged warfare, and widespread hoarding of copper coins by the populace led to the introduction of *jiaozi* (交子) and *huizi* (会子). These new financial instruments were based on *bianhuan* (便换), *jiaoyin* (交引), and *yanyin* (盐引), which had been introduced during the Northern Song Dynasty (960–1127). This marked a significant evolution in negotiable instruments. The adoption of the "payable to the bearer" mechanism greatly enhanced the circulation of these instruments. Furthermore, *jiaozi* spearheaded beneficial innovations in standardized form, total issuance amount, circulation period management, reserve requirements, installment systems, and trade-in procedures.

Jiaozi first gained popularity in the Sichuan region. Small shops initially issued it to facilitate transactions, followed by sixteen larger establishments. As these shops' fortunes waned, *jiaozi* became non-exchangeable, triggering local redemption crises and frequent lawsuits. The government's intervention, backed by its credit, swiftly normalized issuance. Initially, the government maintained traditional issuance methods. However, the Northern Song Dynasty, burdened by prolonged wars and hefty expenditures, altered its approach. To ease the financial strain, they levied substantial seigniorage and promoted *jiaozi* as national paper currency, officially transforming it into a formal tender. Ultimately, severe over-issuance led to *jiaozi*'s significant devaluation, coinciding with the Northern Song's economic decline. The commercial economy of the Ming Dynasty (1368–1644), initially suppressed, gradually rebounded. Yet, credit development stagnated. Money houses emerged but primarily focused on currency exchange. Consequently, negotiable instruments saw little advancement. Notably, the late Ming's *huipiao* (会票), incorporating features from previous dynasties' instruments, laid groundwork for its widespread use in the Qing Dynasty (1644–1911).

SECTION I

Bills in the Zhou Dynasty

During the Zhou Dynasty, the flourishing commercial economy and evolving credit systems gave rise to contractual agreements. Two primary methods emerged for recording these contracts: grand *yueji* (约剂) and small *yueji*. Grand *yueji*, typically inscribed on large bronze vessels, were reserved for significant events such as national sacrifices and royal rewards. In contrast, small *yueji* served to document more mundane affairs. *Zhiji*, *fubie*, and *shuqi*—which functioned as proof of debt, gifting, and commercial transactions—can be considered the embryonic forms of negotiable instruments.

I. Basic Conditions for the Emergence of Early Bills

The earliest forms of bills in China can be traced back to the Zhou Dynasty. While these early forms differed significantly from modern bills, they already embodied the fundamental principles of bills as credit carriers. Essentially, they represented an early prototype—or more accurately, they should be considered contracts and credentials.

Early forms of bills during the Zhou Dynasty emerged from specific historical conditions. The development of a commercial economy and credit systems were crucial factors. In terms of governance, the Zhou Dynasty implemented a system of enfeoffment, where the king distributed land, population, and other resources to nobles and high-ranking officials. These nobles and officials wielded significant authority over their territories and enjoyed hereditary inheritance rights, leading to independent economic units in each region. Initially, commercial transactions primarily occurred within these individual economies. However, as the square-fields system[5] disintegrated, the land was freed from imperial and noble control, entering the market and increasing commercial activities. The practice of borrowing and lending also emerged during this period, with China's earliest lending institution, *quanfu* (泉府), appearing. This institution played a key role in regulating the private economy and maintaining social order. The Zhou Dynasty government provided for its people through two types of loans: interest-bearing and interest-free. These loans, typically offered in kind, supplied daily necessities. Interestingly, interest was usually repaid in real estate rather than in goods or currency.

Commercial documents began to appear to provide proof in transactions and lending relationships, as well as to handle disputes. They became the primary vouchers for these activities. Historical records reveal insights into ancient commercial markets. One ancient book states: "In the past, our late ruler Duke Huan and merchants, both from the Zhou Dynasty, worked together and helped each other. They braved obstacles, developed this land, and then coexisted. At that time, they made an oath to keep their promises to each other. The oath stated: 'I will not betray you, and I will not forcefully take away your interests. If you have a lucrative market, precious treasures, or assets, I will not interfere.' It is through this oath and mutual trust that we have been able to protect each other until today."[6] This commercial covenant demonstrates a system of mutual protection. In these markets, merchants typically used documents for contracts. As the commercial economy grew, the government strengthened its oversight of market transactions. *The Rites of Zhou* mentions that during the Western Zhou Dynasty (1046–771 BCE), specialized officials called "*sishi*" (司士) managed the market, "*xushi*" (胥师) verified goods' authenticity, "*jiashi*" (贾师) managed prices, "*sibao*" (司虣) maintained order, and "*zhiren*" (质人) oversaw measurements.[7] The development of writing was also crucial for the emergence of proto-bills like *zhiji*, *fubie*, and *shuqi*.

II. *Zhiji*, *Fubie*, and *Shuqi*: Bill Prototypes

1. *Zhiji*, *Fubie*, and *Shuqi*

Historical records indicate that during the Zhou Dynasty, contracts were primarily recorded using two methods: grand *yueji* and small *yueji*. Grand *yueji*, closely associated with "rituals," was typically employed for significant events such as national sacrifices and royal rewards. It fulfilled the nobility's need to record, verify, and preserve treaties long-term, with inscriptions made on large vessels. Consequently, the content of grand *yueji* differs substantially from modern transaction records, with only a small portion aligning with contemporary contractual concepts. Grand *yueji* often involved valuable property like land and had a complex establishment process. Usually, one party would first petition a noble, who would then verify the request and dispatch an officer to conduct a survey. As grand *yueji* typically documented important national events, their creation involved a formal signing ceremony with a joint oath among the relevant parties. This oath acted as a guarantee, imbued with religious mystique. For production, artisans used knives and brushes to inscribe the text on bronze ware. According to *The Rites of Zhou*, the government was responsible for preserving these contracts, with multiple copies kept in several official institutions—a practice known as "*dian*" (典, pawn).[8]

Small *yueji*, unlike grand *yueji*, typically documented minor events such as folk activities and transactions. Their content aligned more closely with modern contractual concepts. *Zhiji*, *fubie*, and *shuqi* were classic examples of the Zhou Dynasty's small *yueji*. Due to lower preservation requirements, small *yueji* often used bamboo slips—materials with simple production processes and relatively low-cost. According to *The Rites of Zhou · Heavenly Official Governing Government Decrees*, *zhiji*, *fubie*, and *shuqi* of the Zhou Dynasty seemingly corresponded to three transaction types: debt claiming, giving, and buying and selling, respectively. However, this interpretation lacks substantial historical evidence, and it's questionable whether contracts had evolved to such a clear, standardized level at that time.

Though all three were contracts in essence, they differed significantly in form. Qing Dynasty scholar Sun Yirang (1848–1908) provided a detailed analysis in *Rectified Interpretation of the Book of Rites*, stating: "*Zhiji*, *fubie*, and *shuqi* were all written agreements. For *fubie*, a contract was handwritten on bamboo slips or silk, then cut in half, with each party keeping one half. *Zhiji* involved cutting the bamboo slips in half, but keeping the characters intact. *Shuqi* were written on two separate slips, each party holding one complete copy."

Other historical records offer similar explanations. "In *Huainanzi · Annotations*, Eastern Han Dynasty (25–220) scholar Gao You noted that '*fu*' [傅] was explained as 'to document.' *The Guangyaan*, an early 3rd-century Chinese dictionary, defines '*bie*' [别] as 'to divide,' indicating separation. This terminology refers to the practice of clearly documenting the repayment date and interest amount when borrowing and lending. Both parties would retain part of this document as evidence, much like modern contracts or agreements."[9]

The three methods were used as follows:

- *Fubie.* Transaction details were written on one side of a bamboo slip, which was then divided for both parties to keep. Verification involved matching the two halves.
- *Zhiji.* Two identical documents were written on government-issued bamboo slips, then divided, with each party holding a complete document. *Zhiji* held more authority as it was supervised by a "guarantor" (a government official), serving as legal proof. It came in two types: long rolls for large transactions (e.g., land deals) and short rolls for small transactions (e.g., daily goods).

- *Shuqi.* Two identical documents were written on separate bamboo slips, with each party keeping one—similar to modern contracts.[10]

Zhou Dynasty contracts typically included the signing time and place, parties' names, subject matter, witnesses, and an oath serving as a religiously significant guarantee. Essentially, these documents represented creditor-debtor relationships. As long as *zhiji*, *fubie*, and *shuqi* reflected this relationship and served as vouchers for debt settlement, they can be considered early forms of bills in a broader sense.

2. The Relationship Between Contracts and Bills

In the evolution of contracts, the earliest forms were imprinted bamboo or wood pieces, serving as reminders for parties to fulfill their obligations. These agreements were initially verbal. During the Zhou Dynasty, as the economy grew and writing spread, simple contract terms began to be etched onto bamboo and wood chips, marking the shift from oral to written contracts. *Zhiji*, *fubie*, and *shuqi* exemplified this transition. The Han Dynasty (202 BCE–220 CE) introduced a new contract form: two wooden boards with identical text, where parties or guarantors would draw their fingers together, creating a contract voucher—a precursor to the Tang Dynasty's "finger-drawing voucher." After the Eastern Han Dynasty, paper replaced bamboo and wood for contracts. The Sixteen Kingdoms period (304–439) saw the emergence of "contracts," initially writing "同" where bamboo slips met, later using "和同" (a homophone of "合同" [contract]), and sometimes replacing these with auspicious phrases. The Tang Dynasty standardized contract formats and wording. In the Southern Song Dynasty (1127–1279), all valid contracts required a government stamp; otherwise, they were considered blank, leading to more formal, standardized contracts. Contract use expanded in the Ming Dynasty, with greater variety. The Qing Dynasty saw further complexity in property rights, resulting in diverse contract forms and subjects, including bills of lading and pawn tickets. Early to mid-Qing contracts, though privately written, required a government-issued attachment. Later, officially stamped paper was used, with private contracts still allowed to affix the attachment. Finally, a stamp duty was introduced, making the stamp the basis for a deed's legal validity.[11]

Contracts and bills share numerous similarities while also exhibiting significant differences. Both are products of commercial economic development, evolving in content and form as commerce grows. The Zhou Dynasty's *zhiji*, *fubie*, and *shuqi* were essentially early forms of contracts. Their concepts inspired the creation of bills and marked the beginning of using documents as transaction vouchers. These documents partially replaced the function of bills as withdrawal vouchers before the latter's appearance. *Feiqian*, the first truly significant bill in Chinese history emerging in the Tang Dynasty, inherited and improved upon these earlier contracts.

Contracts reflect the specific content of commercial transactions, while bills are issued based on contract content, whether oral or written. The primary distinction between contracts and bills lies in their content and form. Contracts prioritize transaction standardization, while bills emphasize convenience. Generally, contracts cannot be transferred arbitrarily, whereas bills, at a certain stage of development, can be paid to the bearer. Moreover, bills function as financial instruments, while contracts are commercial documents—a fundamental difference between the two.

SECTION 2

Bills in the Tang Dynasty

After centuries of development since the Zhou Dynasty, the Tang Dynasty saw significant advancements in commercial economy and credit systems. The government and large commercial shops leveraged cross-regional operations and credit, giving rise to *feiqian*—an instrument for cross-regional exchange. As the precursor to bills of exchange, *feiqian* marked the formal introduction of such instruments in China. Despite facing multiple prohibitions, *feiqian* persisted, never entirely restricted. It played a pivotal role in China's financial history by facilitating the transition from physical to bill credit. Additionally, the Tang Dynasty witnessed the emergence of *shutie*, precursors to modern checks, which could be used for withdrawals and transfers. However, both *feiqian* and *shutie* still employed a registered method, requiring individuals to withdraw funds in person. This limitation prevented them from achieving the basic conditions necessary for large-scale circulation.

I. Historical Conditions for the Emergence of *Feiqian*

The thriving commercial economy of the Tang Dynasty paved the way for the emergence of *feiqian*. With its vast territory and well-developed transportation networks, the Tang Dynasty saw remarkable growth in agriculture, handicrafts, and commerce during the "Prosperity of Zhenguan" era and "Kaiyuan Heyday Period." This led to a flourishing and stable society for an extended period. In the mid to late Tang Dynasty, the implementation of the two-tax system triggered the collapse of the equal-fields system, further liberating the economy. As individual small peasants became less dependent, the traditional commodity economy gained vigor, boosting market vitality. The demise of the equal-fields system sparked nationwide commerce, with a wide array of agricultural and handicraft products flooding the market.

The Tang Dynasty fostered a sophisticated financial market and thriving cross-regional trade, evidenced by the constant stream of merchants and the proliferation of inns and taverns along trade routes. An account vividly illustrates this: "From Bianzhou in the east to Qizhou in the west, shops and taverns flanked the roads, serving travelers exquisite wines and sumptuous fare. Each inn offered donkeys for hire—dubbed 'post road donkeys'—enabling guests to cover vast distances swiftly. This network of establishments stretched southward to Jingzhou and Xiangyang, northward to Taiyuan and Fanyang, and westward to Sichuan and Liangfu, catering to merchants and tourists alike. Astonishingly, these travelers traversed thousands of miles without even carrying small weapons for protection."[12] The burgeoning merchant class and increasing commercial taxation necessitated more efficient cross-regional settlements. As transporting large quantities of copper coins across regions proved both perilous and impractical, the stage was set for the advent of *feiqian*, which built upon the legacy of *zhiji*.

The "money shortage," leading to deflation and price decline, was a significant economic challenge in the mid to late Tang Dynasty. This issue, stemming from a lack of copper coins, was rare before but persisted throughout the Tang era. In 732, Emperor Xuanzong's edict highlighted the severity of the problem: "Various commodities—such as silk, cloth, and groceries—should be acceptable as payment in transactions. However, I have been informed that merchants within the markets are insisting upon monetary payments exclusively, a practice I deem unjust and detrimental. I hereby decree that all establishments engaged in trade shall henceforth accept both currency and goods of equivalent value as legitimate means of payment. Any parties found in violation of this edict shall be subject to appropriate legal sanctions."

Two main factors contributed to this shortage. From the demand side, the Tang Dynasty saw Buddhism's peak, with rulers, especially Emperor Gaozong and Empress Wu Zetian, strongly promoting it. This led to Buddhism's ascendancy over Confucianism and Taoism, resulting in a surge in Buddha statue casting—a copper-intensive process that diverted metal from coin production. Moreover, in 780, the Tang Dynasty implemented the two-tax law, shifting state taxation from goods to monetary collection twice yearly. This change further strained the copper coin supply, intensifying the "money shortage." From the supply side, the shortage of copper coins led to deflation. As money became more valuable and goods less so, wealthy merchants began hoarding large amounts of currency. The widespread practice of melting copper coins to cast copper wares further exacerbated the coin shortage. To address this money shortage, the Tang Dynasty government implemented policies prohibiting currency outflow and banning the melting of copper for casting wares. The "Food and Commodity Annals" in *The Old Book of Tang* notes: "At the beginning of the Zhenyuan period of Emperor Dezong's rule, copper coins were prohibited from leaving Luoguan and Sanguan passes. Zhang Pang, the salt and iron envoy, even appealed to the emperor, requesting a ban on the use of copper casting tools in the Yangtze River and the Huaihe River basins." *The New Book of Tang* adds: "Emperor Xianzong reinstated the ban on copper wares due to money scarcity." Both measures aimed to increase the domestic supply of copper coins, but the ban on copper coin outflow severely hampered cross-regional trade. As the Tang Dynasty's military governors gained power, *feiqian* emerged as a potent response to the "money prohibition" policy.[13]

The rapid growth of commercial credit in the Tang Dynasty, the rise of large cross-regional trading firms, and the widespread adoption of papermaking technology catalyzed the creation of *feiqian*. Bills were fundamentally based on credit, relying on mutual trust between parties. This trust allowed *feiqian* users to confidently deposit money with issuing institutions and withdraw it elsewhere. The Tang Dynasty gradually fostered a robust commercial credit environment, evidenced by merchants' adherence to contracts and the emergence of prepayment and credit sales. The use of *feiqian* depended on commercial credit between parties and could only exist once credit practices had sufficiently matured. During this period, deposit services emerged, with counter shops and large stores managing these operations. As the public increasingly embraced the concept of deposits, the credit industry flourished. The Tang Dynasty also saw the rise of large cross-regional trading firms, which later became key players in private *feiqian* exchange operations. Their emergence laid the groundwork for cross-regional transactions. On the technological front, *feiqian* utilized paper materials, with the advancement and spread of papermaking techniques facilitating its widespread adoption.

II. Use of *Feiqian*

Scholars generally agree that *feiqian* emerged during the Yuanhe period (806–820) of Emperor Xianzong's rule. *Feiqian* operations were either official or private. In the Tang Dynasty, each Dao (道, the highest local administrative unit) maintained a liaison office in the capital. These offices facilitated local-capital communication and transferred local revenue to the central government, moving money and goods from local areas to the capital. Conversely, merchants from various regions needed to transport their earnings back from the capital after selling goods there. This two-way flow of funds set the stage for the emergence of *feiqian*. Typically, merchants using *feiqian* would deposit money at the liaison offices for exchange. The offices then issued a "public receipt" split into two parts: one for the merchants and one sent to the local government. Upon return, the merchants could collect their money by presenting their half of the document to match the government's half. *Feiqian* was paper-based and registered, requiring personal appearance for collection.

Private *feiqian* exchange operations were primarily run by large, cross-regional stores. *Feiqian* was mainly used for currency exchange between the capital and local regions. Businesses with operations in both areas utilized their nationwide branch networks to offer exchange services, primarily for fund management and profit generation. Their practices mirrored those of official institutions like the liaison offices. However, private *feiqian* operations had a distinctive feature: most remittances were free, with profits coming mainly from holding funds.[14]

As previously mentioned, the "money prohibition" policy directly led to the emergence of *feiqian*. Being a public response to government policies, the future of *feiqian* was inherently uncertain. Following its widespread use, the Tang government made repeated attempts to ban it. Historical records reveal the first instance coincided with *feiqian*'s implementation: "Pei Wu, the capital governor, requested a ban on *feiqian* transactions with merchants. He ordered thorough searches across neighborhoods and districts, mandating that every ten households form a joint guarantee team to monitor and report any violations." This ban clearly targeted those operating *feiqian* businesses, including liaison offices, armies, military governors, and wealthy families. The second instance occurred in February of the six year of Emperor Xianzong's reign (811). The emperor decreed: "For transactions exceeding ten *guan* [贯, 1 *guan* = 1,000 cash], both public and private, goods must be used alongside money. Ministry of Revenue envoys, salt and iron envoys, and the capital governor must establish specific ratios and rules, which they must submit to the court for review. Additionally, tea merchants and other entities engaged in public and private transactions are prohibited from directly exchanging goods for cash." In the ninth year of Emperor Xianzong's reign (814), "the capital governor is ordered to strictly prohibit individuals of all social standings from engaging in unauthorized *feiqian* exchanges with merchants. Violators would face property confiscation, with punishments meted out based on the severity of the offense." These imperial edicts to officials suggest an attempt to prevent merchants from hoarding coins or diverting them elsewhere through *feiqian* exchanges (*bianhuan*).[15]

Feiqian emerged as a result of financial system reforms in the mid-Tang Dynasty, making it impossible to enforce a complete ban without serious consequences. Historical records from May of the seventh year of Emperor Xianzong's reign (812) reveal, "Recent restrictions on merchant *feiqian* exchanges led to wealth accumulation in households, impeding circulation. This resulted in falling prices and widespread coin hoarding. It seems various departments and administrative bodies have lately permitted merchants to retain large sums within the city, allowing them to collect and store these funds in private residences as they please, effectively bringing circulation to a standstill." This reveals that banning *feiqian* exchanges failed to ease the "money shortage." Copper coins remained hoarded rather than circulating, and prices kept falling. With prohibition proving ineffective, the government sought to bar private merchants, liaison offices, armies, envoys, and wealthy families from the *feiqian* business. It strived to monopolize operations through the "three central government departments," allowing the central government to control currency circulation. This centralization was seen as a crucial step in managing the money supply and addressing the money shortage issue. However, historical records indicate that the three central government departments struggled to operate the *feiqian* business effectively and failed to garner support from merchants. According to records, "after the capital banned *feiqian*, wealth accumulation in households led to falling prices. Officials like Finance Minister Lu Tan, Minister of War Wang Shao, and Salt and Iron Envoy Wang Bo proposed allowing merchants to use *feiqian* through the three departments, offering an incentive of 100 additional coins for every 1,000 *guan* exchanged. Despite these incentives and the option to exchange *feiqian* for equivalent copper coins, merchants showed little interest. The public continued to prefer holding onto money rather than goods."

Since its inception during the Yuanhe period of Emperor Xianzong's rule in the Tang Dynasty, the *feiqian* business persisted, albeit with a tumultuous development. The government repeatedly attempted to suppress the spread of *feiqian*, with the central authorities seeking to monopolize the trade to control currency circulation. In reality, however, private merchants had long dominated the *feiqian* industry. Notably, the central finance department's monopoly on *feiqian* positively influenced national price regulation and currency circulation, offering valuable insights for future monetary policies.

Feiqian, China's earliest bill of exchange, marked the beginning of the bill exchange function. Its emergence was closely linked to a developed commercial economy, a "money shortage" environment, and the rise of cross-regional credit institutions. Merchants, affluent families, and official bodies widely used *feiqian*, which primarily circulated in Chang'an, the capital, and other areas where major merchants gathered. This greatly facilitated long-distance trade and safeguarded merchant wealth. Notably, *feiqian* was mostly issued by government agencies, reflecting official backing—a key characteristic. Simultaneously, *feiqian* symbolized the shift from physical to bill-based credit in ancient China. During the Tang Dynasty, using tokens like hats and sticks for money withdrawal was common. Historical evidence indicates that the mid to late Tang Dynasty saw the transition from physical to bill credit, coinciding with *feiqian*'s emergence and popularity. Furthermore, the promotion of *feiqian* during the Tang Dynasty provided crucial experience and laid the conceptual foundation for the widespread use of bills in the subsequent Song Dynasty.

III. *Shutie*: Predecessor of Checks

Aside from *feiqian*, the Tang Dynasty also saw the creation of *shutie*, a document similar to checks. This innovation facilitated large commercial transactions, eliminating the need for physical cash. After depositing money at a counter shop, customers could transfer funds to others. *Shutie* acted as a transfer voucher, specifying the payment amount, date, and recipient's name. For transactions, only the owner's *shutie* was required. *The Extensive Records of the Taiping Era* illustrates this practice, recounting how a scholar borrowed 500-*guan* cash from Yuchi Gong (585–658), a prominent general in the early Tang Dynasty, using this method.

When discussing *shutie*, it's crucial to mention counter shops, also known as "deposit shops." These establishments stored customers' valuables and emerged as a result of commercial trade development. Merchants found storing and transporting goods both inconvenient and unsafe, necessitating specialized institutions for goods custody. Counter shops also evolved from the development of credit systems, as merchants entrusted their valuable assets to these shops based on these shops' creditworthiness.[16]

Historical records document the significance of counter shops. In May 781 (second year of Emperor Jianzhong's reign), a rebellion of feudal lords prompted the government to raise military funds through increased taxes and reduced debts. By the following year, the government still struggled to collect and distribute taxes effectively. Emperor Dezong then sought advice from Wei Dubin and Chen Jingyan, officials in charge of ritual affairs, who suggested, "To address the country's financial needs, we can borrow money from wealthy merchants in the capital. Each merchant can retain 10,000-*guan* cash for their operations, while the government will acquire their remaining assets and funds. Involving just ten to twenty major merchants in this scheme can significantly alleviate the nation's financial strain."

Emperor Dezong then ordered Wei Zhen, the capital governor, and the magistrates of Chang'an and Wannian "to conduct a large-scale search and seizure of wealthy merchants in the capital. The operation was brutal, with strict law enforcement. Xue Ping, the magistrate of Chang'an, personally led searches through city neighborhoods, wielding torture devices and riding in a vehicle. He mercilessly whipped people, causing unbearable pain that drove some to suicide. The capital descended into chaos and panic, as if ravaged by bandits. Yet, despite the severity and scope of this plundering, the final amount seized was a mere 800,000-*guan* cash."

Wei Zhen then resorted to interrogating rental shops and pawnshops, but the total fund raised amounted to no more than two million-*guan* cash. These events are recorded in both *The Old Books of the Tang Dynasty* and *The New Books of the Tang Dynasty*. The latter further notes, "The government's confiscation of property from wealthy families and their servants in the capital yielded a mere 800,000-*guan* cash. Desperate for more funds, authorities then targeted rental shops, pawnshops, and grain market transactions, demanding a quarter of all transactions as tax or contribution. This harsh measure ignited a strike in Chang'an, with citizens flooding the streets in protest and attempting to intercept the prime minister's carriage. Prime Minister Lu Qi, however, hastily drove past the protesters. Fearing escalating unrest, Wei Zhen proposed exempting transactions below 100-*guan* cash or 50 bushels of grain. Despite these measures, the government's total haul amounted to only two million-*guan* cash."

Historical records indicate that specific vouchers were required to retrieve money and goods stored in counter shops, Persian mansions, and Persian shops. For example, Xiao Li used a cane to withdraw 20,000-*guan* cash from a Persian store, while Lao Li presented an old hat to collect 300-*guan* cash from Wang's pharmacy. Others used personally written notes or letters as withdrawal vouchers. *Shutie* were just one type of acceptable credential. Although the specific forms of identification varied, the consistent requirement was the presentation of some form of proof to collect money and goods.

SECTION 3

Bills in the Song Dynasty

The use of *feiqian* and *shutie* during the Tang Dynasty paved the way for bill circulation in the Song Dynasty. This prior experience made people more receptive to bills. The flourishing commercial economy of the Song Dynasty further fostered the development of *jiaozi* and *huizi*. Unlike *feiqian* and *shutie*, *jiaozi* enhanced bill liquidity by adopting the "payable to the bearer" mechanism. It also introduced valuable innovations in standardized forms, issuance limits, circulation period management, reserve requirements, installment systems, and note replacement policies. These advancements marked substantial progress over the negotiable instruments of previous dynasties.

I. Basic Conditions for the Emergence of *Jiaozi*

The Song Dynasty's commercial prosperity and high demand for currency were crucial factors in the development of *jiaozi*. Following its development in the Tang Dynasty, the commercial economy thrived in the Song Dynasty, reaching its zenith in China's ancient feudal society. The Song Dynasty was one of the few dynasties in Chinese history that primarily relied on commercial taxation. Agricultural advancements—including improved rice varieties, expanded arable land, and widespread multiple cropping in regions south of the Yangtze River—sparked a rice economy boom. This surge enhanced agricultural efficiency, boosted national grain output, and freed rural labor. Surplus grain flooded the market as a commodity, enabling more people to abandon farming for urban commercial endeavors. In foreign trade, China's porcelain and tea found markets in Southeast Asia and Europe, while goods like black pepper and spices flowed into China, strengthening its global ties. This economic upswing intensified the demand for currency. As a result, *jiaozi* emerged as a crucial complement to physical money, marking its debut on the historical stage.

Jiaozi emerged as a crucial solution to the "money shortage" plaguing the Song Dynasty. Ironically, despite being one of the largest issuers of copper coins in Chinese history—minting around 300 million-*guan* copper coins—the Song Dynasty grappled with a severe currency scarcity. This period, aptly dubbed the "Copper Coin Era," saw several factors contributing to the shortage. First, the dynasty's thriving commerce increased currency demand, outstripping supply. Second, bustling trade with foreign nations and ethnic minority regions resulted in a substantial outflow of copper coins. Third, persistent border conflicts and hefty military expenses compelled the government to monopolize copper production and usage. They even confiscated copper items from the public, leading to a severe shortage for everyday use and prompting people to melt coins into household wares. Last, as the scarcity intensified, people began hoarding high-quality copper coins, further diminishing circulation and exacerbating the shortage. To tackle this crisis, paper bills—and eventually paper currency—were introduced, offering an innovative solution to the persistent "money shortage."

The credit system had evolved and improved since the Tang Dynasty. The Tang Dynasty's *feiqian* and the early Song Dynasty's *bianhuan*, *jiaoyin*, and *yanyin*, along with advancements in papermaking and printing, paved the way for the emergence of bills. Merchants adapted to using these financial instruments and mastered their application in trade, fostering the development of *jiaozi*. The rise of *jiaozi* exemplifies the evolution of credit. Before *jiaozi*, various forms of commercial credit—such as currency lending, credit sales, and prepayments—were already common in goods production and circulation. *Jiaoyin* and similar bills, representing commercial credit, circulated widely. The government also established financial institutions to manage trade, tax collection, and bill operations.

The Song Dynasty boasted a broader, more diverse array of lending institutions than the previous dynasty, with heightened government involvement in lending activities. Two notable government borrowing practices were the "young shoots law" and the "market exchange law." The young shoots law, a key component of Wang Anshi's (1021–1086) reforms, primarily supported agriculture by providing spring loans to the poor for seeds and necessities, to be repaid with interest after the autumn harvest. The market exchange law sought to stabilize private goods prices and offer lending services to cash-strapped merchants. Borrowers were required to provide collateral such as land, houses, or valuables—or secure three guarantors if tangible collateral wasn't available—earning it the alternative name "guarantee loan law." To implement this system, the Song Dynasty established Market Exchange Affairs offices in major cities and border regions. Despite its eventual bankruptcy due to funding shortfalls, this initiative significantly advanced the Song Dynasty's financial and credit development.

Private entities such as landlords, wealthy merchants, and temples had become increasingly active in lending. They offered loans to commoners, officials, and nobles at much higher interest rates than official sources. During the Xining period (1068–1077), Wang Anshi, a Song Dynasty statesman, observed, "In every prefecture and county, there are families amassing wealth through acquisitions. These families can earn tens of thousands-*guan* copper coins annually from interest alone ... The wealthy now acquired property not just from ordinary people, but even from nobles. Meanwhile, the poor may end up displaced and dying in ditches." Regarding credit sales, Su Shi (1037–1101), a famous Song Dynasty poet and politician, noted, "Merchants seldom use cash for direct trades, as it yields no interest. Instead, they typically collect payment for the previous year's sales in the current year, and for this year's credit sales in the following year. This system facilitates fund turnover and calculations, ensuring smooth transactions and economic interconnectivity. However, this practice of credit sales and delayed payments has led to decreased alcohol tax and other tax revenues, which often rely on cash transactions. Consequently, commercial activities have slowed, leaving city shops and houses increasingly vacant."

Credit sales had thus become crucial for ensuring smooth circulation of goods. Merchants often made prepayments, particularly in the tea trade. Historical records show that tea merchants typically prepaid tea plantation owners for the following year's harvest. Lü Tao (1027–1103), a well-known writer in the Northern Song Dynasty, remarked, "Some farmers produce 30,000 to 50,000 catties annually, while others manage only 100 to 200 catties. Traditionally, these farmers have either collected deposits from customers the year before harvest or used tea seedlings as collateral for the next year's crop." Notably, when private entities provided the government with grain, fodder, or currency, they received *jiaoyin* in return. These notes could be exchanged for cash or goods at different locations, indicating that they had begun to function as a form of currency. This development significantly accelerated the evolution of credit-based money.[17]

Jiaoyin was a collective term for credit notes in the Song Dynasty, encompassing tea notes, salt notes, alum notes, and cash notes. These could be exchanged for physical goods or cash. The Jiaoyin Office and the Trade and Tax Office were specialized institutions responsible for issuing, storing, distributing, and redeeming these notes. They played a crucial role in ensuring the smooth operation of the *jiaoyin* system. The "Food and Commodity Annals" in *The History of the Song Dynasty* states: "During emperors Yongzheng and Kangxi period, urgent military needs prompted the court to order merchants to transport grain and forage to border areas. Prices were set based on travel distance and exceeded market rates. In return, merchants received certificates called *jiaoyin*. These vouchers could be exchanged for money in the capital or for tea and salt in the Yangtze River and the Huaihe River basins or the Hubei and Hunan regions." This system emerged from the Song Dynasty's thriving trade activities, where merchants frequently engaged in cross-regional commerce. To ensure ample military grain supply at the frontlines and minimize transportation time, the government implemented a direct grain delivery system. Merchants received vouchers redeemable for cash in the capital or goods like tea and salt in regions south of the Yangtze River. "The court offered generous compensation to merchants transporting grain to the capital, allowing them to obtain commodities in the Yangtze River and the Huaihe River basins." This innovative approach not only secured frontline supplies but also stabilized grain and currency supply in the capital.

It is worth noting that after obtaining *jiaoyin*, merchants could not only exchange these vouchers for physical goods or cash but also engage in buying and selling them. The trading partners were usually shops specializing in tea and salt note operations, which acted as guarantors for merchants to exchange *jiaoyin* for cash or replacement of *jiaoyin*. These shops either received remuneration for their services or directly engaged in trading to make substantial profits. The "Book of Food and Commodities" in *The History of the Song Dynasty* records that in the early Northern Song Dynasty, border residents brought grain to the central region. After receiving tea notes, "they were unaware of the profit margins of tea business and were eager to exchange the vouchers for money. After obtaining tea notes, they sold them to tea merchants or tea shops in the capital, but their profit was minimal. Some tea merchants and tea shops used tea notes to buy tea leaves, while others hoarded them for trading to seek higher profits." Some merchants brought tea notes to the capital but "for several months" failed to exchange them for cash. Consequently, they had to "lower the price and sell tea notes to merchant families who hoarded them." This indicates that *jiaoyin* had already acquired a certain degree of liquidity. The emergence of *jiaoyin* was an important foundation for the later creation of paper currency such as *jiaozi*. Its circulation and use further deepened the influence of credit notes in people's daily lives and promoted the transition from credit notes to currency.

II. Use of *Jiaozi* and *Huizi*

Jiaozi, China's earliest paper currency, emerged in Sichuan due to unique circumstances. While copper coins were the primary currency during the Song Dynasty, Sichuan used iron coins because of its geographical isolation and complex history. *The Facts of the Song Dynasty* illustrates this: "In Sichuan, iron coins were commonly used. Ten *guan* of small iron coins weighed 65 catties, equivalent in value to one *guan* of large coins. A single *guan* of large coins weighed 12 catties. For market transactions involving three to five *guan*, iron coins proved cumbersome to carry." Iron coins had significantly lower value than copper coins, requiring ten times the weight for equivalent transactions. As trade rapidly expanded, the inconvenience of carrying iron coins became a pressing issue in Sichuan. The urgent need for a more practical currency in daily trade led to the creation of *jiaozi*.

The issuance of *jiaozi* evolved through three stages: private free issuance, official issuance, and decline.[18] During the private free issuance stage, individual merchant shops issued *jiaozi* without authorization. People exchanged their iron coins for *jiaozi* vouchers, which bore the issuer's stamp and a secret seal. These vouchers varied between shops and lacked uniformity. Unlike previous dynasties' bills, anyone could redeem *jiaozi* for iron coins at the issuing shop without identification. The official issuance stage began when individual shops' credit could no longer support the payment and circulation of *jiaozi*. To maintain the credit of *jiaozi*, sixteen affluent merchants in Chengdu established a *jiaozi* shop. They issued vouchers printed on uniform colored paper with house, tree, and figure designs, along with shop "secret seals." The face value was customized for each recipient, and *jiaozi* could be cashed anytime for a 30-*wen* (文, 1 *guan* = 1,000 *wen*, 100 *wen* = 1 tael) fee per *guan*. However, this stage of *jiaozi* had significant drawbacks. It lacked fixed face values, circulation periods, issuance reserve requirements, and unified exchange and withdrawal mechanisms—all of which introduced potential risks.

As the sixteen shops' operations faltered, instances emerged where *jiaozi* couldn't be exchanged, sparking minor redemption crises and numerous lawsuits. The government stepped in to regulate private *jiaozi* operations, and backed by government credit, *jiaozi* quickly resumed normal issuance, marking its transition to official status. Initially, government-issued *jiaozi* retained its original issuance method. However, faced with prolonged warfare and severe financial strain, the Northern Song government devised a new *jiaozi* issuance strategy to alleviate fiscal pressure. This approach involved levying substantial seigniorage on the populace. *Jiaozi* was then promoted and adopted as a national paper currency, solidifying its transformation into a formal legal tender. *Jiaozi*, now officially sanctioned, had evolved into a sophisticated paper currency with well-defined mechanisms for issuance, circulation, exchange, and recovery. Its key features include the following:

- Term-based issuance. Each term lasting three years (effectively two years), with a total issuance amount of 1,256,340 *guan* per term.
- Reserve capital. A reserve of 360,000 *guan* in cash was set aside to allow holders to exchange for cash when needed.
- Anti-forgery measures. Fixed denominations stamped with an official seal, with all transactions recorded in a ledger and tracked by account number.
- Upfront fee. A 30-*wen* deduction for the official account upon deposit, replacing the previous practice of charging interest only upon redemption.
- Limited circulation period. A specified three-year circulation period, after which old currency was replaced with new.[19]

It is evident that, during the Northern Song Dynasty, the initial issuance of *jiaozi* was designed based on previous experiences, creating optimized operating mechanisms. Had this been maintained long-term, *jiaozi* might have significantly boosted the commodity economy and paper currency circulation. However, this was not the case. As *jiaozi* was later issued for improper purposes, the system's collapse became inevitable. After "official *jiaozi*" was issued for just one term, the second term's amount exceeded the prescribed limit. Subsequently, issuance increased dramatically. In 1047, Qinzhou of Gansu obtained 600,000 *guan* of *jiaozi* from Sichuan for grain and forage funds, but it was "a false printing"—*jiaozi* was issued without a reserve capital. During the Xining period, the Song Dynasty twice attempted to issue *jiaozi* in Shaanxi but abandoned it because *jiaozi* "was not real money and was not accepted." During the Chongning and Daguan periods (1102–1110) of Emperor Huizong's rule, *jiaozi* was issued indiscriminately, leading to its complete depreciation. It became waste paper and ceased to circulate. In 1109, the Song Dynasty was forced to change its policy, replacing *jiaozi* with *qianyin* (钱引). Following the old practice during the Tiansheng Period (1023–1032), it resumed issuing *qianyin* of 1.25 million *guan* per term, with a reserve capital of 500,000 *guan*. With *qianyin*'s issuance, the paper currency's value stabilized. During the Southern Song Dynasty, the government introduced a new paper currency called *huizi*, which was used for both official transactions and everyday commerce. This currency proved particularly useful during emergencies. For instance, when severe drought struck a province, *huizi* became the primary means of purchasing grain. Officials "urgently tapped into county granaries and borrowed *huizi* from the Finance and Taxation Office. Working tirelessly around the clock, they purchased rice—amassing approximately 40,000 *dan* [石, a unit of dry measure equivalent to about 200 catties] in total."

Unlike the *jiaozi* of the Northern Song Dynasty, the *huizi* of the Southern Song Dynasty could be valued not only in copper coins but also in commodities such as salt, iron, and silver. The Southern Song Dynasty faced a more dire military situation, leading to a scarcity of physical currency. This, coupled with rampant government corruption in its later years, resulted in a prolonged financial crisis. To alleviate this, some officials resorted to issuing paper currency, ultimately leading to oversupply and devastating the national economy. In the first year of the Qingyuan era (1195), the government issued 30 million *guan* of *huizi* per term. This amount escalated to 36.32 million *guan* in the 11th term and a staggering 116.98 million *guan* in the 15th term. The Song Dynasty also banned the exchange of gold, silver, and copper coins for *huizi*. When exchanging 14th-term *huizi* for previously issued *huizi*, the old currency was devalued by half. As a result, *huizi* flooded the market, causing a sharp decline in currency value, soaring prices, and widespread poverty.

During its early stages of private issuance, *jiaozi* functioned as a negotiable instrument. Its liquidity significantly improved compared to instruments from previous dynasties, primarily due to its "payable to the bearer" mechanism. *Jiaozi* also made beneficial advancements in unified form, total issuance amount, circulation period management, reserve system, installment system, and trade-in system. Upon becoming official, *jiaozi* emerged as the world's earliest paper currency—a significant contribution of the Chinese nation to global monetary development. As a credit currency, it boosted commercial trade and credit development substantially. It also provided invaluable lessons for future paper currency issuance, highlighting the importance of currency issuance management. Notably, the Song Dynasty's introduction of salt note discounting greatly influenced the development of future bill business.

SECTION 4

Bills in the Ming Dynasty

The commodity economy saw significant growth during the Song Dynasty but somewhat declined when the Yuan Dynasty (1271–1368) began to rule the country. The southern regions adhered to the Han ethnic system, while the north was under the Yuan government's direct control, leading to a noticeable economic difference between the areas. Regarding currency, the Yuan Dynasty was the first to use silver as a measure of value, a significant milestone in the history of Chinese currency. Another characteristic of the Yuan Dynasty monetary system was the continued use of paper currency. However, the overall development of bills during the Yuan Dynasty was limited. Initially, the Zhongtong note, a national paper currency officially printed and issued by the government in the era of Kublai Khan in the first year of the Zhongtong period (1260) in the Yuan Dynasty, was a convertible currency used in daily and cross-regional transactions. Copper or silver was often used in some market transactions according to local customs. Paper money holders needed to convert their currency at exchange shops to adapt to local trading mechanisms. At this point, Yuan Dynasty paper currency could be considered alternative negotiable instruments. Using silver as a value benchmark distinguished Yuan Dynasty bills from those of previous dynasties. In the 24th year of the Zhiyuan era (1287), the Yuan Dynasty began issuing non-convertible paper currency, becoming the first country in global currency history to establish a paper currency standard system. Building on the Song Dynasty's experience with paper currency issuance, the Yuan Dynasty adopted a more prudent issuance policy and made beneficial explorations into the system and theory of paper currency issuance and circulation.

The early Ming Dynasty prioritized agriculture over commerce, which hindered the recovery of the commercial economy. It was only in the mid to late Ming Dynasty that commerce and credit began to see gradual growth. Early money houses also appeared, initially dealing in currency exchange, then gradually expanding into deposit and lending businesses. The Ming Dynasty can be seen as a transitional stage in the development of ancient bills. While it inherited bills from previous dynasties, they did not achieve widespread use. Both the mid to late Ming Dynasty and the Qing Dynasty had a currency structure featuring the concurrent use of silver and paper currency. The emergence and development of money houses and *huipiao* in the Ming Dynasty laid the groundwork for the large-scale circulation of bills in the Qing Dynasty. Given the limited development of bills in the Yuan Dynasty, the author will not explore them in detail here. The rest of the text will focus on the development of bills during the Ming Dynasty.

I. Basic Conditions for the Emergence of *Huipiao*

In the early days of the Ming Dynasty, Zhu Yuanzhang (1328–1398), founding emperor of the dynasty, implemented strict measures in the regions south of the Yangtze River to amass wealth for post-war construction, significantly undermining the regions' commercial foundation. Additionally, the early Ming Dynasty prioritized agriculture over commerce and employed a system of collecting taxes in kind. As a result, the commercial economy was severely underdeveloped, with most transactions being exchange of physical goods. However, after the maritime ban was lifted in 1567, a substantial amount of silver flowed in, stimulating the commodity market and triggering an economic upturn. Regarding credit, money houses began to appear, initially conducting currency exchange transactions before expanding into deposit and loan businesses. These money houses played a crucial role in the evolution of ancient Chinese bills and laid a solid foundation for their further development in the Qing Dynasty.

During the Zhengtong period (1436–1449), Ming Dynasty paper currency witnessed depreciation. Consequently, the Ming government eased restrictions on silver use, allowing silver coins to circulate freely. This created a more complex currency market, with dozens of varying currencies in terms of weight and quality. The fluctuating silver prices resulted in the emergence of financial organizations specializing in silver exchange, invariably known as money shops, money houses, exchange shops, money tables, or money stalls. During the eighth year of Emperor Jiajing's reign (1529), rampant copper coin smuggling led the government to ban copper coin sales, resulting in private contracts between currency exchange businesses, causing high prices. In the fifth year of Emperor Wanli's reign (1577), Pang Shangpeng (1524–1580), a prominent minister, approved the establishment of a money shop, marking the beginning of the legal system for such shops. He appointed wealthy city and town residents as money house owners to buy standard currency from the government and facilitate transactions. By the end of the Ming Dynasty, the business scope of money houses included not just silver and currency exchange, but also lending, bill issuance, and other operations. Small-scale money exchange shops and rice and money shops were also active in rural areas. As money houses became more numerous and developed, various guild organizations of money houses emerged during the Qing Dynasty.

II. Ming Dynasty *Huipiao*

While the Ming Dynasty's *baochao* (宝钞) was a paper currency, it was state-mandated to be non-exchangeable, making it hard to classify as a negotiable instrument. This inconvertible national paper currency, due to the absence of a corresponding monetary system, faced collapse shortly after its issuance, thus failing to showcase the power of national credit.

In addition to national paper currency, bills from previous dynasties were still used for private lending. This is illustrated in the novel *The Plum in the Golden Vase*: "Jiang Wenhui, a county doctor, borrowed thirty taels of silver from Lu, with Zhang Sheng as his guarantor, to manage his wife's funeral. It is agreed on a monthly interest rate of 3% on the borrowed funds and repay the principal and interest in full by the following year. To secure the agreement, a loan bill is issued."[20] The novel doesn't specify a fixed repayment date for this bill, and the usage aligns with that of the Song and Yuan dynasties.

In borrowing and lending activities, the government typically needed to issue bills as proof. "During spring plowing, if there are impoverished community members lacking seeds, they should report to the head of the community and inform the village contract official to issue a loan bill. Borrowing less than five *dou* [斗, about 90 catties] does not incur any interest, but borrowing more than one *dan* will incur one *dou* of interest. In winter, the seeds should be returned to refill the warehouse, and the person in charge will mark the original loan bill with the words 'Repayment Received.'"[21]

During the Ming Dynasty, money bills, silver bills, and *huipiao* emerged. *Huipiao*, in particular, emerged in the late Ming Dynasty and persisted into the Qing Dynasty. These bills were obtained either by depositing funds at a store that managed the bills or issued by reputable establishments or high-ranking officials in a specific area, specifying the amount and bearing a special seal. Holders could then redeem the full amount at designated stores and cities. Historical materials suggest that *huipiao* was widely used during the Ming Dynasty, often featuring in literary works. The late Ming novel *Idle Talk Under the Bean Arbor: A Seventeenth-Century Chinese Story Collection* illustrates this, recounting how Wang Yan, a pawnbroker in Huizhou, Anhui Province, entrusted his son Wang Hua with 10,000 taels of silver to open a pawnshop in Suzhou, Jiangsu Province. Wang Hua, proving inept at business, squandered the entire sum within a month. In desperation, he turned to "his fellow townsman, who issued a *huipiao* to help him pull through."

The Collected Works of Xu Guangqi contains family letters that mention the use of *huipiao*, providing evidence for the circulation of private *huipiao* during the late Ming Dynasty. Here are some excerpts.

> I received Sun Pan's letter only yesterday due to a processing delay of a few days. The *huipiao* has also arrived, but I'm hesitant to collect it, suspecting Wang Yin to be a secret agent from the capital. I've sent my payment ahead. As he wasn't home again, I'll deliver it tomorrow, on the seventh day of the lunar new year. I'll then retrieve the reply and arrange for someone to bring it back.
>
> Lord Fu's family has returned, and the letter sent on the 19th will undoubtedly arrive. The three contracts of Ding, Sun, and Tang were enclosed in the letter and can be collected promptly. The collection of bills is a pressing matter.
>
> Xi Hongqiao has mortgaged his house for three taels of silver to cover imperial examination expenses and now owes interest. I'm sending the receipts back, and you can use this money for household needs without touching the Ding, Sun, and Tang families' silver. Please collect the silver from these three families promptly and remit it to Tianjin.
>
> Uncle Zhao intends to remit 100 taels of silver. When he delivers it, please accept it. You may use these funds for future expenses such as weddings or other matters if needed. If not immediately necessary, consider investing in some business ventures.

Alternatively, you could use it to redeem the Xu family's house, which your son-in-law Ai has mortgaged. Upon receiving the silver, please write a *huipiao* and bring it to me when I return to Beijing.

The first, third, and fourth family letters mention *huipiao* from Songjiang, Shanghai (Xu Guangqi's hometown), to the capital, while the second mentioned *huipiao* from the capital to Songjiang. The first letter suggests that Sun Pan, possibly a fellow villager or relative of Xu Guangqi, entrusted the Xu family or a third party to remit money from Songjiang to the capital in Xu Guangqi's name. This letter and the *huipiao* were sent to Xu, who did not redeem the funds, thus using Xu Guangqi's silver first. The second letter describes Xu Guangqi sending money to his family with urgent instructions to redeem it. The third letter requests the family to remit money from Songjiang to Tianjin. In the fourth letter, Xu's family issued a *huipiao*, and used the cash from Mr. Zhao, the sender. This suggests the Xu family facilitated a 100-tael silver transfer from Songjiang to the capital for Zhao, issuing the *huipiao* in Songjiang before remitting it to the capital.

The above analysis reveals several scenarios of exchange transactions between Xu Guangqi, stationed in the capital, and his hometown. First, the Xu family entrusted others to manage their fund exchanges. Second, they commissioned third parties to issue *huipiao* on their behalf. Last, they accepted remittance commissions from others. In essence, the Xu family both delegated to and accepted commissions from others to facilitate exchange transactions between Beijing and Shanghai.

Summary

From the Zhou to the Ming Dynasty, the commercial economy experienced fluctuations, with periods of growth and decline, but overall, it progressed. The evolution of credit was closely tied to the commercial economy. Generally, dynasties with more advanced commercial economies fostered stronger credit systems, creating favorable conditions for the growth of bills. A scarcity of physical currency often spurred societal demand for bills. However, the development of bills also required time and a gradual shift in public perception of their use. An examination of bill history during these eras reveals significant advancements, particularly during the Tang and Song dynasties when economic and credit systems flourished. This period saw credit carriers evolve from physical objects to bills. Financially, bills emerged as a solution to physical currency shortages, carving out a niche in the monetary and financial system. Functionally, bills evolved from simple loan receipts and withdrawal vouchers to more sophisticated instruments. The Tang Dynasty's *feiqian* introduced exchange functions, while the Song Dynasty's *jiaozi* and *huizi* enhanced payment and settlement capabilities. As the economy, finance, and credit systems developed, the role of bills continuously expanded and improved.

NOTES

1. Sales deeds used in the Western Zhou Dynasty.—Trans.
2. An ancient Chinese contract bearing the character "中" in its center, split in half for each contracting party to hold a portion.—Trans.
3. A bamboo or wooden voucher deed with written characters on the front and engraved teeth on the side for verification. It is a document with a contractual nature.—Trans.
4. Exchange vouchers from the Tang and Song dynasties allowed withdrawing money using paper coupons without physical transportation. This system, where "money flies without wings," earned the nickname "*feiqian*" (flying money).—Trans.
5. "井田制" in Chinese. Also the "nine squares" system (of land ownership in China's slave society) with one large square divided into nine small ones (like the Chinese character "井"), the eight outer ones being allocated to serfs who had to cultivate the central one for the serf owner.—Trans.
6. Du Yu, "Spring and Autumn Annals with Annotations," vol. 47, in *Annotated Edition of the Thirteen Classics in the Song Dynasty by Nanchang Prefecture School*, 1045.
7. Liu Fang, "On the Development of Commerce in the Western Zhou Dynasty," *Journal of Baoji Normal University* (Philosophy and Social Sciences Edition), no. 2 (1989): 52.
8. Wang Xu, "A Study on the Evolution of Traditional Chinese Contracts: Yueji," *Journal of Liaoning University (Philosophy and Social Sciences Edition)* 43, no. 5 (2015): 137–145.
9. Lin Yin, *The Rites of Zhou: Current Annotations and Translations* (Beijing: Bibliographic Literature Publishing House, 1988).
10. Ding Haibin and Yang Lulu, "Research on Commercial Documents in the Pre-Qin Period," *Archives*, no. 3 (2019): 4–11.
11. Bai Xiaoping, "Research on Ancient Chinese Sales Contracts" (Master's diss., Lanzhou University, 2006).
12. Du You, "Food and Goods 7," in vol. 7 of *Tongdian*, Qingwu Yingdian engraved edition.
13. Hou Guangqing and Zhao Xueqin, "On the Origin and Nature of Feiqian," *Journal of Shanxi University of Finance and Economics*, no. 4 (1997): 72–73, 84.
14. Wang Jijie, "Research on Several Issues of 'Flying Money' in the Tang Dynasty," *Hubei Numismatics Special Issue*, no. 14 (2015): 40–42.
15. Zhu Ruigen, "Feiqian During the Tang Dynasty," *China Numismatics*, no. 2 (1992): 78.
16. Xue Pingshuan, "On the Financial Industry of Chang'an, the Capital of Tang Dynasty," in *Collection of Tang History Essays*, ed. Du Wenyu, vol. 8 (Xi'an: Sanqin Publishing House, 2006), 296–321.
17. Jia Daquan, "The Emergence of *Jiaozi*," *Sichuan Finance*, no. S1 (1994): 5–29.
18. Dai Zhiqiang, "Several Questions About Jiaozi in the Northern Song Dynasty," *China Numismatics*, no. 3 (2006): 43–46, 95–96.
19. Du Wenyu and Wang Kexi, "The Issuance, Recovery, Exchange, and Trading of Banknotes in the Song Dynasty," *Historical Monthly*, no. 1 (1992): 24–30.
20. Xiaoxiaosheng, *Plums in a Golden Vase*, vol. 4, edition engraved during Emperor Chongzhen's reign in the Ming Dynasty.
21. Huang Zuo, "Taiquan Township Rites," in *The Complete Library of Four Books in the Qingyuan Pavilion*, vol. 4.

CHAPTER TWO

Bills in the Qing Dynasty

After initial accumulation and development, the use of bills had become somewhat popular. In the Qing Dynasty, following the gradual recovery and development of the commercial economy post-Kangxi era, many types of bills such as *huipiao*, silver bills, and money bills circulated in large quantities. These featured more standardized forms, stronger credit enhancement measures like guarantees and mortgages, improved anti-counterfeiting measures, and significantly expanded circulation. Money houses and bill shops played a pivotal role in this evolution. The development of money houses can be divided into four key stages: pre-Opium War, post-Opium War, after the Second Opium War, and following the Revolution of 1911. Despite fluctuations, their importance in bill development remained constant. Money houses primarily issued bills such as silver bills, money bills, money house bills, and bills of exchange, each with multiple subtypes. Bill operations proved lucrative, with money house bills exerting the most significant influence. In modern Sino-foreign trade, Chinese merchants, money houses, and foreign banks gradually established a stable operating model, their financial relationships interwoven through money house bills.

Scholars disagree on when bill shops emerged, though many place their origin in the early 1820s. These experts contend that Rishengchang, established in 1823 from the restructured Xiyucheng Pigment Shop, was the first bill shop. They regard Lei Lütai, who spearheaded Rishengchang's creation, as the founder of bill shops. The evolution of bill shops can be split into five stages: initial development, decline, recovery, peak, and eventual decline. This century-old system significantly enhanced China's bill exchange industry. Bill shops played a pivotal role in promoting the bill industry, expanding the scope of bill circulation and instituting innovative systems. For example, a thorough and rigorous management system was developed for bill shops' exchange business, which adopted a strategy of "allocating funds between the main shop and its branches and increasing lending to expand profits." The system prioritized the mechanism of "payable to the bearer" and merged exchange operations with deposit and lending services.

To combat counterfeiting, measures included using special paper, employing dedicated personnel to write bills with unique seals, creating multiple copies, and implementing a confidentiality system. In accounting, the exchange difference settlement system was adopted, fostering the development of related bill systems. As bill circulation increased and bills became exchangeable at non-issuing institutions, a high demand for bill clearing arose, leading to the emergence of the posting system. Later, the establishment of the remittance association led to the introduction of a remittance system using public bills for clearing. This significantly improved bill clearing efficiency and marked the initial establishment of a centralized clearing system—a major advancement in China's financial system.

Following the Opium War, modern China became the target of foreign aggression due to its poor national strength and was forced down a semi-colonial and semi-feudal path. Foreign invaders introduced their financial and bill systems, spurring the establishment of both foreign and Chinese-funded banks. These institutions issued what are known as modern bills, including bills of exchange, promissory notes, and checks, marking a period of integration between Chinese and Western systems. Notably, a trend of learning from the West emerged in modern China. Influenced by this trend, the Qing government began formulating laws and bill-related regulations to regulate commercial behavior. These initially manifested as ideas and attempts of the reformist legislative movement. Although a comprehensive commercial legal system didn't fully materialize, these early efforts laid a solid foundation for the development of future laws and signaled the dawn of China's commercial legislative awareness. Regulations such as the *Qing Dynasty Commercial Law Compiled by Imperial Order*, *Company Registration Trial Charter*, *Trademark Registration Trial Charter*, *Bankruptcy Law*, *Insurance Industry Charter*, *Draft Qing Dynasty Commercial Law*, and *Revised Qing Dynasty Commercial Law* were enacted. These regulations provided basic guidelines for commercial behavior, played a crucial role in the development of bill regulations, and paved the way for the subsequent *The Negotiable Instrument Law of the People's Republic of China* (hereafter referred to as *The Negotiable Instrument Law*).

SECTION I

Huipiao, Silver Bills, and Money Bills in the Qing Dynasty

During the Qing Dynasty, the large-scale circulation of bills had a strong foundation, aligned with the dynasty's currency structure where silver and paper currency were used in tandem. The circulation of *huipiao*, silver bills, and money bills significantly facilitated people's lives and commodity transactions. The Qing Dynasty saw a greater variety of bills than previous dynasties, with more institutions issuing them. While bills from different institutions had unique features, their content became more comprehensive, approaching that of modern bills. As circulation increased, so did the need for anti-counterfeiting measures. Bill design improved, incorporating special paper, seals, watermarks, and secret codes. Credit enhancement measures also diversified, bolstering bill credibility and promoting wider use. In rural markets, bills primarily served as payment for land deals and agricultural transactions, providing credit guarantees. Rural bill credit stemmed largely from land and land-based social networks, often requiring mortgages, guarantees, and other credit-boosting measures.

I. Historical Conditions of the Early and Middle Qing Dynasty

In its early days, the Qing Dynasty grappled with internal and external challenges: an unstable social environment, frequent wars, and inadequate economic foundations. However, during Emperor Kangxi's reign, China achieved internal and external unity, fostering a peaceful environment conducive to economic growth. Agriculture and handicrafts flourished during this period. Kangxi's lenient approach to commerce and his pro-business policies further catalyzed economic prosperity, contributing to the prosperous period known as the "Golden Age of Kangxi and Qianlong" (also the High Qing). Additionally, the interest-bearing silver system, implemented during the Kangxi, Yongzheng, and Qianlong eras, emerged as a distinctive government lending mechanism. This system played a pivotal role in accommodating various social strata and maintaining internal stability within the empire.

II. *Huipiao*, Silver Bills, and Money Bills

Over thousands of years, the practice of "payable to the bearer" had gained widespread acceptance. By the Qing Dynasty, using bills for transactions had become commonplace. As the influence of bills continued to expand, their design evolved and a standardized institutional arrangement was formed. Anti-counterfeiting measures also improved, and the emergence of financial institutions like money houses and silver shops provided crucial credit support, fueling the popularity of bills. The early to middle Qing Dynasty saw various bill types, such as *huipiao*, money bills, silver bills, and voucher bills, which already exhibited the basic functions of modern bills. The elements of these bills were quite similar to modern ones, with credit bolstered by guarantees and mortgages. However, the lack of standardization in design and elements led to significant variations among bills issued by different institutions.

Huipiao emerged as early as the late Ming Dynasty and saw further development during the early and mid-Qing Dynasty. Its circulation rapidly expanded, and the standardization of its design gradually improved. The *huipiao* in the Qing Dynasty featured a distinctive style, with detailed text and unique patterns that served as certain anti-counterfeiting measures. Typically written on a single sheet of paper without a stub, these bills employed vermilion seals as both anti-counterfeiting and authentication marks. The complex seal engravings served as an important anti-counterfeiting method. Analysis of historical records reveals two methods for indicating the date of presentation: payments on a designated date and payments scheduled after issuance. The usage of *huipiao* can be categorized into three scenarios. The first scenario resembles modern bank transfers: moving funds from one location to another using *huipiao*.

Historical materials reveal that currency exchange via vouchers began as early as the Ming Dynasty. The silver specified on *huipiao* could be withdrawn in parts, but this required signing and keeping a separate check. To prevent unauthorized withdrawals, precautions needed to be filled in. While not a formal endorsement, this practice can be seen as the precursor to endorsement. The promissory note was both liquid and transferable; any bearer could exchange it for silver, provided someone accepted and signed it. The second scenario involved long-distance merchants or store retailers who issued *huipiao* due to insufficient funds when purchasing goods from other merchants or stores. This method allowed transactions to proceed smoothly despite temporary funding shortages, thereby facilitating the circulation of goods. In the third scenario, *huipiao* primarily denoted a borrowing and lending behavior with monetary funds.[1]

Money bills, a type of bills issued by money houses based on their own credit, functioned as a redeemable instrument akin to a modern promissory note and served as a substitute for silver. Its development peaked from Emperor Daoguang's reign to the early years of Emperor Xianfeng's reign (1851–1861) in the early to mid-Qing Dynasty. Financial historians dub this era the "age of using silver and copper as standard currency in tandem," which saw little advancement in China's modern monetary relationships. Despite the silver yuan's increased circulation in south China, it didn't significantly impact the overall currency development. In the mainland, it was not uncommon for silver coins to be melted and recast into silver ingots. In the silver-copper dual currency system, money bills emerged as a crucial supplement. Its issuance and circulation expanded considerably, with some estimates suggesting that Chinese money bills accounted for one-third of the total currency in circulation during this period.[2]

In the early and mid-Qing Dynasty, the bill system remained largely unchanged from the previous dynasty, with little innovation. The government made no unified institutional arrangements for bill development. Although bills could circulate and transfer in market transactions, continuous endorsements were not mandatory, and the holder's right of recourse against the endorser lacked adequate protection. The practice of "payable to the bearer" necessitated stronger anti-counterfeiting measures. By this time, anti-counterfeiting methods had become quite sophisticated, primarily consisting of

- printing watermark text on the paper used for *huipiao*;
- modifying or adding a secret code to a certain character or place in the seal or text;
- adding text and numbers or stamping on the junction to achieve overall anti-counterfeiting; and
- splitting a coin into two halves, sewing one half onto the bill and the other half onto the counterfoil, with fitting the two halves together perfectly as the basis for redemption.

Regarding credit enhancement, the discovered Qing Dynasty bills reveal that bills were widely circulated in both economically developed cities and small rural markets. These bills primarily facilitated land transactions and trades in agricultural and sideline products, providing credit guarantees. Rural bill credit mainly stemmed from land and land-based networks, often necessitating mortgages, guarantees, and other credit enhancement measures. Notably, the evolution of *huipiao* laid solid groundwork for future exchange operations by bill shops and paved the way for the establishment of a bill exchange system.

SECTION 2

Money House and Money House Bills: Enduring Financial Legend

Money houses played a crucial role in bill issuance, profoundly shaping their evolution during the Qing Dynasty. Money houses, which emerged in the mid to late Ming Dynasty, initially specialized in the exchange of silver coins. Over time, its business scope expanded to include deposits, loans, and bill issuance. They issued various types of bills such as silver bills, money bills, money house bills, and *huipiao*, which were widely circulated during the Qing Dynasty. Money house bills, in particular, were omnipresent, from bustling commercial ports to remote regions. Their sterling reputation made them a preferred medium for both domestic inter-port and international trade during the Qing Dynasty.

I. Development Stages of Money Houses

The evolution of money houses during the Qing Dynasty can be divided into four key phases: before the Opium War, after the Opium War, following the Second Opium War, and after the Revolution of 1911. In the early to mid-Qing Dynasty, money houses primarily focused on silver currency exchange, operating within a narrow scope. However, from the mid-18th century onward, as economic credit expanded and social needs evolved, money houses broadened their services. They began accepting deposits, offering loans, and issuing bills alongside their silver exchange operations, transforming into full-fledged credit institutions. By the dawn of the 20th century, the significance of money houses had grown substantially, paralleling the progress of modern Chinese industry, commerce, and international trade.

Money houses emerged before the Qing Dynasty. Historical documents from the Qing Dynasty referred to these institutions as "shops for exchanging money." In the early Qing Dynasty, money houses primarily facilitated silver coin exchange. However, by the late Qianlong period, their functions expanded to include credit services, with deposits and lending becoming a significant aspect of their business. An official's 1749 observation illustrates this shift: "Unlike most provincial garrison leaders who relied solely on their salaries and had few savings, Nuo Musan, a leader of the same rank, was notably wealthy. An investigation revealed that, in addition to his properties, Nuo had 1,000 taels of silver stored in hat shops and 2,000 taels in money shops." In short, before the Opium War, money houses conducting currency operations in areas with thriving commodity economies exhibited robust financial capabilities, with their role evolving from mere currency exchange to providing credit services.

After the Opium War, the influx of foreign powers and merchants into China created an urgent need for currency exchange and financial settlement solutions. Money houses became instrumental, offering crucial financial services like cash custody and bill issuance, playing an indispensable role in Sino-foreign trade. Most money houses were linked to commerce, with few solely engaged in silver exchange. They accepted two types of deposits from merchants: interest-free deposits withdrawable at any time, and interest-bearing deposits (up to 12% annually) requiring advance notice several days before withdrawal. During this period, money houses primarily focused on deposits, foreign exchange, and commercial bill issuance, expanding their operational scope and financial capacity. Simultaneously, China's traditional socioeconomic structures grappled with the need for reform and innovation, risking obsolescence if they failed to adapt.

After the Second Opium War, China's increased openness led to a surge in foreign traders exploiting the domestic economy. Money houses became a crucial tool for foreign powers to penetrate the Chinese economic landscape. They offered credit facilities to importers and exporters, inadvertently helping promote foreign goods and extract domestic resources. "Some major foreign banks have shown considerable interest in local money houses. This interest manifested in foreign banks using credit relationships to expand trade-in port cities and inland markets. Concurrently, money houses utilized foreign banks' funds to broaden their financial activities. The potent combination of foreign capital and mutual exploitation catalyzed a transformation of money houses into compradors."[3]

With the development of society and economy, financial interactions between local money houses and foreign banks intensified. By the 1860s and 1870s, foreign banks were accepting commercial bills from money houses as collateral for loans. This practice allowed foreign powers to deepen their involvement in the Chinese economy while increasing local money houses' dependence on foreign banks. Concurrently, money houses used their domestic influence to ease the entry of foreign goods into China, unwittingly becoming conduits for these imports. In Zhenjiang, Jiangsu, for instance, imported goods were typically paid for using bills of exchange from money houses in Shanghai. Merchants would transport copper coins or silver ingots to Suzhou to acquire local products, which were then transported to Shanghai for payment.

During this phase, money houses often assumed a comprador role, with many integrating this function into their operations. This dual identity enabled them to engage with foreign banks while managing their own banking business, reaping profits from both ventures. The following is an example, "Wang Yiting, hailing from a prominent merchant family in Zhejiang, began as an assistant manager at a money house before becoming a manager of Dingxin, a Japanese consignment store specializing in matches and cotton yarn. After 1900, he also acted as a comprador for Osaka Shipping Company and Nisshin Shipping Company. Simultaneously, he was a shareholder of Tongtai Money House in Nanshi, Shanghai."

During this phase, money houses experienced significant shifts in their functions, roles, and overall development. This evolution, however, wasn't solely driven by internal reform and innovation. In the prevailing social climate, money houses were largely influenced by external forces, relying on the profits these connections brought for their growth. Concurrently, money houses during this phase fueled economic progress. Although it served as a conduit for external economic influences to penetrate the mainland, in the long run, this process helped dismantle China's traditional natural economy, enabling adaptation to the demands of a changing era.

The Revolution of 1911 marked a tumultuous period for China's financial industry, beset by both external exploitation and internal strife. Money houses, unsurprisingly, faced severe business crises, necessitating constant vigilance against bank runs and currency fluctuations. They were forced to limit bill issuance to peer-to-peer transfers, temporarily suspending cash payments. Despite these challenges, money houses proactively sought new clientele, capitalizing on the burgeoning modern industrial and mining sectors. This period saw banks eagerly extending financial support to these enterprises—a positive and significant business venture. For instance, historical records indicate that Fukang Money House substantially increased its factory credit loans after 1899. However, later speculative operations of money houses led to their downfall. The 1910 rubber stock boom triggered a major financial crisis, further destabilizing China's already fragile financial system. Consequently, numerous money houses faltered, with many shuttering their doors. A reprieve came during World War I, as imperialist pressures on China eased, allowing for a swift recovery in money house operations. This resurgence persisted until the establishment of the PRC in 1949, which ultimately resulted in either the bankruptcy of these money houses or their transformation into banks.

II. Bills Issued by Money Houses

Money houses primarily issued four types of bills: silver bills, money bills, money house bills, and *huipiao*. Silver bills and money bills represented specific amounts of silver and money, respectively. These bills clearly state the issuing bank, the specific amount, and other relevant information. They effectively replaced physical currency in circulation, addressing the inconvenience and safety issues associated with cash transportation. Holders can exchange these bills for cash as needed, and money houses would redeem them upon verification. Historical records show that as early as Emperor Qianlong's reign, money bills issued by money houses had already circulated in many cities. By Emperor Daoguang's reign in the early to mid-18th century, these bills were widely used in over ten provinces nationwide, with their quantity significantly increased. "Silver bills" and "money bills" are general terms, encompassing various subtypes. "In the capital's folk market, money bills were used for transactions exceeding 500 yuan. These bills were also common in parts of Anhui Province, such as Chuzhou, Fengyang, and Luying. Remarkably, money bills from one location could be used to withdraw funds from money houses up to 200–300 miles away, making them more versatile than those confined to the capital. It is reported that money bills were also in use in Shengjing [present-day Shenyang] and Shandong regions." Money bills used widely in Shanxi had three subtypes: bills issued by the shop itself, those exchanged between shops, and those given to money shops by pawnshops. All three were equivalent to cash, payable upon presentation. During Emperor Xianfeng's reign, various types of silver and money bills continued to develop. Even when official bills stagnated, various private bills still circulated effectively in the folk market.

Issuing bills could generate substantial profits for money houses. As in the previous dynasty, money houses could earn transaction fees when exchanging silver and money bills. For instance, Money houses in Beijing could directly earn a 2% to 4% profit by offering a 98% or 96% discount during the exchange process. Unfortunately, some unscrupulous merchants exploited this system for illicit gains. They would issue large quantities of money bills, then abruptly close their shops and disappear. Others would purchase low-quality currency cheaply, hire people to trigger bank runs, and use this inferior currency to pay off money bills. Some even went as far as producing counterfeit bills to cash out at other money shops.

Money houses, while responsible for honoring credit, could amass significant cash reserves by issuing silver and money bills. This practice increased their operating funds and expanded working capital. After 1900, when silver yuan replaced the standard money to become the primary currency, money houses capitalized on this shift by issuing "silver bills" in denominations of five, ten, fifty, and one hundred taels. From 1904, they also issued silver yuan bills in denominations of one, three, and five yuan. These proved popular among merchants and civilians due to their convenience. Since it was rare for all holders to cash out at once, money houses could utilize their cash more effectively. They increasingly relied on issuing non-convertible silver and money bills to further expand their working capital.[4]

Money house bills, issued by money houses, were the most prevalent and influential type of bills. "Money house bills are promissory notes issued by money houses." With their long history and robust financial backing, they exerted significant market influence, "especially in Shanghai where they circulated freely in domestic financial, industrial, and commercial sectors, and even among foreign banks and stores." These bills enjoyed exceptional credibility. "Regardless of who held them, they were considered as cash." Money house bills could replace cash in circulation, addressing the shortage of gold and silver supply while eliminating the inconvenience of transporting the precious metals during transactions.

Money houses and foreign merchants shared a unique relationship. Foreign merchants placed their trust in money houses, utilizing them as intermediaries in Sino-foreign trade for credit guarantees. Money houses, in turn, used their domestic resources to assist foreign merchants in developing sales channels and obtaining local specialties at competitive prices. This process gradually unveiled the comprador nature of money houses. Consequently, money house bills evolved into a crucial means of payment for domestic trade and significantly propelled the development of Sino-foreign trade.

In Sino-foreign trade, a relatively fixed operating model had emerged among Chinese merchants, money houses, and foreign firms, facilitated by money house bills, which linked the financial credit relationship between these entities. When foreign banks received money house bills, they didn't need to cash them individually at the issuing bank. Chinese merchants selling local specialties to foreign merchants often received checks, which they used to offset their money house loans. The money house then forwarded these checks to foreign banks for cashing. This process allowed foreign banks to use money house bills to offset checks, eliminating the need for physical cash transfers. Money house bills had thus replaced cash in circulation, serving as vouchers for merchants to settle accounts. They played a crucial role in both domestic and international trade. As one account notes, "When a broker dealt with a foreign firm, they used money house bills, and the firm withdrew funds from the issuing money house when the bills matured." By the late 19th century, money house bills had become indispensable credit instruments in industry and commerce. One Chinese scholar even observed that commodity market transactions were settled exclusively with money house bills. These bills had a profound influence, circulating widely in Shanghai and appearing across commercial ports. Their presence even in remote areas highlighted their far-reaching impact on trade and finance.

Money house bills fell into two categories: sight bills and forward bills. Sight bills were payable at sight, while forward bills had set expiration dates, typically five days, ten days, or twenty days. Forward bills could not be cashed before their due date but could be discounted if needed. Each bill must clearly show the payable amount in silver and the issuing money house's name. For a forward bill, the expiration date should also be included. The money house then stamped the bill and split it in two: keeping the counterfoil and giving the main part to the client.

Bills of exchange were a crucial part of money house bills. "A bill of exchange was a written order from the issuer to a third party—typically a money house—instructing them to pay a specified sum to the bearer or a designated person, either immediately or at a future date, free of charge. The third party (a money house) is the drawer, while the bearer or designated person is the payee." Money houses in Shanghai used bills of exchange to settle creditor-debtor relations during trade in the mainland. "When local debtors wished to remit money to creditors in a different location and settle debts, they could make a payment to a money house, which would then issue a bill of exchange. This bill specified payment at a local branch or agency. The drawer would mail the bill to the drawee, while the bank sent the bill counterfoil to the paying money house as proof of future payment." These bills of exchange were specialized instruments used by money houses to facilitate fund exchange between different locations.

Bills of exchange were a vital component of *shenhui* (申汇, Shanghai bills). With the growth of inter-port trade, *shenhui* had evolved into a financial link connecting various regions of China with Shanghai. With notable creditworthiness, *shenhui* could be monetized and sold in the market at any time, making it a "cash chip." Major commercial port cities could adjust their financial positions through *shenhui* trading, making it a versatile fund transfer method that combined exchange, settlement, and credit. *Shenhui* markets had been established in cities like Tianjin, Hankou, Chongqing, Nanchang, Ningbo, Hangzhou, Nanjing, Xi'an, Qingdao, and Xiamen, creating a national financial network centered around Shanghai.

SECTION 3

Bill Shops and Bills of Exchange: Century-Long Journey of Bill Shops

Bill shops, prominent financial institutions in the late Qing Dynasty, dominated the domestic financial sector with its substantial capital and extensive operations before modern banks emerged. Its far-reaching influence significantly shaped China's financial industry. While scholars debate the precise origins of bill shops, most agree that Rishengchang Bill Shop—established in 1823 from the restructured Xiyucheng Pigment Shop—was China's first. Its swift growth spurred the creation of numerous Shanxi-based bill shops. The development of bill shops can be divided into five stages: initial growth, decline, recovery, peak, and eventual decline. This century-long journey mirrors the socioeconomic transformations during the late Qing Dynasty. Bill shops played a crucial role in advancing ancient bills. They introduced innovative bill types, encouraged wider usage among the populace, and expanded the circulation range of these financial instruments. By building a nationwide exchange network, bill shops significantly enhanced the transferability of bills. Furthermore, bill shops established sophisticated exchange systems, including innovative strategies such as "allocating funds between the main shop and its branches, and increase lending to expand profits." They also implemented confidential codes and exchange rate settlement methods. These flexible practices not only improved operations but also effectively managed risks.

I. Emergence and Development of Century-Old Bill Shops

Currently, there is ongoing debate within the academic community about the origin of bill shops. Some argue they originated in the Tang and Song dynasties, while others suggest the middle of the Ming Dynasty.[5] However, the majority believe bill shops first appeared in the early 1920s. Advocates of this latter view consider Rishengchang, restructured from the Xiyucheng Pigment Shop in 1823, as the pioneer of bill shops. They regard Lei Lütai, the founder of Rishengchang, as the industry's progenitor. During the late Qing Dynasty, spanning nearly a century, Rishengchang made significant contributions to Chinese financial history through its astute management and sterling reputation. It is no exaggeration to call it the "leader of national finance." Its operations provided valuable insights for modern Chinese banks, fostering the growth of China's financial industry. The emergence of bill shops was a historical inevitability—a natural product of commercial and financial evolution. To fully understand bill shops, one must consider their historical context.

Bill shops were financial organizations that primarily supported commercial development through services such as exchange and deposit. The thriving commercial environment nurtured the growth of bill shops, underscoring that these institutions could not exist without robust commercial development. Since the establishment of the Qing Dynasty in 1644, internal and external conflicts had gradually subsided, creating a stable social environment conducive to commercial development. From Emperor Kangxi's reign onwards, China's social productivity began to recover, with commodity exchanges expanding significantly in both volume and geographical reach. By the early years of Emperor Daoguang's reign, the society was peaceful, and commerce had reached a substantial scale. The resurgence of mercantilism during the Ming and Qing dynasties greatly boosted China's commercial development. Among scholars, farmers, artisans and merchants, merchants traditionally held the lowest status in ancient Chinese society. Despite this, their role gained recognition and their status elevated with the rise of mercantilism. Historical records indicate that from the 17th to the early 19th century, an increasing number of people in China abandoned Confucian pursuit to engage in commerce. Marriages between scholar and merchant families became commonplace, with the two groups often interchanging roles. During Emperor Qianlong's reign, the total capital of Shanxi and Anhui merchants in Yangzhou reached 70–80 million taels of silver, with some prominent salt merchants (such as Wang Jiaoru, Jiang Chun, and Bao Zhidao) holding millions of taels in assets. At the peak of the Qing Dynasty, the imperial treasury held only 700,000 taels of silver, indicating that increasing social wealth was concentrated in the hands of merchants. This trend led the country to value commercial development more, attracting talented individuals to the business sector and promoting rapid commercial growth. As commerce flourished, traders sought to expand beyond regional limits, leading to inter-port trade development. However, the need for long-distance cash transportation, which was time-consuming, labor-intensive, and insecure, impeded further growth in inter-port trade. To address this issue, financially stable shops with numerous national branches began offering exchange services. As inter-port trade prospered, a need arose for specialized organizations to manage this business, resulting in the emergence of bill shops.

The emergence of old and well-known commercial families supplied ample talent and capital for the establishment of bill shops. During the late Qing Dynasty, several new commercial families rose to prominence in Shanxi, including the Li family in Pingyao, the Hou family in Jiexiu, the Qiao family in Qi County, the Cao family in Taigu, and the Ji family in Jiexiu.[6] These families had substantial capital and owned diverse industries across the country. They faced a pressing need to manage long-distance cash flows and had ample capital to invest and generate value. Consequently, they were highly motivated to establish financial institutions such as bill shops.

The evolution of the financial industry and exchange during the Qing Dynasty paved the way for the advent of bill shops. Earlier financial institutions such as pawnshops, money houses, and accounting bureaus provided valuable experience that shaped the development of bill shops. While these institutions differed from bill shops in some aspects, they shared many operational similarities. The exchange business in our country dates back to the Tang Dynasty, with bills of exchange appearing as early as the 9th century. The Ming and Qing dynasties saw the rise of *huipiao*, marking the transition of exchange from an individual to a commercial practice. Lu Shiyi, a scholar in the late Ming and early Qing eras, noted in *On Currency*: "Many people today transfer large sums to the capital. To avoid travel risks, they entrust their money to wealthy merchants in the capital, who issue bills redeemable for the value, known as '*huipiao*,' similar to *feiqian* used in the Tang Dynasty."[7] This account vividly illustrates the use of *huipiao* during that period.

Shanxi was the birthplace of bill shops, owing to several deep-rooted factors. First, Pingyao boasted excellent transportation links. An official road network connected the east to Beijing, Tianjin, and West of Shanhai Pass; the west to Shaanxi, Gansu, and Xinjiang; the north to Guihua, Mongolia, and Russia; and the south to Hunan, Hubei, Guangdong, and Guangxi provinces. Second, by Emperor Daoguang's reign, Pingyao had evolved into a national cargo distribution hub, drawing merchants from across the country. Last, Pingyao was renowned for its merchant families who passed down their businesses through generations. This practice nurtured a wealth of elite talent and formed agricultural merchant families with substantial capital. Many Pingyao merchants established branches or chain shops nationwide, weaving an extensive trading network.[8] These conditions paved the way for bill shops to first emerge in Pingyao. The Xiyucheng Pigment Shop was restructured into Rishengchang Bill Shop, with its name "Rishengchang" symbolizing prosperity and growth. The establishment of the bill shop heralded a new era in China's financial development, marking a significant milestone in the country's thousand-year history of feudal finance.

1. Initial Development (1823-1850)

In 1823, China's first bill shop, Rishengchang, was established, evolving from the Xiyucheng Pigment Shop in Pingyao. This marked the emergence of bill shops as a new type of financial institution. Rishengchang was initially funded by Li Daquan from Dapu Village in Pingyao, Caidong, who invested a total of 360,000 taels of silver. Lei Lütai served as the general manager, with Mao Honghui as the assistant manager and Cheng Dapei as a deputy assistant manager. Each of the top managers received a salary share. Rishengchang initially set up eight branches in Chengdu, Chongqing, Hankou, Liaocheng, Peking, Tianjin, Baoding, and Shenyang, each staffed by four to seven people. Branch managers oversaw operations, assisted by their deputies. The branches ceased their involvement in the pigment business, maintaining only the "Risheng Rice Mill" business in Hanyang as a nod to their roots. Though the mill was considered a branch, it kept its own accounts. Rishengchang's services included remittance, deposit, lending, donation handling, and the issuance of silver bills.

Following Rishengchang's establishment, its business flourished and grew increasingly prosperous. Consequently, wealthy merchants and tycoons in the area soon followed suit and began operating similar businesses. A businessman from Beijia Village, Jiexiu, who was known as "Millionaire Hou," was the first to see the potential of bill shop business. Three years later, in the sixth year of Emperor Daoguang's reign (1826), he reorganized five existing shops in Pingyao, with names all beginning with "蔚" (Wei), into bill shops. In the seventeenth year of Emperor Daoguang's reign (1837), Heshengyuan, the first bill shop in Qi County, was established. In the eighteenth year of Emperor Daoguang's reign (1838), Rishengchang invested additional funds to establish a bill shop named Rixinzhong. They then opened Rixinzhong branches in 14 locations, including Beijing, Zhangjiakou, Guihua, Sanyuan, Ji'nan, Zhoucun, Yingkou, Zhoukou, Nanjing, Suzhou, Zhenjiang, Wuhu, Tunxi, and Hankou.[9]

From 1823 to 1850, the continuous development of commerce and the rising demand for exchanges, deposits, and loans drove the bill shops into the first period of significant growth. During this period, the number of bill shops rapidly increased, and their reach expanded quickly. According to statistics, from 1823 to 1853, there were a total of 16 bill shops in Pingyao, including Chengguangqing and Guangtaixing, which closed shortly after their establishment. In 1853, three new bill shops, namely Xiehexin, Xietongqing, and Baichuantong, were established. By 1853, Pingyao boasted 17 bill shops. As these establishments expanded their operations, their reputation soared. This was due to their exceptional service and adherence to a business philosophy of "seeking profit through integrity and righteousness." Consequently, the bill shops' social credit rapidly improved. In the third year of Emperor Xianfeng's reign (1853), Yang Yizeng, the Governor General of the Jiangnan Dao, emphasized in a memorial, "Owing to their good credit status, bill shops in each province can exchange for millions of taels of silver using only pieces of paper [bills] as proof."[10] In the second year of Emperor Xianfeng's reign (1852), Feng Guifen (1809–1874), a prominent thinker in the late Qing Dynasty, praised Shanxi bill shops in an article titled "On Using Copper Coins Without Phasing Out the Use of Silver," saying, "Nowadays, bill shops in Shanxi often have several dozen branches scattered across provinces, and the *huipiao* they issue can circulate smoothly in different locations."[11] These statements reflect the high social reputation of bill shops at that time.

Bill shop businesses saw rapid growth during this period. Besides exchange operations, the deposit businesses of bill shops were also expanding quickly, with their geographical coverage steadily increasing. Previously, financial institutions such as accounting bureaus only offered deposit and withdrawal services locally. However, to manage exchange businesses, bill shops now had branches across the country. As a result, they could gather deposits and issue loans on a larger scale, aiding in nationwide fund adjustment. Deposit and lending by bill shops can be executed in tandem with, or separate from, exchange operations. These deposit and lending methods transformed bill shops into full-fledged financial institutions, conducting exchange, deposit, and lending businesses. They began performing the fundamental functions of modern banks. Beyond managing these operations, bill shops during this period also started operating donation businesses. According to historical records, since at least 1841 (the 21st year of Emperor Daoguang's reign), bill shops had been processing sizable donations. During the donation exchange management process from various provinces to Beijing, bill shops also collaborated with silver shops in Beijing to handle registration and licensing affairs on behalf of donors exchanging money for official positions or titles. Consequently, bill shops became intermediaries facilitating donations. While operating the donation business did not bring significant direct benefits, the potential advantages were numerous and varied.

2. Decline (1851-1861)

The Taiping Rebellion (1851–1864) plunged many southern provinces into conflict. Areas where the Taiping Army and the Qing Army clashed suffered severe damage to their urban economies. Market buildings were destroyed, populations fled, and industrial and commercial enterprises shut down, leaving many industrial and commercial towns and cities in a state of decay. In October 1856, the Second Opium War broke out, forcing the Qing government to sign the *Tianjin Treaty* and *Beijing Treaty*, which further entrenched China's semi-colonial status. Under these circumstances, bill shops had to close and lay off employees.

During this period, the domestic situation was highly unstable due to frequent wars, which severely impacted the urban economy. Industrial and commercial closures, market depression, and silver outflows worsened the bill shops' operating environment, causing a sharp decline in business demand. The prolonged wars also hindered the development of exchange business, leading to a slump in bill shop operations. However, many bill shops scaled back their operations and downsized, which helped them maintain their original strength. This prudent approach laid a solid foundation for later recovery and development. Although many bill shops closed down during this period, many others emerged, and some operated while reducing their branch networks. Despite setbacks faced by bill shops, some still yielded considerable profits. For instance, in the ninth year of Emperor Xianfeng's reign (1859), Weifenghou Bill Shop paid dividends after making a total profit of 82,499 taels over four years. At that time, the capital was only 30,000 taels, and the annual profit margin was 68.74%, with a total of 17.7 capital and human shares, yielding a dividend of 4,660.96 or more per share.[12] Overall, although bill shop operations were sluggish during this period, they didn't suffer a major blow. Once the war ended and the domestic environment stabilized, a slight stimulus could quickly revive and develop bill shops.

3. Recovery and Development (1862-1894)

The Taiping Rebellion and the Second Opium War had both positive and negative impacts on the development of bill shops. On the negative size, these wars forced bill shops to downsize and lay off employees, leading to a downturn in operations. However, they also disrupted the transportation channels for the tribute paid by each province to the court, which led the Qing government to temporarily allow its transportation through bill shop exchange, creating a new opportunity for bill shops to grow rapidly. Moreover, after the Second Opium War, the expansion of trading ports increased import and export trade, integrating China further into the world market and boosting the commodity currency economy. This, in turn, paved the way for the further development of bill shops.

In the first year of Emperor Tongzhi's reign (1862), the Qing government started allowing tribute from Guangdong to be exchanged in Beijing, marking the beginning of public fund remittance through bill shops, and operations flourished from a low point. The salaries of Qing government officials, wages of Eight Banners (military-administrative organizations of the Man nationality in the Qing Dynasty) soldiers, and imperial palace expenses relied on collecting silver from various provincial and customs sources like land, food, salt, and tariffs. These resources were transported to the capital to ensure supply and were then known as "capital tribute." Prior to 1862, capital tribute could only be paid through cash transportation, not remittance. However, due to the impact of the Taiping Rebellion, many provinces struggled to pay the tribute on time. Consequently, the Qing government began to accept tribute payments through remittance out of necessity.

After capital tribute could be exchanged in Beijing, provincial tribute also started being paid through remittance and exchange. In the fourth year of Emperor Tongzhi's reign (1865), Hedong Dao in Shanxi Province received three aid fund payments from Lanzhou, Gansu Province, totaling 80,000 taels of silver. All funds were exchanged by bill shops in Pingyao.[13] In the same year, Sichuan Province allocated 20,000 taels of official silver ingots, which were transferred to the Shaanxi treasury through bills shops like Yuanfengjiu.[14] In the seventh year of Emperor Tongzhi's reign (1868), under the 40% foreign tax of the Fujian Customs, 10,000 taels of silver were allocated each month as aid funds to Shaanxi. These were remitted by the Fukang Silver Shop in Fuzhou, which then transferred the funds to Hubei and subsequently to Shaanxi Province for use via the Shaanxi-Gansu Field Commissariat, an official office responsible for food and fund supplies.[15] According to incomplete statistics, by 1893, each province had remitted over 4.6 million taels of aid funds to Shaanxi, Gansu, and Xinjiang through bill shops.[16]

Aside from capital tribute and aid funds, bill shops also played a significant role in handling funds that supported the Westernization Movement. This movement, which began in the 1870s, involved comprehensive planning for coastal defense and the purchase of warships, both of which required substantial funding. These funds generally came from various provinces and were usually transported through remittance. Moreover, bill shops provided financial support for military salary payments and activities, underscoring their strong support for the Qing government.

Building on their experience with capital tribute, aid funds remittance and exchange businesses, bill shops gradually expanded into advance payment operations. During the remittance and exchange process, when provincial governments lacked sufficient funds, the bill shops provided advance payments, effectively offering loans to these local governments. This arrangement had led to a long-lasting dependency of the government on bill shops. According to historical records, places like Guangdong, Fujian, Zhejiang, Guangdong Customs, and Fujian Customs had all relied on advance payments from bill shops to alleviate inadequate public finances, with Guangdong and Guangdong Customs being the most notable cases.

Following the end of the Second Opium War and the Taiping Rebellion, relative domestic stability led to significant growth in bill shops, spurred by the introduction of public fund remittance and exchange services. During this period, bill shops quickly recovered their operations and surpassed previous development levels. Public fund remittance and exchange services brought bill shops closer to the Qing government. These services offered substantial benefits to these shops. First, the fees for remittance and exchange of public funds were generally higher. Second, the lead time for public funds was longer, typically between 80 days to three months, nearly two months longer than the one-month limit for regular industrial and commercial remittances. Last, the large amount of public funds allowed bill shops to gain substantial profits through interest, even without capital.

For local governments, the advance payments from bill shops alleviated the issue of insufficient funds. Bill shops would pay approximately half of the high remittance fees from the government as commissions to relevant officials. For the central government, the financial power of bill shops offered strong fiscal support, aiding in maintaining and consolidating feudal rule to some extent. During this period, bill shops and the Qing government formed a relationship of mutual utilization and interdependence. This marked a significant shift in the development of bill shops compared to earlier times. It was also during this period that bill shops increasingly relied on the Qing government's support, and their growth became closely tied to the Qing government.

4. Heyday (1895–1910)

The *Treaty of Shimonoseki*, which marked the end of the Sino-Japanese War of 1894, was signed in Shimonoseki, Japan on April 17, 1895. To finance the war and pay reparations, the Qing government borrowed money from England, Germany, Russia, France, and several foreign banks. The repayment of these loans and other foreign debts was managed by the government office of Jianghaiguan Dao, Shanghai, and delivered to various foreign banks in China as scheduled. Additionally, bill shops were responsible for handling the reparations of the *Boxer Protocol of 1901*, making substantial profits in the process. The large compensation brought significant remittance and exchange fee income to the bill shops, allowing them to acquire a substantial amount of low-cost funds, which were lent out to generate huge profits.

Table 2-1 Statistics of exchange of public funds by bill shops (1894–1911)

Item	Amount (tael)
Capital tribute	28,864,983
Imperial House expenditures	2,145,055
Expenditures of other types	908,413
Interest-bearing silver	314,067
Repayment of four-country loans	37,210,918
Reparations of new treaties	49,690,138
Repayment of other loans	7,099,314
Shanxi and Gansu salary funds	5,267,357
Salary funds of other types	8,208,011
Copper-based silver	666,000

(Continued)

Item	Amount (tael)
Navy funds for the Westernization Movement	968,219
Railway funds for the Westernization Movement	392,000
Other funds for the Westernization Movement	130,000
Total	141,864,475

Source: PBC Shanxi Branch, Shanxi University of Finance and Economics, and Compilation Group of Historical Materials of Shanxi Bill Shops, *Historical Materials of Shanxi Bill Shops*, rev. ed. (Taiyuan: Shanxi Economic Publishing House, 2002).

The further advancement of national industry and commerce contributed to bill shops reaching their peak. The Westernization Movement from the early 1860s to mid-1890s positively impacted the growth of modern industry and commerce in China. This movement involved the Qing government's efforts to maintain feudal rule by adopting advanced Western science and technology, establishing modern military and civilian industries, and reforming military, diplomatic, cultural, and educational sectors, as well as some government agencies. The movement's slogan was "striving to become stronger and richer," advocating for the development of military and private industries and the establishment of new education systems. This movement objectively promoted the development of China's modern industry and commerce, paving the way for modernization by the end of the 19th century. Within this context, bill shops also further developed.

Large companies had always been primary customers of bill shops, and their remittance and exchange amounts, along with those of business owners and private funds, accounted for the majority of the total remittance and exchange amount of bill shops. After the turn of the 20th century, with the initial development of modern Chinese enterprises, these enterprises began to emerge in the lending business of bill shops. Moreover, bill shops contributed positively to the construction of railways and the development of mines in the late Qing Dynasty. Some modern enterprises entrusted bill shops to collect and deposit stock funds nationwide. For example, in 1904, Henan Jun Kiln Porcelain Industry Company entrusted Dadetong Bill Shop's branch offices in various locations like Kaifeng, Shanghai, Hankou, and Beijing to raise stock funds and issue stocks on its behalf.[17] Similarly, Tianjin Wanyi Machine-Made Felt Co., Ltd. entrusted the local Yuanfengrun Bill Shop to collect the stock funds for the company.[18]

The surge in import and export trade was a significant factor contributing to the peak development of bill shops. As semi-colonialism deepened in China during the late Qing Dynasty, the number of foreign firms involved in import and export trade grew rapidly. According to statistics, there were 440 firms in 1882, 579 in 1892, and a sharp increase to 3,805 in 1913.[19] In just two decades, foreign firms increased by 5.57 times. These firms expanded their branches from various trading ports to China's hinterland to promote industrial products and plunder raw materials. For instance, some Tianjin-based foreign firms established institutions or agents in Zhangjiakou, Urga (now Ulaan Baatar), Guihua, Ningxia, and other areas to acquire China's fur and other raw materials. Consequently, foreign firms often needed to transfer funds between their trading ports and mainland branches, commonly using remittance and exchange services offered by bill shops. As import and export trade grew, the remittance and exchange business for foreign firms also expanded, making them important new customers for bill shops.

In brief, during this era, bill shop development was at its peak, with the total number of bill shops, especially their branches, rapidly growing. The financial network, consisting of headquarters and branches, spanned the entire country. With the introduction of telegrams, bill shops could genuinely connect to the world. During this period, bill shops not only established many branches in China but also opened branches abroad. For instance, in April 1907, Heshengyuan Bill Shop in Shanxi opened a sub-branch in Kobe, Japan, and advertised in Japanese newspapers. Six months later, the same shop opened branches in Tokyo, Yokohama, and Osaka in Japan, and Incheon in North Korea, all managed by the Kobe Sub-Branch.[20]

During this period, the profits and dividends of bill shops also increased several times over. For example, the Dadetong Bill Shop's dividend per share rose from 850 taels in 1888 to 4,024 taels in 1900—a 3.7-fold increase. By 1908, the dividend per share had skyrocketed to 17,000 taels, 20 times its initial value. Bill shops' various businesses also experienced rapid growth. In the remittance and exchange business, bill shops dominated the market through their financial network covering key towns and cities. In terms of deposit and lending, particularly deposits, bill shops held a significant position in the financial industry during the late Qing Dynasty due to their substantial deposit amounts. In conclusion, the term "leading national financial development" aptly describes bill shops in their peak period of development.

Table 2-2 Capital and dividends of Dadetong Bill Shop (1896–1908)

Year	Capital (tael)	Dividend per share (tael)
1896	140,000	3,150
1900	160,000	4,024
1904	180,000	6,850
1908	220,000	17,000

Source: Huang Jianhui, *A History of Shanxi Bill Shops*, rev. ed. (Taiyuan: Shanxi Economic Publishing House, 2002), 415.

5. Eventual Decline (1912–1932)

On October 10, 1911, the Wuchang Uprising began, signaling the start of the Revolution of 1911, the Chinese bourgeois democratic revolution led by Sun Yat-sen which overthrew the Qing Dynasty. From then until 1912, the urban economy suffered significant damage due to the Qing army's counterattack and Yuan Shikai's initiation of the "Beijing mutiny," leading to years of war and turmoil. Following the Xinren Incident, the subsequent war against Yuan Shikai in 1913 further devastated the economy and society, with bill shops incurring substantial losses in both conflicts.

Table 2-3 Statistics on losses of 12 bill shops in the Xinren Incident

Silver and property looted	Number of looted bill shops (tael)							
	Chengdu	Xi'an	Hankou	Taiyuan	Beijing	Tianjin	Ziliujing	Ningxia
Silver	738,931	439,850	65,690	2,700	6,475	9,550	3,500	69,200
Property	33,800	74,700	181,370	11,800		3,500	3,400	

Source: PBC Shanxi Branch, Shanxi University of Finance and Economics, and Compilation Group of Historical Materials of Shanxi Bill Shops, *Historical Materials of Shanxi Bill Shops*, rev. ed. (Taiyuan: Shanxi Economic Publishing House, 2002), 487–488.

The Revolution of 1911 overthrew the Qing Dynasty's rule, ending China's over two-thousand-year feudal autocracy. This upheaval stripped bill shops of their political backing, eliminating their lucrative public funds exchange business. It also severed the financial practice of "storing in the north and lending in the south," dealing bill shops a deadly blow. Furthermore, the rise of modern banks began to encroach upon the business of bill shops. The Imperial Bank of China (later translated as the Commercial Bank of China), established in 1897, was China's first self-operated bank. By 1911, the number of official and commercial banks in China had grown to 17. These well-capitalized banks started to conduct exchange business, a domain previously monopolized by bill shops, resulting in a loss of business for the latter. Two official banks established after the Commercial Bank of China, namely the Ministry of Revenue Bank (renamed the Ta-Ching Government Bank in 1908) founded in 1905 and the Bank of Communications (BOCOM) established in 1908, posed significant threats to the exchange business of bill shops.

The rapid growth of foreign banking in China also posed a significant threat to bill shops. Li Mianlin, the Governor of Jiangxi Province, noted in the early 20th century, "Recently, many foreign merchants have established banks in trade port cities, slightly eroding the benefits of Shanxi bill shops."[21] Consider the changes in Tianjin's currency exchange: the annual transfer of funds from Tianjin to Shanghai, primarily for cotton yarn, amounted to approximately ten million taels. Foreign banks handled half of these transactions, money houses and silver shops 30%, and bill shops merely 20%.[22] This demonstrated foreign banks' substantial impact on bill shops' currency exchange business in Tianjin. Similar shifts in currency transactions had occurred in all Chinese port cities with foreign bank branches and sub-branches, although the extent varied.

Drastic changes in the external environment, coupled with money shops' management system limitations and conservative, change-resistant leadership, caused them to miss a favorable restructuring opportunity. As a result, its operations declined, making recovery challenging. On the eve of the Revolution of 1911, there were 26 bill shops across various groups—24 bill shops operated by Shanxi merchants and 2 bill shops established by merchants for southern provinces like Zhejiang, Jiangsu, and Yunnan. From 1912 to 1921, 21 of the 24 Shanxi bill shops went bankrupt.[23] In the 1920s, the remaining bill shops either folded or transitioned to other businesses. These institutions, which had weathered a century of changes and once held a significant position in late Qing Dynasty finance, ended their remarkable journey and exited the historical stage—a truly regrettable outcome.

II. Bill Business of Bill Shops

1. Bills Issued by Bill Shops

Exchange was the primary business of bill shops, which extensively utilized bills in their operations. Exchange methods predated these shops in China. During Emperor Xianzong's reign (806–828) in the Tang Dynasty, *feiqian* or "flying money" emerged as a rudimentary form of exchange. However, *feiqian* was primarily used on a small scale by military and political groups, while wealthy merchants only engaged in informal exchange. Throughout the Song, Yuan, Ming, and mid-Qing dynasties, exchange practices surfaced sporadically but remained limited in scope. The late Qing Dynasty saw a significant expansion of the exchange business, marked by the rise of specialized institutions known as bill shops. These establishments primarily focused on bill exchange while also offering deposit and withdrawal services. They developed and refined comprehensive management systems for conducting exchange business.

Bill shops used various forms of exchange, including mail transfer and telegraphic transfer, with favorable and reverse transfers as specific methods. For mail transfers, money shops issued bills of exchange, which remitters then took to the designated location within a specified timeframe to redeem their funds. Telegraphic transfers, introduced by the official post office in the mid-Qing Guangxu period, were similar but used unique telegraphic codes to prevent disputes and ensure safety. Favorable exchange was the main method of bill shop exchange. This meant that if a customer from location A wanted to transfer money to location B, they would deliver a certain amount of silver of a specific quality to a bill shop at location A. They would then take the bill of exchange to location B, where the bill shop branch was located, to redeem the exchanged silver after evaluating the quality of the silver. Reverse exchange was an auxiliary method of bill shop exchange, used for trusted customers or to balance cash shortages between locations. In this process, the bill shop in location A would initiate the exchange business. Then, the bill shop in location B would either make or receive the payment first. Subsequently, the bill shop in location A would complete the transaction by either receiving or making the payment. The essence of this practice was "combining deposit and loan operations with exchange business, incorporating capital financing into silver transfers. When location B made a payment before receiving funds from location A, it merged loans with the exchange. Conversely, when location B received funds before location A made a payment, it combined deposits with the exchange."[24]

For reverse exchanges, both merchants and bill shops paid remittance fees and interest based on prevailing market rates. Although this method was supplementary, it offered significant advantages. It enabled bill shops to attract deposit and loan business while eliminating the need for physical silver transfers between locations. This arrangement proved highly convenient for merchants. A reverse exchange example appears in the 27th letter from the Zhangjiakou Branch of Rishengchang Bill Shop to Bianliang on the tenth day of the first lunar month in 1850 (30th year of Emperor Daoguang's reign): "We will make the payment upon receiving the previous letter. On September 1, 3,000 taels of high-quality silver were remitted from the Hankou Branch of Rishengchang Bill Shop. Our branch charges according to the standard rate of four taels of silver per year. Starting from the day we receive the silver, in addition to providing interest as per each party's regulations, our branch will offer an additional subsidy of six taels for every thousand taels of silver."

Bills of exchange were the most common instruments used in the exchange process. While styles varied among bills from different bill shops, the content remained largely consistent. These bills come in forms of single, double, or triple folds, with the single-fold form being predominant. The Rishengchang Bill Shop's bill of exchange serves as an illustrative example. Their blank bill is a four-fold document, structured from left to right as follows:

- The first fold features "Honest and Trustworthy" in light red vertical script in the upper middle part.
- The second fold displays either "Daoguang" or "Xianfeng" at the top in vertical script, with "*Li Huipiao*" (立会票) written below, slightly lower than the fold.
- The third fold contains the main body of the "*huipiao*," comprising four vertical rows of blank bars. The leftmost row, positioned higher than the others, is reserved for merchants' names.
- The fourth fold is split in two: the upper half bears the character "*Huijuan*" (会卷) in regular script, while the lower half showcases a colorful painting titled "Red, Yellow, Orange, Green, and Blue" alongside a vertical "Blessing from Heavenly Officials" pattern.

The blank bill matches the size of the bill actually used, measuring 25.3 cm high and 45.8 cm wide. The paper, likely rice paper, is flat yet resilient to creasing.[25]

After bill shops emerged in Shanxi, they continuously innovated their bill business, resulting in diverse bill types. According to historical records, these shops introduced various bill formats, including proof vouchers, exchange vouchers, posting vouchers, pot and bottle vouchers, posting bills, promissory vouchers, remittance vouchers, and traveler's checks. Among them, proof vouchers, exchange vouchers, and posting vouchers functioned like cash and were payable at sight. In contrast, the pot and bottle vouchers, posting bills, and promissory vouchers allowed for delayed payment, typically settled a few days after presentation.

2. Innovation of Bill Systems

Bill shops introduced innovations in the bill systems, primarily in risk management and accounting practices for bill exchange businesses. Preventing and controlling risks are vital for financial activities, necessitating a robust and efficient risk management system for financial organizations. Bill shops were long renowned for their prudent operations, reflecting their emphasis on risk management. Over time, they developed an efficient risk management system tailored to their unique business needs, resulting in few risk events. Effective accounting management also played a crucial role in helping these financial organizations understand their business status and enhance operational efficiency. The exchange rate settlement system used in bill account accounting stood out as a significant institutional innovation.

(1) Risk Control Mechanism for Exchange Business

Careful Selection of Customers and Exchange Locations

Each branch of bill shops operated under unique conditions, resulting in variances in the amount of exchange received and paid out. Consequently, some branches accumulated excess silver, while others faced shortages. To address cash flow issues stemming from these imbalances, daily correspondence occurred between the main shop and its branches, as well as among the branches themselves. These letters reported the amounts paid and received, along with current business conditions, allowing for more strategic operations. With this information at its disposal, the main shop could orchestrate the overall situation, allocating funds across its network and expanding lending to maximize profits. For example, if the Beijing Branch discovered that the Xi'an Branch had received substantial payments, it would actively seek business opportunities to exchange money with Xi'an. "In extreme cases, to swiftly correct imbalances, they would not only waive the remittance fee but even compensate the remitter."[26]

Risk Prevention for Bills of Exchange

Bills of exchange were the primary payment instruments in bill exchange transactions. As drawers could obtain funds using these documents, verifying their authenticity and preventing counterfeiting was crucial. A successfully cashed counterfeit bill could inflict severe financial damage on a bill shop. To counter this risk, bill shops employed several key anti-counterfeiting measures:

- Using special paper. Bill shops used specially crafted paper for their bills of exchange, which was difficult to counterfeit. For example, the Weitaihou Bill Shop in Pingyao County used paper with green lines and red grids, all printed at a single location in the county. This paper was used for bills at all branches across the country. If a bill was damaged, it had to be sent to the main shop for recording. The paper used by the shop was also imprinted with "蔚泰厚" (Weitaihou, the shop name).
- Appointing dedicated persons and using special seals. "A designated individual crafted each bill shop's bills of exchange using a brush, creating a handwriting record for the main office and all branches. Upon receiving a bill, the bill shop or its branch verified

it against the reserved handwriting sample. Payment was only authorized if there were no discrepancies. After the bill's completion, it was authenticated with various seals: header, deposit, landing, paging, typeface, and anti-counterfeiting seals."[27]

- Affixing secret codes to prevent fraudulent claims. Bills of exchange contained secret codes within the amount and date, known as the silver amount code and time code. Only authorized personnel could decipher these codes, while remitters and holders remained unaware of their meaning. To maintain security, bill shops changed these codes every few years. A mnemonic song helps in learning the codes: "Monthly Code:[28] Beware of fraudulent claims, and don't forget to verify handwriting and seals. Daily Code:[29] Life's unfair, but justice prevails, and selfishness harms; good and evil face consequences. Silver Code:[30] Exercise caution with strangers, act wisely. Additional Code:[31] Scrutinize deceit to ensure security."
- Using multiple copies to protect the rights and interests of both parties. Bills of exchange were typically issued in triplicate. "For outward remittance, the three parts were: the bill stub (kept at the issuing bill shop), the delivery note (serving as a payment notice), and the bill of exchange itself (given to the remitter)." The Dadetong Bill Shop used a similar "three-copy" format: one bill stub sent to the main shop or payment branches, the bill of exchange given to the remitter,[32] and another stub kept as a record by the remitting bill shop.[33] If a remitter or payee lost their bill, they could report it to the bill shop. The report would be verified against the shop or branch's retained stub. If correct, this proved no fraud had occurred, and the corresponding silver could be released. This system prevented fraudulent claims from lost bills, provided evidence for the bill shop, and deterred customers from falsely reporting amounts to gain wealth dishonestly.

To mitigate payment difficulties upon presentation, bill shops established regulations for deferred payment. "Bills of exchange came in two types: bills at sight, requiring immediate payment, and promissory notes, allowing payment within a few days."[34] To address potential issues with large payment amounts, provisions for deferred payment were implemented, typically "allowing three to five days after presentation."[35] The Wuhu Branch of Sanjinyuan Bill Shop set specific deferred payment periods: "ten days after sight or twelve days after remittance for Shanghai; ten days after sight or fifteen days after remittance for Hankou; sixteen days after remittance for Suzhou; and seventeen days after remittance for Shanxi—not exceeding seventeen days overall."[36] Despite these measures to reduce payment risks, clients with urgent needs could still cash unexpired bills, albeit with a fee. This "double fee" was two hundred *wen* per thousand taels, halved to a "single fee" for payees within the same industry.[37]

To prevent payment errors, rules of "Guarantee Required for Payment" and "Guarantee Required for Strangers" were established. Bill shops' exchange business used a system of "payable upon presentation and payable to the bearer." However, for large transfers, to ensure complete security, bill shops would stamp "Guarantee Required for Payment" and "Guarantee Required for Strangers" on bills of exchange. Any bill labeled "Guarantee Required for Payment" must obtain a commercial guarantee at the time of payment, while bills marked "Guarantee Required for Strangers" only required a guarantee when the payee was unfamiliar.[38]

To mitigate payment risks, bill shops employed "redemption notes" as a specific internal review measure for verification. The redemption note process worked as follows: Party A handed money to the bill shop to remit to Party B. The bill shop then issued a note, tearing it in half. The top half went to Party A, while the bottom half was sent to the bill shop's branch (Party C). Party A sent their half to Party D, who then presented it to Party C for payment. This process occurred without any guarantee.[39] To further deter forgery, bill shops cut the "redemption notes" into curved shapes.

(2) Exchange Difference Settlement System

The bill shops' system innovation extended to the accounting management system. Bill shops' settlement of exchange differences could be divided into internal clearing and external settlement. Internal clearing refers to the settlement within each bill shop, between the main shop and its branches, and among branches. For instance, if there was a remittance difference between branches over a certain period, it was reported to the main shop in two accounts: "monthly clearing and annual settlement." These accounts were categorized as "remittance received" and "remittance delivered," with detailed and total amounts, all cleared according to business with each branch and the main shop.

After the main shop received and verified the reported clearing, it recorded the monthly clearing collection and remittance difference separately in the transaction accounts between each branch and the main shop. If the received amount exceeded the delivered amount, the difference was deposited by the branch into the main store. Conversely, if the delivered amount was greater, the difference represented the main shop's debt to the branch, without interest. The entire shop implemented unified accounting.[40] External clearing refers to settlement between different bill shops, resulting from transfer settlements between merchants and forming creditor-debtor relationships among various financial institutions. Under the organization of money and banking industry associations, it was settled through a "verifying meeting." At a specified time, representatives from the money and commercial sectors gathered with the financial association to conduct a general check, verifying accounts with each other. If errors or missing items were discovered, payments could be recovered—a process known as "account recovery." Even amounts transferred through multiple shops or delayed for years could be recovered based on each shop's accounts, a unique method in the money market.[41] Bill shops in Shanxi stipulated regular "verifying meetings" (usually based on the standard period) for mutual offsetting and settlement of differences.

3. The Role of Bill Shops in Financial and Bill Development

Bill shops and modern banks shared numerous operational similarities, including exchange, deposit, and lending services. The strategies employed by bill shops offer valuable insights for modern banks in conducting related businesses. Moreover, the challenges bill shops faced during their transformation serve as crucial lessons. Modern banks had taken note of these issues in designing their management systems. They'd addressed problems such as inadequate supervision of general managers and the unlimited liability system. Bill shops had also made significant contributions by providing skilled personnel. Given the operational similarities, the management expertise from bill shops was highly relevant to modern banks. Through their rigorous talent selection and training processes, bill shops produced many business-savvy professionals. As bill shops declined, many of these experts transitioned to modern banking, substantially contributing to its evolution.

Modern financial institutions can draw valuable lessons from the history of bill shops. They should prioritize building credit and brand reputation, enhance human resource systems to boost employee engagement, and develop market-oriented enterprise systems. Additionally, these institutions should embrace reform and innovation to keep pace with current trends, strengthen risk management capabilities, cultivate effective government-business relationships, and improve both financial and information management practices.

Bill shops were important financial institutions in the history of ancient bills. They contributed to the diversification of bill types, promotion of bill usage, expansion of bill circulation, and improvement of bill systems. During their operations, bill shops extensively used various types of bills, especially bills of exchange. They innovated by creating promissory vouchers, exchange vouchers, posting vouchers, pot and bottle vouchers, posting bills, and traveler's checks. As bill shops proliferated, these bills became part of people's daily lives. The main business of bill shops was exchange, primarily using bills of exchange as vouchers. Through years of practice, they organized a nationwide exchange network, greatly enhancing the exchange function of bills. Bill shops also established a rigorous and comprehensive management system for exchange transactions, adopting a business strategy of "allocating funds between the main shop and it branches, and expanding lending to maximize profits" They promoted the concept of "payable to the bearer," and integrated exchange transactions with deposit and loan services. To prevent counterfeit bills, they implemented various measures such as using special paper, assigning dedicated personnel to write bills of exchange with special seals, creating multiple copies of bills, and establishing a confidential system. In accounting management, they used an exchange difference settlement system, which further promoted the development of related bill systems.

SECTION 4

Posting and Remittance Systems: Prototypes of the Bill Exchange System

As bills gained widespread circulation, efforts were made to enhance their convenience. Bills issued by one institution could be exchanged at others, necessitating clearance between the issuing and receiving institutions. This marked the birth of bill clearing. The system progressed from the initial posting system to the remittance system, culminating in the bill exchange system during the Republic of China period. Over time, a centralized clearing system emerged, significantly boosting bill clearing efficiency. This improvement, in turn, further propelled the circulation of bills.

I. Posting System

Compelling evidence shows that, at least by the mid-19th century, the money industry in Ningbo had implemented a posting system. Using Shanghai as a hub, this system spread nationwide, becoming a widely adopted and effective management practice in the national money industry. The posting system in Ningbo comprised three procedural steps:

- The buyer and seller record payments and receipts at their respective money houses, confirming these transactions.
- The following day, money houses settle accounts with their peers. Settlements are based on balances rather than individual merchants. When income exceeds payment, it's called a "surplus account," and the difference is collected in cash from the debtor who pays more than they receive. This process, akin to modern bank clearing houses, settles debts through exchange.
- Money houses and account-holding customers confirm receipts and payments to prevent errors.

Posting primarily facilitated bulk trade, with small transactions still using cash to maintain efficiency. While intra-money house postings had no minimum limit, inter-money house transactions did. The system evolved into six forms: account book, discount, money house bill, letter, special methods, and error correction. Initially limited to account book posting, it expanded to address various situations, reaching maturity by the late 19th century. Despite being a direct clearing method, its cumbersome procedures, time-consuming nature, labor intensity, and poor security rendered it inadequate for contemporary needs.

II. Remittance System

Around 1890, the Shanghai Money Industry Association established a remittance association within its premises on Ningbo Road and introduced a novel remittance system. This remittance association, a subsidiary of the Shanghai Money Industry Association, became the central institution for bill clearing. The remittance system was an indirect settlement method that used "public bills" as a medium, with the remittance association at its center. The settlement procedure was as follows:

- Bills were submitted for inspection and exchange for public bills (vouchers used by Shanghai money houses in old China to offset funds during the bill clearing process). Money houses collecting bills would send a senior steward or apprentice to the issuing money house for verification and collection of public bills before 3 p.m. daily. The minimum limit for a public bill was 500 taels (yuan), with any lesser amount termed a "small amount" and settled directly between the two money houses. Creditors received public bills while debtors sent them. The number of bills was specified on the public bills, which would then be stamped by the issuing money house after receiving them to prove their authenticity.
- The remittance association checked public bills. Every afternoon around 6 or 7 p.m., each remittance money house sent all collected public bills to the remittance association. The association's officer (known as "Mr. Public Bill") checked the bills and determined the balances, with any differences paid by the money house using vouchers.

The remittance system functioned for both member and non-member money houses. The remittance association served two key roles: it cleared bills between Chinese merchant banks and money houses, and it mediated interbank bill clearance among Chinese merchant banks.

In the late Qing Dynasty, the increasing use of bills and the growing need for clearing among peers led to the creation of the initial bill clearing system—the posting system. This system improved bill clearing efficiency and promoted the circulation of bills. However, it had notable drawbacks: decentralized clearing, complex procedures, time-consuming one-by-one account reconciliations with peers, and security risks associated with cash payments. Around 1890, the Shanghai Money Industry Association established a remittance association, providing a centralized venue for bill settlement. This centralized system further boosted efficiency, marking a significant step toward the maturity of China's modern bill system. Later, the bill exchange established during the Republic of China period also used a centralized clearing system, but with further improvements to the bill clearing method.

SECTION 5

Rise of Western-Style Bills: Unveiling the "Chaotic Era"

The late Qing Dynasty saw China's market forcibly opened to foreign invaders through unequal treaties, paving the way for foreign banks to enter the country. These banks introduced Western financial instruments—bills of exchange, promissory notes, and checks—leading to a fusion of Chinese and Western bill practices. This merger expanded bill types and refined trading and settlement systems, profoundly altering China's financial landscape. Concurrently, the Westernization Movement ignited a passion for Western learning, bringing foreign commercial laws to China. In response, the Qing government began enacting specific laws, including bill-related regulations, to regulate commercial behavior. These new laws and regulations established a framework for commercial activities, enhancing market regulation and safeguarding the rights of transaction parties. The exploration of bill-related laws during this period marked a significant ideological shift. It not only deeply influenced the subsequent development of bills but also laid a robust foundation for the future *Negotiable Instrument Law*.

I. Historical Conditions of the Late Qing Dynasty

The late Qing Dynasty heralded the dawn of modern Chinese history. Following the British army's forced opening of China's doors in 1840, the nation gradually shifted from a closed feudal state to a semi-colonial, semi-feudal country. This era witnessed an intense clash and blending of feudal and Western capitalist systems. The Chinese people embarked on an arduous yet extraordinary journey of development and exploration, with "change" as the period's defining characteristic. Politically, movements like the 1898 Reform ushered in explorations of constitutional monarchy, democracy, and republicanism. Economically, the Westernization Movement spurred the establishment of numerous modern enterprises, nurturing China's burgeoning industry and capitalism. Culturally, the influx of Western ideas and the exodus of young Chinese students to the West catalyzed a continuous collision between traditional Chinese thought and Western culture. Progressive intellectuals grappled with finding development models suited to China's unique context.

The Western powers' occupation and plunder of China through wars yielded both negative and positive outcomes. On the one hand, it disrupted peaceful life, inflicted deep humiliation, and subjected the Chinese people to prolonged oppression and economic damage. On the other, it starkly revealed to the Chinese people that backwardness invited aggression. It also connected China to the global community, integrating it into the world market and accelerating its modernization process. Notably, during the late Qing Dynasty, astute individuals, recognizing the vast economic disparity between China and the West, advocated emulating Western industrial and commercial development. This elevated the status of commerce in the economic landscape. The Qing government began enacting specific commercial laws and regulations, including those related to bills. From the preliminary plans and attempts of reformist legislation to the introduction of regulations such as the *Qing Dynasty Commercial Law by Imperial Order*, *Company Registration Trial Charter*, *Trademark Registration Trial Charter*, *Bankruptcy Law*, *Insurance Industry Charter*, *Draft Qing Dynasty Commercial Law*, and *Revised Draft Qing Dynasty Commercial Law* established fundamental guidelines for commercial conduct, while a comprehensive commercial legal system didn't fully materialize, these efforts laid crucial groundwork for future legislation, marked the emergence of commercial legislative awareness in China, and established fundamental guidelines for commercial conduct, fostering economic development. In terms of credit, the growing influence of Western countries spurred the rise of foreign and Chinese banks, significantly contributing to the modernization of China's credit industry. Concurrently, the modern Chinese banking and money industries developed their own credit reporting system, further exemplifying the period's credit system evolution. This system also bolstered the development of bills during this time.

During the late Qing Dynasty, money houses, bill shops, and new-style banks widely promoted bills, leading to their expanded use in domestic and international trade, as well as daily life. Bills' exchange function significantly improved, and their financing role gradually emerged. This enhanced their impact on commercial economy and foreign trade. Moreover, traditional Chinese bills began to merge with new Western-style bills.

II. New-Style Banks

The previous sections detailed old-style bills issued by money houses and bill shops. Now, we'll focus on modern bills issued by new-style banks. Since these new-style banks were the primary issuers of modern bills, we'll begin by exploring their origins and evolution.

China's modern banking landscape included foreign banks and Chinese-funded banks. After the Opium War, China's market was forcibly opened, resulting in an influx of foreign banks engaging in Sino-foreign trade. This created a demand for international exchange, deposit, and loan services. Consequently, foreign banks began offering specialized financial services at various port cities. As society developed and foreign banks proliferated, the Qing government recognized the necessity of establishing its own modern banks. Although China's modern banking industry did not develop concurrently with its capitalist industry and commerce, it eventually took shape. The Qing government played a crucial role in this development, notably through the establishment of institutions like the Imperial Bank of China, the Ministry of Revenue Bank, and the BOCOM.

In 1897, China's first domestic bank, the Imperial Bank of China, was established. Its founder, Sheng Xuanhuai (1844–1916), noted that "railway profits are distant but thin, while bank profits are close but thick." This remark indirectly reveals the Qing government's motive for establishing the bank—to alleviate its financial crisis. In 1905, the Ministry of Revenue Bank was founded. Though not directly controlled by the Qing government, its key participants were officials. "At its inception, it was poorly received as merchants viewed officialdom with caution." "The bank was created by officials, and the public hesitated to use its services." In 1908, the Qing government's Postal and Communications Department established the BOCOM as a joint government-commercial venture. Its aim was to "facilitate communications and invigorate four key areas: transportation, roads, electricity, and postal services." Despite its appearance as a joint venture between officials and businesses, it remained essentially under Qing government control.

Foreign banks engaged in various operations, including issuing, buying, and selling bills of exchange, discounting bills, and handling outward bills. In 1852, an overseas merchant observed that the Oriental Bank "wasn't performing typical banking functions but merely trading bills of exchange." Zhou Jingui, a comprador of the Commercial Bank Corporation of India and the East, remarked that bill transactions were "daily occurrences." The Shanghai Branch of Yokohama Specie Bank specifically managed bill settlements for all branches. Likewise, the Hongkong and Shanghai Banking Corporation (HSBC) focused on international exchange transactions—primarily buying and selling bills of exchange—as its core business.

Bill discounting and outward bills were a crucial part of the foreign bank lending business. "During the early stages of port openings, banks focused on discounting and rediscounting bills from the opium and cotton trade." However, as bill discounting carried inherent risks, banks typically required guarantees for bill discounting. HSBC's Hong Kong headquarters initially advertised their bill discounting services openly. In the mid-1870s, the Oriental Bank shifted its focus to large-scale discounting and lending operations. The outward bill of exchange business emerged as early as the 1860s, facilitating foreign trade financing. Contemporary records note, "When purchasing export bills of exchange, the ship's bill of lading, insurance policy, and original invoice detailing the goods must be included, with the consignee responsible for any future payment shortfalls." *Regulations of the Commercial Bank Corporation of India and the East* stated, "For goods to be shipped to various ports, the delivery note should be handed to the bank for withdrawal, and the bill of exchange calculated at current prices. Upon arrival, the bank will act as an agent to sell the goods. When the bill of exchange expires, the parties will exchange silver and goods."

Chinese banks progressively standardized their bill operations, establishing a bill system inspired by foreign banks. The Ta-Ching Government Bank's *Rules for the Ta-Ching Government Bank* explicitly listed "discounting and selling various promissory notes," "collecting bills issued by businesses and banks," and "issuing diverse bills" as its core operations.

Chinese banks also considered discounting a crucial part of their operations. Major institutions, including the Bank of China, BOCOM, and others known as "the three southern banks" and "the four northern banks," explicitly included discounting in their charters. However, due to inherent risks, banks approached this business cautiously. For example, the Bank of China's *Discounting and Lending Rules* prohibited customers from discounting bills if they were the drawees or the money house owners. The rules also stipulated that "customers seeking discounting should provide a guarantor, though this requirement may be waived in special circumstances or if the bank deems the customer financially secure and trustworthy." The National Industrial Bank of China stipulated that "discounting should be limited to partner banks, and the creditworthiness of the payer, drawer, and discounting party should be carefully scrutinized."

III. New-Style Bills

Modern banks primarily issued three types of bills: bills of exchange, promissory notes, and checks.

1. Bills of Exchange

Foreign banks were established to facilitate their merchants' trade in China. These banks provided financing by offering international exchange services, which promoted the use and development of foreign bank bills. By the 19th century, bills of exchange had become a crucial instrument for both domestic and international trade. Contemporary accounts note: "Trade transactions use an average of 600,000 pounds in bills monthly—about 7.2 million pounds annually. This mainly covers foreign exchange for opium purchases and bills for silk and other exports." As Sino-foreign trade expanded, China's money and banking industries increasingly accepted and used foreign bank bills. An 1886 *Xiamen News* report stated, "HSBC's bills, in particular, have long enjoyed the trust of the gentry and merchants." From the 1880s, more money houses in Hankou began using foreign bills of exchange to remit money to Shanghai. In 1899, a *North China Daily News* correspondent in Chongqing reported, "Those having connections with Shanghai banks have reaped significant profits, and both local and foreign bills of exchange are in high demand."

The Imperial Bank of China, like other Chinese banks, issued bills of exchange and conducted bill business. "Each branch must assess the bank's liquidity, support one another, and be cautious when accepting various bills of exchange." At its founding, the bank held 50,000 taels in bills payable and 1,105,000 taels in bills receivable. By 1909, however, the bank's bills payable had surged to 913,000 taels, while bills receivable dwindled to just 188,000 taels. These figures highlight the bank's rapid expansion in bill issuance.

2. Promissory Notes and Checks

Foreign banks in China issued bank bills on a large scale, which were essentially a unique form of bank promissory notes. For example, the Oriental Bank issued silver bills in denominations of five, ten, fifty, one hundred, and five hundred taels. In 1865, the five-hundred-tael silver bills issued by the bank bore the English inscription "Silver Bill of the Imperial Bank Corporation in Shanghai" and the Chinese characters "凭票取规银伍佰两" (Payable for Five Hundred Taels of Standard Silver). Later, in 1905, Citibank issued silver dollar bills in denominations of five, ten, and one hundred yuan.

In 1898, the Imperial Bank of China issued silver dollar bills of 1 million yuan and silver bills of 100,000 taels. These notes featured Chinese phrases such as "Promises to Pay the Bearer on Demand at Its Office Here" and "Pay to Bearer." This marked China's first self-issued bank bills, ushering in a new era of Chinese bills. The BOCOM's *Articles of Association* allowed it to "emulate various banks and print flat-colored silver bills and other bills commonly used in the local market." In its inaugural year, the BOCOM printed its own promissory notes, bearing the phrases "Promises to Pay the Bearer on Demand at Its Office Here" and "98 Standard Silver."

Foreign merchants also used checks to pay for raw materials and local products. After receiving these foreign bank checks, Chinese merchants entrusted them to money houses for collection. Chinese banks also issued their own checks.

Summary

From the Kangxi period of the Qing Dynasty, the commercial economy rapidly recovered and developed, leading to widespread circulation of bills. In the late Qing Dynasty, the rise of money houses and bill shops significantly increased their use. Foreign banks introduced novel types of bills to China, blending Chinese and Western practices. By the late Qing Dynasty, bills had evolved into reliable payment and settlement instruments, enhancing daily life and bolstering both domestic and international trade. The large-scale issuance of bills satisfied the growing demand for currency and effectively regulated the finances during that era. Bill discounting emerged during the Qing Dynasty, gradually unveiling the financing potential of bills. This development laid the foundation for bills' strengthened financing role in the Republic of China period.

NOTES

1. Liu Qiugen and Xie Xiuli, "The Preliminary Development of Paper-Form Commercial Credit in the Ming and Qing Dynasties: Centered on Bills and Exchange," *China Numismatics*, no. 1 (2006): 3–11, 79.
2. Dai Jianbing, "A Brief Exploration of Modern Chinese Money Bills," *Journal of Hebei University of Economics and Trade*, no. 5 (1996): 73–78.
3. Zhang Guohui, *A Study on Late Qing Dynasty Money Houses and Bill Shops* (Beijing: Social Sciences Literature Press, 1989), 58.
4. Yan Hongzhong, *A History of Chinese Finance* (Shanghai University of Finance and Economics Press, 2020).
5. *The Bankers Weekly*, no. 7 and no. 8.
6. Zhang Guiping, *A Study on the Management System of Shanxi Bill Shop Operations* (Beijing: China Economic Publishing House, 2005), 21.
7. "On Currency," "The Household Administration" (Volume 27), in *Continuation of Imperial Classics and Chronicles* (Volume 52).
8. Wang Yidian, *A Century's Vicissitudes of Rishengchang Money House* (Taiyuan: Shanxi Economic Publishing House, 2013), 5.
9. Ibid., 7–8.
10. Shi Ruomin, *The Rise and Fall of Bill Merchants* (Beijing: China Economic Publishing House, 1999), 143.
11. "On Currency," in *Continuation of Imperial Classics and Chronicles* (Volume 58).
12. Huang Jianhui, *A History of Shanxi Bill Shops*, rev. ed. (Taiyuan: Shanxi Economic Publishing House, 2002), 185.
13. "Wang Rongji's Memorial for Remitting Salary Funds to Gansu" (5th day, 8th month, the 4th year of Emperor Tongzhi's reign [1865]), in *The Grand Council Records.*
14. "Luo Bingzhang's Memorial Annex" (September of the fourth year of Emperor Tongzhi's reign [1865]), in *The Grand Council Records.*
15. Ying Gui et al., "Memorial" (April 20 of the seventh year of Emperor Tongzhi's reign [1868]), in *The Grand Council Records.*
16. People's Bank of China Shanxi Provincial Branch, Shanxi University of Finance and Economics, Compilation Group of Historical Materials of Shanxi Bill Shops, *Historical Materials of Shanxi Bill Shops (Oil Print)* (Taiyuan: Shanxi People's Publishing House, 2002).
17. *Oriental Magazine 1*, no. 8 (August 1904): 115.

18. *Ta Kung Pao*, September 18, 1906.
19. Wu Chengming, *Imperialism's Investment in Old China* (Beijing: People's Publishing House, 1956), 41.
20. Zhang Zhengming, *Shanxi Merchants and Business Culture* (Beijing: World Book Publishing Company, 1998), 7.
21. Li Mianlin, "Revised Version on the Flexible Government Policy," *Shun Pao*, July 2, 1901.
22. Kichi Negishi, "Tianjin Bill Shops," in *An Overview of Qing Dynasty Business*, vol. 4 (Tokyo: Maruyama Corporation, 1906), 412–413.
23. People's Bank of China Shanxi Branch, Shanxi University of Finance and Economics, and Compilation Group of Historical Materials of Shanxi Bill Shops, *Historical Materials of Shanxi Bill Shops*, rev. ed. (Taiyuan: Shanxi Economic Publishing House, 2002), 660–664.
24. Huang Jianhui, *A History of Shanxi Bill Shops*, rev. ed. (Taiyuan: Shanxi Economic Publishing House, 2002), 106.
25. Wang Yidian, *A Century's Vicissitudes of Rishengchang Bill Shop* (Taiyuan: Shanxi Economic Publishing House, 2013), 81–85.
26. People's Bank of China Shanxi Branch, Shanxi University of Finance and Economics, and Compilation Group of Historical Materials of Shanxi Bill Shops, *Historical Materials of Shanxi Bill Shops*, rev. ed. (Taiyuan: Shanxi Economic Publishing House, 2002), 222.
27. Kong Xiangyi, "The Enterprise System of Shanxi Merchants," *Journal of Shanxi Finance and Taxation College*, no. 6 (2007).
28. The month code used 12 characters to represent the 12 months of a year.
29. The day code used 30 characters to represent the 30 days of a month.
30. The silver code is represented by ten characters in the original complex form (壹, 贰, 叁, 肆, 伍, 陆, 柒, 捌,玖, 拾), meaning 1, 2, 3, 4, 5, 6, 7, 8, 9, and 10.
31. To prevent the leakage of month, day, and silver codes, a layer of anti-counterfeiting code is added, that is, the additional code.
32. People's Bank of China Shanxi Branch, Shanxi University of Finance and Economics, and Compilation Group of Historical Materials of Shanxi Bill Shops, *Historical Materials of Shanxi Bill Shops*, rev. ed. (Taiyuan: Shanxi Economic Publishing House, 2002), 375.
33. Wei Juxian, *A History of Shanxi Bill Shops* (Chongqing: Chongqing Shuowen Society, 1944), 145.
34. People's Bank of China Shanxi Branch, Shanxi University of Finance and Economics, and Compilation Group of Historical Materials of Shanxi Bill Shops, *Historical Materials of Shanxi Bill Shops*, rev. ed. (Taiyuan: Shanxi Economic Publishing House, 2002), 377.
35. Ibid., 388.
36. Ibid., 215.
37. Jun Shi, "Shanxi Bill Shops," *The Oriental Magazine*, no. 6 (1917): 7.
38. People's Bank of China Shanxi Branch, Shanxi University of Finance and Economics, and Compilation Group of Historical Materials of Shanxi Bill Shops, *Historical Materials of Shanxi Bill Shops*, rev. ed. (Taiyuan: Shanxi Economic Publishing House, 2002), 405.
39. Chen Qitian, *A Brief Study of Shanxi Bill Shops* (Beijing: Commercial Press, 1937), 302.
40. Kong Xiangyi, "The Enterprise System of Jin Merchants," *Journal of Shanxi Finance and Taxation College*, no. 6 (2005): 5.
41. Ibid., 4.

PART TWO

BILLS IN THE PERIOD OF THE REPUBLIC OF CHINA

CHAPTER THREE

Negotiable Instruments Before the Promulgation of *The Negotiable Instrument Law* and Its Promulgation

Following the Revolution of 1911, traditional financial institutions such as bill shops experienced a decline. Influenced by bill speculation and rubber stock rush, the number of money houses diminished dramatically and the credit of bill shops plummeted. However, during World War I, weakened imperialist forces in China led to the emergence of national industry and commerce. This provided sufficient funds for the development of money houses, leading to a revival in the money house business. Modern banks also entered a golden development period. A tripartite competition arose among money houses, foreign banks, and modern Chinese banks. The market was flooded with old-style bills represented by money house bills, new-style bills from foreign banks, and Chinese new-style bills. Due to the lack of unified institutional norms, the types, names, and customs of bills varied across regions. The bills in the market were a mix of Chinese and Western elements, and new and old bills were intermingled, leading to extremely chaotic circulation. The book *Research on the Negotiable Instrument Law*, published by the Shanghai-based *The Bankers Weekly* in 1922, enumerated over 100 types of bills.[1] The circulation of bills varied across regions, with different regions having unique and chaotic practices.

Long-term disarray in bill management severely hampered sustained and healthy development of the bill market. In March 1923, the Bank of China, BOCOM, Shanghai Bank, and Bank of Jiangsu jointly established the Anhui Bengbu Discount Office to standardize interbank discounting operations. The money and banking industries had strived to regulate bill development by introducing unified industry regulations. However, due to socioeconomic factors, the financial industry alone couldn't fully achieve this. The five-year legislation attempts by the Beiyang Government (1912–1928) also ended in failure. In 1929, the Republic of China officially promulgated *The Negotiable Instrument Law*, the first of its kind in China, marking the initial establishment of China's modern bill legal system.

SECTION I

Bengbu Discount Office: Institution Specialized in Bills

During the early days of the Republic of China, bill trading methods were primarily limited to discounting and remittance business. Chinese-funded banks also lent money to money houses through interbank discounting. New-style banks and traditional money houses each had their own focus when handling bill business, with traditional banks handling more discounting business. Despite many new-style banks listing discounting as an important part of their business in their charters and regulations, many did not actually engage in discounting business. Typically, buyers would first discount the bills they received at money houses, and these money houses would then discount these already discounted bills at banks, which could be regarded as interbank discounting. In March 1923, the Bank of China, BOCOM, Shanghai Bank, and Bank of Jiangsu jointly established the first specialized bill institution in modern China, known as the Bengbu Discount Office. This institution, which specializes in interbank discounting, has significant relevance to the development of the bill market.

I. Background of Establishment

Bengbu, located at the north-south transportation hub along the Jin–Pu (Tianjin–Pukou) Railway and the Huaihe River, formed a land and water transportation center and became a distribution center for goods across northern Anhui, western Anhui, and southeastern Henan. Rapid commercial development was seen, especially in the salt, grain, and transportation industries. Merchants flocked here to "buy rice and wheat, transporting bills of lading via railway to secure funds with banks. However, demand exceeded supply each year."[2] The difficulty of investigating customers' credit status, stagnation in goods transportation, frequent payment delays, and the widespread practice of picking up goods without a bill of lading had all posed significant business risks to banks. In response, banks discontinued their remittance business. They instead purchased discounted promissory notes from other places, guaranteed by various forwarding companies. These notes, with short terms and high profits, are foolproof, making them the primary bulk transaction in Bengbu.[3] Over the years, the discount bill business had surged. Banks often competed blindly, continuously lowering interest rates to attract business. This led to a perception of thin profits and heavy responsibilities among banks. "To avoid disputes, prevent merchant exploitation, and adjust finances, a discount office was established through public consultation."[4] The Bengbu Discount Office in Anhui, officially opened on March 19, 1923, strictly prohibited private operations and unified the market. This led to clearer information, less risk, increased interest, and greater unity among banks. Its operation had been very successful.

II. Organizational Structure

The Bengbu Discount Office consisted of four banks: Bank of China, BOCOM, Shanghai Bank, and Bank of Jiangsu, and was affiliated with the Bank of China. Each bank appointed one staff member to handle its affairs.

III. Explanation of Discounted Bills[5]

1. Drawers and Payees

Bengbu was a grain-producing area in northern Anhui. Numerous groups, including the Tianjin Faction, Shandong Faction, Zhenjiang Faction, Changzhou Faction, and Wuxi Faction, conducted their business in Bengbu, typically without carrying cash. If the discount office offered low rates, they would issue promissory notes guaranteed by their companies, and then discounted and cashed them at the headquarters. This kind of discounting was most prevalent among Zhenjiang, Changzhou, and Wuxi factions, followed by Tianjin factions, while they were rarely used by the Shanghai Faction. These were all examples of discounted bills. Moreover, there was a covert form of bill discounting where bills were backed by guarantors, which reduced the risk.

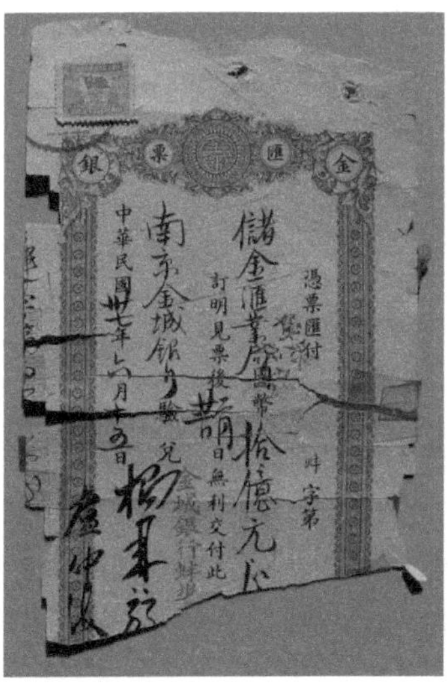

Figure 3-1 Acceptance bill of Bank of Jiangsu in Bengbu

Source: Collected by Guo Kai.

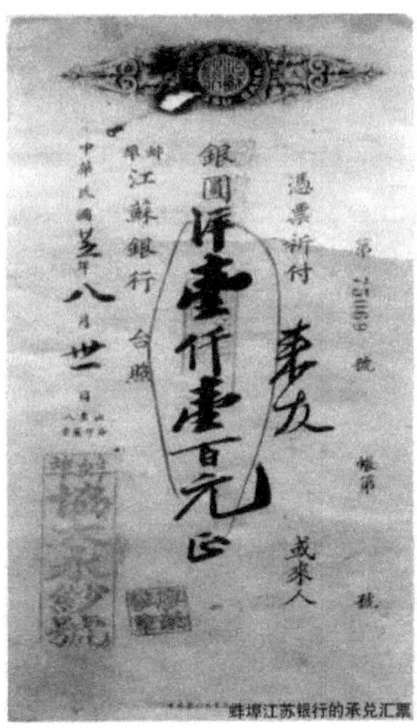

Figure 3-2 Acceptance bill of Bank of Jiangsu in Bengbu

Source: Wan Liming, "Bengbu Discount Office," *China Finance*, no. 17 (2015): 98–99.

2. Terms of Discounting Bills

The discounting period at the Bengbu Discount Office was typically three to five days after sight. For board-dated bills,[6] the maximum period did not exceed ten days after sight. However, it's worth noting that bills paid ten days after sight were extremely rare.

3. Guarantee for Discounted Bills

Discounted bills were often jointly guaranteed by one or two companies and must be endorsed by the forwarding company. Occasionally, the money house might also provide an endorsement. It was rare for customers to directly discount them at the bank.

4. Risks of the Bengbu Discount Office

Since the establishment of the Bengbu Discount Office, two risk events had occurred. In one instance, the guarantor compensated for the principal, while reducing the interest by approximately ten yuan. In the other instance, the guarantor compensated both the principal and interest in full.

5. Purpose of Discounted Funds

The discounted funds should be used for proper purposes and collected by each entity for purchasing goods. Since the establishment of the Bengbu Discount Office, incidents of cashing out through discounting had occurred. Transactions were immediately halted once such activity was detected. Guarantors were very prudent as they were unwilling to become involved in violations. Therefore, banks maintained confidence in ensuring the proper use of such funds.

6. Approximate Monthly Discount Amount

From March 1923 to June 1926, the highest monthly discount amount exceeded 1.09 million yuan, while the lowest was just over 10,000 yuan. The discount amount was influenced by the stability of the situation and the availability of trucks.

IV. Functions

1. Stabilizing Discount Interest Rate

The Bengbu Discount Office was established by the four leading banks in Bengbu, namely Bank of China, BOCOM, Shanghai Bank, and Bank of Jiangsu. "As such, its discount rate could at least serve as the standard interest rate for these four banks. Given the influence of these banks, the city's interest rates could only fluctuate based on this rate. Therefore, this system could establish a powerful central bank discount rate."[7]

2. Preventing Multiple Discounting of Individual Bills and Reducing Risks

The bills were uniformly discounted at the Bengbu Discount Office. The Bank of China paid the necessary amount for discounting upfront. Once the account was checked on the same day, other banks separately transferred or delivered the cash. This allowed the Bengbu Discount Office to accurately understand the credit status of customers, prevented multiple discounting of individual bills, and effectively minimized the operational risks associated with bills.

3. Adjusting Deposit Funds and Standardizing Financial Markets

The market trade in Bengbu experienced significant fluctuations, posing a challenge for banks to comprehend the relationship between currency supply and demand. The Bengbu Discount Office centralized the discounting business of diverse banks within its office. This approach not only lowered information collection costs, but also standardized the use of discount funds. Consequently, it optimized the allocation of financial resources and fostered stable development of the financial market.[8]

V. Operation Modes

Discounted bills must be stamped, signed, and guaranteed by money houses and transfer companies recognized by the Bengbu Discount Office to be accepted. After the bill was discounted, the payee could receive payment at the Bank of China using a receipt. The Bank of China advanced the discount payment, which, after being processed by the office at 4 p.m. on the same day, was transferred or cashed out at each receiving bank. After 4 p.m. each day, the office distributed the bills received that day to various banks. Then the office filled out the receipts, which were stamped and verified by the discounting companies and money houses. The daily discounted bill prices were negotiated jointly by four banks at 10 a.m. each

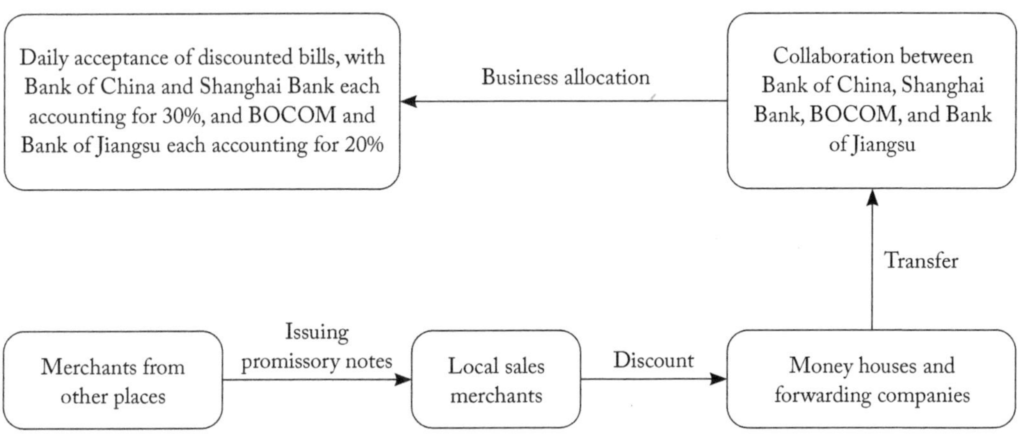

Figure 3-3 Schematic diagram of the Bengbu Discount Office operation

Source: Wan Liming, *Research on the Institutional Evolution of the Modern Chinese Bill Market* (Shanghai Far East Publishing House, 2014), 202.

day. The daily discounted bills were recognized and distributed proportionately by the Bank of China, and it was agreed that each bank would deposit a certain amount of funds in the Bank of China as a reserve.[9]

VI. Limitations

1. Limited Discount Scope

The types of bills discounted by the Bengbu Discount Office were limited to promissory notes exchanged between money houses and transfer companies, a scope that was too narrow. Consequently, each bank inevitably ended up discounting other bills independently.

2. Rigid Division of Responsibilities Among Different Banks

Each bank's allotment of discount bills was percentage-based, which often failed to meet each bank's unique supply and demand of discount. The Bank of China advanced the discount funds, leading to a rigid division of responsibilities.

3. Potential for Monopoly

Bills from money houses and transfer companies needed to be discounted at the Bengbu Discount Office, which could easily lead to a monopoly.[10]

VII. Significance

The Bengbu Discount Office, an institution specializing in interbank discounting, was established to better facilitate loans to money houses. Upon receiving discounted bills from customers, money houses could transfer these to the Bengbu Discount Office for interbank discounting. This process leveraged the strengths of both parties and promoted the development of banking business. It was a primary financing method for Chinese-funded banks. The establishment of the Bengbu Discount Office, the first specialized institution in modern Chinese bill history, revolutionized the previous unhealthy interbank bill trading competition. It also standardized the local bill market and fostered the healthy growth of the financial market in Bengbu. Additionally, it spurred the development of China's discount industry at the time, serving as a driving force and model for the evolution of the bill market.

SECTION 2

The Negotiable Instrument Law: Unification and Institutionalization of Bills

Before replacing the tael with the yuan as the currency unit in 1933, China's currency system was in disarray, leading to the widespread use of various bills as substitutes for currency circulation. The market was flooded with a mix of domestic and foreign bills, both new and old.

The lack of sufficient legal regulations for these bills resulted in long-term chaos and disorder in China's bill market, with numerous negative effects. Various money and banking institutions introduced a series of systems and norms to regulate bill circulation, and the Beiyang Government also worked toward bill legislation. These efforts by modern China to establish a bill legal system were crucial for maintaining order and promoting standardization of bills. They also laid a solid theoretical foundation for the enactment of *The Negotiable Instrument Law*. In 1929, *The Negotiable Instrument Law* was officially enacted. This marked the first official bill legal system in China, setting the stage for the institutionalization of the Chinese bill market.

I. Exploration of the Bill System in the Banking and Monetary Industries

The bill business played a pivotal role in the banking and monetary industries, making the standardized development of the bill market crucial. Before *The Negotiable Instrument Law* was officially enacted in 1929, the banking and monetary industries had issued several business regulations, including provisions on bills. These regulations held significant importance in maintaining order in the bill market and promoting standardized development of bills, especially in the absence of bill laws.

The monetary industry had made significant efforts in standardizing bill practices, with the industry in Shanghai making the most notable contributions. *The Regulations on the Reorganization of Shanghai's Monetary Industry* issued in 1900 was the city's first written regulation in its monetary industry. It placed high emphasis on the credit of money house bills and provided clear guidelines on reporting and suspension of payments of money house bills, as well as handling their loss. These regulations also established rules for issuing due receipts for promissory notes and checks. Out of the seven business regulations, five were related to bills. *The Reorganization Regulations* issued in 1904 added rules for using money house bills, introducing regulations on bill power, collection charges, and other related matters.

The Reorganization Regulations issued in 1905 included specific measures for handling unfamiliar individuals who needed to redeem cash with money house bills. It demanded that all promissory notes be dated. In 1907, these regulations were augmented with content related to risk prevention, risk sharing, and procedures in case of accidents. *The Business Rules* of the Shanghai monetary industry, issued in 1917, thoroughly examined issues pertaining to bills and introduced regulations on topics such as bills of exchange and checks. *The Business Rules of 1923* were the first to explicitly state that the credit of a money house bill could be "considered as cash." However, the status of money house bills declined due to the policy of replacing tael with yuan. In *The Regulations of Shanghai Monetary Industry* issued in 1933, the provision considering money house bills as "cash" was removed.[11]

Beside the Shanghai money industry, money industry associations in other regions also established regulations related to bills. Around 1921, the Yangzhou Money Industry Association specifically outlined the types of bills, procedures for reporting and stopping payment of lost bills, and down payment of bills in its business rules. In 1925, the *Wuxi County Money*

Industry Business Rules outlined regulations on bill types, money house bills, bills of exchange, and checks. In 1931, the *Business Regulations for Members of the Hankou Money Industry Association* provided detailed regulations on collection charges, bill collection and distribution, bill types, reporting and stop payment of lost bills, along with other bill-related issues.[12]

The banking industry also established specific regulations regarding bill transactions. In September 1920, the Shanghai Bank implemented the *Shanghai Bank Business Regulations*, identifying bill discounting, domestic and foreign exchange, and bill remittance as key business areas. It provided detailed procedures on sealing promissory notes, checks, and bills of exchange. It also covered reporting and halting payment of lost promissory notes and bills of exchange, as well as exchanging checks for promissory notes.[13] In 1937, the *Revised Shanghai Banking Industry Regulations* identified the acceptance, exchange, and remittance, as well as the discounting of promissory notes, as significant banking operations. Chapters 7, 8, and 9 of the document offered detailed regulations on significant bills, bill procedures, loss reporting, and payment suspension.[14] However, due to the different regulations on bill circulation in various banking and monetary industries, China's bill system was extremely chaotic and inconsistent before the formal introduction of *The Negotiable Instrument Law*.

II. Promulgation

Legislative work on bills in China started in the late Qing Dynasty. However, the true legislative process began during the Beiyang Government era. In 1921, the Beiyang Government initiated its legislative work on bills.[15]

1. Background of the Promulgation of *The Negotiable Instrument Law*

After the Opium War, China was invaded by Western powers, which significantly violated its judicial sovereignty, and undermined its national economy and the livelihood of its people. As a result of a series of unequal treaties, an increasing number of ambitious individuals began to demand the development of national industry and commerce. After the Republic of China was established in 1912, Western powers were preoccupied with wars, and Chinese national capitalist industry and commerce had opportunities to develop. The industrial development brought prosperity to trade, and bills, as instruments for payment and settlement, were widely used. However, after World War I, China's proposal to abolish the consular jurisdiction of foreign countries in China was rejected at the Paris Peace Conference, despite its participation as a victorious country. This rejection was largely due to the dismissive behavior of Western countries. In response, the Nationalist Government unilaterally abolished the consular jurisdiction of Western powers in China and ordered a revision of various laws, including the negotiable instrument law. The absence of a modern Chinese bill legal system was detrimental to the development of bills. Especially in the early Republic of China period. As the types, quantities, and circulation scope of bills expanded, numerous bill disputes arose. This situation highlighted the urgent need for a comprehensive bill system to standardize the bill business process.[16]

2. Tortuous Process of Bill Legal System Building in the Early Republic of China Period

Banking and money industry groups had been instrumental in promoting the development of bill legislation. In 1921, the Hangzhou and Beijing banking associations each submitted a proposal urging the government to swiftly enact the negotiable instrument law, directly influencing the Beiyang Government's legislative efforts concerning bills. The Shanghai Banking Association took note of the proposal and promptly established a Negotiable Instrument Law Committee to select member banks for discussion. By 1925, the Law Revision Office had crafted five draft bills, with the Shanghai Bank Association actively contributing numerous suggestions. However, due to the reorganization of the office, bill legislation efforts during the Beiyang Government period came to a halt.

The five-year legislative work of the Beiyang Government established the groundwork for the introduction of *The Negotiable Instrument Law*. In 1928, the Nationalist Government in Nanjing set up the Ministry of Industry and Commerce and formed the Industrial and Commercial Regulations Committee. With the suggestion of Xu Jigu, an influential financier during the Republic of China period, the drafting of *The Negotiable Instrument Law* resumed. The Industrial and Commercial Regulations Committee drafted *The Negotiable Instrument Law (Draft)*, based on the negotiable instrument law drafted by the Law Revision Office and also considering the negotiable instrument laws of countries like the United States, as well as previous drafts and opinions. *The Negotiable Instrument Law (Second Draft)* was then completed, and the Ministry of Industry and Commerce immediately submitted the draft to the Executive Yuan to be forwarded to the Legislative Yuan for review. It was also sent to the Ministry of Finance for review, which, with its review opinions, also forwarded the document to the Legislative Yuan. The Legislative Yuan's Commercial Law Drafting Committee wrote a new draft based on the Legislative Yuan's resolution. This new draft consisted of five chapters,

Figure 3-4 Cover of *The Negotiable Instrument Law*

Source: Collected by Guo Kai.

12 sections, and 139 articles, which became the text of the forthcoming *Negotiable Instrument Law*. On October 30, 1929, *The Negotiable Instrument Law* was officially enacted,[17] signifying the initial establishment of China's modern bill legal system and the progress in credit-based commodity economy.

The Shanghai Banking Association contended that the negotiable instrument law had significant relevance to the banking industry. However, many provisions in the law lacked alignment with banking business practices. As such, shortly after *The Negotiable Instrument Law* was enacted, a new Negotiable Instrument Law Research Association was established to scrutinize the negotiable instrument law, clause by clause, and presented its findings to the Shanghai Banking Association. The Shanghai Banking Association consequently drafted *Opinions on the Supplementation and Interpretation of the Negotiable Instrument Law*, which was then submitted to the Legislative Yuan. Subsequently, the Shanghai Banking Association conducted another discussion regarding the unpassed bill. In March 1930, the Ministry of Industry and Commerce compiled the *Implementation Law of the Negotiable Instrument Law (Draft)* and submitted it to the Executive Yuan to be forwarded to the Ministry of Finance for review. On July 1, the implementation law was officially announced and enforced. This law, comprising 20 articles, provides additional explanations for *The Negotiable Instrument Law*.

Following this, the Shanghai Banking Association issued a directive to banking societies, instructing them to partake in the discussion on the revision of *The Negotiable Instrument Law*. Even though the law remained unamended, the Shanghai Banking Association's efforts to protect banks' interests and its contributions to bill legislation deserve recognition.

III. Content and Features[18]

1. Analysis of Articles in the Law

(1) Types and Nature of Bills

The Negotiable Instrument Law drew from the relevant laws of the United Kingdom, the United States, Japan, and other countries. It adapted these rules to China's specific national conditions and categorized negotiable instruments into three types: bills of exchange, promissory notes, and checks.

Negotiable instruments had formality, non-causality, inherent value, suggestive power, literalness, and independence. According to *The Negotiable Instrument Law*, "The person who signs the negotiable instrument is held accountable as per the meaning stated on it." "Even if a person without legal capacity signs the instrument, it doesn't impact the rights and obligations of other signatories." "The debtor of the instrument cannot use defenses previously held between themselves and the drawer or holder against the latter. However, this limitation doesn't apply if the holder acquires the instrument through malicious intent or fraud." "The forgery of instruments or signatures on them doesn't affect the validity of genuine signatures."[19]

(2) Negotiable Instrument Behavior System

Issuance involves recording essential information on a negotiable instrument, signed by the issuer and then handed over to the recipient. "The issuer guarantees acceptance and payment as per the terms of the bills of exchange. However, the obligation of ensuring acceptance and payment can be waived by special agreement. If a record on the bill of exchange exempts the guarantee payment, that record is deemed invalid."[20]

Acceptance refers to the promise of payment by the acceptor to the bearer. *The Negotiable Instrument Law* sets a time limit for acceptance, stating that "for bills of exchange payable at regular intervals after sight, the presentation for acceptance must be made within six months from the issuance date. The drawer may shorten or extend this period through a special agreement. However, the extended period should not exceed six months."[21]

Endorsement involves transferring the rights of a negotiable instrument through marking its back or an attached note. "The endorser makes this endorsement on the back of a negotiable instrument or its attached note, recording the name or business name of the endorsee and the date of the endorsement. The endorser signs the endorsement. If the endorsee only signs the negotiable instrument without recording, it is essentially a blank endorsement."[22] "The bearer proves their rights through a chain of endorsements. If there's a blank endorsement among them, the subsequent endorser is considered the endorsee of the preceding blank endorsement."[23]

(3) Negotiable Instrument Rights

Negotiable instrument rights refer to the rights of the bearer to request payment of the bill amount from the debtor. These include the rights of payment request and recourse.

The right to request payment, often known as the right of first claim, allows the bearer to demand payment from the main debtor of the negotiable instrument (such as the acceptor of the bill, the drawer of the promissory note, or the check guarantor). *The Negotiable Instrument Law* states that the payer has absolute responsibility for the debt: "The bearer of the bill should provide a payment reminder within two days after the due date. If a payer is recorded on the bill of exchange, the payment reminder must be provided to this individual."[24]

The right of recourse, also known as the right to demand repayment, allows the bearer of a negotiable instrument to request the return of the face amount and associated legally-guaranteed fees from any previous bearer, if the right of first claim is lost. "This right can be exercised against the endorser, drawer, and other debtors on a negotiable instrument when the instrument is not paid upon the due date, following the exercise or preservation of rights on the instrument." "The bearer can also exercise this right under the following circumstances, even before the due date: when a negotiable instrument is refused to be accepted; if the payer or acceptor evades or cannot present for acceptance due to death or other reasons; if the payer or acceptor is declared bankrupt."[25]

2. Features of *The Negotiable Instrument Law*

(1) One Law for Three Types of Negotiable Instruments

In China, bills of exchange, promissory notes, and checks were often used interchangeably. In 1929, *The Negotiable Instrument Law* amalgamated bills of exchange, promissory notes, and checks into one legal system, demonstrating the scientific and rational nature of bill legislation. This law, based on the commonalities of the three types of negotiable instruments, included specific general provisions that established the general rules for these bills. This not only simplified the bill legal system but also showcased the progressive nature of China's legislation.

(2) Integration of Chinese and Western Elements

The Negotiable Instrument Law was formulated based on traditional Chinese negotiable instrument customs and experience from the negotiable instrument laws of multiple countries. It borrowed ideas from countries such as the United Kingdom, the United States, Germany, Japan, and France, advocating for the separation of the basic relationship and bill relationship of negotiable instruments to accelerate their circulation.

(3) Emphasis on Non-Causality and Independence

Bills are primarily used to facilitate commercial transactions. Therefore, *The Negotiable Instrument Law* emphasized the independence and non-causality of negotiable instruments, aiming to alleviate any constraints on their circulation.

IV. Judicial Practice

According to the Supreme Court's *Civil Cases Journal*, on April 4, 1930, three bills of exchange were issued by Chubao Firm, with Fuyuanzheng Company currently holding them. All three bills bore the words "Accepted by Chongyu," but lacked an endorsement on the back for transferring it from "Chongyu" to Fuyuanzheng Company. Luo Jingshan, the subsequent acceptor stamped his acceptance on the back of the negotiable instruments but later refused to make payment to Fuyuanzheng Company, claiming that there was no endorsement by "Chongyu" for the transfer. In the original and first instance, it was found that Luo Jingshan had stamped the back of the negotiable instruments, indicating his acceptance. According to local customs, the person who stamped should make the payment. Therefore, Luo Jingshan was ruled to bear payment responsibility. However, Luo Jingshan lodged an appeal to the court. The Supreme Court found that despite Luo Jingshan's stamped acceptance, the bearer in this case did not have an endorsement on the back of the negotiable instruments for the transfer from "Chongyu," meaning the endorsement was discontinuous and couldn't validate the authenticity of the negotiable instrument rights. Despite the inconsistency between local customs and legal provisions, the Supreme Court highlighted the unified legal application and ruled that Luo Jingshan was not responsible for payment, in accordance with the provisions in *The Negotiable Instrument Law*.[26]

V. Significance and Inspirations

The Negotiable Instrument Law was the first written legal norm for the modern Chinese bill market. This law signified a breakthrough in bill legislation, effectively promoting the standardized development of bills during the Republic of China period. The law's formulation carefully considered traditional Chinese bill customs, while also incorporating Western bill legislation experiences. It categorized negotiable instruments into bills of exchange, promissory notes, and checks. It also established standardized systems for various aspects of bills, such as issuance, guarantee, acceptance, endorsement, and writing-off. This further promoted standardization in China's bill market and ensured the effective use and circulation of bills. Consequently, it served as an initial result of the exploration and development in the early Republic of China period.

1. Improving the Legal System

The Negotiable Instrument Law was developed on the basis of the bill drafts from the late Qing Dynasty and early Republic of China period. It borrowed extensively from the bill systems of the United Kingdom, the United States, Germany, and Japan, and integrated them with traditional Chinese customs. Its enactment greatly advanced the modern Chinese bill legal system. This can be summed up in the following way, "The success or failure of businesses hinges on finance, and financial health is often gauged by the effective use of bills. Thus, finance serves as the lifeblood of business, with bills acting as its backbone."[27]

2. Delivering Economic Benefits

The Negotiable Instrument Law standardized the issuance and format of bills issued by money houses and banks to expedite their circulation. This, in turn, promoted trade prosperity and boosted the national economy. The total value of commercial goods traded in 1930 saw an increase of approximately 20,000 taels compared to that in 1928. Similarly, the total value of goods exchanged among ports also rose by more than 2,000 taels.[28] These figures clearly demonstrate the economic benefits delivered by the law.

Summary

In the early days of the Republic of China, the negotiable instrument was an essential instrument for financing and played an important role in promoting trade. The dominant money house bills functioned as "cash with equivalent value." Merchants used these bills for payment and settlement, which helped stimulate Sino-foreign trade. Shanghai bills of exchange, a significant method of fund allocation, could be monetized and sold anytime in the market. It functioned as a "cash chip," allowing major commercial ports to adjust their fund positions through its purchase and sale. It served as a financial link between various regions and Shanghai, promoting both domestic and foreign trade. The establishment of the Bengbu Discount

Office in Anhui was a significant step toward creating a specialized institution for modern Chinese bills. This move held substantial importance in regulating the orderly development of regional bill markets, promoting the healthy operation of regional financial markets, and advancing the development of the modern Chinese discounting industry. However, the chaotic circulation of bills in the early Republic of China period persisted. The banking and money industries remained committed to regulating bill circulation and introducing systems for its control. The Beiyang Government made significant strides in building the legal framework for bills. The enactment of *The Negotiable Instrument Law* laid the legal foundation for the modern Chinese bill market, leading the market toward standardized development.

NOTES

1. Hu Mengjia, "Advice to the Research Committee on the *Negotiable Instrument Law*," in *Research on the Negotiable Instrument Law*, ed. The Bankers Weekly Editorial Office (Shanghai: The Bankers Weekly, 1922), 1–26.
2. Ma Yinchu, *The Complete Works of Ma Yinchu*, vol. 4 (Hangzhou: Zhejiang People's Publishing House, 1999), 323.
3. Ibid.
4. Ibid., 324.
5. Ibid., 324–326.
6. Board-dated bills refer to bills that require payment on a specified date.
7. Wan Liming, *Research on the Institutional Evolution of the Modern Chinese Bill Market* (Shanghai Far East Publishing House, 2014), 204.
8. Joint Institute for Commercial Paper of JUFE and BOJJ, *A History of Bills* (Beijing: China Financial Publishing House, 2020), 128.
9. Ma Yinchu, *The Complete Works of Ma Yinchu*, vol. 4 (Hangzhou: Zhejiang People's Publishing House, 1999), 324, 326–327.
10. "Observation of the Bengbu Discount Office," *The Bankers Weekly*, no. 27 (1923): 24–42.
11. Du Xuncheng, *The Common Law of Modern Chinese Money Industry: From the Perspective of Shanghai Money Industry* (Shanghai University of Finance and Economics Press, 2006), 32–45.
12. Wan Liming, *Research on the Institutional Evolution of the Modern Chinese Bill Market* (Shanghai Far East Publishing House, 2014), 28.
13. "Shanghai Bank's Articles of Association," in *Principles of the Negotiable Instrument Law*, ed. Wang Dunchang (Beijing: The Commercial Press, 2016), 116–119.
14. "Revisions to the Shanghai Banking Industry Regulations," in *An Economic History of the Republic of China: The Bankers Weekly 30th Anniversary Commemorative Issue*, ed. Zhu Sihuang (Shanghai: The Bankers Weekly, 1948), 580–582.
15. Wan Liming, *Research on the Institutional Evolution of the Modern Chinese Bill Market* (Shanghai Far East Publishing House, 2014), 26.
16. Joint Institute for Commercial Paper of JUFE and BOJJ, *A History of Bills* (Beijing: China Financial Publishing House, 2020), 128.
17. Wan Liming, "The Shanghai Bank Association and Bill Legislation in the 1920s and 1930s," *Social Science Research*, no. 5 (2007): 169–174.
18. Joint Institute for Commercial Paper of JUFE and BOJJ, *A History of Bills* (Beijing: China Financial Publishing House, 2020), 133–137.
19. *The Negotiable Instrument Law of the Republic of China* (1929), Articles 2, 5, 10, and 12.

20. Ibid., Article 26.
21. Ibid., Article 42.
22. Ibid., Article 28.
23. Ibid., Article 34.
24. Ibid., Article 66.
25. Ibid., Article 82.
26. Joint Institute for Commercial Paper of JUFE and BOJJ, *A History of Bills* (Beijing: China Financial Publishing House, 2020), 137–138.
27. Xu Cangshui and Yao Zhongba, *Suggestions on Research Regarding the Negotiable Instrument Law* (Shanghai: The Bankers Weekly, 1922).
28. Lu Yangyuan and Fang Qingqiu, *A Social and Economic History of the Republic of China* (Beijing: China Economic Publishing House, 1991).

CHAPTER FOUR

Negotiable Instruments After the Promulgation of *The Negotiable Instrument Law*

In the late 1920s and early 1930s, the introduction of foreign bill theory led to the emergence of acceptance bills and discounting businesses. From 1930 to 1931, the banking industry, led by the BOCOM, began promoting these services, triggering a movement in Shanghai's financial industry. The BOCOM not only designed and created acceptance bills, handled acceptance bills and discounting business for itself and other banks, but it also issued the first specialized regulations on bill acceptance and discounting. By 1932, businesses, represented by domestic enamel shops, had joined this movement, starting to handle commercial acceptance bills and discounting businesses. This first wave of acceptance bills in modern China, promoted by theorists and embraced by the banking and business communities, significantly advanced acceptance bills and discounting businesses in the country.

However, the "Silver Wave" of 1934, a financial crisis caused by the massive outflow of silver from China, led to a tightened monetary policy and a subsequent industrial and commercial depression in Shanghai. In response, industry organizations advocated for commercial acceptance bills in 1935, sparking a second wave. This led to the establishment of the Shanghai Bank Bill Acceptance Office, marking the formation of a regional bill market in Shanghai and leading to the rapid development of the bill discounting business in modern China. After the full-scale outbreak of the War of Resistance Against Japan in 1937, with the fall of Shanghai and Wuhan, the Nationalist Government relocated to Chongqing, which became the political and wartime financial center. The government promoted the Chongqing bill market and the discount market, issuing regulations to encourage the development of acceptance bills and stabilize wartime finance, in an effort to promote wartime economic development and support the development of industries such as industry, agriculture, commerce, and mining. During this period, the bill exchange system also saw significant development. The establishment of the Shanghai Commercial Paper Exchange Company Ltd. led to the emergence of a new type of bill exchange system that gradually became dominant. During the war, the Chongqing United Bill Acceptance Office was established. As of June 1, 1942, the Central Bank officially took charge of the Chongqing bill exchange work, marking the establishment of the central bank's bill clearing function. The central bank also considered rediscounting as one of its essential functions. Although the *Central Bank Regulations* of 1927 had clearly defined rediscounting as a business operation, it was not until the *Measures for Bill Acceptance and Discount During Extraordinary Period* were issued in 1943 that the rediscount system was officially established. In July 1943, the central bank began handling rediscount business and established a rediscount review committee, officially affirming the rediscount function.

Following the victory of the War of Resistance Against Japanese Aggression, various financial institutions became active again, reaffirming Shanghai's role as a financial center. To encourage active finance use, support economic growth, enhance the bill acceptance and discount system, and promote the system nationwide, the Nationalist Government introduced the *Measures for Acceptance and Discount of Negotiable Instruments* on December 9, 1945. The *Banking Law of the Republic of China* (hereafter referred to as *Banking Law*) was enacted in September 1947, outlining "bill acceptance" and "handling various loans and bill discounting" as the primary operations of commercial banks.[1] During this period, numerous commercial banks enacted their own regulations to administer bill acceptance and discounting. The bill acceptance and discounting business saw rapid growth in the post-war era, and industrial and commercial enterprises began to regularly use acceptance and discounting to secure funds.

To solidify the absolute advantage of bureaucratic capitalist finance, the Nationalist Government imposed various restrictions on the national financial industry. They issued the *Interim Measures for Restricting the Use of Bills of the Day*, which stated that bills, except promissory notes, bills of exchange, remittance receipts, or guaranteed checks, could not be used on the same day they were required. This regulation prompted the public to withdraw cash from money houses and banks or exchange for promissory notes, leading to a significant increase in market cash and a proliferation of promissory notes.[2] The result was escalating inflation, with the fiat currency nearing collapse. The over-issuance of gold yuan notes (paper money issued by Kuomingtang in 1948) became a serious issue, and large-denomination banknotes were in short supply. Consequently, banks vied to issue large-denomination promissory notes to replace cash in circulation. When the central bank couldn't issue promissory notes promptly, it released large-denomination fixed-amount promissory notes, further stimulating price increases. To curb the growth of the national financial industry, the central bank limited the lending interest rates of private money houses and banks. Under this policy, deposit interest rates were extremely low, driving depositors to withdraw their money for black market transactions. This gave rise to underground money houses and posting notes[3] became increasingly rampant.

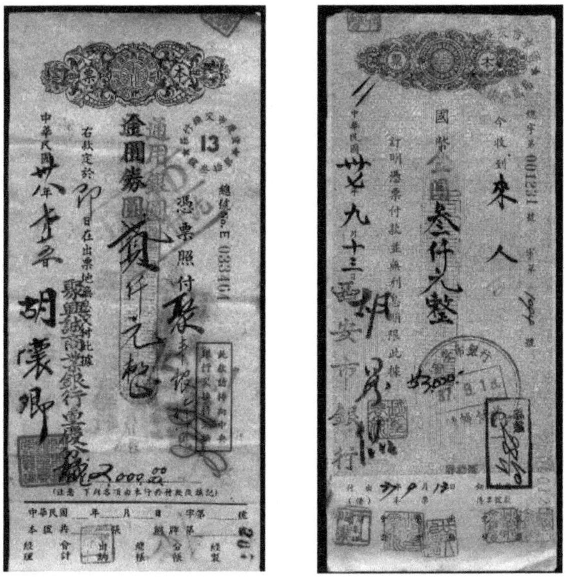

Figure 4-1 Bank promissory notes during the Liberation War

Source: Collected by Guo Kai.

SECTION I

Rise of Bill Theory: First Wave of Acceptance Bills

From 1912 to 1928, many new-style banks in China were opened and then closed. This phenomenon was largely due to these banks investing heavily in government loans, bonds, and real estate. The use of short-term funds for long-term investments often led to significant losses amid instability and turmoil. After the 1920s, there were few new industrial enterprises, and most struggled with capital turnover due to poor management. Some businesses even faced bankruptcy shortly after starting operations. In June 1928, the price of silver started a four-year-long decline, severely affecting political and economic development. Various sectors sought solutions, and the idea of establishing an acceptance and discount market emerged. This proposal was positively received by the theoretical, banking, and business communities.[4]

I. Spread of Acceptance and Discounting Theory

On November 27, 1917, *The Bankers Weekly* published an article titled "On Negotiable Instrument Discounting,"[5] introducing the theory of bill business for the first time. Subsequently, the journal often featured articles related to bank acceptance bills, commercial acceptance bills, and discount businesses in countries like the United States and the United Kingdom. Concurrently, other publications like the *Economic Quarterly* and the *Current Affairs News* began to feature articles on acceptance bills and discount businesses and gradually shifted the focus of discussion toward domestic implementation.[6]

In his monograph *On Chinese Banks*, Ma Yinchu (1882–1982), a prominent Chinese economist and banker, provided a detailed discussion on the principles, advantages, and status quo of the discount business in the Chinese banking industry. He analyzed the reasons behind its underdevelopment and proposed specific methods and strategies for its advancement. Ma argued that the discount business benefited both the banking industry and commercial sectors. First, it facilitated transactions, as merchants could settle debts through forward bills at the time of transaction. Otherwise, a lack of funds could prevent the completion of a deal. Second, the drawer, endorser, and bill bearer were collectively responsible and obligated to fulfill their debts, ensuring fund recovery upon the bill's maturity. Third, the longest period for discounting bills did not exceed four months, aligning with the principle of utilizing short-term funds. Last, discounted bills could be rediscounted with the central bank or other banks when funds were needed, offering high liquidity. Therefore, funds could be secured by selling through endorsement or rediscounting.[7] Regarding the implementation of discounting, Ma Yinchu suggested a few strategies. First, since China had never habitually used discounting, loan contracts could be used as bills of exchange after slight modification of its terms. As a transitional method, they could be rediscounted with the central bank after the bank provides a discount. Second, the government could offer tax incentives, such as exempting discounted bills from being stamped. Third, banks should lower discount rates while increasing mortgage lending rates. Last, the circulation and use of commercial bills should be encouraged, and money houses and banks should be allowed to use these bills instead of government bonds as preparation for receiving cash from large banks.[8]

Financial scientist Yang Yinpu (1898–1966), in his monograph *A Summary of Shanghai Financial Organizations*, argued that compared to other types of loans, discounting has a shorter term and easier fund recovery. In times of insufficient funds, banks can buy and discount bills to other banks for further lending. Yang saw discounting as a beneficial method for banks to utilize their funds.[9] He stressed the urgency of "promoting the enactment of the negotiable instrument law," recognizing its importance in the development of bill discounting. Without this law, he noted, "The use of bills cannot be standardized, limiting their popularity and hindering the development of bank discounting. This will result in an underdeveloped credit system that impedes the flow of funds."[10] Yang Yinpu also urged the construction of banking infrastructure, proposing the establishment of a bill exchange office and a credit information bureau. In his book *On Chinese Finance*, he emphasized that the discounting business "is a beneficial method for the financial industry to use funds and a potent instrument to aid industrial and commercial enterprises. It is more advantageous than lending." However, as bills were not widely used in transactions in China, the discounting business in the financial industry was underdeveloped. The average discount amount from various banks that also offered discounting services was less than 1% of the lending amount, which was surprisingly small.[11]

Table 4-1 Lending and discount amounts of Shanghai Banks at the end of 1927

Bank	Lending amounts (yuan)				Discount amount (yuan)
	Fixed lending	Current lending	Mortgage	Total	
BOCOM	9,044,489	34,686,752	13,496,183	57,227,424	101,930
Zhejiang Industrial Bank	1,141,959	12,732,069	12,190,924	26,064,952	17,773
Salt Industry Bank	6,873,669	14,848,754	16,270,250	37,992,673	688,078
Continent Bank	3,263,710	3,839,315	5,908,138	13,011,163	515,787
Rural Commercial Bank	652,032	950,208	2,057,011	3,659,251	263,192
Ho Hong Bank	175,411	1,100,093	1,139,785	2,415,289	43,836
Total	21,151,270	6,8157,191	51,062,291	140,370,752	1,630,596

Source: Yang Yinpu, *On China Finance* (Beijing: The Commercial Press, 1930), 253.

Yang Yinpu provided a detailed analysis of the reasons why the discount business in China was underdeveloped, primarily focusing on the following six points:

(1) The slow development of industrial and commercial enterprises has hindered the growth of discounting. Discounting relies on bills, which are based on trade, which in turn depends on enterprise growth. Historically, our country's enterprises have been underdeveloped—an undeniable fact. Low production volumes have resulted in fewer transactions. With underdeveloped credit systems and the prevalent use of cash, opportunities for using bills have been limited, leading to slow growth in the discounting business. This is a primary reason for the slow development.

(2) The relatively recent enactment of the negotiable instrument law is another reason. A bill's repayment at maturity hinges on the merchant's creditworthiness. However, legal sanctions are crucial to deter unscrupulous individuals—making negotiable instrument law an essential guarantee for bill circulation. In our country, this law is relatively new, and its initial impact has been limited. Merchants have yet to fully grasp its content, and the financial industry hasn't fully developed the discounting business.

(3) The lack of agencies supporting bill business development is a significant issue. Our country urgently needs auxiliary agencies for bills. There are no bill brokers to balance the supply and demand of bills, nor is there a rediscount system to ensure smooth acceptance and issuance. Due to this deficiency, banks often struggle with bill handling, especially in urgent situations. This reluctance to engage in discount business is the third major reason for the slow development of the industry.

(4) The allure of government bond speculation is another reason. Banks, with their substantial capital, inevitably seek prudent investments. In our country's current climate, beyond lending, many are drawn to trading government bonds, which offer higher returns than traditional lending and discounting. If the financial sector focuses on profiting from government bonds, discounting may be neglected due to a lack of available credit funds. As a result, the essential function of discounting is often overshadowed by government bond trading.

(5) The fifth reason stems from the practices of Chinese merchants, who often rely solely on credit for transactions. When purchasing goods, they don't need to make immediate payments. Instead, they can buy on credit and pay in installments later. This practice eliminates the need for bills, consequently removing the necessity for discounting.

(6) Discounting carries significant risks. Currently, it's challenging to verify the creditworthiness of each issuer and payer involved in discounting bills of exchange. These risks can lead to severe, often unmanageable consequences. In contrast, overdrafts and credit loans typically involve local businesses. These transactions often occur between familiar parties, making credit status investigations easier. With careful monitoring, risk control is more manageable. Consequently, the financial industry tends to favor outright lending over discounting loans.[12]

Notable figures in the banking industry had also significantly contributed to the propagation of the discount theory. These include Zhang Jiaao, General Manager of Bank of China; Xu Qiqing, Executive Director of Zhejiang Industrial Bank; Zhang Naiqi, Deputy Manager of Zhejiang Industrial Bank; and Jin Guobao, Deputy General Manager of the Business Department at Shanghai Communications Bank.

Zhang Naiqi asserts that acceptance bills serve as exceptional credit instruments. He states, "Its primary advantage is to enable businesses to convert stagnant 'book debts' into tradable 'face debts.' Through discounting, the financial industry can similarly transform these debts. Typically, the financial sector supports industrial and commercial enterprises via discounting, while obtaining its own backing from the central bank through rediscounting. This system facilitates smooth financial turnover and ensures unhindered financing for industrial and commercial funds."[13] As a result, he advocates for the abolition of the "three-festival" accounting system in favor of bill credit.[14]

Jin Guobao has made significant contributions to the banking industry, particularly in promoting acceptance bills and establishing a discount market. In his speech titled "How to Develop Industry and Commerce," he asserted, "Funding is crucial for revitalizing industry and commerce. Without adequate capital, these sectors cannot thrive. Creating a bill market serves as an effective strategy to attract both domestic and foreign investments.[15] Banks can utilize their funds to purchase bills, allowing the discount market to absorb excess capital and promote smoother fund circulation."[16] Jin Guobao pioneered the idea that creating a bill market is crucial for industrial and commercial development. He drew an apt comparison between China's situation at the time and the United States before the establishment of the Federal Reserve System in 1913. He observed that both countries primarily relied on accounting methods for transactions. The market consisted mainly of checks, promissory notes, and a few bills of exchange, with no established discount market. This significantly contributed to the decline of industrial and commercial sectors. In the US, before the Federal Reserve System was established, national banks couldn't accept on behalf of others, hindering the formation of a discount market. However, once the Federal Reserve System was established and member banks gained acceptance rights, bank acceptance bills surged, resulting in the rapid development of the discount market.[17] Reflecting on China's contemporary situation, Jin Guobao proposed seven key points for establishing a bill market.

(1) The Banking Association and the Money Industry Association should establish a discount agency to buy and sell bills on behalf of customers. This agency will include a credit investigation department.
(2) The central bank can rediscount commercial bills endorsed by Bank Association member banks if they meet these criteria: mature within 90 days; serve production purposes, not speculation; bear at least two signatures (for individuals discounting bills to the central bank, endorsement by two or three individuals with equivalent collateral is required).
(3) An Acceptance Bill Promotion Association should be formed to organize and guide the use of acceptance bills.
(4) Inter-bank silver lending rates should be eliminated. The central bank and banking association should set public interest rates and market discount rates.
(5) A bill exchange should be established, with the central bank managing account transfers and settlements.
(6) A Warehouse Law should be enacted. More warehouses should be built in major commercial ports, transportation should be improved, and bank bill business should be promoted.
(7) The central bank should be urged to manage the discounting business.[18]

Jin Guobao authored articles like "Bill-Related Issues in the *Banking Law*," suggesting that "bill acceptance" should be incorporated into banking operations. In the prevailing banking law, bill acceptance was neither a primary nor a secondary business for banks. Furthermore, Article 9 of the *Banking Law* forbade banks from engaging in other businesses, implying that the acceptance business was among the banks' prohibited activities. However, the acceptance business has a great bearing on the development of the discount market. Laws in European and American countries allowed banks to handle acceptance businesses concurrently. Despite the gradual completion of China's financial structure, its discount market had not been formed. "To establish a discount market, we must first promote bank acceptance bills. To promote bank acceptance bills, we must first grant banks the acceptance rights," Jin argued. He advocated for amending Article 1, Paragraph 2 of the *Banking Law* from "bill discounting" to "bill acceptance and discounting." Jin insisted that the acceptance business of bank bills needed careful consideration by judges and legislators[19] to fundamentally eliminate concerns about banks' inability to handle acceptance business.[20] To safeguard the rights and interests of banks, Jin Guobao proposed adding the following clauses in the *Banking Law* to regulate the acceptance business.

> Article ——: Bank acceptance bills shall be limited to those maturing within three months and falling under any of the following categories:
>
> (1) Foreign trade transactions
> (2) Domestic transportation, with bills of lading or other relevant documents serving as collateral at the time of acceptance
> (3) Agricultural product warehouse receipts, which can be readily liquidated to cover potential losses during acceptance
>
> Banks must not allow acceptance bills from any individual, corporation, or unincorporated entity to exceed 10% of the bank's actual paid-in capital and provident fund. This restriction does not apply to bills backed by genuine collateral such as bills of lading. The total amount of bank acceptances shall not exceed 50% of the bank's actual paid-in capital and provident fund. However, this limit may be increased to 100% with joint approval from the Ministry of Finance and the Central Bank.[21]

Jin Guobao proposed an amendment to Article 34, suggesting: "Banks' total loans to any individual, corporation, or unincorporated entity should not exceed 10% of their paid-in capital and provident fund. However, this limit shouldn't apply to discounting goods-related bills."[22] In April 1931, Jin's advocacy for a discount market gained traction in Shanghai's business community. The following month, he delivered a speech titled "Issues Related to Bill Acceptance," highlighting the benefits of bill acceptance and discounting for industrial and commercial financing.[23] After the September 18 Incident in 1931, which marked the beginning of the 14-year Chinese People's War of Resistance Against Japanese Aggression, Shanghai faced financial turmoil. During this period, Jin again promoted commercial bills to foster the development of the discount market.

II. Boom of Bank Acceptance and Discount Business

From 1930 to 1931, the banking industry spearheaded the promotion of bill acceptance and discounting. Prominent institutions, including the BOCOM, China State Bank, Shanghai Commercial Savings Bank, the Continent Bank, China National Commercial Bank, China and South Sea Bank, Zhejiang Industrial Bank, Ho Hong Bank, and Donglai Bank, joined the initiative in succession. This concerted effort sparked a movement within Shanghai's financial community, championing the practices of bill acceptance and discounting.[24]

In 1930, Jin Guobao pioneered bill acceptance and discount services at the BOCOM, leading to the creation of acceptance bills. To facilitate the circulation of these bills, the BOCOM issued the *Rules for Handling Bill of Credit and Acceptance and Discounting Business* in the same year. This was the first specialized regulation on bill acceptance and discounting in the history of China's bill discount market. "The BOCOM decided to issue two types of credit letter: Type A, suitable for commercial acceptance, and Type B, suitable for bank acceptance."[25] It stipulated that commercial acceptance bills and bank acceptance bills should generated using these two types of credit letter, which were then discounted by local branches of the BOCOM or entrusted banks. For instance, if a manufacturer in Shanghai wanted to conduct business in Wuxi, they could arrange for the Shanghai Branch to issue a Type A credit letter. This would be sent to the Wuxi Branch along with detailed information about the goods and purchase amount. At the same time, they would notify the seller to issue a bill of exchange and submit it to Wuxi BOCOM with the bill of lading and insurance policy. Wuxi BOCOM would purchase the bill of exchange and send it to Shanghai BOCOM. Shanghai BOCOM would notify the manufacturer to make the payment and collect the bill of lading for shipment. If a manufacturer from Wuxi sold goods to a business in Shanghai, the manufacturer could issue a bill of exchange along with the bill of lading and insurance policy. Wuxi BOCOM can discount these documents to achieve the same purpose. For a Type B credit letter, if the manufacturers in Shanghai and Wuxi have never had any contact and the manufacturer in Wuxi required the bill of exchange to be accepted by the bank, the manufacturer in Shanghai could negotiate with the Shanghai BOCOM to request the issuance of a Type B letter of credit, which should detail the drawer's name, the bill of exchange amount, and other relevant information. The letter of credit could be sent either by the bank or the manufacturer. After receiving the letter of credit, the seller could proceed with the delivery of goods. When the goods were loaded, the invoice, bill of lading, insurance policy, and bill of exchange would be handed over to the Wuxi BOCOM for acceptance. At the same time, the letter of credit must be sent to the Wuxi BOCOM for inspection to ensure it validity. Wuxi BOCOM must indicate the amount and purchase date of each letter of credit. When the total amount on the letter of credit was used up, Wuxi BOCOM would retrieve the letter of credit and send it to Shanghai BOCOM along with the last bill of exchange.[26] The *Rules for Handling Bill of Credit and Acceptance and Discounting Business* were based on foreign Acceptance Procedure and Letter of Credit regulations, adapted to the local Chinese context. They aimed to build a discounting market through bills. The introduction of these rules standardized, normalized, and institutionalized the BOCOM's discounting business, marking the beginning of modernization in China's banking business.

According to the *Rules for Handling Bill of Credit and Acceptance and Discounting Business*, acceptance bills were categorized into bank acceptance bills and commercial acceptance bills. In the case of commercial acceptance bills, the seller sold goods, issued a bill to the buyer, and submitted it to the payer for acceptance. Once accepted, the payer became the acceptor. These bills can be further divided based on whether they were attached with documents. Bills with complete sets of documents like bills of lading and insurance policies were known as documentary bills. Those without were termed non-documentary bills or clean bills. Documentary bills could be discounted before acceptance, while non-documentary bills must be accepted before discounting. On the other hand, bank acceptance bills had the bank as the acceptor. There were four ways to generate these bills: in import trade, in export trade (both derived from international trade), in domestic trade, and in warehouse goods trading.[27] The credit of bank acceptance bills was considered significantly higher than commercial acceptance bills. This was due to the outdated accounting system in China's business community, which made it challenging to investigate the credit status of acceptors, issuers, and endorsers.[28]

The BOCOM also managed the acceptance and discounting of commercial bills from other banks.[29] In early 1931, Jin Guobao's proposal to expand the acceptance business in the banking sector was endorsed by Ma Yinchu, the Chairman of the Economic Committee of the Legislative Yuan. That same year, the BOCOM started its business of buying and selling acceptance bills.

In the spring of 1931, China State Bank, Shanghai Bank, Continent Bank, and China National Commercial Bank began offering bill acceptance and discounting services, following the lead of the BOCOM. Specifically, China State Bank began to conduct remittance, acceptance, and discount business in 1931. They formulated the *Rules for Acceptance and Discount* and *General Rules for Handling Acceptance and Discount Business*, and decided to "officially start acceptance and discount service in 1932."[30]

In January 1932, the central bank developed a rediscount charter and guidelines. Additionally, the Bill Research Association of the Shanghai Banking Industry Association created a unified bill acceptance contract and documents related to letters of credit.[31] Although the rediscount charter wasn't officially promulgated, these initiatives by the banking industry positively influenced the evolution of bill acceptance and discounting practices.

In promoting bill acceptance and discounting, banks like BOCOM, Shanghai Bank, China State Bank, Bank of China, and Zhejiang Industrial and Commercial Bank have been influential advocates of the two types of bills: bank acceptance bills and commercial acceptance bills. BOCOM and China State Bank issued the majority of bank acceptance bills, with a total amount of no less than 1 million yuan. However, this came to a halt following the September 18 Incident in 1931. There was a surplus of money at that time, and the businesses preferred stability over uncertainties, so the total amount of commercial acceptance bills was not large. Since 1931, the BOCOM has been handling them without interruption, albeit in small quantities. From March 1931 to the present, over 700 bills totaling about 400,000 yuan have been processed.[32] From the beginning of 1931 to the end of 1932, the amount of bill acceptance and discount services managed by the banking industry reached no less than 1 million yuan. This activity gained significant momentum, progressing swiftly day by day.[33] The boom propelled the development of bill acceptance and discount businesses in the banking industry. The discount amounts of 12 major banks rose from 1,367,600 yuan in 1927 to 9,437,000 yuan in 1934, achieving an impressive average annual growth rate of 98.57%.

Table 4-2 Bills accepted and discounted by BOCOM (Shanghai)

Time	Number (piece)	Amount (yuan)
March to December, 1931	248	48,274.58
1932	313	274,253.55
1933	81	50,412.71
1934	44	35,561.45
January to February, 1935	11	1,428,530

Source: Jin Guobao, "The Promotion of Commercial Acceptance Bills," in *Bill-Related Issues and Banking Legislation*, ed. Jin Baoguo (Beijing: Zhonghua Book Company, 1947), 53–54.

Table 4-3 Discount operations of twelve major banks

Year	Absolute number (yuan)	Month-on-month increase (%)	Fixed-base speed of development (%)	Notes
1927	1,367,641	100.00	100.00	These 12 banks were among those offering discount service in old China: BOCOM, Zhejiang Industrial Bank, Bank of Jiangsu, Yancheng Bank, Continent Bank, Juxingcheng Bank, Agricultural and Industrial Bank of China, Yung Hung Bank, Ningpo Commercial and Savings Bank, Donglai Bank, East Asia Bank, and Chun Foo Bank.
1928	1,606,102	117.44	117.44	
1929	1,923,702	119.77	140.66	
1930	2,667,917	138.69	195.07	
1931	1,833,391	68.72	134.05	
1932	4,021,479	219.35	294.04	
1933	5,837,193	145.15	426.80	
1934	9,437,026	161.67	690.02	

Source: Hong Jiaguan and Zhang Jifeng, *Modern Shanghai Financial Market* (Shanghai People's Publishing House, 1989), 62.

III. Trial Implementation of Enterprise and Commercial Acceptance Bills

Societal prosperity is closely tied to the commercial boom, which, in turn, relies on substantial capital and a flexible economic turnover. Typically, merchants must settle their accounts upon selling goods due to market influences. However, purchasing goods often requires cash. Thus, those involved in sales and wholesale need at least two sources of capital: one for purchasing goods and the other for settling accounts. This requirement makes growth challenging, especially for larger businesses that need more capital.[34] In 1932, following the January 28 Incident, Shanghai underwent a financial crisis, resulting in a tight money supply and an economic downturn. This situation prompted the business community to recognize the importance of acceptance bills for commercial development. As a result, they embraced this trend, beginning to handle commercial bill acceptance and discount businesses.

To resolve the conflict between customers purchasing goods and making payments, domestic enamel trading companies pioneered the use of commercial acceptance bills. In 1932, an article titled "Initial Discussion on the Trial Issuance of Commercial Acceptance Bills by Domestic Enamel Trading Companies" was published in *The Bankers Weekly*. They also published "A Notice to Customers about the Launch of Commercial Acceptance Bills" on the same journal, signifying the start of this trial.

If a customer agrees to use a commercial acceptance bill to payment, our company can negotiate a payment term with them—20 days, 30 days, or even longer—as long as it is clearly stated in the bill that the customer agrees to ensure payment on the specified date. Our company can then discount this bill at the bank, which collects payment from the customer when due. For customers, this approach frees them from strict payment regulations (like payment within ten days or by sight draft and cash), allowing them to sell goods before settling their account. This reduces upfront capital needs and facilitates increased sales. For our company, processing these bills through banks enables business expansion. New customers wanting to trial products can avoid advance payments by obtaining a letter of credit from their local bank for goods delivery. In essence, accepting bills of exchange proves advantageous for both customers and our company.[35]

According to the domestic enamel companies' commercial acceptance bill regulations, local customers could set a payment date when purchasing goods. They must declare the use of the acceptance bill and include "Bill of Exchange with —— Day Term" on the order form. Once a domestic enamel company delivered the goods to the local customer's store, they also gave the customer an invoice along with the bill of exchange. The customers must verify the bill's face value and the invoice's accuracy before filling in the date, signing, and stamping the bill of exchange's acceptance column. The payment was made when the bill was due. If the customer ordered goods from another place, they could include a "Bill of Exchange with —— Day Term" on the shipping letter. The enamel branches would handle shipping, complete all customs procedures, and send the necessary documents, including invoices, bills of lading, insurance policies, and the draft to the bank. Customers would be notified to sign, stamp, and date the draft's acceptance column when collecting the other documents from the bank. On the draft's due date, the bank could use the draft to redeem payment from the customer.[36]

Scholars noted that the introduction of commercial acceptance bills by domestic enamel companies had "provided a model for the business community and played a pivotal role in popularizing the use of commercial acceptance bills. This influence was stronger than general theoretical promotion and held a pioneering position in the development history of Chinese bills and their market."[37]

SECTION 2

Shanghai Bank Bill Acceptance Office: Preliminary Formation of Regional Acceptance and Discount Market

The nationwide "Silver Wave" of 1934 led to deflation in the Shanghai market, a tight money supply, and a substantial slowdown in the industrial and commercial sectors. This caused a lack of short-term market credit tools and financial stagnation. The credit system and mortgage lending methods resulted in a serious solidification of funds and a subsequent shortage of funds in the banking industry. By 1935, industry organizations understood the importance of acceptance bills for economic development and promoted commercial acceptance bills. This sparked a second wave of acceptance bills. To foster the development of the banking industry, stimulate industrial and commercial recovery, enhance liquidity, and increase financial market resources, the Shanghai Banking Industry Association passed a resolution to establish a bank bill acceptance office.[38]

I. Second Wave of Acceptance Bills

In early 1935, Shanghai-based Marya Silk Mills proposed the use of commercial acceptance bills in the silk industry to address fund shortages.[39] After several discussions, the Shanghai Silk and Satin Industry Association agreed to implement this solution. On March 4 of the same year, Luo Qinghua, the Chairman of the Shanghai Silk and Satin Industry Association, sent a letter to the Shanghai Chamber of Commerce. The letter stated, "Following a resolution at a special general meeting of members, a commercial acceptance bill has been created in line with the negotiable instrument law to shorten the account opening period and boost currency usage. Please ensure these bills are accepted across all industries and encourage the banking and monetary sectors to discount them as much as possible. It would be appreciated if you could send a special letter to the central bank for rediscounting, thus increasing currency usage while maintaining low cash amounts. This initiative will benefit industry, commerce, and finance alike."[40] After discussion, the Shanghai Chamber of Commerce agreed to the proposal. The decision was to communicate all industries through correspondence and send separate letters to the banking and monetary industries. An official letter was also sent to the central bank to request for rediscounting.[41] The decision to use acceptance bills in the silk and satin industry was well-received by the Mechanical and Electrical Industry Association. Both associations jointly issued a letter on April 1 announcing the implementation of commercial acceptance bills.

On April 2, 1935, the Shanghai Banking Association convened a committee to discuss the implementation of commercial acceptance bills. Subsequently, the association held several meetings to further discuss issues related to these bills. In July, it officially proposed the implementation of bank acceptance bills. In October, the Shanghai Industrial and Commercial Loan Committee approved the *Measures for Promoting Acceptance Bills*, deciding to allocate three million yuan from the loan fund to support the promotion of these bills, which further advanced the development of commercial acceptance bills.[42]

During this period, other cities followed suit and scrambled to promote acceptance bills. Organizations such as the Hankou Banking Industry Association and Ningbo Chamber of Commerce joined this trend. The head of the Hankou Banking Industry Association suggested that "if Hankou adopts commercial acceptance bills, the city's banking industry should provide discount services." The head of the Hankou Central Bank also voiced support for discount and rediscount operations. However, due to a market downturn, progress in bill discounting stalled. It wasn't until after the victory of the War Against Japanese Aggression that discounting gradually took hold in commercial banks.

Additionally, while commercial acceptance bills and discount services were in progress, the development of commercial promissory note services was also underway. In 1936, promoted by the banking and silk industries in Shanghai, banks and silk factories engaged in commercial promissory note discounting activities.

II. Establishment

The establishment of the Shanghai Bank Bill Acceptance Office after the second wave of acceptance bills marked the gradual formation of a regional bill market in Shanghai. Its inception in 1936 signified the early stages of China's bill discounting market and triggered the rapid expansion of the bill discounting business. In its first year, the office handled 84 acceptance bills totaling over 4 million yuan and the discount amount reached 6.71 million yuan, with affiliated banks discounting a total of 4.66 million yuan and the office discounting 2.05 million yuan.[43]

1. Evolution of Regional Acceptance and Discount Markets

In March 1935, the Joint Preparatory Committee of the Shanghai Banking Industry Association proposed to establish a bill acceptance office. On June 24, the representatives of the Joint Preparatory Commission convened a meeting to draft the rules for this office. After several meetings, the articles of association, conventions, and detailed rules of procedure were revised. On February 20, 1936, a general meeting of member bank representatives was held by the Joint Preparatory Committee. They approved the articles of association and draft conventions of the acceptance exchange, and submitted them to the Shanghai Banking Association for approval and filing. This marked the beginning of the planning and implementation stage for the bank bill acceptance office. Subsequently, the Committee of the Bill Acceptance Office, the Committee of the Collateral Evaluation Group, and the Committee of the Collateral Custody Group were established. They carried out various preparatory work, leading to the official establishment of the Shanghai Bank Bill Acceptance Office on March 16, 1936. However, with ample money supply in the Shanghai market, the Joint Preparatory Committee decided to suspend the operation of the bill acceptance office on June 25, 1941.[44]

2. Organizational of Shanghai Bank Bill Acceptance Office

The bank bill acceptance office was a limited liability company, overseen by the Board of Directors. Membership was mandatory for member banks and exchange banks of the Joint Preparatory Committee. To join the office, member banks must fill out an application form, sign an agreement, and pay an entry fee of either 300, 500, or 1,000 in national currency.[45] At its inception, the acceptance office had 34 member banks, and 4 more banks joined later, bringing the total to 38.

3. Functions of Shanghai Bank Bill Acceptance Office

The Shanghai Bank Bill Acceptance Office was a mutual-aid organization formed by banks in Shanghai with the strength of the Joint Preparatory Committee and created in an unfavorable credit environment. Its aim was to manage economic crises and promote the circulation of interbank funds. The Shanghai Bank Bill Acceptance operated on a profit and loss sharing mechanism. As per the member bank agreement, the bill acceptance fund was contributed by the member banks in a one-time payment. Each bank deposited an amount equal to 6.25% of its total paid-in capital and provident fund. Of the bill acceptance fund deposited by each bank, 5% was kept as a reserve in the acceptance office, and the remaining 95% was deposited into the originating bank for future needs. For member banks, the required deposit amount was merely 0.31% of the total paid-in capital and provident fund. This rate did not impose a significant economic burden on the banks. Each member bank shared responsibility according to the proportion of the subscribed funds in the total fund amount. Similarly, the net profits (excluding the discretionary provident fund) and losses generated were shared proportionately. For any advance payment generated from bill acceptance, the reserve fund deposited by the member bank was used. Only when the reserve funds were insufficient to cover the advance payments would the member banks contribute funds based on their respective shares.[46] In essence, the Shanghai Bank Bill Acceptance Office was a public credit organization, which pooled the strength of its member banks and used bill acceptance funds as guarantees, offering a credit level much higher than individual banks.

4. Main Business Services of Shanghai Bank Bill Acceptance Office

The Shanghai Bank Bill Acceptance Office handled various tasks including issuing, accepting, buying and selling, discounting, and rediscounting acceptance bills, and setting and announcing discount interest rates.

(1) Issuance and Acceptance

Member banks must provide a list of collateral in accordance with regulations and submit it to the acceptance office for review. The collateral mainly includes the following types:

(1) Domestic primary commodities.

(2) Domestic commercial bills and other promissory notes.
(3) Commercial bills payable abroad.
(4) Marketable securities, including government bonds, corporate bonds, and stocks, but the proportion of these securities should not exceed half of the total collateral.
(5) Real estate located in the city, including collateral directly invested or received by member banks, with a proportion not exceeding 25% of the total collateral.
(6) Other goods and property approved by the Joint Preparatory Committee, such as the Public Treasury Certificate issued and subsequently approved by the Joint Preparatory Committee, with the proportion not exceeding 40% of the total collateral.[47]

The acceptance office was also responsible for evaluating the qualification and value of the collateral. Upon approval, the affiliated bank deposited the collateral. After this evaluation, each affiliated bank could complete the Acceptance Bill Application Form, issue a certain sum of money for the payers' bills of exchange, and request the acceptance office to accept these bills.[48] The handling fee for bill acceptance was determined by the Executive Committee of the Acceptance Office. It was charged at a rate of 2.5‰ every ten days based on the face value of the bills as the minimum standard. If the period was less than ten days, it was calculated as ten days. According to the Joint Preparatory Committee regulations, the acceptance office's bill acceptance amount for each bank should not exceed 25% of the bank's paid-in capital and total provident fund. Additionally, the term should not exceed ninety days.[49]

Unlike traditional commercial bills, bank acceptance bills were bills accepted by the acceptance office, a novel credit tool developed by the Shanghai Bank Bill Acceptance Office at its inception based on the actual situation at that time. Essentially, they were financing bills, which were different from traditional bills in the following aspects:

- Different drawers. Commercial bills were typically issued by industrial and commercial enterprises, while bank acceptance bills were issued by affiliated banks.
- Different acceptors. Commercial bills were accepted by banks or financial companies, while bank acceptance bills were accepted by the Shanghai Bank Bill Acceptance Office.
- Different financing objects. Commercial bills were typically used for industrial and commercial enterprise financing, while bank acceptance bills were used for inter-bank financing.
- Different generation methods. Commercial bills usually arose from domestic and foreign import/export trades or domestic warehouse inventories, whereas bank acceptance bills were generated after being accepted by the Shanghai Bank Bill Acceptance Office when a member bank deposited eligible collateral, filled out the Acceptance Bill Application Form, and submitted it for acceptance.

(2) Bill Buying and Selling, Discounting, and Rediscounting

Acceptance bills could stimulate market funds due to their high liquidity. They could be bought, sold, discounted, and rediscounted among affiliated banks. To encourage the growth of the bill discounting market, the Executive Committee of Joint Preparatory Committee issued the *Interim Measures for Discounting of Acceptance Bills by Member Banks* on March 13, 1936, outlining specific regulations for buying, selling, discounting, and rediscounting acceptance bills.[50]

The trading of bills was confined to transactions between associated banks. Sellers and buyers could inform the acceptance office of the amount and interest rate at which they wished to trade, before 2 p.m. and 3:30 p.m. each day respectively. If the purchase and sale prices were close, the acceptance office would inform both parties to proceed with the handling procedures. If a sale price matched multiple purchase prices, the acceptance office might distribute the seller's bills equally among the buyers. If an equal distribution wasn't possible, it would be allocated at the acceptance office's discretion. If there were only sellers with no buyers on a given day, the acceptance office would purchase and discount the bills at the set discount rate. The face value of bills varied from 10,000 yuan to 50,000 yuan, and the minimum trading amount was 50,000 yuan.[51]

The discounting of bills was restricted to member banks, who could request discounting from other banks or the acceptance office. If needed, each bank could rediscount their bills with the Bank of China, the Central Bank, and the BOCOM. To ensure the smooth execution of rediscounting, the Joint Preparatory Committee sent a letter on March 19 to these banks, asking them "to handle rediscounting of bills that have already been discounted at our office when needed. We will announce daily rediscount rates for your reference."[52] To absorb market funds, the Bank of China, the Central Bank of China, and the BOCOM could also publicly sell discounted acceptance bills.

(3) Setting and Announcement of Discount Interest Rates

The discount interest rate for acceptance bills was calculated in fen (分, a fractional unit of money in China, 1/100 of a yuan) per 1,000 yuan per day. The rate fluctuated in units of 2.5 li (厘, 1/1,000 of a yuan).[53] The discount rate was publicly announced after 3 p.m. daily. On days with only sell orders and no buy orders, the acceptance office would announce its own rate. When both buy and sell orders existed, the daily transaction discount rate was announced. Based on a 90-day period, the rate was announced daily starting March 31. The discount interest rate could be adjusted according to term length, with a 20-day term as the base level and approximately 2.5-li difference between each level.[54]

5. Management System of Shanghai Bank Bill Acceptance Office

The Shanghai Bank Bill Acceptance Office, established by the Joint Preparatory Committee, operated under its administration. It adopted a committee system, creating a Bill Acceptance

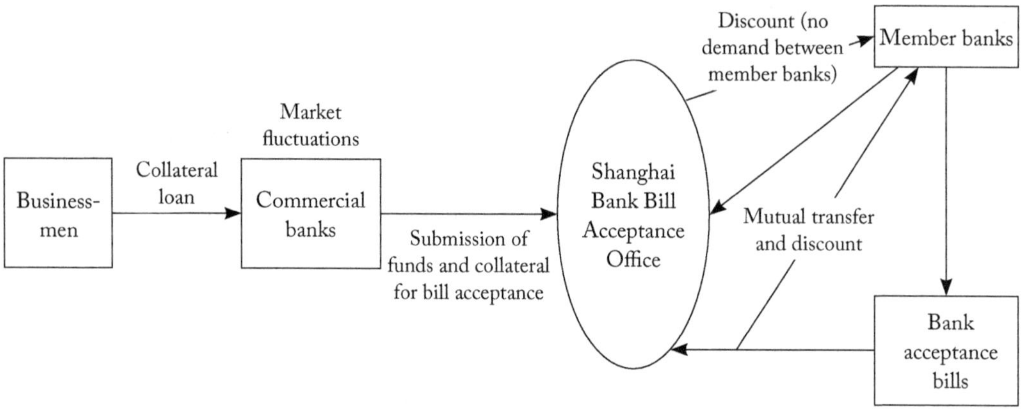

Figure 4-2 Operation of Shanghai Bank Bill Acceptance Office

Source: Wan Liming, *Research on the Institutional Evolution of the Modern Chinese Bill Market* (Shanghai Far East Publishing House, 2014), 210.

Committee with 12 elected members responsible for handling the office's bill acceptance affairs. The Joint Preparatory Committee manager served as an ex officio member, while the other 11 members were elected from key staff of affiliated banks by the member banks' representative assembly. The acceptance office appointed five standing committee members to assist the manager with daily operations. The committee was divided into two groups, a collateral evaluation group and a collateral management group, each with several members and a chairman.[55] On February 27, 1936, the first committee of the Shanghai Bank Bill Acceptance Office was established. Zhu Boquan, the Joint Preparatory Committee manager, concurrently held the position of the first committee manager.[56]

6. Significance and Inspirations of Shanghai Bank Bill Acceptance Office

The creation of regional acceptance and discount markets revolutionized the traditional "buying-on-credit" settlement method by introducing a new credit tool to the market. The modern discount market in China emerged during a period of stringent monetary policy, economic downturn, and a decline in commerce and industry. Various sectors were working to expedite fund turnover through bill acceptance and discounting operations, which facilitated fund financing and debt securitization, and positively contributed to the recovery and development of the industrial and commercial sectors.

(1) The Embryonic Form of Modern China's Discount Market

The Shanghai Bank Bill Acceptance Office was the second institution specializing in bill discounting, following the Anhui Bengbu Discount Office. It facilitated bill trading and discounting between affiliated banks or directly with the office. These bills could be rediscounted at the Bank of China, Central Bank of China, and BOCOM, which were also authorized to sell discounted bills publicly. The discount interest rate, determined by market supply and demand, was announced daily. These features established the foundations of the discount market, shaping the basic structure of China's modern discount market.

(2) Improving Fund Operation

The Shanghai Bank Bill Acceptance Office, a unique intermediary for bills, played a crucial role in revitalizing the dormant assets of its affiliated banks, facilitating asset securitization, and promoting fund financing. It allowed these banks to use commodities, loan collateral, and discounted bills as security to request the issuance of acceptance bills. These bills were then circulated through buying, selling, discounting, and rediscounting. Renowned for their safety, reliability, and high liquidity, these bills increased market credit instruments, activated stagnant bank funds, fostered asset securitization, and enhanced the operational capacity of market funds. The funds obtained from discounting could be used to support industrial and commercial development. Moreover, the loan collateral acquired could be reused as security to apply for additional acceptance bills, thereby improving fund utilization efficiency.

(3) Reducing Transaction Costs

The establishment of the Shanghai Bank Bill Acceptance Office facilitated the matching of information between buyers and sellers, thus reducing the cost of market information collection. The acceptance office not only paired buyers and sellers for transactions but also discounted bills from its member banks, which increased the likelihood of transactions, balanced market supply and demand, and aided in reducing market transaction costs.

(4) Promoting Innovation

From its inception, the Shanghai Bank Bill Acceptance Office innovated in organizational structure, trading tools, and operational methods to suit China's unique conditions. The office introduced the "acceptance office-accepted bill," a financing bill that required all member banks to share profits and losses within a set fund deposit limit. Commercial bills could serve as collateral for issuing acceptance bills, which helped stimulate the discount market's growth. These innovations had profound implications for the development of both the bill market and the bill system of the time.

(5) Providing Bill Intermediary Services

The Shanghai Bank Bill Acceptance Office was a mutual-aid organization established to manage interbank funds and bolster industrial and commercial growth during challenging credit conditions. While it had some limitations in curbing market speculation, its creation and effective operation proved that acceptance bills could successfully foster industry, commerce, and economic circulation. This provided a viable approach for developing industry and commerce in other parts of modern China, especially when facing financial shortages and circulation challenges. The office acted as a bill intermediary, offering transaction information and matching services for bill buyers and sellers. Furthermore, it released daily market price data based on supply and demand, yielding valuable insights for the evolution of modern bill intermediary institutions.

7. Limitations of Shanghai Bank Bill Acceptance Office

The Shanghai Bank Bill Acceptance Office had certain limitations when it came to curbing market speculative behavior.

8. Suspension of the Shanghai Bank Bill Acceptance Office

The full-scale outbreak of the War of Resistance Against Japanese Aggression in July 1937 led to the relocation of political and economic centers, causing abnormal economic development in Shanghai and a decline in the Shanghai Bank Bill Acceptance Office's business. By June 25, 1941, the situation had deteriorated further due to a surge in speculative money and loosening monetary conditions. As a result, the Standing Committee of the Joint Preparatory Committee decided to suspend the acceptance office's operations.[57]

SECTION 3

Chongqing United Bill Acceptance Office: Formation and Development of Multi-Regional Acceptance and Discount Markets

In July 1937, Japan launched a full-scale invasion of China. After the fall of Shanghai and Wuhan, the Nationalist Government and various factories gradually relocated, transforming Chongqing into a political and wartime financial hub. To stimulate wartime economic growth and support the development of diverse sectors including industry, agriculture, commerce, and mining, the Nationalist Government actively fostered the discount market. They aimed to replace working capital loans with discounts, thereby stabilizing wartime finance. To expedite the formation of the Chongqing bill market, the Nationalist Government issued a series of institutional regulations to promote the development of acceptance bills. Additionally, the Ministry of Finance and the Joint General Office of the Central Bank, Bank of China, BOCOM, and China Agricultural Bank (Joint General Office of Four Banks) began organizing the establishment of the Chongqing United Bill Acceptance Office.

I. Relocation of the Joint General Office to Chongqing

Japan's full-scale invasion of China in July 1937 severely disrupted the Chinese discount market. The outbreak of the war caused financial market instability and widespread anxiety. The situation worsened after the August 13 Incident of 1937 as depositors scrambled to withdraw their money, leading to a sharp decrease in bank deposits and a shortage of money in the market, which stagnated various industrial and commercial sectors. The high relocation costs of factories and enterprises in regions like Shanghai were unbearable for businesses and bank credit. To alleviate the wartime money shortage and sustain the stable development of industrial, agricultural, commercial, and mining sectors, the Ministry of Finance actively promoted the establishment of joint discount and rediscount systems.

To pool financial resources for addressing the crisis, the Ministry of Finance authorized the Central Bank, Bank of China, BOCOM, and China Rural Bank on July 29, 1937, to form a Joint Discount Committee, which was tasked with handling interbank discount business. Given the urgent need for capital financing in industries like agriculture, industry, commerce, and mining during the war, the committee was renamed the Joint Discount and Lending Committee to give equal importance to discount and lending operations. On August 9, 1937, the Joint Discount and Lending Committee was officially established in Shanghai, with representatives from the four banks rotating as chairs. To standardize the discount and loan services, the committee introduced the *Measures for Handling Interbank Discount and Loan Business by the Discount and Loan Committee* and *Detailed Rules for the Operation of the Discount and Loan Committee*. These regulations dictated that the discount and loan interest rates would be decided by the committee and publicly announced by the central bank. They also removed the term "interbank" for ordinary interbank lending to facilitate financing.

On August 13, the Nationalist Government ordered the establishment of a joint office under the Joint Discount and Lending Committee, which was first led by Soong Tse-ven and then by Kung Hsiang-hsi. To regulate the flow of funds in industries like finance, agriculture, mining, industry, and commerce in the mainland, the Joint General Office of the Four Banks issued the *Joint Measures for Discount and Lending Business by the Central Bank, Bank of China, Bank of Communications, and China Rural Bank* on August 26, 1937. These measures provided detailed rules on discount and lending scope and collateral, and stated that the discount and lending interest rates should be determined by the local Joint Discount and Lending Committee based on market conditions.[58]

On November 14, the *Detailed Rules for Handling Discount and Lending Business in the Mainland by the Central Bank, Bank of China, Bank of Communications, and China Rural Bank* was issued, which clarified that the discount and loan funds would be shared by the Central Bank, Bank of China, BOCOM, and China Rural Bank in the proportions of 35%, 35%, 20%, and 10%, respectively. The document also stated that the discount and lending interest rates should be based on a monthly interest rate of 0.7%, and the transfer collateral interest rate should be appropriately reduced.[59] To operate in mainland China, the Joint Discount and Lending Committee of the Four Banks set up joint discount and lending committees and joint offices in the locations of its branches and sub-branches. With the establishment of joint discount and lending committees in 15 cities including Nanjing, Hankou, and Chongqing, a nationwide discount and lending network was formed.[60] The joint discount and lending business in these regions expanded from lending to banks to lending to industry and commerce.

On November 25, the Joint Discount and Lending Committee was relocated to Wuhan and renamed the Joint General Office of the Four Banks. In late November, the Shanghai Banking Association called Kung Hsiang-hsi and said, "The headquarters of the Central Bank,

Bank of China, BOCOM, and China Rural Bank have all relocated to Wuhan, and the financial center will inevitably shift accordingly. However, the majority of commercial banks still operate in the Shanghai market and rely on the government and banks for their operations. It is difficult to maintain stable operation, and in case of major accidents, each bank would struggle to cope." The Ministry of Finance, considering the significant impact of the Shanghai financial market on the mainland market, had not stopped joint discount and lending business for the Shanghai banking industry and other sectors. Instead, it had increased discount and lending efforts.[61] Despite the relocation of the Joint General Office of the Four Banks, most commercial banks remained concentrated in the Shanghai Concession.

In early 1938, the Joint General Office moved to Chongqing. On September 8, 1939, the Nationalist Government issued the *Measures for Strengthening Central Financial Institutions in Wartime*, and the Joint General Office was transformed into the highest financial supervisory, guiding, and decision-making body under the Nationalist Government. The joint discount and lending businesses were transferred to the discount and lending department under the Wartime Financial Committee for supervision.[62] In October of the same year, the Joint General Office was officially established in Chongqing, known as the Joint General Offices of the Four Banks.[63] The implementation of the joint discount and lending system was successful. From September 1937 to December 1939, the total amount of joint discount and lending by the four banks reached 634.56 million yuan. Ordinary discount and lending accounted for 16.4% (104.06 million yuan), and special discount and lending[64] accounted for 83.6% (530.5 million yuan).[65]

In 1940, the office stopped handling ordinary discount and lending business to focus on special discount and lending. In 1941, the Joint General Office handled business totaling 1.5 billion yuan for special projects. By the end of December, the actual discount and lending amount reached over 12.257 billion yuan and 900,000 Hong Kong dollars, covering multiple areas such as grain, industry and mining, transportation, and local expenditure and finance.[66] In 1942, the four banks divided their businesses and implemented specialized operations, which made joint discount and lending no longer suitable, resulting in the halt of such business operations.[67] After the outbreak of the War of Resistance Against Japan, the Joint General Office invested a large amount of funds in the market through joint discounts and lending businesses to meet wartime needs. This helped ease capital turnover difficulties in the industrial, commercial, and financial sectors, supported the relocation of coastal factories, aided the development of industries in rear areas (such as supporting industrial and mining production, transportation development, and the purchase of materials for war zones), and maintained financial market stability.

II. Formation of Chongqing Bill Discounting Market

The Nationalist Government recognized the importance of developing bill business to address the lack of funds in the rear areas and to achieve financial adjustments. With the relocation of the Joint General Office, bill acceptance and discounting saw broader development space, and their significance became prominent. The establishment of a bill market was seen as an effective way to solve fund shortages in the rear areas and adjust finances. The government acknowledged, "Only by utilizing the acceptance and discounting of bills can we fulfill their mission to the national economy and finance."[68] On April 28, 1938, the Ministry of Finance issued the *Outline of Measures for Improving Local Financial Institutions*, stating that "local financial institutions should increase the acceptance or discounting of agricultural bills, commercial bills and other businesses."[69] The document aimed to encourage local financial institutions to handle the acceptance and discounting of bills. However, due to wartime fund shortages, the implementation was slow and inefficient.

To stabilize the discount rate and avoid financial market turmoil, on October 27, the Joint General Office sent a letter to the Ministry of Finance, stating, "The inventory of the four banks is relatively abundant. For the implementation of discount rate management, it may be possible for the four banks in each province to publish a daily discount rate based on market conditions. The types of products should still be limited to those specified by the Ministry of Finance." Kung Hsiang-hsi soon approved the proposal, recommending a pilot in Chongqing and other areas, with potential expansion to other provinces following successful results.[70] In February 1940, the Joint General Office issued the *Interim Measures for Promoting Bank Acceptance and Discount Business*, the government's first specialized regulation on acceptance and discount business. It detailed provisions for acceptance, discount, and rediscount procedures and stated that "the Central Bank, Bank of China, BOCOM, and China Rural Bank should join hands to set up an acceptance committee to hand bill acceptance business ... All bills accepted by the committee should apply for discounting with the four banks ... The interest rate of acceptance bills shall be published daily by the Central Bank, Bank of China, BOCOM, and China Rural Bank, which shall be moderately lower that the local lending rate." The rediscount was handled by the Central Bank, Bank of China, BOCOM, and China Rural Bank, and its interest rate was determined and announced by the four banks at any time based on market conditions. The document put forward requirements for the true trade background of bills, stipulating that "acceptance bills should be guaranteed by goods and a complete set of documents, including bills of lading and insurance policies, and must have sufficient insurance."[71] However, the implementation of these measures was not ideal due to limiting conditions.

On September 17, 1942, the Joint General Office passed the *Resolution on the Use of Bill Discounting for Working Capital Loans*, viewing it as a significant aid in adjusting the money market. It suggested that "when businesses need funds for transactions, banks can issue, guarantee, or accept bills on their behalf to be discounted at other banks. In this way, the funds of commercial banks can be used in a prudent and reliable way."[72] Commercial banks could apply for discounting from the central bank when necessary. On October 9, the *Draft Interim Measures for the Guarantee, Acceptance, and Discounting of Production-Related Bills by the Joint General Office of the Four Banks* was issued, which provided detailed explanations on the types, terms, and procedures for acceptance and discounting of production-related bills. The implementation of regulations on borrowing working capital for production operations, and the use of bill issuance, guarantee, acceptance, and discount as much as possible,[73] has promoted the development of production in the rear areas and furthered the progress of acceptance bills and discount business.

On April 28, 1943, the General Administrative Office of the Bank of China issued a copy of the *Measures for the Administration of Bill Acceptance and Discount Business During Special Period*, stating that "controlling currency should be aimed at meeting the needs of market production and sales. Bills are based on the production and sales of goods, making them the ideal instruments for financing needs. Central banks worldwide use bill rediscounting and open market trading as essential financial control tools." Historically, China's credit system, whether it was the accounting method commonly used in commercial industries or the loan contracts prevalent in the financial sector, was all about book debts. This often led to stagnant funds, poor turnover, and hindered production development. Issuing currency could also easily spark credit inflation. During the time of emergency, implementing the bill system and developing the discount market not only strengthened the central bank's control over finance, but also saved cash reserves and facilitated flexible capital turnover.[74] To invigorate wartime finance, support production development, and establish a discount market, the Ministry of Finance issued and implemented the *Measures for the Administration of Bill Acceptance and Discount Business During Special Period* in April 1943, defining the types, terms, discount rates, and rediscount rates of bills. The types of bills were restricted to industrial and commercial acceptance bills, agricultural acceptance bills, and bank acceptance bills. The issuance of bills was to be accompanied by legitimate commercial activities.

After six months of implementing these measures, discounting became increasingly common. However, due to insufficient improvements in commercial credit and a lack of robust credit reporting institutions, the circulation of commercial acceptance bills was not as good as that of bank acceptance bills. Bank acceptance bills dominated the market because they didn't require cash payment, but this could easily lead to credit risks if not handled carefully. To enhance the credit of bills and improve the foundation, the Ministry of Finance issued three other measures to regulate the amount and responsibility of bank acceptance business and require banks to record each transaction when accepting bills, further standardizing bank acceptance business.[75]

The Nationalist Government proposed the creation of a bill acceptance office to promote the *Measures for the Administration of Bill Acceptance and Discount Business During Special Period*, address wartime fund shortages, support production development, and gradually establish a bill market. In October 1944, the Chongqing United Bill Acceptance Office was officially established, leading to the gradual formation of the Chongqing bill market. Along with this, the United Credit Information Bureau was also established, marking the inception of China's official credit reporting system.

During the War of Resistance Against Japan, the KMT-controlled areas were once prosperous. However, Haikou became isolated, and land routes were blocked. This interruption led to machinery, equipment, parts, and raw material shortages. Consequently, industrial production faced severe difficulties, and supplies became scarce, fueling speculation in the market. Speculative sales, hoarding, and stockpiling were rampant as hot money flowed in and out of Myanmar and Vietnam as well as Hong Kong, Chongqing, Kunming, and other places in China. This situation sidelined normal industry and commerce, leading to a shrinkage in commodity exchange. Soaring prices resulted in currency being tied up in speculative transactions, with funds concentrated on hoarding and speculation. This led to depleted bank deposits, tight lending, currency depreciation, and reduced bank credit. Despite the Nationalist Government's repeated advocacy for acceptance bills and discounting business to support the development of various sectors like mining, agriculture, industry, commerce, and finance, progress was slow. This was because bills relied on the full development of commodity transactions, whose foundation had been severely undermined. For instance, in 1943, the National Bank of the Nationalist Government conducted only 82 discounting transactions. Although 1944 saw a slight improvement, there were still only 257 discounting transactions.[76]

During this period, the development of bill exchange in Chongqing was quite complex. From 1938 to 1940, the Chongqing Bill Exchange was suspended, and it was not until 1942 that the exchange officially resumed operations.

To address the fiat currency shortage and increase credit chips, the bill market in Chongqing issued promissory notes as a replacement for fiat currency. Demand for fiat currency was growing in 1940, but supply was limited. The Joint General Office set up a research group to discuss measures for promoting promissory notes. In September, the General Office passed the *Measures for the Issuance of Fixed-Amount Promissory Notes by the Four Banks*, stipulating that, to facilitate market transactions, the Ministry of Finance authorized the issuance of fixed-amount promissory notes. Bearers could redeem fiat currency from local issuing banks or designated acceptance banks. On June 4, 1944, the Central Bank issued sight promissory notes of six denominations (5,000, 10,000, 20,000, 30,000, 40,000, and 50,000) in Chongqing, which could be used equally with fiat currency and exchanged for cash.

The issuance and denomination of promissory notes continued to increase, causing exchange price differences and discounts between fiat currency and promissory notes. This led to a crisis in speculative exchange. A large number of promissory notes circulated in the market, spurring price increases. Commercial banks began issuing promissory notes to expand credit. The discount rate for exchanging promissory notes for fiat currency gradually increased, causing continuous price increases and triggering financial market instability. After the victory of the War of Resistance Against Japan, the demand for fiat currency in the recaptured areas soared. The Nationalist Government and the Joint General Office approved the issuance of fixed-amount promissory notes in places like Peking, Tianjin, Shanghai, Hankou, Guangzhou, and the Northeast. Two months after the victory, the fixed-amount promissory notes issued by the Bank of China, BOCOM, China Rural Bank, Central Trust of China, and Postal Remittances and Savings Bank alone exceeded 110 billion yuan. In November 1945, with the supply of fiat currency gradually increasing, it was decided to stop issuing fixed-amount promissory notes. At the same time, five measures were formulated to restrict the issuance of promissory notes by commercial banks, effectively restricting the excessive issuance of such notes.[77]

III. Establishment of Chongqing United Bill Acceptance Office

During the War of Resistance Against Japan, the economic center shifted southwestward to the rear area. To stimulate wartime finance, the Nationalist Government supported wartime production, creating a surge in the demand for funds in this area. Consequently, the government began to promote bill acceptance, discounting, and rediscount business. As the Joint General Office of the Four Banks relocated inland, these financial services found a broader space for development. To hasten the establishment of a regional bill market in Chongqing, the Ministry of Finance and the Joint General Office organized the creation of the Chongqing United Bill Acceptance Office.

1. Establishment Process of Chongqing United Bill Acceptance Office

To stimulate wartime finance, boost production, and encourage bill acceptance and discounting, the Ministry of Finance issued the *Outline of Measures for Improving Local Financial Institutions* in April 1938, stating clearly that efforts should be made to increase the acceptance and discounting of agricultural and commercial bills.[78] To meet market fund demands and foster independent development of acceptance and discount business, the Joint General Office drafted the *Interim Measures for Promoting Bank Acceptance and Discount Business*, which was officially enacted on January 29, 1940, distinguishing "lending" from "acceptance" to a certain extent.

In April 1943, the Ministry of Finance issued the *Measures for the Administrating Bill Acceptance and Discount Business During Special Period*, which facilitated the development of bill businesses in the rear areas. To actively implement these measures and establish a bill market, the Ministry of Finance proposed the creation of a bill acceptance institution with a credit reporting organization. Upon approval from the Joint General Office, the relevant personnel began drafting measures for establishing such an institution. Endorsed by Kung Hsiang-hsi, Vice Chairman of the Joint General Office, on October 6, 1943, a preparatory committee was established to draft the organizational charter of the acceptance office and to make preparations for related matters. Finally, the Chongqing United Bill Acceptance Office officially opened on October 2, 1944.[79]

2. Organization of Chongqing United Bill Acceptance Office

The Chongqing United Bill Acceptance Office was a government-organized and supervised entity that operated under a membership system. It involved participation from the Ministry of Finance, the Joint General Office of the Four Banks, and the Central Bank. Fundamental members included the Bank of China, BOCOM, China Rural Bank, Central Trust Bureau of China, and the Postal Remittances and Savings Bureau (commonly referred to as "Three Banks and Two Bureaus"). Commercial banks and money houses approved by the Ministry of Finance were required to join the acceptance office as general members. The Chongqing United Bill Acceptance Office has established a one-time, fully paid acceptance fund of 25 million yuan, with subscriptions from affiliated banks. The "Three Banks and Two Bureaus" should subscribe to no less than half of the total fund amount. The office operated in groups to manage affairs and it may include credit reporting agencies and joint warehouses when necessary.[80]

3. Functions of Chongqing United Bill Acceptance Office

Except for the banking and monetary industries, all those engaging in legitimate commercial activities related to production could apply for acceptance. The Chongqing United Bill Acceptance Office was established to "assist industry and commerce, promote production, and ensure that the funds from accepted bills are used for production."[81] The acceptance of such bills could enhance the credit of industrial and commercial bills. Once accepted, the bills could be circulated in the market for discounting, transfer, and rediscounting.

4. Main Business Lines of Chongqing United Bill Acceptance Office

The main business of Chongqing United Bill Acceptance Office included acceptance, discounting, and rediscounting.

(1) Acceptance

Industrial and commercial enterprises that met the requirements could apply for acceptance at the Chongqing United Bill Acceptance Office. To apply, they needed to provide collateral, a usage application, and legal business conduct documents to verify the legality of their business operations. The Joint Credit Reporting Office, affiliated with the Chongqing United Bill Acceptance Office, conducted investigations across various industries. To minimize risks, the acceptance office required that the collateral provided during acceptance be physically secured and stored at the joint warehouse for protection. Additionally, an acceptance fee equal to 0.5% of the bill's face value was charged.

(2) Discounting and Rediscounting

Accepted bills could be bought and sold freely or discounted at any money house or bank. If necessary, they could be rediscounted at the central bank.

5. Management System of Chongqing United Bill Acceptance Office

The Chongqing United Bill Acceptance Office operated as a joint organization, initiated and promoted by government departments. Its organization and operation were fully governed by these departments, with the government leading the way. The office consisted of 11 directors. One director was appointed by each of the following: the Ministry of Finance, the Joint General Office of the Four Banks, the Central Bank, and the "Three Banks and Two Bureaus." The remaining three directors were elected by the general assembly of members. Among these

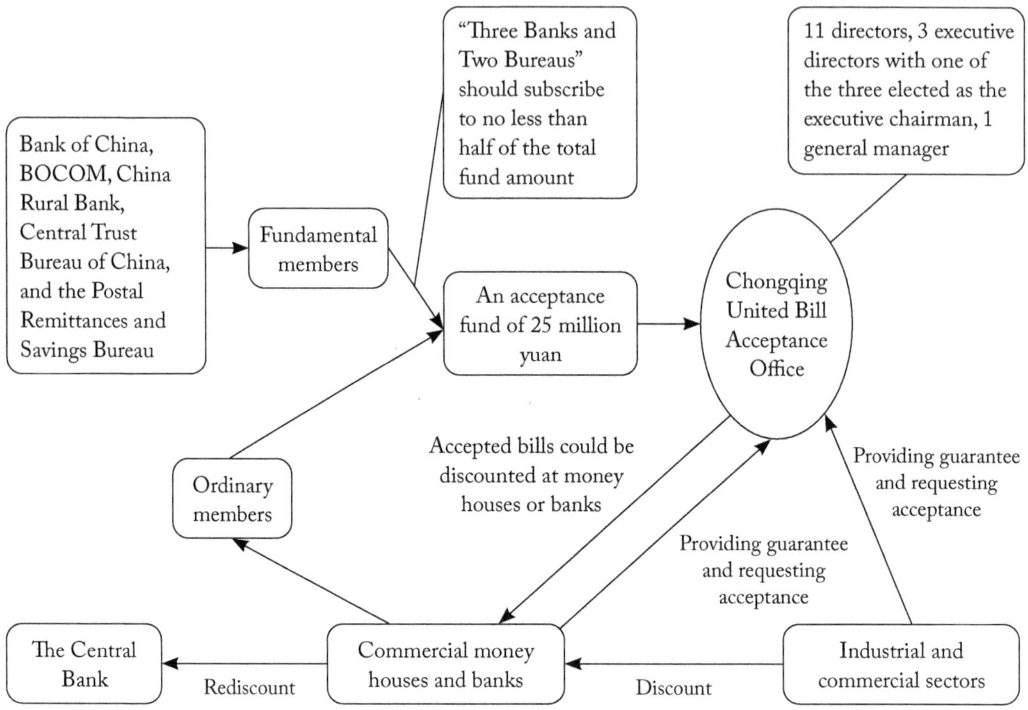

Figure 4-3 Operation of Chongqing United Bill Acceptance Office

Source: Wan Liming, *Research on the Institutional Evolution of the Modern Chinese Bill Market* (Shanghai Far East Publishing House, 2014), 212.

directors, eight represented the government. This was an acceptance institution established by consolidating government forces. The acceptance office appointed three executive directors, with Kung Hsiang-hsi, one of the three, elected as the executive chairman (represented by Guo Jingkun in his absence), and Wang Zhishen was appointed as the general manager. Two assistants were also assigned to manage the daily affairs of the acceptance office as per the chairman's instructions.

6. Significance and Inspirations of Chongqing United Bill Acceptance Office

The Chongqing United Bill Acceptance Office was established during the War of Resistance Against Japanese Aggression. The office enhanced the credit of commercial and industrial enterprise bills, improved their circulation, and played a crucial role in activating fund usage in rear areas and promoting industrial, commercial, and production development. Its establishment fostered the evolution of the bill discount system, extended the central bank's rediscounting application, and became the core of the bill market in the rear areas. It contributed to the prosperity and growth of the bill market in Chongqing.

The Chongqing United Bill Acceptance Office was a specialized institution for bill acceptance. By accepting qualified industrial and commercial bills, it enhanced credit and served as a significant reference for fostering industrial and commercial credit.

SECTION 4

Shanghai Commercial Paper Exchange Company Ltd.: Establishment and Development of Bill Exchange System

The bill exchange system, also known as the bill settlement system, emerged at the turn of the 20th century. With the rise of both money houses and foreign banks, a bill clearing pattern dominated by bank bill clearing, alongside foreign bank bill clearing, had emerged in the market. After the Shanghai Commercial Paper Exchange Company Ltd. was established in 1933, a new type of bill exchange system emerged and gradually dominated the market. With the expansion of new-style banks, Bank of China, as the central clearing center for new bank bills, and the China International Settlement Association joined the Shanghai Commercial Paper Exchange Company Ltd. as members. Since then, the new bill exchange system had gradually replaced the old one.

The Chongqing Bill Exchange was established in May of the same year. During the War of Resistance Against Japanese Aggression, the Chongqing Bill Exchange underwent several changes. These changes included periods when the Bank of China Chongqing Branch was in charge, the Sichuan Provincial Bank and other banks jointly maintained the exchange, and the central bank managed its affairs.[82] Despite the *Central Bank Law* of 1935 stating that "handling bill exchange and interbank transfer settlement"[83] was part of its business scope, it was largely nominal. However, from June 1, 1942, the Central Bank established the Bill Business Department and officially took over the management of the Chongqing Bill Exchange.[84] With this, the central bank's bill clearing function was established, marking the completion of the transformation of the Chongqing bill exchange system from being jointly maintained by banks to being administered by the central bank.

Before 1945, the bill clearing institution of the monetary industry remained a central part of the bill clearing business. After the victory of the War of Resistance Against Japanese Aggression, the Shanghai Commercial Paper Exchange Company Ltd. was reorganized, ending the division in bill business and establishing a unified bill exchange system. During the War of Liberation (1946–1950), the central bank's oversight of bill exchange gradually extended to the entire country, formally establishing its role in national settlement affairs. Consequently, the bill exchange system transitioned from a combination of direct and institution exchange systems to a direct exchange system.

I. Exchange System Before the Shanghai Commercial Paper Exchange Company Ltd.

Before the emergence of Chinese-funded banks, money houses and foreign banks had established their own unique bill clearing systems. Before the Shanghai Commercial Paper Exchange Company Ltd. was created in 1933, Chinese-funded banks relied on these banks for bill clearing. The bill market at the time featured a coexistence of the money house remittance system, led by the remittance association, and the foreign bank bill clearing system, headed by HSBC.

1. Money House Bill Settlement System

Before 1890, money houses in Shanghai utilized a clearing method combining "remittance" and "silver transfer." "Remittance" involved offsetting accounts receivable and payable among money houses to simplify collection and settlement.[85] Any remaining balance was settled through cash transfer. In this method, the manager would distribute silver to peers with the accounts receivable every night. While this was a direct clearing method, it was also cumbersome, time-consuming, and labor-intensive, and lacked inadequate security. It could not meet the needs of the time.

Around 1890, the Shanghai Money Industry Association established a remittance system (also known as the public bill clearing system) through the creation of a remittance association. This central institution for clearing bills was located on Ningbo Road within the premises of the Shanghai Money Industry Association, and functioned as a subsidiary of the association.

Before the Shanghai Commercial Paper Exchange Company Ltd. was established, the remittance association had always served as the bill clearing center. In 1925, the remittance association handled silver bills of about 7.3 billion taels, increasing to nearly 16.6 billion taels by 1931. The volume of silver-dollar public bills also increased, from over 1.1 billion yuan in 1925 to about 4 billion yuan in 1931, indicating rapid growth. However, the January 28 Incident in 1932 significantly reduced the number of public bills handled by the remittance association. Overall, the remittance system was an institutional innovation in the development of modern Chinese bill exchange. It already exhibited some characteristics of modern bill exchange, representing its embryonic form. However, the remittance system also had certain limitations.

Table 4-4 The Remittance Association business (1924–1932)

	Public receipts		Silver public receipts	Total
Year	Silver (thousand taels)	Silver yuan (thousand yuan)	(thousand yuan)	(thousand yuan)
1925	7,311,970	10,065,393	1,189,877	11,255,270
1926	9,861,303	13,684,107	1,590,127	15,274,234
1927	8,092,653	11,318,396	1,506,198	12,824,594
1928	9,471,590	13,246,979	1,849,292	15,096,127
1929	10,463,162	14,633,793	2,309,687	16,943,480
1930	13,416,373	18,764,158	2,918,304	21,682,462
1931	16,622,098	23,247,690	4,066,081	27,313,771
1932	10,640,504	14,881,824	2,649,704	17,531,528

Source: PBC Shanghai Branch, ed., *Historical Materials of Shanghai Money Houses* (Shanghai People's Publishing House, 1960), 203; Cui Xiaocen, *Central Bank Theory* (Beijing: The Commercial Press, 1935), appendix 47.

Additionally, similar bill exchange systems also emerged in other locations, such as the posting system in Ningbo and the transfer system in Tianjin. Of these, the posting system in Ningbo had a significant impact.[86] The posting system in Ningbo, implemented from 1843–1844, used accounting books instead of bills. This unique system combined the clearing system with the bill exchange system. The term "posting" means that when a trade in need of receiving or settling money with a money house can notify each other of their respective banks. The payer would transfer money from their own account to the money house that the payee dealt with, effectively collecting an additional sum from the payee's deposit. Therefore, the claims and debts between the two parties would not be settled in cash but in the account books of their respective money houses.[87] The posting system was highly successful and popular among customers. It was implemented in Ningbo for nearly a hundred years and was not abolished until 1941 with the fall of Ningbo into Japanese hands.[88]

2. Foreign Bank Bill Clearing System

Foreign banks in China, also known as the "bund banks," issued and utilized bills known as "clearing notes." These notes could be withdrawn on the same day of its maturity. The clearing of these bills between foreign banks was overseen by the comprador's office. Instead of paying in cash, the comprador's office of the paying bank issued a bill called a "large header note" to settle differences nightly. HSBC, with its substantial strength, established control over the clearing of silver deposits. This control had formed a bill clearing pattern centered around HSBC and managed by its compradors. After checking accounts between peers every day, the accounts to be settled were separately sent to HSBC with "large header notes." Once the business was completed, the comprador's office issued a detailed list of accounts receivable and payable, as well as a list of differences for the day. It included the received "large transfer notes" for cross-checking with the comprador's office of HSBC Bank. The differences in accounts receivable and payable were deposited with HSBC Bank, while the payable differences were deposited with the paying bank by HSBC.[89]

HSBC also oversaw the clearing of bills between money houses and foreign banks. In Sino-foreign trade, Chinese merchants received checks issued by foreign merchants, while foreign merchants received money house bills from Chinese merchants. Consequently, the bill settlement between foreign banks and money houses involved offsetting foreign bank checks with money house bills. Typically, after this offsetting process, the accounts of both parties were roughly balanced.

Due to the lack of safety and convenience in using cash for direct collection and settlement of header silver dollar bills, it was decided after several discussions that from January 5, 1931, all exchanges of silver dollar bills with foreign banks would be handled by the Bank of China, which made the Bank of China the center for clearing header silver dollar bills. Following the implementation of the policy replacing tael with yuan, silver dollar bills ceased to exist, and the Bank of China took on the role of clearing external bills in the banking industry. After the fiat currency policy was put into effect in November 1935, the Bank of China officially replaced HSBC as the sole institution to handle bill settlement for foreign banks.[90]

3. Chinese-Funded Bank Bill Clearing System

Since Chinese-funded banks didn't have their own bill clearing institution, they had to rely on money houses and foreign banks for bill clearing. The Chinese-funded banks used a variety of bills, including specialized remittance bills and header bills, and some used both types. New-style banks using remittance bills needed to entrust money houses for clearing, while those using header bills needed to entrust foreign banks for the same purpose.

II. Establishment

In the 1920s and 1930s, the rise of modern Chinese banks led to the decline of the money industry. The absence of clearing institutions necessitated that the settlement of bills between new Chinese banks and money houses and among new Chinese banks be managed through the remittance association, which dispersed funds among money houses: "As the banking industry grew larger than the money industry and handled a significant volume of bill clearings, relying on remittance association for bill exchange became impractical. This arrangement increased commission costs" and hindered the development of China's banking industry.[91] The implementation of *The Negotiable Instrument Law* in 1929 spurred the circulation of bills, stimulating commercial banks' demand for a bill exchange system. The establishment of the Joint Preparatory Committee of the Shanghai Banking Industry Association in 1932 directly led to the creation of the Shanghai Commercial Paper Exchange Company Ltd.

1. Establishment of the Shanghai Commercial Paper Exchange Company Ltd.

From 1922 to 1932, the Shanghai Bank Association made five unsuccessful attempts to establish the Shanghai Commercial Paper Exchange Company Ltd. The January 28 Incident made the banking community in Shanghai realize the importance of unity among peers and financial development. On March 15, 1932, the Joint Preparatory Committee of the Shanghai Banking Industry Association was officially established, following a proposal by Zhang Jiaao, the General Manager of the Bank of China.[92] Shortly after the establishment of the committee, the Shanghai Banking Association entrusted the preparation work for creating the Shanghai Commercial Paper Exchange Company Ltd. to it. In June 1932, the Joint Preparatory Committee began planning to establish a bill exchange, and by November, the committee had decided to set up an exchange office committee, led by Zhu Boquan, to draft various rules and regulations. The Joint Preparatory Committee, after careful planning and discussions, finally drafted rules and regulations for bill exchange matters. To ensure the smooth operation of the bill exchange after its opening, exchange officers from each bank conducted a three-day trial run on January 6, 7, and 9, 1933, under the guidance of Zhu Boquan.[93] On January 10, the Shanghai Commercial Paper Exchange Company Ltd. officially opened in the lobby of the Shanghai Bank Association Building at 59 Hong Kong Road. The Shanghai Commercial Paper Exchange Company Ltd., established solely by commercial banks, was the first formal bill exchange in Chinese history. Its establishment marked a significant step forward for Shanghai bankers in modern business activities.

Figure 4-4 Outside of Shanghai Commercial Paper Exchange Company Ltd.

Source: Wan Liming, *Research on Shanghai Commercial Paper Exchange Company Ltd. (1933–1951)* (Beijing: China Book Publishing House, 2019), 36.

2. Preliminary Development of the Shanghai Commercial Paper Exchange Company Ltd.

The Shanghai Commercial Paper Exchange Company Ltd. initially only dealt with the exchange of silver dollar bills upon its establishment. However, from February or March of 1933, it expanded to include the remittance of silver dollar bills and silver bills, and the exchange of silver bills. In April of the same year, following the implementation of the "replacing tael with yuan" policy, the collection and payment of silver bills were discontinued.[94]

In February 1933, the Shanghai Commercial Paper Exchange Company Ltd. Committee decided that "all local branches and affiliated institutions of exchange banks, such as the savings departments, trust departments, and real estate departments, should join the exchange on March 16. Each exchange bank should act as its own agent."[95] This decision expanded the scope of the exchange from downtown areas to the whole city. At that time, the central bank had not yet joined the bill exchange. Therefore, the Bank of China and the BOCOM acted as intermediaries for the bill exchange during this period. As the exchange business expanded, the frequency of fund collection and payment from exchange banks increased. In June 1935, the Bank of China and the BOCOM established a joint office under the Joint Preparatory Committee to handle fund collection and settlement from exchange banks. Influenced by the financial crisis, the money industry experienced a significant panic and began to implement centralized bill exchange. The Shanghai Commercial Paper Exchange Company Ltd. started to collect money house bills on behalf of its members. In July of the same year, the Joint Preparatory Committee also joined the Shanghai Commercial Paper Exchange Company Ltd. When it was first established, the Shanghai Commercial Paper Exchange Company Ltd. had a total of 32 exchange banks, and by 1937, this number had increased to 46.[96]

The bill exchange data from 1933 to 1936 indicates an upward trend in the Shanghai Commercial Paper Exchange Company Ltd., seen in the exchange amount, number of exchanged bills, and average amount per bill. These changes in the data effectively illustrate the expansion of the bill exchange business. In 1937, due to the full-scale of the Japanese invasion, there was a slight decline in the bill exchange data, but the overall change was not significant.

Table 4-5 Statistics of bill business in Shanghai Commercial Paper Exchange Company Ltd. (1933–1937)

Year	Exchange amount (yuan)	Pieces	Average amount of a single bill (yuan)
1933	1,966,451,761.83	902,660	2,178.51
1934	3,222,116,609.54	162,774	1,979.45
1935	3,715,828,325.01	1,859,231	1,998.58
1936	5,984,308,071.10	2,578,913	2,320.48
1937	5,808,128,309.49	2,396,617	2,423.47

Source: Wan Liming, *Research on Shanghai Commercial Paper Exchange Company Ltd. (1933–1951)* (Beijing: China Book Publishing House, 2019), 58.

Note: (1) Before the policy of "replacing tael with yuan," it was calculated and incorporated into silver dollars in a ratio of 715:1. (2) The various numbers exchanged by the entrusted agent are not included in the total number.

3. The Shanghai Commercial Paper Exchange Company Ltd.'s Efforts to Maintain Its Operation

In 1937, the Battle of Shanghai erupted. After resisting for three months, Shanghai fell. Only branches of the Bank of China, the Central Bank, and the BOCOM continued operating within the concessions.[97] Japan attempted to undermine the Chinese economy by establishing Japanese-controlled banks and promoting the use of Japanese-controlled currency. The Japanese puppet regime gradually took control of various financial institutions in Shanghai and manipulated the entire financial market through organizational and institutional changes. Despite these challenges, the Shanghai Commercial Paper Exchange Company Ltd. struggled to sustain its operations.[98]

Following the outbreak of the Pacific War in 1941, the Japanese invaded the Shanghai concessions, taking over the former Central Bank, Bank of China, BOCOM, China Rural Bank, Central Savings Association, and various foreign banks. The coercive policies of the Japanese puppet regime forced the Shanghai Commercial Paper Exchange Company Ltd. to adopt "China Central Reserve Bank notes" as its base currency. Each exchange bank was required to convert its existing legal currency deposits and debts to this new currency for bill exchange. Alongside exchanging bills for the base currency, the Japanese puppet regime plotted to control bill exchange deposits and differential transfers. Despite the efforts of the Joint Preparatory Commission, the puppet regime gained the right to handle cash exchange differential transfers from exchange banks. However, the transfer of exchange differential transfers, as well as the collection, payment, and lending of agent exchange banks and correspondent banks, remained under the control of the Joint Preparatory Commission and the Shanghai Commercial Paper Exchange Company Ltd. The puppet regime also attempted to alter the exchange's articles of association, proposing to include the "China Central Reserve Bank" in the Shanghai Commercial Paper Exchange Company Ltd., making it an ex officio member of the exchange, and assigning it to undertake differential bank transfers. They instructed the Shanghai Commercial Paper Exchange Company Ltd. to place the exchange affairs of its exchange banks under the control the China Central Reserve Bank. Through these calculated measures, they attempted to achieve control over the Shanghai Commercial Paper Exchange Company Ltd. Despite efforts to maintain independence, the Shanghai Commercial Paper Exchange Company Ltd. eventually became a subsidiary institution of the "China Central Reserve Bank" due to the circumstances.[99]

The bill exchange data shows a significant decrease followed by a steady increase in the amount and number of bills exchanged and collected during this period. From 1943 to 1945, there was a linear upward trend, reflecting the abnormal prosperity of Shanghai's financial industry after the outbreak of the Pacific War and the sharp increase in the number of exchange banks. Furthermore, it highlighted the uncontrollable inflation and the predatory nature of the "China Central Reserve Bank notes" at the time.

Table 4-6 Statistics of bill exchange in Shanghai Commercial Paper Exchange Company Ltd. (1937–1945) (unit: China Central Reserve Bank notes)

Year		Amount (fiat currency)	Number (piece)	Collection amount	Number of collected bills (piece)
1937		5,808,128,309.49	2,396,617	913,549,095.08	1,004,683
1938		2,176,335,120.89	1,423,501	485,851,818.51	435,577
1939		5,031,003,127.92	2,348,770	830,923,121.62	515,758
1940		11,080,089,722.44	3,115,442	3,838,350,611.83	1,058,945
1941		15,290,652,878.94	3,090,149	18,084,467,596.50	3,064,665
1942	Jan to May	4,086,201,619.99	645,777	8,055,711,928.82	837,932
	Jun to Dec	8,397,533,971.62	858,584	11,123,490,927.39	1,001,634
1943		57,709,631,757.11	2,643,758	82,910,560,148.95	3,103,766
1944		258,700,980,947.95	3,422,827	530,600,863,981.71	5,177,398
1945		4,091,839,382,940.53	—	—	—

Source: Zhu Sihuang, *Economic History of the Republic of China: The Bankers Weekly 30th Anniversary Commemorative Issue* (Shanghai: The Banking Society, Bankers Weekly, 1948), 514–516.

Note: The unit in the table was in fiat currency before June 1942, and it was changed to China Central Reserve Bank notes starting from June 1942.

4. Reorganization and Expansion of the Shanghai Commercial Paper Exchange Company Ltd.

Following the victory in the War of Resistance Against Japan, the Nationalist Government gradually established a financial system, primarily through the National Capital banks, using methods like demobilization, acceptance, and liquidation, enabling Shanghai to resume its status as a national financial center. There were differing opinions among factions about whether to accept the Shanghai Commercial Paper Exchange Company Ltd. Facing a stalemate, a compromise was made, deciding that the exchange would be restructured. Upon the financial regulatory authorities' request, the Shanghai Commercial Paper Exchange Company Ltd. implemented a series of measures to counteract the impact of Japanese control, gradually restoring the bill exchange units to fiat currency. To fortify the financial industry's management, the financial authorities used the acceptance and liquidation of the Shanghai Commercial Paper Exchange Company Ltd. as an opportunity to consolidate the original three exchange centers into one. They also mandated that money houses and foreign banks join the Shanghai Commercial Paper Exchange Company Ltd., establishing it as the city's sole bill exchange institution and creating a unified bill exchange system throughout the city. It's important to note that the restructured Shanghai Commercial Paper Exchange Company Ltd. was essentially entrusted by the central bank to manage the bill exchange business in Shanghai on its behalf.[100]

Table 4-7 Statistics of bill exchange in Shanghai Commercial Paper Exchange Company Ltd. (November 1945–May 1949) (unit: gold yuan notes)

Time	Amount (fiat currency)	Number (piece)	Average amount of a single exchange bill
November to December 1945	286,002,105,465.13	699,815	408,682.45
1946	45,732,586,713,184.08	18,834,615	2,428,113.70
1947	523,007,906,496,886.85	38,283,600	13,661,408.71
1948	54,020,606,139.50	57,508,979	939.34
January to May 1948	109,167,228,952,789.09	41,397,940	2,637,020.80

Source: "Monthly Report of the Clearing House in 1950," in *Archives of Shanghai Commercial Paper Exchange Company Ltd.*: Q52-2-22.

Note: Prior to July 1948, fiat currency was the standard. From August 1948 to May 1949, gold yuan notes took its place. The 1948 figures were then converted to gold yuan notes at a 300:1 ratio.

Due to the restructuring of the Shanghai Commercial Paper Exchange Company Ltd. and the post-war abnormal boom in Shanghai's financial industry, the number of banks and money houses joining the exchange rose from 133 in 1946 to 232 in 1949. The growth was primarily driven by money houses. As inflation escalated, the volume of bill exchange soared. Zhu Boquan noted that "on the eve of liberation in 1949, inflation ran wild like an untamed horse, triggering a daily credit surge. Numerous types of bills circulated, and the number and value of exchanged bills surged, making them hard to process. On April 14, the Bank of China received 210,000 bills. A large truck was needed to transport them from the exchange. The sight overwhelmed the processing staff, and they couldn't finish sorting the bills even though they stayed up all night. The exchange personnel were swamped with work, working for months without a good rest. They were mentally drained and lacked time to do a thorough check of the bills."[101] This situation highlighted the extent of the depreciation of fiat currency and gold yuan notes at that time.

5. Closure of the Shanghai Commercial Paper Exchange Company Ltd.

On the eve of Shanghai's liberation, the Nationalist Government was busy enough with its own affairs, and the central bank, unwilling to fulfill its responsibilities, entrusted them to the Shanghai Commercial Paper Exchange Company Ltd. During this critical period, the Shanghai Commercial Paper Exchange Company Ltd. was solely responsible for the exchange and clearing of bills. However, on May 25, 1949, most of the urban area south of the Suzhou River in Shanghai was liberated, creating a turbulent situation. The banking and money industries in Shanghai awaited instructions from the authorities and suspended their collection and payment business, forcing the Shanghai Commercial Paper Exchange Company Ltd. to announce its closure.[102]

6. Relaunch of Shanghai Commercial Paper Exchange Company Ltd. and Takeover by the PBC

Following Shanghai's liberation in May 1949, the Financial Department of the Financial and Economic Takeover Committee, under the Shanghai Military Control Commission of the People's Liberation Army, assumed control and supervision of Shanghai's financial industry. Consequently, the Shanghai Commercial Paper Exchange Company Ltd. was promptly taken over, restructured, and officially resumed operations on June 2. It was mandated that the Chinese yuan should be used as the standard currency in bill exchange, exchange reserves should be transferred to the PBC, and any exchange differences should be managed by the PBC. It was also prescribed that all pre-liberation exchange balances should be converted at a rate of 100,000 gold yuan notes to one Chinese yuan, and then deposited into the PBC. This marked the end of any connection between the exchange banks and money houses and the former central bank, and the beginning of a new relationship with the Shanghai Branch of the PBC.[103] Although the Shanghai Commercial Paper Exchange Company Ltd. still handled the daily management and operation, it was in reality under the control of the PBC.[104] After the Shanghai Commercial Paper Exchange Company Ltd. resumed its operations, the number of member exchange money houses and banks dropped significantly from 230 to 81, and the number of exchange venues was reduced from four to two. This led to staff redundancies and reduced funds, making it challenging for the exchange to operate normally.[105] On February 1, 1951, the Shanghai Branch of the PBC officially took over the Shanghai Commercial Paper

Exchange Company Ltd. and began overseeing credit adjustment, cash management, and money house and bank inspections.

Table 4-8 Statistics of Shanghai Commercial Paper Exchange Company Ltd.'s business after liberation

Time	Amount (yuan)	Number (piece)	Average amount of a single exchange bill (yuan)
June to December 1949	11,283,015,154,160.03	14,692,144	767,962.47
1950	67,016,458,775,650.00	21,119,154	3,173,254.89

Source: "Monthly Report of Shanghai Commercial Paper Exchange Company Ltd. 1949 (Issue 12)," in *Shanghai Bill Coking Archive*: Q52-2-21; "Bill Exchange Report 1950," in *Shanghai Bank Association Archives*: S172-4-34.

III. Bill Exchange System After the Shanghai Commercial Paper Exchange Company Ltd.

The Nationalist Government established a central bank in November 1928 and enacted the *Central Bank Law* in May 1935, aiming to shift the bill clearing responsibilities to the central bank. In November of the same year, there were plans to reorganize the central bank to handle national bill clearing. However, these plans were not successfully carried out due to the prevailing circumstances. On January 26, 1936, the Central Bank became a member of the Shanghai Commercial Paper Exchange Company Ltd. The Shanghai Commercial Paper Exchange Company Ltd., created in the absence of the central bank's bill clearing system, represented another financial innovation. It was the first clearing institution independently established by commercial banks in China, marking the beginning of a bill exchange system independently operated by Chinese commercial banks. The establishment of the Shanghai Commercial Paper Exchange Company Ltd. provided Chinese-funded commercial banks with their own bill exchange, improving the efficiency of internal operations and reducing operating costs. The total amount of bills exchanged at the Shanghai Commercial Paper Exchange Company Ltd. steadily increased, reaching 59.8 billion yuan in 1936, doubling the amount in 1933, and the number of exchanged bills reached 2.58 million, more than 1.8 time that of 1933.

Table 4-9 Statistics of bill exchange amount at Shanghai Commercial Paper Exchange Company Ltd. (1933–1936)

Year	Total amount (yuan)	Number (piece)
1933	1,966,341,761.83	902,660
1934	3,222,116,609.54	1,627,748
1935	3,715,828,325.01	1,859,231
1936	5,984,308,071.10	2,578,913

Source: Wan Liming, *Research on Shanghai Commercial Paper Exchange Company Ltd. (1933–1951)* (Beijing: China Book Publishing House, 2019), 48–81.

For some time after the establishment of the Shanghai Commercial Paper Exchange Company Ltd., bill transactions between Chinese-funded banks and money houses were still handled through the remittance association. This didn't change until June 10, 1936, when the Shanghai Money Industry Joint Reserve became part of the Shanghai Commercial Paper Exchange Company Ltd. Following this, the exchange of bills between banks and money houses was managed by the Shanghai Commercial Paper Exchange Company Ltd., officially taking over the role of the Money Industry Bill Clearing Center. In 1937, following the full-scale War of Resistance Against Japan began, the Shanghai Money Industry Association decided to establish a bill exchange. The effectiveness of this new system led to its permanent implementation.[106] Consequently, the money house exchange system, which had been in place for over half a century, was declared obsolete and officially replaced by the bill exchange system.

During the War of Resistance Against Japan, Chongqing faced soaring inflation and a shortage of monetary resources. To stabilize the financial market and activate the money market, the central bank initiated the establishment of a bill exchange. On June 1, 1942, the Central Bank set up the Bill Business Department, marking the start of its bill exchange operations. Upon victory in the War of Resistance Against Japan, Chen Xing, the Central Bank's Vice President, pushed for the takeover of the Shanghai Commercial Paper Exchange Company Ltd. Despite opposition from Bei Songsun and Zhang Gongquan, he succeeded with the backing of Soong Tse-ven. Subsequently, the Shanghai Commercial Paper Exchange Company Ltd. was restructured, and a new committee was formed. On October 18, 1945, the committee held its first meeting and issued a resolution, stating that the Central Bank would entrust the Shanghai Banking and Money industry associations with the task of creating a bill exchange to handle exchange business. The total number and allocation of seats in the exchange were set, the list of exchange banks was compiled, and the position of exchange and agency banks and money houses was rearranged. A bill exchange system combining prewar direct exchange and entrusted agent exchange was adopted for key personnel selection. After all preparations were completed, the restructured Shanghai Commercial Paper Exchange Company Ltd. was officially established on November 1, 1945, at the former site of the Shanghai Commercial Paper Exchange Company Ltd. In December of the same year, foreign banks began to resume operations and joined the Shanghai Commercial Paper Exchange Company Ltd. This expanded the scope of the bill exchange and ended the division of bill exchange in Shanghai. It became the only exchange institution in the city, operating under the supervision of the central bank.[107]

Following the victory in the War of Resistance Against Japan, the number of entrusted agent exchange banks and money houses in the Shanghai Commercial Paper Exchange Company Ltd. significantly increased, surpassing that of direct exchange money houses and banks. However, these entrusted agent exchange banks and money houses were less convenient compared to direct exchange banks and money houses, leading to dissatisfaction with the system. The Shanghai Commercial Paper Exchange Company Ltd. started designing exchange plans in October 1946. Despite several letters sent to relevant institutions regarding the plans' feasibility, they didn't receive approval. It wasn't until July 1947 that the group direct exchange system was chosen, and it was officially implemented on February 21, 1948. This institutional change represented a gradual and exploratory approach initiated by the grassroots, starting from the existing institutional structure. This method aligned more closely with the internal laws of financial system development.[108]

SECTION 5

The Central Bank and Bill Development

The creation of modern China's central bank began in 1905 with the establishment of the Qing government's Ministry of Revenue Bank. Its development spanned three historical periods: the late Qing Dynasty, Beiyang Government, and Nationalist Government.[109] In 1908, the Ministry of Revenue Bank was renamed the Ta-Ching Government Bank and introduced the *Regulations on Ta-Ching Government Bank*, which was China's first official central bank law. During the Republic of China period, the Bank of China and the BOCOM took on the role of a central bank. However, due to the unclear division of tasks and overlapping business activities, competition and contradictions arose, exerting a negative impact on the development of national finance.[110] It led some scholars to argue that "despite the Bank of China and BOCOM having the authority of managing the national treasury and issuing paper currency, they failed to fulfill the central bank's mission."[111] After the Nationalist Government was established in Nanjing, preparations began for the creation of the Central Bank. Although the Nationalist regime established the Guangzhou Central Bank and the Hankou Central Bank in 1924 and 1927 respectively, these central banks were primarily for the purpose of serving military operations. They bore the name of the central bank but lacked its essence.[112] Notably, the Guangzhou Central Bank was the first to use the term "central bank," significantly influencing the design of the central banking system under the Nationalist Government in Nanjing. As such, many regard it as the precursor to the central bank during the Republic of China period.[113] In November 1928, the Central Bank of the Nationalist Government, modern China's central bank, was officially established in Shanghai.

I. Background

The central bank of modern China emerged against a backdrop of various factors, including the rapid development of world central banks, the unification of domestic currency systems, an absence of credit institutions, and the consolidation of the Nationalist Government's political power.

1. Trends in Financial Development After World War I

Following the outbreak of World War I, the governments of the countries involved heavily borrowed from their central banks or discounted treasury bills to finance their military expenses. This caused a sharp increase in the issuance of central bank notes, leading to inflation and a rise in prices. This, in turn, stimulated an expansion in government fiscal expenditure. As a result, governments became increasingly reliant on issuing central bank notes, creating a vicious cycle that culminated in significant financial chaos during the war. After the war, while seeking currency price stability and economic recovery, various governments and economic sectors began to acknowledge the unique functions of central banks. In 1920, the Brussels International Financial Conference encouraged central banks worldwide to maintain relative independence through financial regulation and credit management, instead of blindly extending unrestricted payments to governments. The conference highlighted the central banks' role in restoring and maintaining stability in currency and banking systems. It also urged countries without central banks to establish them as soon as possible. Following this, in 1921, countries with central banks began seeking reforms while those without joined in forming central banks. By the time World War II broke out, nearly all countries had their own central banks.[114]

2. The Need for Currency Unification

Following the Opium War, trade and economic exchanges through the five port cities of Guangzhou, Xiamen, Fuzhou, Ningbo, and Shanghai fostered the development of modern China's monetary system. After the establishment of the Republic of China, the Beijing Government (Beiyang Government) devised the *National Currency Regulations* and the *Rules for the Implementation of the National Currency Regulations*. These abolished the silver standard system and implemented the silver dollar standard system. However, because foreign banks and associated money houses continued to use silver as the accounting unit, a situation arose where silver ingots and silver coins coexisted in the market. During the circulation of silver coins, different regions began minting their own silver currency to aid in the distribution of silver coins. The varying quality of silver coins minted by different regions led to regional circulation and amplified the disarray of modern Chinese currency values. Moreover, the influx of foreign banks resulted in the illegal circulation of foreign banknotes within China, causing significant disruptions to the social and economic order. After the establishment of the Republic of China, banknote circulation became even more chaotic. Despite attempts by the Beiyang Government to centralize the issuance of banknotes through the Bank of China, the efforts produced very little effect. The call for currency system unification highlighted the need for establishing a strong central bank responsible specifically for currency issuance.[115]

3. Development and Shortcomings of Credit Institutions

Following the Opium War, foreign powers established banks in port cities to facilitate trade with China and strengthen economic exploitation. These foreign banks, along with traditional financial institutions such as money houses, silver shops, and bill offices, evolved into significant credit institutions in modern China. After the Sino-Japanese War of 1894–1895, foreign banks intensified their economic and financial aggression in China to accommodate their needs of factory establishment. They directly or indirectly controlled China's national finance, basic industries, and transportation lifelines. This had a detrimental impact on China's economic and financial development and posed a substantial threat to national consolidation and the survival of the nation. Traditional Chinese financial institutions did not have the strength to compete with foreign banks. Some even relied on foreign banks' support to influence the financial market, significantly undermining the development of China's financial industry. The invasion of foreign banks spurred the enthusiasm of China's self-operated banks, leading to the emergence of new-style Chinese banks in the late 19th century. However, because most of these new-style banks blindly imitated foreign ones and had weak capital and insufficient strength, they faced oppression and couldn't compete with the oppressive foreign banks with strong capital and financial strength.[116]

4. The Need for the Nationalist Government to Consolidate Its Political Power

During the early days of the Nationalist Government, political instability was high. The government faced internal factional struggles and external aggression from Japan. To consolidate its power, a strong financial and economic foundation was crucial. However, substantial military expenses and the Ministry of Finance's inability to raise funds threatened the stability of the new regime. Nationalist figures, like Chiang Kai-shek, understood the importance of banks for governance. To stabilize political power, spur economic growth, and resolve the financial crisis, Chiang Kai-shek appointed Soong Tse-ven as the Minister of Finance in 1928 and began to prepare for the establishment of the central bank.[117]

II. Evolution

Following the establishment of the Nanjing Nationalist Government in 1927, efforts were directed toward establishing the Central Bank. By November 1928, the Nationalist Government's Central Bank was officially set up in Shanghai. As it developed, the Central Bank's operations expanded, its functions improved, and its market position significantly enhanced.[118]

1. Initial Development (1928-1937)

Modern China's central bank faced numerous obstacles during its early stage of development, including weak capital and unstable credit. They encountered fierce competition from foreign banks, as well as established institutions like the Bank of China and BOCOM. These factors created significant disparities between the central bank and its competitors, making it difficult for the central bank to regulate the national financial industry effectively. In response, the Nationalist Government implemented a series of measures to increase the capital and improve the status of the central bank.

Table 4-10 Comparison of strength between Central Bank, Bank of China, and BOCOM (unit: 100 million yuan)

		Central Bank		Bank of China		BOCOM		
Item	Year	Amount	%	Amount	%	Amount	%	Total
Paid-in capital	1932	0.20	37.45	0.247	46.26	0.087	16.29	0.534
	1934	1.00	74.79	0.25	18.70	0.087	6.51	1.337
Total assets	1932	2.49	18.04	8.05	58.34	3.26	23.62	13.800
	1934	4.78	25.44	9.776	51.94	4.25	22.62	18.790
Amount issued	1932	0.40	12.54	1.84	57.68	0.95	29.78	3.190
	1934	0.86	21.34	2.05	50.87	1.12	27.79	4.030
Deposits	1932	1.69	17.98	5.57	59.26	2.14	22.77	9.400
	1934	2.73	21.82	6.85	54.76	2.93	23.42	12.510
Loans	1932	1.63	20.61	4.55	57.52	1.73	21.87	7.910
	1934	1.67	15.11	6.74	61.00	2.64	23.89	11.050
Net profit	1932	0.12	83.91	0.018	12.59	0.005	3.50	0.143
	1934	0.15	84.27	0.019	10.67	0.009	5.06	0.178

Source: Shi Tao, *A History of Modern Chinese Central Banks* (Beijing: The Commercial Press, 2021), 141–142.

(1) Restructuring Bank of China and BOCOM

The Nationalist Government, looking to establish a national monopoly financial system, started restructuring the Bank of China and BOCOM during the preparation for the establishment of the central bank. They removed these banks' national statuses, increased the share of government investment, and took control of their personnel rights. Through these actions, the Nationalist Government aimed to create a banking system with the central bank as the main body and the Bank of China and the BOCOM as the wings. After two rounds of capital increase and restructuring, "the central bank's capital grew stronger, and its status improved."[119] Under the Nationalist Government's control, the Bank of China and BOCOM developed into "auxiliary banks of the central bank,"[120] leading to the formation of a government banking system with the central bank at its core. During the second round of capital increase and restructuring in 1935, the Nationalist Government established the China Rural Bank and the Central Trust (Bureau) of China. They also reorganized and expanded the Postal Remittance and Savings Bureau, officially forming the "Four Banks and Two Bureaus" government financial system.[121]

Table 4-11 Statistics of paid-in capital of Central Bank, Bank of China, and BOCOM

	1933		1935	
Bank	Capital (yuan)	%	Capital (yuan)	%
Central Bank	20,000,000	7.97	100,000,000	24.97
Bank of China	24,712,200	9.85	40,000,000	9.99
BOCOM	8,715,600	3.47	19,715,750	4.92
Total	53,427,800	21.30	159,715,750	29.88
Total of banks nationwide	250,835,332	100.00	400,496,027	100

Source: Economic Research Office of the General Administration of Bank of China, *National Bank Yearbook 1936* (Shanghai: Hanwen Regular Script Printing Company, 1936), 10–15.

(2) Promulgating the *Central Bank Law*

As the central bank continued to develop and grow, the *Central Bank Regulations* enacted in 1927 became outdated. Consequently, the Nationalist Government officially promulgated and implemented the *Central Bank Law* in May 1935. This law offered detailed provisions regarding the central bank's capital, organization, privileges, operations, final settlement of accounts, and reporting. It further clarified the central bank's responsibilities and privileges, thereby improving its status. Compared to the previous *Central Bank Regulations*, the *Central Bank Law* increased the central bank's capital from 20 million yuan to 100 million yuan, fully funded by the national treasury. It established the headquarters in the capital and set up new branches. It also expanded the number of directors and vice presidents. Additionally, it decreased the proportion of commercial stocks in the total capital to no more than 40%.

(3) Reforming the Currency System

During the Silver Crisis, a significant amount of silver flowed out, pushing China's silver standard system to the verge of collapse. In response to this crisis, the Nationalist Government abandoned the silver standard system and adopted a fiat currency policy. The central bank, as a key policymaker and implementer of the fiat currency policy, saw its functions like currency issuance, foreign currency management, and national treasury agency significantly strengthened. This improved its status,[122] marking what is often considered the "starting point of a strong central bank."[123]

At this stage, the central bank used the political privileges of the Nationalist Government to continuously bolster its strength, increase its assets, and steadily conduct its operations. However, due to various constraints, the central bank "was still in its infancy and unable to perform its intended functions. Its structure was relatively simplistic, its operations were basic, and its branches were not nationwide."[124]

Table 4-12 Statistics on the development of Central Banks

Year		End of 1928 (yuan)	End of June 1937 (yuan)
Capital	Regular	20,000,000	100,000,000
	Index	100	500
Total asset	Regular	47,470,796	1,477,147,078
	Index	100	3,112
Deposits	Regular	15,410,468	923,885,255
	Index	100	5,995
Cash	Regular	18,358,010	532,298,205
	Index	100	2,899
Exchange vouchers issued	Regular	11,712,923	377,961,513
	Index	100	3,227
Net profit	Regular	239,360	7,859,532
	Index	100	3,284

Source: Shi Tao, "Functional Improvement (1937–1945)," in *A History of Modern Chinese Central Banks* (Beijing: The Commercial Press, 2021), 212.

2. Functional Improvement (1937–1945)

The successful implementation of the fiat currency policy required a robust central bank for currency management. Accordingly, during the fiat currency reform, the Nationalist Government committed to restructuring the central bank. In early 1936, Kung Hsiang-hsi appointed an expert committee to devise a restructuring plan. They drew on global experiences, aiming to transform the central bank into a modern, fully functional central bank. Here are the key points of this restructuring.

(1) Concentrated efforts should be made to ensure a significant proportion of commercial banks' deposit reserves are stored in the Central Reserve Bank. This reserve can be withdrawn at any time and used as a transfer fund for bill exchange differences. By adjusting the deposit-reserve ratio, credit control can be achieved, monetary policy can be adjusted, and financial emergencies can be managed.

(2) The central bank is responsible for overseeing national bank clearing and managing financial transfers.

(3) The central bank handles bill discounting and rediscounting, establishing rediscount interest rate standards. These standards serve as the basis for deposit interest rates and market discount rates, facilitating macroeconomic regulation of finance.

(4) The central bank manages the unified national paper currency issuance. This ensures price and exchange rate stability, and allows for the control of the basic currency supply according to societal demand.

(5) Short-term, minor adjustments are primarily used for government borrowing. The central bank encourages general banks and the public to subscribe to government bonds and contribute fiscal funds. Concurrently, through public market activities, the central bank trades bonds, adjusts currency policy, and regulates credit.[125]

Following a year of deliberation and efforts, the Legislative Yuan approved the *Draft Central Reserve Bank Law* and *Measures for the Restructuring and Transition of the Central Bank* on June 25, 1937. The draft law proposed that the Nationalist Government restructure the existing central bank into the Central Reserve Bank, also known as the Central Bank, to manage finance and stabilize currency. However, the outbreak of the War of Resistance Against Japan put this restructuring plan on hold.

Following the outbreak of the War of Resistance Against Japan, the national economy contracted significantly due to severe damage to productivity. However, the central bank lacked the exclusive right to issue currency and did not fully collect its treasury funds, rendering it incapable of independently managing wartime finance. In response, the Ministry of Finance directed the Central Bank, Bank of China, BOCOM, and China Rural Bank to establish a joint office. This office, later restructured as the Joint General Office of the Four Banks, was tasked with managing various special operations of the government's wartime financial policies. With the support of the Joint General Office, the central bank's leading role gradually emerged, and its functions became more comprehensive, as reflected in the following aspects:

(1) The central bank acted as fiscal agent. In October 1939, the *Public Treasury Law* was officially implemented, establishing a unified agency for the national treasury. From that point onwards, the central bank gained the authority to centrally manage the collection and allocation of national treasury funds.
(2) The central bank collected and stored reserve funds from various banks. It centralized the exchange of bills in major cities, handled loan services such as rediscounting, collateral transfer, and foreign exchange collateral transfer, and set loan interest rates.
(3) It was tasked with managing foreign exchange audit affairs and gradually gaining foreign exchange management rights.
(4) It was responsible for overseeing and ensuring that the operations of commercial banks and money houses aligned with financial policies and national wartime economic strategies.
(5) It possessed exclusive fiat currency issuance rights. Starting from July 1, 1942, the central bank monopolized the issuance of fiat currency. All fiat currency, along with foreign exchange and gold used as fiat currency reserve, was consolidated in the central bank. This marked an end to the previous situation where the four

banks issued banknotes simultaneously and competed for issuance rights. The central bank's role as the issuing bank was a significant indicator of a fully-realized national central bank.[126]

In 1942, the Joint General Office created the *Measures for Four Banks Business Division and Assessment* and *Measures for the Implementation of Unified Issuance*, significantly enhancing the central bank's financial regulatory capacity. The revised Articles of Association for the Joint General Office of the Four Banks, established in June of that year, further emphasized the powers of the central bank.[127]

3. Toward Decline (1945–1949)

Following the conclusion of the War of Resistance Against Japan, the central bank received a substantial amount of financial assets from the Japanese puppet regime, significantly bolstering its strength. To combat the severe inflation during the civil war, the central bank was assigned additional tasks, leading to a more comprehensive system, a more rigorous organizational structure, and a significant increase in business volume. However, in challenging environments, a sound financial system could not be maintained, and the central bank could not fully perform its role. As inflation escalated, the central bank struggled to exercise its monetary function, lost all credit, and could no longer operate normally.[128]

III. Main Functions

The functions of the central bank continually evolved with its development. Its primary roles were threefold: serving as the issuing bank, the government's bank, and the banks' bank.

1. Issuing Currency

As the issuing bank, the central bank's most basic and important function was currency issuance. This is a significant reason for and symbol of the formation of the modern central bank system. It also distinguishes the central bank from other financial institutions.[129]

2. Acting as Fiscal Agent

As the government's bank, the bank central provided services to the government and aided in implementing national fiscal and financial policies. It managed all fiscal revenues and expenditures on behalf of the government.

3. Managing Government Bonds

Government bonds represent debt incurred by the government when it borrows or issues bonds to domestic and foreign sources. This is done based on its creditworthiness to raise funds. These bonds fall into two categories: domestic and foreign. Management of government bonds was another financial service provided by the central bank as the government's bank.

4. Exercising Centralized Management of Gold and Silver and Foreign Exchange

Gold, silver, and foreign exchange are significant international reserve assets and reflect the value of a country's currency. Governments usually delegate the centralized management of these assets to central banks. This was an important function of the central bank as the government's bank.

5. Exercising Custody of Deposit Reserves

Once banks accumulate a certain amount of deposits, they are required to set aside a portion of cash as reserves, which are necessary to fulfill the needs of depositors who may wish to withdraw at any time. A part of these reserves is kept as cash on hand by the bank, while the remaining reserves are deposited into the central bank. This is why the central bank is termed the banks' bank.

6. Acting as the "Lender of Last Resort"

As the banks' bank, the central bank served as the "lender of last resort" during financial emergencies or poor daily capital turnover in general financial institutions. This role of the central bank was primarily reflected through operations such as rediscounting, collateral transfers, and transfer of foreign exchange collateral, with rediscounting being the most significant.

7. Supervising Bill Settlement

Bill settlement, also known as bill exchange, involved the daily exchange of bills received by banks within a specific city or region. After balancing debts and credits, the remaining difference was transferred and cleared through the central bank accounts of each bank.

8. Carrying Out Supervision and Management

A country's highest financial regulatory authority is responsible for overseeing, inspecting, and managing the financial system, business, market, and the macro implementation of policies. The central bank, due to its unique status and influence, was well-equipped to shoulder the responsibility of financial supervision and management.

9. Carrying Out Macro Regulation

As a key department for government intervention, control, and regulation of the economy and finance, the central bank was a crucial instrument for macroeconomic regulation. Its responsibilities included issuing currency, managing credit, regulating currency circulation, redistributing funds, implementing monetary policies, and ensuring financial stability.

IV. The Central Bank and Bill Clearing

Bill clearing traditionally fell under the central bank's purview. The 1927 *Central Bank Regulations* included "collecting and clearing various bills on behalf of banks and enterprises" as one of its tasks. This description remained largely unchanged in the *Central Bank Regulations* revised in 1928, stating that one of its tasks was "collecting and clearing various bills." During the early establishment phase of the central bank, its functions were still incomplete. To meet business needs, local banks set up their own bill clearing institutions. In May 1935, the *Central Bank Law* officially marked "handling the exchange of bills and the transfer and settlement of various banks" as one of the central bank's responsibilities. However, this provision wasn't effectively implemented due to prevailing conditions. Therefore, before the onset of the War of Resistance Against Japan, bill clearing in Shanghai was not unified. Foreign banks, the money industry, and modern Chinese banks independently managed their bill clearing businesses. The central bank only participated in the Shanghai Commercial Paper Exchange Company Ltd. as a member for bill clearing.

Following Japan's full-scale invasion, the Communist Party of China (CPC) took measures to alleviate the market's tight monetary policy. On September 9, 1940, the Joint General Office issued the *Interim Measures for Checking Accounts in the Four Banks* and the *Measures for the Implementation of Centralized Account Checking and Interest Calculation in the Four Banks.* These measures transferred the responsibility of checking accounts of the Central Bank, Bank of China, BOCOM, and Agricultural Bank of China (ABC) to the Central Bank.[130] This move laid the groundwork for the Central Bank to take over the bill exchange operations in Chongqing.

In 1941, Chongqing faced significant inflation and a tight monetary policy. The Ministry of Finance began to recognize the importance of bill exchange. To stabilize finance and activate monetary resources, the Central Bank initiated the establishment of a bill exchange institution. They drafted *Measures for Central Bank to Handle Bill Exchange* and *Regulations for Central Bank-Affiliated Bill Exchange Banks and Money Houses to Ensure the Preparation of Stock Price Committees.* The first document stated that "bill exchange and transfer matters are to be handled by the central bank in a centralized manner. Participation is limited to member banks and money houses of the bank and money industry associations. All local association member banks and money houses could join the exchange banks through the introduction of their associations."[131] The conditions for participating in the exchange, the supervision and management of exchange banks and money houses, and the types of exchange bills were all specified. The document also detailed exchange methods, rules, refunds, penalties, and more, making the central bank a center for bill exchange in terms of the system. In January 1942, the Central Bank Business Bureau established a Bill Exchange Department specializing in bill exchange business, which started operations in May of the same year. From June 1, bill exchange business was conducted in Chongqing. This marked the beginning of the central bank's leadership in the bill exchange business in China, laying the groundwork for a national bill clearing pattern led by the central bank. Data from 1942–1948 shows a significant upward trend in the total amount and number of bills exchanged after the Central Bank took charge of the Chongqing Bill Exchange. From January to July 1948 alone, the Chongqing Bill Exchange processed 4.86 million bills, totaling 50.3 trillion fiat yuan, demonstrating significant results.

Table 4-13 Statistics of Chongqing Bill Exchange's exchange business (June 1942–July 1948)

Time	Total amount (10,000 fiat currency)	Number (piece)
June–December 1942	3,283,529	343,762
1943	13,911,056	777,606
1944	58,104,193	1,409,566
1945	261,042,916	2,028,825
1946	510,182,000	1,119,756
1947	3,849,276,886	3,224,840
January–July 1948	50,386,907,776	4,867,747

Source: Chongqing Financial Writing Group, ed., *Chongqing Finance (Volume 1)* (Chongqing: Chongqing Publishing House, 1991), 303.

Afterward, the central bank successively opened bill exchanges in cities such as Chengdu and Guilin.

Table 4-14 Statistics of Central Banks handling bill exchanges in various regions during the War of Resistance Against Japan

Location	Launch date
Chengdu	May 25, 1943
Guilin	February 5, 1944
Xi'an	May 16, 1944
Kunming	November 27, 1944
Guiyang	February 19, 1945
Lanzhou	June 15, 1945

Source: Chongqing Archives and Financial Research Institute of the People's Bank of Chongqing, *Historical Materials of the Joint General Office of the Four Banks (Part 1)* (Beijing: Archives Publishing House, 1993), 633.

The establishment of the Chongqing Bill Exchange in 1942 signified the onset of the central bank's supervision over bill exchange operations. Following the victory in the War of Resistance Against Japan, the Shanghai Commercial Paper Exchange Company Ltd. was restructured and integrated into the central bank's clearing system. With the central bank's strong promotion, bill clearing business in other regions were managed by the central bank's various branches. On February 12, 1947, the Central Bank introduced the revised *Measures for Central Bank to Handle Bill Exchange*, clearly stipulating the disposal, entrusted exchange, types of exchange bills, and the rules for exchange banks and money houses. The measures split the banks and money houses participating in the exchange into two categories: those established with government approval and those approved and registered by the Ministry of Finance. Entities accepting funds were regarded as banks. This expanded the scope of bill exchange to the national banking industry and affirmed the Central Bank's status as the national bill exchange center. All bills received by the exchange banks and money houses were required to apply for exchange, and transfer applications and interbank loan vouchers were included in the scope of exchange bills.[132] In March of the same year, the Central Bank revised and issued the *Measures for Handling the Collection and Settlement of Bills Between the Four Banks and Two Bureaus at Each Branch of the Central Bank.* This was a supplement to the *Measures for Handling the Exchange of Bills by the Central Bank.* Through this, the Central Bank enhanced its management of the bill collection and settlement operations of banks and bureaus. The central bank's bill exchange system was largely complete, becoming a national settlement center for financial institutions.[133] The central bank's function to supervise national clearing affairs was officially established. Subsequently, the central bank implemented the bill exchange regulations nationwide, and by around 1948, a bill exchange system led by the central bank had been essentially established nationwide.[134]

Table 4-15 Statistics on Central Bank's handling of bill exchange in various regions after the victory of the War of Resistance Against Japan

Location	Launch date
Tianjin	January 7, 1946
Peking	January 7, 1946
Nanjing	May 1, 1946
Hankou	June 1, 1944
Guangzhou	August 1, 1946
Hangzhou	September 2, 1946
Qingdao	September 2, 1946
Shenyang	November 1, 1946

Source: "Central Bank's 1946 Annual Business Report," in *Compilation of Historical Archives of the Republic of China (Volume 5)*, ed. Second Historical Archives of China (Nanjing: Phoenix Publishing House, 2010), 593–596.

However, due to the impending collapse of China's economy at that time, the bill exchange was not promising and bill withdrawals were ongoing. In March 1948, despite some improvement after the Central Bank revised the *Measures for Banning Bill Withdrawals*, the situation improved, but was still far from ideal. In June of that same year, the total amount of bill exchange in Shanghai was 33.93 trillion fiat yuan, with a difference of 2.77 trillion fiat yuan, and bills withdrawn amounted to approximately 300 billion fiat yuan.[135]

V. The Central Bank and Rediscounting

In 1927, the *Central Bank Regulations* included "discounting or rediscounting of treasury securities and commercial bills" as part of the central bank's business operations. The revised regulations in 1928 expanded this scope to include "discounting or buying of commercial promissory notes and bills of exchange." In 1935, the Shanghai Chamber of Commerce suggested the creation of acceptance bills. It wrote to the central bank requesting support by providing a rediscounting service. The *Central Bank Law*, enacted in May of that same year, further specified that treasury securities, government bonds issued or guaranteed by the Nationalist Government, domestic bank acceptance bills, domestic commercial bills, and promissory notes could all be rediscounted by the central bank. This was done to encourage the central bank to conduct rediscounting operations.

In the early stages of the War of Resistance Against Japan, the Central Bank, Bank of China, BOCOM, and China Rural Bank managed rediscounting services. However, due to the central bank's limited functions, the development of rediscounting in modern China was significantly delayed. In 1942, the Joint General Office of the Four Banks issued the *Measures for the Division of Lending and Investment Business of the Four Banks*, leading to specialized development within these banks. The central bank obtained the exclusive right to undertake rediscounting. In 1943, the *Measures for the Administration of Bill Acceptance and Discounting During Special Period* was enacted, requiring each bank to apply for rediscounting from the central bank. This legislation officially established the central bank's rediscount system for the first time. In July of the same year, the Central Bank began processing rediscount transactions, established a rediscount review committee, and made specific regulations on rediscount procedures, officially defining its rediscounting function. However, during this period, the central bank's rediscount system was only initially established. From 1942 to 1945, the central bank primarily focused on the financing operations of national banks and bureaus and rarely conducted rediscounting for general banks and money houses, resulting in a relatively small rediscount volume.[136]

Table 4-16 Central Bank discounting business (1938–1946)

Year	Discount and rediscount amount (fiat currency yuan)	Total lending amount (fiat currency yuan)	%
1938	3,975,507	1,268,904,473	0.31
1939	3,974,105	3,730,979,405	0.11
1940	3,971,342	6,036,661,462	0.07
1941	22,750,000	9,238,802,413	0.25
1942	Total: 71,850,000 Discount: 68,850,000 Rediscount: 3,000,000	39,210,025,518	0.18
1943	Total: 615,571,250 Discount: 595,771,250 Rediscount: 19,800,000	89,969,662,013	0.71
1944	253,614,500	281,232,667,468	0.09

(Continued)

Year	Discount and rediscount amount (fiat currency yuan)	Total lending amount (fiat currency yuan)	%
1945	653,860,000	1,613,289,796,934	0.04
1946	4,271,527,400,000	8,682,995,375,491	0.05

Source: Liu Huiyu, *Research on the Central Bank of China (1928–1949)* (Beijing: China Economic Publishing House, 1999), 196.

Note: The total discount and rediscount figures for 1944–1946 represent only the rediscount amounts.

In April 1947, the Central Bank established the Central Bank Discount and Lending Committee and consecutively released the *General Rules for Handling Discount and Lending for Commercial Banks and Money Houses in Shanghai* and *Notice for Commercial Banks and Money Houses to Apply to the Central Bank for Rediscounting, Transfer of Collateral, and Transfer of Bill of Lading*. These guidelines targeted individual commercial banks and money houses for rediscounting and outlined the procedures and requirements for it. The criteria for commercial banks to rediscount was eased.[137] In June 1947, the draft amendment to the *Central Bank Law* was reviewed and approved, stating that the central bank should form a rediscount committee to oversee the discounting business. However, this law was not formally pronounced and enforced.[138] In April 1948, the Joint General Office approved the *Guidelines for Loans to Meet Production Purposes*, stating that "the central bank should form a discount and lending committee to review matters related to transfer of collateral, transfer of bills of exchange, and rediscounting of general business lending handled by various banks and bureaus, and consider market conditions to determine the amount and interest rate. The committee should also accept applications from commercial banks and money houses for transfer of collateral, transfer of bills of exchange, and rediscounting."[139] In March of the same year, the *Supplementary Methods to the Policy Regarding Lending for Production Purposes* outlined the method for determining the rediscount interest rate. This involved calculating and confirming the transfer of collateral, transfer of bills of exchange, and rediscount interest rates for general business with market interest rates as reference.[140] The Central Bank Discount and Lending Committee was re-established in Shanghai on April 27, 1948. This committee had advisory committees for industry, mining, agriculture, and export, and was responsible for reviewing related cases.[141] The committee also specifically formulated the *Rules for Handling Interbank Discounting and Lending by the Central Bank Discount and Lending Committee*. These rules stated that the application for rediscounting, transfer of collateral, and transfer of collateral foreign exchange should be based on the principle of separate application by banks, including national banks, provincial and municipal banks, and banks under the *Banking Law*. The total lending amount was limited to the bank's deposit, and the maximum rediscount period was set at 15 days, which did not exceed the original loan maturity date. The discount and interest rate for rediscounting, transfer of collateral, and transfer of documentary bills would be determined by the discount and lending committee at any time.[142]

The above regulations indicate that the central bank's rediscount system was becoming more robust, with the central bank taking on specific roles in managing the discounting business. The rediscount interest rate, set by the central bank, aligned more closely with market interest rates. However, the central bank's rediscounting often blended with acceptance, discounting, and mortgage loans. The relatively small proportion of rediscount business limited the central bank's function of carrying out rediscounting.

Summary

In the late 1920s and early 1930s, social unrest was commonplace, and the advancement of industry and commerce faced challenges, primarily due to funding issues. Acceptance bills and discount services were actively promoted as effective solutions to these crises. This provided new credit options for the market, enhancing fund financing. The Shanghai Bank Bill Acceptance Office, in particular, provided banks with credit support with its own credit, promoting the growth of acceptance bills and discount business. This was instrumental in revitalizing the banks' stagnant assets and facilitating fund financing. During the initial stages of the War of Resistance Against Japan, the Joint General Office of the Four Banks infused a significant amount of capital into the market via joint discount and lending services. This eased capital turnover difficulties in various sectors, including industry, commerce, and finance. It supported the relocation of industrial enterprises, the transport and reserve of wartime materials, and production development in rear areas.

The Nationalist Government actively developed bill business in rear areas and encouraged the establishment of a discount market. This not only bolstered the central bank's control over finance but also activated wartime finance and preserved cash reserves by developing bill business. It effectively addressed the issue of poor fund circulation under the earlier credit system and supported the development of various rear area industries, including mining, agriculture, industry, commerce, and finance. The Chongqing United Bill Acceptance Office provided credit support for the acceptance of industrial and agricultural bills, and the joint credit reporting agency supported the production in rear areas and promoted industrial and commercial credit development. After the victory in the War of Resistance Against Japan, the Nationalist Government implemented bill acceptance and discounting to stimulate finance and aid economic growth. During the post-war period, bill business positively impacted the development of industry and commerce. After the establishment of the Republic of China, a bill exchange system led by modern Chinese banks was gradually established, exerting a significant impact on reducing speculation, preventing capital flight and bank runs, and ensuring the smooth turnover of industrial and commercial funds. The central bank gradually established its function of overseeing national bill clearing and rediscounting, further encouraging the development of modern China's bill market.

NOTES

1. *Banking Law*, in *Compilation of Chinese and Foreign Financial Regulations*, vol. 3, ed. Financial Research Institute of the Head Office of the People's Bank of China (1988), 114–123.
2. Sun Fei and Zhao Wenkai, *A-Century Thrilling Journey: Major County Finance (1912–2012)* (Beijing: China Legal Publishing House, 1988), 177–178.
3. Posting notes, also known as black market lending, is a short-term borrowing method that uses forward checks as a borrowing tool.
4. Hong Jiaguan and Zhang Jifeng, *Modern Shanghai Financial Market* (Shanghai People's Publishing House, 1989), 62–63.
5. Wan Liming, *Research on the Institutional Evolution of the Modern Chinese Bill Market* (Shanghai Far East Publishing House, 2014), 42.
6. Hong Jiaguan and Zhang Jifeng, *Modern Shanghai Financial Market* (Shanghai People's Publishing House, 1989), 63.
7. Ma Yinchu, *On China's Banks* (Beijing: The Commercial Press, 1929), 147.
8. Ibid.
9. Yang Yinpu, *A Glimpse of Shanghai Financial Organizations* (Beijing: The Commercial Press, 1930), 136.
10. Ibid.
11. Ibid., 253.
12. Ibid., 254–255.
13. Zhang Naiqi, "China's Bill Market," *Central Bank Monthly*, no. 1 (1936).
14. The "Three-Festival" accounting system refers to a practice where transaction amounts are initially recorded in the account and then uniformly settled during the three major festivals: Dragon Boat Festival, Mid-Autumn Festival, and Spring Festival.
15. Jin Guobao, "How to Develop the Industrial and Commercial Sectors," in *Bill-Related Issues and Banking Legislation*, ed. Jin Baoguo (Beijing: Zhonghua Book Company, 1947), 1.
16. Jin Guobao, "Why and How to Create a Discount Market," *The Bankers Weekly* 15, no. 16 (1931).
17. Jin Guobao, "How to Develop the Industrial and Commercial Sectors," in *Bill-Related Issues and Banking Legislation*, ed. Jin Baoguo (Beijing: Zhonghua Book Company, 1947), 5.
18. Ibid., 6–7.
19. Ibid., 74–76.
20. Hong Jiaguan and Zhang Jifeng, *Modern Shanghai Financial Market* (Shanghai People's Publishing House, 1989), 69.
21. Jin Guobao, "The Bill-Related Issues in the *Banking Law*," in *Bill-Related Issues and Banking Legislation*, ed. Jin Baoguo (Beijing: Zhonghua Book Company, 1947), 76.
22. Ibid., 76–79.
23. Jin Guobao, "Speech at the 7th Star Five Dinner Party of the China Association for Domestic Production and Marketing Cooperation on May 6, 2021," in *A Collection of Insightful Quotes at Dinner Tables.*
24. Hong Jiaguan and Zhang Jifeng, *Modern Shanghai Financial Market* (Shanghai People's Publishing House, 1989), 69.
25. Jin Guobao, "A Brief Discussion on Acceptance Bills," in *Bill-Related Issues and Banking Legislation*, ed. Jin Baoguo (Beijing: Zhonghua Book Company, 1947), 12.
26. Ibid., 12–15.
27. Ibid., 19–20.
28. Ibid., 22.
29. Hong Jiaguan and Zhang Jifeng, *Modern Shanghai Financial Market* (Shanghai People's Publishing House, 1989), 71.
30. "Information on the Establishment of Bill Advance Acceptance and Discounting Business by China State Bank (1931)," in *China State Bank Archives*: Q278-1-109-85.

31. Jin Guobao, "Why and How to Create a Discount Market," *The Bankers Weekly* 15, no. 16 (1931).
32. Jin Guobao, "The Promotion of Commercial Acceptance Bills," in *Bill-Related Issues and Banking Legislation*, ed. Jin Baoguo (Beijing: Zhonghua Book Company, 1947), 53.
33. Financial History Research Office, Financial Research Institute, Head Office of the People's Bank of China, *The Financial Market in Modern China* (Beijing: China Financial Publishing House, 1987).
34. Cheng Nianpeng, "Notice of Domestic Enamel Business Offices on Issuing Commercial Acceptance Bills," *The Bankers Weekly*, no. 42 (1932): 33–36.
35. Ibid.
36. Ibid.
37. Hong Jiaguan and Zhang Jifeng, *Modern Shanghai Financial Market* (Shanghai People's Publishing House, 1989), 76.
38. Wan Liming, *Research on the Institutional Evolution of the Modern Chinese Bill Market* (Shanghai Far East Publishing House, 2014), 63.
39. Ibid., 55.
40. "Issues Regarding the Revitalization of the Shanghai Market," *The Bankers Weekly*, no. 19 (1935): 9.
41. "Relief for Industrial, Commercial, and Financial Issues," *Industrial and Commercial Semi-Monthly*, no. 7 (1935): 7.
42. Financial History Research Office, Financial Research Institute, Head Office of the People's Bank of China, *The Financial Market in Modern China* (Beijing: China Financial Publishing House, 1987), 111.
43. Hong Jiaguan, *Shanghai Finance in the 20th Century* (Shanghai People's Publishing House, 2004), 208.
44. Wan Liming, *Research on the Institutional Evolution of the Modern Chinese Bill Market* (Shanghai Far East Publishing House, 2014), 65.
45. "Opening of Bank Bill Acceptance Office," *The Bankers Weekly*, no. 20 (1936): 10.
46. Wan Liming, "Institutional Innovation of Modern Chinese Bill Intermediary Institutions and Its Implications—Taking Shanghai Bank Bill Acceptance Office as an Example," *Journal of Shanghai University of Administration*, no. 2 (2008): 59–67.
47. Hong Jiaguan and Zhang Jifeng, *Modern Shanghai Financial Market* (Shanghai People's Publishing House, 1989): 85.
48. Detailed Rules for the Operations of Bank Bill Acceptance Office (March 13, 1936), collected by Shanghai Archives, Archives of the Joint Preparatory Commission: S177-1-72.
49. "Organizational Regulations of the Committee of the Bank Bill Acceptance Office and the Convention on Members Banks," *The Bankers Weekly*, no. 20 (1936): 11.
50. Financial History Research Office, Financial Research Institute, Head Office of the People's Bank of China, *The Financial Market in Modern China* (Beijing: China Financial Publishing House, 1987), 424.
51. Acceptance Bill Instructions (May 1936), collected by Shanghai Archives, Archives of the Joint Preparatory Commission: S177-1-72.
52. Letter to the Bank of China, the Central Bank, and Bank of Communications (March 19, 1936), collected by Shanghai Archives, Archives of the Joint Preparatory Commission: S177-2-606.
53. "The First Conference of the Bank Bill Acceptance Office (March 31, 1936)," *The Bankers Weekly*, no. 20 (1936): 12.
54. "The Discount Rate Announced by the Bank Bill Acceptance Office (April 7, 1936)," *The Bankers Weekly*, no. 20 (1936): 13.
55. "The First Conference of the Bank Bill Acceptance Office (March 31, 1936)," *The Bankers Weekly*, no. 20 (1936): 11.
56. First Meeting of Members of the Bill Acceptance Office, collected by Shanghai Archives, Archives of the Joint Preparatory Commission: S177-1-21.
57. Financial History Research Office, Financial Research Institute, Head Office of the People's Bank of China, *The Financial Market in Modern China* (Beijing: China Financial Publishing House, 1987), 425.

58. Chongqing Archives, ed., "Financial Research Institute of the People's Bank of Chongqing," in *Historical Materials of the Joint General Office of the Four Banks (Part 2)* (Beijing: Archives Publishing House, 1993), 344–345.
59. Zhuo Hanping, *A Brief History of Modern Chinese Monetary Banks* (Nanjing University Press, 1992), 135.
60. Jingshi Xueyi Society, ed., *Modern Economic Dynamics* (Beijing: World Book Company, 1939), 28–29.
61. Wang Hongman, *The Joint General Office of the Four Banks and the Economy of the Southwest Region During the War* (Shanghai: Fudan University Press, 2011), 34.
62. Ibid., 36.
63. Hong Jiaguan, *Central Bank Historical Materials* (Beijing: China Financial Publishing House, 2005), 770–772.
64. The discount and lending business falls into two categories: ordinary and special. Ordinary discount and lending typically involves small to medium-sized short-term loans. Special discount and lending, on the other hand, pertains to large, long-term loans that require approval from the Ministry of Finance before processing.
65. Yuan Yuanfu and Miao Mingyang, *A Brief History of Chinese Finance* (Beijing: China Financial Publishing House, 2001), 159.
66. "Work Report of the Joint General Office of the Four Banks 1941," in *Compilation of Historical Archives of the Republic of China (Volume 5, Part 2, Finance and Economy 4)*, ed. Second Historical Archives of China (Nanjing: Phoenix Publishing House, 2010), 38–39.
67. Yuan Yuanfu and Miao Mingyang, *A Brief History of Chinese Finance* (Beijing: China Financial Publishing House, 2001), 159–160.
68. Liu Huiyu, *Research on the Central Bank of China (1928–1949)* (Beijing: China Economic Publishing House, 1999), 194.
69. "Outline of Measures for Improving Local Financial Institutions Issued by the Ministry of Finance (April 28, 1938)," in *Selected Financial Regulations of the Republic of China*, ed. the Second Historical Archives of China, Jiangsu Branch of the People's Bank of China, etc. (Beijing: Archives Publishing House, 1989), 629.
70. "Letter on Implementing Discount Rate Management Policy and Signing Opinions by the Central Business Bureau (October 27, 1938)." Unpublished archives in the Chongqing Branch of the Joint Office of the Central Bank, Bank of China, Bank of Communications, and China Rural Bank: 02920001380000147000.
71. "Interim Measures for Promoting Bank Acceptance and Discount Business," in *Historical Materials of the Joint General Office of the Four Banks (Part 2)*, collected by Chongqing Archives and Chongqing Financial Research Institute of the People's Bank of China (Beijing: Archives Publishing House, 1993), 571–572.
72. "Resolution of the Joint General Office of the Four Banks on the Proposed Use of Bill Discounting Method for Working Capital Loans," in *Historical Materials of the Joint General Office of the Four Banks (Part 2)*, collected by Chongqing Archives and Chongqing Financial Research Institute of the People's Bank of China (Beijing: Archives Publishing House, 1993), 572–574.
73. "Interim Measures for Promoting Bank Acceptance and Discount Business," in *Historical Materials of the Joint General Office of the Four Banks (Part 2)*, collected by Chongqing Archives and Chongqing Financial Research Institute of the People's Bank of China (Beijing: Archives Publishing House, 1993), 574–576.
74. "The General Management Office of the Bank of China's Letter on the Acceptance and Discount Methods for Special Period Bills During Special Period," in *Historical Materials of the Joint General Office of the Four Banks (Part 2)*, collected by Chongqing Archives and Chongqing Financial Research Institute of the People's Bank of China (Beijing: Archives Publishing House, 1993), 577–580.
75. Ibid., 587–588.
76. Financial Research Editorial Department, ed., *Acceptance and Discount of Bills* (Shanghai Financial Society, 1983), 72–74.

77. Chongqing Financial Writing Group, ed., *Chongqing Finance (Volume 1)* (Chongqing: Chongqing Publishing House, 1991), 337–338.
78. Ministry of Finance, "The Ministry of Finance Has Formulated an Outline of Measures to Improve Local Financial Institutions," *Commercial Monthly Report* 18, no. 5 (1938): 57.
79. Wan Liming, *Research on the Institutional Evolution of the Modern Chinese Bill Market* (Shanghai Far East Publishing House, 2014), 77–78.
80. Chongqing Archives, ed., "Financial Research Institute of the People's Bank of Chongqing," in *Historical Materials of the Joint General Office of the Four Banks (Part 3)* (Beijing: Archives Publishing House, 1993), 594–596.
81. "A bouquet of market news," *Xinhua Daily*, no. 3, November 29, 1944.
82. Zhang Ge, "Research on Chongqing's Financial Market During the War of Resistance Against Japanese Aggression (1937–1945)" (PhD diss., Southwest University, 2019).
83. Financial History Research Office of the Financial Research Institute, People's Bank of China, *Management of Modern Chinese Financial Industry* (Beijing: People's Publishing House, 1990), 264.
84. "The central bank also handles the bill exchange business," *Ta Kung Pao* (Chongqing Edition), June 3, 1942.
85. PBC Shanghai Branch, *Historical Materials of Shanghai Money Houses* (Shanghai People's Publishing House, 1960), 493.
86. Wan Liming, *Research on Shanghai Commercial Paper Exchange Company Ltd. (1933–1951)* (Beijing: China Book Publishing House, 2019), 12.
87. "Created by Our Own Country," trans. Tao Yue, in *Research on the Posting System in Ningbo (1). The Bankers Weekly* 15, no. 35 (1931).
88. Financial History Research Office, Financial Research Institute, Head Office of the People's Bank of China, *The Financial Market in Modern China* (Beijing: China Financial Publishing House, 1987), 212.
89. Shi Tao, "An Analysis of the Evolution of the Bill Exchange System in Modern China," *Journal of Harbin University of Commerce* (Social Sciences Edition), no. 1 (2012): 69–77.
90. Ibid.
91. Du Xuncheng, "The Evolution of China's Credit System in the 1920s and 1930s," *Chinese Social Sciences*, no. 4 (2002).
92. Shi Tao, "An Analysis of the Evolution of the Bill Exchange System in Modern China," *Journal of Harbin University of Commerce* (Social Sciences Edition), no. 1 (2012): 69–77.
93. Wan Liming, *Research on Shanghai Commercial Paper Exchange Company Ltd. (1933–1951)* (Beijing: China Book Publishing House, 2019), 40, 44.
94. Ibid., 52.
95. Minutes of the Seventh Meeting of the Clearing House Committee (February 22, 1933), The Joint Preparatory Commission Archives: S177-1-18.
96. Wan Liming, *Research on Shanghai Commercial Paper Exchange Company Ltd. (1933–1951)* (Beijing: China Book Publishing House, 2019), 52–53.
97. Joint Institute for Commercial Paper of JUFE and BOJJ, *A History of Bills* (Beijing: China Financial Publishing House, 2020), 142.
98. Wan Liming, *Research on Shanghai Commercial Paper Exchange Company Ltd. (1933–1951)* (Beijing: China Book Publishing House, 2019), 60–61.
99. Ibid., 73–84.
100. Ibid., 97–105.
101. Zhu Boquan, "Shanghai Commercial Paper Exchange Company Ltd.," in *20th Century Shanghai Cultural and Historical Data Library (Volume 5)*, ed. Lu Jianxin and Wanyan Shaoyuan (Shanghai Bookstore Publishing House, 1999).
102. Wan Liming, *Research on Shanghai Commercial Paper Exchange Company Ltd. (1933–1951)* (Beijing: China Book Publishing House, 2019), 118–119.

103. Joint Institute for Commercial Paper of JUFE and BOJJ, *A History of Bills* (Beijing: China Financial Publishing House, 2020), 143.
104. Wan Liming, *Research on Shanghai Commercial Paper Exchange Company Ltd. (1933–1951)* (Beijing: China Book Publishing House, 2019), 133–135.
105. Joint Institute for Commercial Paper of JUFE and BOJJ, *A History of Bills* (Beijing: China Financial Publishing House, 2020), 143–144.
106. PBC Shanghai Branch, *Historical Materials of Shanghai Money Houses* (Shanghai People's Publishing House, 1960), 541.
107. Wan Liming, "On the Institutional Changes of Shanghai Commercial Paper Exchange Company Ltd. After World War II," in *Research on the Changes of China's Financial System*, ed. Fudan University Center for the Study of Chinese Financial History (Shanghai: Fudan University Press, 2008), 243–257.
108. Ibid.
109. Shi Tao, *A History of Modern Chinese Central Banks* (Beijing: The Commercial Press, 2021), 1–2.
110. Ibid., 48–96.
111. Yang Yinpu, *Yang Zhu's Theory of Chinese Finance* (Shanghai: Dawn Book Company, 1932), 35.
112. Cui Xiaocen, *Central Bank Theory* (Beijing: The Commercial Press, 1935), 244.
113. Shi Tao, *A History of Modern Chinese Central Banks* (Beijing: The Commercial Press, 2021), 129–130.
114. Liu Huiyu, *Research on the Central Banks of China (1928–1949)* (Beijing: China Economic Publishing House, 1999), 5–6.
115. Ibid., 8–11.
116. Ibid., 11–20.
117. Ibid., 20–25.
118. Shi Tao, *A History of Modern Chinese Central Banks* (Beijing: The Commercial Press, 2021), 124.
119. The Second Historical Archives of China, *Compilation of Historical Archives of the Republic of China* (Nanjing: Phoenix Publishing House, 2010), 331.
120. Guo Rongsheng, *A Chronicle of Mr. Kung Hsiang-hsi's Life in the Republic of China Period* (Taipei: Taiwan Commercial Press, 1981), 96.
121. Shi Tao, *A History of Modern Chinese Central Banks* (Beijing: The Commercial Press, 2021), 143–144.
122. Ibid., 145–147.
123. Sheng Mujie, "On the Discount and Lending Policy of the Central Bank," *Economic Review* 1, no. 5 (1947).
124. Zhang Du, "The Evolution of the Central Bank in the Past 20 Years," Collected by China's Second Historical Archives.
125. Liu Huiyu, *Research on the Central Bank of China (1928–1949)* (Beijing: China Economic Publishing House, 1999), 57.
126. Ibid., 59–60.
127. Ibid., 60.
128. Ibid., 60–61.
129. Shi Tao, "Functional Improvement (1937–1945)," in *A History of Modern Chinese Central Banks* (Beijing: The Commercial Press, 2021), 190.
130. Sun Jianhua, *Financial Development and Institutional Changes in Modern China (1840–1945)* (Beijing: China Financial and Economic Publishing House, 2008), 585.
131. The Second Historical Archives of China, Jiangsu Branch of the People's Bank of China, et al., *Selected Financial Regulations of the Republic of China* (Beijing: Archives Publishing House, 1989), 903–908.
132. Ibid., 936–941.
133. Liu Huiyu, *Research on the Central Bank of China (1928–1949)* (Beijing: China Economic Publishing House, 1999), 214–216.
134. Shi Tao, "An Analysis of the Evolution of the Bill Exchange System in Modern China," *Journal of Harbin University of Commerce* (Social Sciences Edition), no. 1 (2012): 69–77.

135. Liu Huiyu, *Research on the Central Bank of China (1928–1949)* (Beijing: China Economic Publishing House, 1999), 216.
136. Ibid., 196–197.
137. "General Rules for the Central Bank Discount and Lending Committee to Handle Discount and Lending Business for Shanghai Commercial Banks and Money Houses," in *Complete Collection of Financial Regulations (Continued)*, ed. Economic Research Department of the Central Bank (Taipei: Taiwan Student Bookstore, 1971), 53–54; "Commercial Banks Apply to the Central Bank for Rediscounting, Pledging, and Transfer Exchange Operations," in *Selected Financial Regulations of the Republic of China*, ed. The Second Historical Archives of China, Jiangsu Branch of the People's Bank of China, et al. (Beijing: Archives Publishing House, 1989), 1204–1206.
138. "Draft Amendment to the *Central Bank Law*," in *Compilation of Chinese and Foreign Financial Regulations (Volume 3)*, ed. Financial Research Institute of the Head Office of the People's Bank of China (1988), 89–93.
139. "Loan Policy for Production Enterprises," in *Selected Financial Regulations of the Republic of China*, ed. The Second Historical Archives of China, Jiangsu Branch of the People's Bank of China, et al. (Beijing: Archives Publishing House, 1989), 1229–1231.
140. "Supplementary Measures to the Policy on Loans for Production Enterprises," in *Selected Financial Regulations of the Republic of China*, ed. The Second Historical Archives of China, Jiangsu Branch of the People's Bank of China, et al. (Beijing: Archives Publishing House, 1989), 1231–1233.
141. "Resolution of the Council on the Approval of the 1948 Production Enterprise Loan Policy," in *Historical Materials of the Joint General Office of the Four Banks (Part 2)*, ed. Chongqing Archives and Chongqing Financial Research Institute of the People's Bank of China (Beijing: Archives Publishing House, 1993), 428–430.
142. "Regulations of the Central Bank Discount and Lending Committee on Handling Interbank Discount and Lending Operations," *Financial Weekly*, no. 2 (1948).

CHAPTER FIVE

Bills in Revolutionary Base Areas

During the New Democratic Revolution (1919–1949), the CPC led the people to establish revolutionary bases and develop various forms of financial instruments such as promissory notes, checks, and bills of exchange. These were used in their effort to overthrow imperialism, feudalism, and bureaucrat capitalism while striving for national independence and liberation. During the Agrarian Revolution (1927–1937), the Farmers Association of Jingang Township, Liuyang County, Hunan Province, established a Public Property Preservation Office. This office issued promissory notes with public property as a guarantee to develop the peasant economy. To ensure the Red Army's food supply, the Soviet government of Xiang-Gan Province issued promissory notes for rice purchases. The State Bank of the Chinese Soviet Republic, established in Ruijin, Jiangxi Province, also incorporated bill business into its charter.

During the War of Resistance Against Japan, banks in the base and liberated areas issued promissory notes, checks, and bills of exchange to support production development, contributing to economic development in these areas. The Beihai Bank in the Shandong Revolutionary Base also established a bill exchange to handle bill exchange business and a bill of exchange office to manage the buying and selling of bills of exchange. The Shanxi-Hebei-Shandong-Henan Border Area issued the *Interim Measures for the Administration of Foreign Exchange* to strictly regulate foreign exchange, including promissory notes, checks, and bills of exchange. During the Liberation War (1946–1950), the base areas used bills of exchange and promissory notes as weapons in financial struggles against the enemy. In the First Division of Central China, the Huangqiao Bill Exchange was established to regulate finance, promote market prosperity, and manage foreign exchange bills. A foreign exchange bill exchange was also established in central Hebei, transitioning the bill business model to mass operation. To alleviate deflation, Beihai Bank, Central China Bank, Central Jiangsu, North Jiangsu, and Northeast Bank issued promissory notes of different denominations. These promissory notes replaced currency in circulation, helping to stabilize wartime finance.

SECTION I

Bills in Revolutionary Base Areas During the Agrarian Revolution

Following the August 1 Nanchang Uprising in 1927, the CPC led the armed masses of workers and peasants in an armed uprising, resulting in the creation of over ten revolutionary bases, including Jinggang Mountain and the Central Revolutionary bases. During the Agrarian Revolution, the banks in these base areas issued and circulated a number of bills, and some even conducted bill business. However, the circulation of these bills was largely confined to the base areas and primarily intended to meet the demand for agricultural products.

I. Bills in Base Areas During the Agrarian Revolution

1. Promissory Notes Issued by Farmers Association in Jingang Township

Jingang Township in Nanxiang, Liuyang County, Hunan Province, was an economically prosperous market town known for its firecracker production. Local farmers relied heavily on firecracker making as a primary source of income. During the height of the peasant movement, several large firecracker shop owners in the area fled with funds out of fear of the revolution. This led to shop closures, worker unemployment, and a lack of firecracker sales opportunities for farmers, resulting in tough living conditions. In early 1927, the Jingang Township established a farmers' association to revitalize the regional economy and help farmers with firecracker transportation and sales. The association set up a Public Property Preservation Office, which held all public property such as school properties, ancestral halls, temples, bridge associations, and road associations as collateral for issuing promissory notes. These notes were used to buy firecrackers from farmers via the Shop Staff Association. After selling the firecrackers, the notes were cashed in, providing farmers with their earnings. This arrangement marked the earliest instance of town-level promissory notes known to us. These promissory notes, with a typical term of three months, came in three fixed denominations: one jiao (角, 10 jiao = 1 yuan), two jiao, and one yuan. They served as a means for farmers to raise funds. Owing to their strong credit, these notes were widely used as currency in Jingang Township and the Dayao area, and were well-received by the public.[1]

2. Promissory Notes for Rice Purchase Issued by Xiang-Gan Province of the Chinese Soviet Republic

In the latter half of 1933, Chiang Kai-shek rallied one million troops to assault the central revolutionary base areas and the Red Army in various regions, marking the commencement of the fifth "encirclement and suppression" campaign against the revolutionary base areas.[2] To counter the Nationalist army's attack and secure the Red Army's food supply, the Xiang-Gan Provincial Party Committee and the Provincial Soviet Government implemented a series of measures. These included collecting land taxes and public bonds and initiating grain borrowing movements to actively raise funds and food for the Red Army.[3] Despite these efforts, the problem of food shortage became increasingly severe as the scale of the anti-encirclement campaign and the number of Red Army soldiers expanded. A significant issue of having money but no rice to purchase emerged around the Red Army base areas following the victories of the 17th and 8th Red Army divisions in the Shashi and Tianli wars.[4]

To ensure food supply, Xiang-Gan Provincial Party Committee took several extraordinary measures,[5] include launching a grain collection campaign, a rice conservation campaign, collecting 40,000 yuan in government bonds for grain, and issuing Xiang-Gan Province's promissory notes for grain purchase.[6] To ensure the food supply for the Red Army and secure victory in the Agrarian Revolution, the Soviet government of Xiang-Gan Province instructed all levels of government to use 40,000 yuan of unsold government bonds to encourage the masses' grain sales. They also allowed full payment of national taxes upon maturity. Consequently, on April 20, 1934, promissory notes for rice purchases were issued in Yongxin County, Jiangxi Province. Each of these promissory notes was equivalent to one silver yuan. Each voter purchased one promissory note with grain and was paid one yuan upon maturity within four months.[7] This promissory note used bamboo-made writing paper using the lithographic printing method with a vertical block diagram structure. The upper part is titled "Grain Sales in Xiang-Gan Province of the Chinese Soviet Republic," and there are diamond-shaped flower decorations on the left and right sides of the middle. A circle is left in the middle of the flower decoration, with the words "Promissory" and "Note" written inside the blank circle. The lower part is printed with the number, an explanation of the issuance, the signature, and the issuance time. The two large words "Promissory Note" have a plum blossom pattern as the background, and it is numbered 002243. The explanation of the issuance is as follows: "(1) To ensure the complete victory of the Agrarian Revolution and sufficient food for the Red Army, a promissory note worth 40,000 yuan is issued to and purchased by each voter or household with rice. (2) After the four-month period (starting from August 1) expires, it can be cashed in with the enterprises, government agencies, or national branches, and will be recollected upon the full payment of national taxes." The signature is "Chen Xiyun, Minister of the Provincial Ministry of Finance," and the date is "April 20, 1934." The note is stamped with the oval seal of the "Executive Committee of the Xiang-Gan Soviet Ministry of Finance" and the private seal of Chen Xiyun, which had a round inner circle and a square outer circle. This marked the first promissory note issued by a provincial government in Chinese history, paving the way for future government promissory notes.[8]

Historical records reveal that the State Bank of the Soviet Republic of China issued a unique bill of exchange. This special bill had a vertical block diagram structure. It bore the inscription "Special Bill of the Soviet Republic of China" at the top, while the bottom displayed the bill number, the explanations for issuance, signature, and date of issuance.

II. The Bill System of Base Areas During the Agrarian Revolution

Some banks in the base and liberated areas mentioned bill business in their articles. For instance, in 1930, the West Fujian Industrial and Agricultural Bank included "exchange and purchase of promissory notes" in its business scope according to its articles of association. Similarly, the State Bank of the Soviet Republic of China, established in Ruijin, Jiangxi in 1932, included "discounting or rediscounting of commercial bills," "buying and selling of gold, silver, foreign currency securities or bills of exchange," and "handling various exchanges and issuing promissory notes" as standard business types in its articles of association. It even established a separate Lending and Discounting Committee in its head office, branches, and sub-branches.[9] In 1933, to regulate the discount business, the national bank specially formulated *The Interim Rules for Discount and Lending*.

(1) Article 1: Any deferred payment bills for the sale of goods by the CPC in a store, which are not yet expired and are in urgent need of payment, may be discounted with the permission of the bank in accordance with regulations.
(2) Article 2: If the payer of a bill is the discounting party or the discounting party's own store, it shall not be discounted to this bank.
(3) Article 3: Any bill that the bank deems impossible to discount shall not be discounted.
(4) Article 4: Those seeking a discount from this bank must provide a sufficient guarantor or sufficient collateral. However, if the bank deems the party reliable, the process may be simplified.
(5) Article 5: The discount interest must be paid in full before discounting.
(6) Article 6: If the payer of a discounted bill fails to make payment by the due date, the discounting party must settle the payment, and the guarantor bears joint and several liabilities.
(7) Article 7: If the discounting party has provided collateral, it will be managed according to the mortgage lending rules.[10]

The Interim Rules for Discount and Lending reveal that the national bank imposed strict requirements for bill discounting. Generally, a guarantor must be present or a significant amount of collateral must be provided, and self-issued bills are not permitted for discounting.

SECTION 2

Bills in Revolutionary Base Areas During the War of Resistance Against Japan

During the War of Resistance Against Japan, the Central Red Army set up the Northwest Soviet regime in northern Shaanxi, becoming the center of revolutionary construction at the time. During this period, revolutionary base areas were widespread, and banks in these areas or liberated territories issued promissory notes, checks, and bills of exchange to support production, alleviate the scarcity of fiat currency, and meet the needs of the revolutionary cause. The varieties and institutional rules of these bills were more diverse during this period than in the Agrarian Revolution period.

I. Bills in Base Areas During the War of Resistance Against Japan

1. Huainan Bank Promissory Notes

Huainan Bank (Bank of Huai Nau) once issued a type of promissory note. Preserved, invalidated notes reveal that there were handwritten words using steel plate oil printing methods, and a promissory note consists of two parts: the counterfoil and the note. The junction of the two parts is stamped with a square official seal, and the note number is printed in a blank space. "Promissory Note of Huainan Bank" was written horizontally on the left side of the note, while the main text was arranged vertically. It said, "This note is equivalent to one thousand yuan of fiat currency and can be used to offset grain tax payments." In the bottom right corner were the words "Commissioner Zheng Baozhen, President Zhou Jizhi, and —— Zhao Luqing."[11] The presence of Commissioner Zheng Baozhen's name indicates that the note was a cash check voucher used in the Luxi Base Area and valued in fiat currency.[12]

2. East Zhejiang Bank Promissory Notes

East Zhejiang Bank publicly issued anti-Japanese currency to fortify economic resistance against the enemy, develop agriculture, industry, and commerce, stabilize finance and prices, promote economic development in the base areas, and actively prepare for a counterattack. East Zhejiang Bank's currency was classified into head office currency and sub-branch office currency. The head office currency was further divided into three types: primary currency, auxiliary currency, and promissory notes. The promissory notes were available in two denominations, 50 yuan and 100 yuan, in a vertical format using a slate ink printing method. The perimeter of the note's face is adorned with a floral frame, with the words of the issuing entity "East Zhejiang Currency FIFTY YUAN" or "East Zhejiang Currency ONE HUNDRED YUAN" listed horizontally at the top and the words "Promissory Note" printed below. The issuance number and denomination are vertically marked on the right. The note bears the inscription "East Zhejiang Bank No. —— Anti-Japanese Currency ONE HUNDRED YUAN" or "East Zhejiang Bank No. —— Anti-Japanese Currency FIFTY YUAN," and the junction is stamped with a square seal with a floral diamond-shaped frame saying "East Zhejiang Bank." Inside the frame, the words "Bills for Payment" are printed vertically on the right side, and a six-digit red number seal is affixed below it. The note's center bears the face value printed with the words "Anti-Japanese Currency ONE HUNDRED YUAN" or "Anti-Japanese Currency FIFTY YUAN," surmounted by the red seal font "East Zhejiang Bank." The lower left part is divided into two rows with the words "General Manager" and "Deputy Manager" printed vertically, with the respective red official seals of "East Zhejiang

Bank General Manager" and "East Zhejiang Bank Deputy Manager" stamped below. The issuance date is indicated vertically on the left side, with the words "—— (month) —— (day) of the 34th Year of the Republic of China" printed.[13]

3. South Hebei Bank Promissory Notes

From 1941 to 1942, the Shanxi-Hebei-Shandong-Henan Base Area experienced extreme difficulties due to the Japanese mopping-up campaigns. Additionally, a severe locust disaster hit many counties in 1942, causing significant losses to the base area. The social order became chaotic, resources were scarce, prices skyrocketed, and food supplies dwindled, resulting in widespread public anxiety. The continuous price increase led to a sharp decline in the purchasing power of the bills in South Hebei, seriously harming their credit. To adapt to the wartime environment, South Hebei Bank began issuing promissory notes to facilitate currency use, control currency supply, replace some paper currency issuance, and strengthen currency management. This was also done to adjust the financial market, stimulate production, prevent counterfeit bills, improve bill credit, encourage capital turnover, and support the banking business. The South Hebei Bank promissory note, similar in style, design, and printing to the South Hebei promissory note, contained images and denominations. It was slightly larger than the South Hebei promissory note, and included "transferor," "guarantor" tables, and "Note Usage Explanation" in the "endorsement column" on the back of the promissory note.

(1) This note can be used in the South Hebei Administrative Region to address commercial transaction issues and improve portability.
(2) This note can be fully exchanged for local currency throughout the South Hebei Administrative Region.
(3) To prevent fraud during the transfer, securing a guarantor's endorsement is necessary.
(4) This note cannot be exchanged if it is worn, stained, or if its authenticity is doubtful or the denomination is illegible.
(5) It will not be replaced if lost.
(6) It is essential to redeem the note upon expiration, as it cannot be used after that date.[14]

4. Beihai Bank Promissory Notes

To boost production and trade in the base area, Beihai Bank in Shandong started issuing promissory notes in August 1942. These notes were meant to replace some cash in circulation, gradually resolving the issue of monetary tightening and the shortage of banknotes in the north. The rules for their issuance and use are detailed below:

(1) This promissory note is a type of bill issued by the bank. It serves as a substitute for cash in circulation and acts as a tool for transactions and payments.
(2) For ease of calculation, promissory notes are assigned fixed face values. They come in three denominations: 100 yuan, 500 yuan, and 1,000 yuan.
(3) Promissory notes are unique negotiable instruments. As such, they do not require endorsement (a stamp or signature on the back) during transfers. They are payable to the bearer upon presentation.[15]

Due to the large face value of the promissory notes, bearers were required to remember their number to ensure smooth circulation when first issued. In case of loss, the bearer could report it. If no one redeemed it within two months from the loss report date, the owner could provide a reliable guarantee, and the issuing bank could pay cash according to the face value, invalidating the promissory note. Because of the high risk of fraud from lost promissory notes, it was later stipulated that promissory notes entirely replace cash in circulation. Lost promissory notes could not be reported, and were stamped with the words "This note will not be replaced if lost." According to statistics from Beihai Bank's shareholder branches, the bank issued promissory notes totaling 1,572,000 yuan in 1943. In the first half of 1944 alone, promissory notes issued by the bank amounted to 6,872,000 yuan.[16]

During the War of Resistance Against Japanese Aggression, several sub-branches of Beihai Bank issued promissory notes with slightly varying designs. Historical records indicate that on November 15, 1943, the Qinghe Branch of Beihai Bank started issuing 100-yuan promissory notes printed using *xuan* paper (宣纸, a high-quality paper made in Xuancheng, Anhui Province). These notes were rectangular and straight, featuring a tender yellow-green background with blue characters. They had a square seal at the top, and the 100-yuan note displayed 长兴 (Changxing, a place in Zhejiang famous for seal making) seal characters, with Arabic characters below it enclosed by an oval seal. Contrarily, the 100-yuan promissory note issued by the Bohai Branch of Beihai Bank had a distinct design. It had a background of pink curved lines, with flower clusters and characters printed in yellow, and numbers and seals in blue. An additional red seal was stamped at the edge of the top.[17]

5. Beihai Bank Checks

During the fishing season in central and east Shandong, there was a strong demand for foreign exchange as Qingdao fish merchants extensively used these bills to purchase fish and shrimp, prompting the Administration for Industry and Commerce to implement new foreign exchange management measures in various coastal counties along the East China Sea to store foreign exchange funds and adjust foreign exchange in other sea areas. It was stipulated that the Administration for Industry and Commerce's exchange office must fully collect and exchange the foreign exchange earned from exporting fish and shrimp, resulting in a high demand for cash. To alleviate this cash shortage and the inconvenience of using cash to collect and accept bills, the method of replacing cash with checks was implemented. Banks in each county issued bulk checks to the Administration for Industry and Commerce, which were then filled out and distributed by the county's Administration for Industry and Commerce. Each check had a fixed face value, ranging from 500 to 1,000 yuan, and was only circulated within the jurisdiction of the county's Administration for Industry and Commerce. The bank was responsible for cashing the checks, ensuring they were payable to the bearer. The cashed checks could then be recycled and reused with great convenience.[18]

6. Jianghuai Bank Promissory Notes

The Third Sub-Branch of Jianghuai Bank issued three types of promissory notes in denominations of 20, 50, and 100 yuan, all made using the woodblock printing method. The value of the notes issued totaled 900,000 yuan, with a redemption period not exceeding one year. However, due to extensive destruction after being recollected, few notes remained in private hands. Historical records describe the 100-yuan note as featuring a five-pointed star between the two big words of "Promissory Note," with the seal of Huang Yuming, the issuer. The note read, "Honored New Anti-Japanese Currency 100-Yuan," with the word "Bank" printed at all four corners. The date was hand-filled with a writing brush. The 100-yuan Jianghuai Bank promissory note is straight, printed in coffee color. The words "Promissory Note" are written horizontally at the top of the bill, and "Bank No. 07507" is stamped above it using a manual numbering machine. The vertical text in the middle of the note reads, "Payable New Anti-Japanese Currency 100-Yuan," with the date "1945.8.6.S·M" printed at the bottom. The words "Jianghuai Bank" appear in the top left and right corners, and "100" is written in the bottom left and right corners.[19]

7. Promissory Notes of Other Base Areas

Most base and liberated areas issued promissory notes to replace currency in circulation. During the War of Resistance Against Japanese Aggression, the issuance of these notes was at its peak, resulting in a diverse range of types.

Table 5-1 Statistics of promissory notes issued by banks in base areas during the full-scale the War of Resistance period

		Year			Main scene		Dominant color		
Issuer	Denomination	Front	Back	Size (length × width) (mm)	Front	Back	Front	Back	Note
Shanxi-Gansu-Ningxia Border Region bank	500 yuan				The Shanxi-Gansu-Ningxia Border Region Promissory Note 500 yuan; President Zhu Lizhi, Vice President Huang Yaguang				
	10,000 yuan	35th year of the Republic of China	1946		Patterns: "Exchange for 10,000 yuan upon presentation"; Huang Yaguang, Feng Zhiguo	Camel			
	50,000 yuan	35th year of the Republic of China			Patterns: "Exchange for 50,000 yuan upon presentation"; Huang Yaguang, Feng Zhiguo				
Beihai Bank	25 yuan	January 20, 33rd year of the Republic of China		146 × 68			Red		
	50 yuan	January 20, 33rd year of the Republic of China		146 × 69			Red		
	100 yuan	33rd year of the Republic of China		70 × 161			Red		
	500 yuan	33rd year of the Republic of China					Purple		
	1,000 yuan	33rd year of the Republic of China					Purple		
East Shandong Bank	200 yuan			130 × 65	Planting rice by the seaside (right)	Endorsement	Brown	Blue	

(Continued)

Issuer	Denomination	Year		Size (length × width) (mm)	Main scene		Dominant color		Note
		Front	Back		Front	Back	Front	Back	
South Hebei Bank	100 yuan	"This promissory note shall be valid until December 31 of the 32nd year of the Republic of China."		164 × 80	Building (left)	This promissory note contains six instructions.			
	200 yuan	"This promissory note shall be valid until December 31 of the 32nd year of the Republic of China."		160 × 80		This promissory note contains six instructions.	Red		
	200 yuan			153 × 73	Hills and village houses (middle)	"This note is used for both public and private funds in the South Hebei Region from October 1 of the 33rd year of the Republic of China to September of the 34th year of the Republic of China. Please exchange it for Hebei banknotes at banks and public stores in the region."			[Plain] printed in bill face
	200 yuan	32nd year of the Republic of China		172 × 88	Water surface and tower (left). "Issued on September 15, 32nd year of the Republic of China; due on June 30, 33rd year of the Republic of China." "Payment upon Presentation."		Red		

(Continued)

Issuer	Denomination	Year		Size (length × width) (mm)	Main scene		Dominant color		Note
		Front	Back		Front	Back	Front	Back	
South Hebei Bank	500 yuan	32nd year of the Republic of China		159 × 78	Water surface and tower (left). "Issued on September 15, 32nd year of the Republic of China; due on June 30, 33rd year of the Republic of China." "Payment upon Presentation."		Blue		[Plain] printed in bill face
	500 yuan			154 × 69	Village houses (middle)		Blue		
	500 yuan	32nd year of the Republic of China		143 × 73	House, Pavilion, Tree (left). "Date of Issue: Early January of the 34th year of the Republic of China; Expiration Date: Late December of the 34th year of the Republic of China."		Purple		
	500 yuan	34th year of the Republic of China		148 × 75	House, Pavilion, Tree (left). "Date of Issue: Early January of the 35th year of the Republic of China; Expiration Date: Late December of the 35th year of the Republic of China."		Green		
	1,000 yuan	32nd year of the Republic of China	June 30, 33rd year of the Republic of China	167 × 80	House, Pavilion, Tree (left). "Date of Issue: September 15, the 32nd year of the Republic of China; Expiration Date: June 30, the 34th year of the Republic of China." "Payment upon Presentation."		Green		
Yanfu Bank	100 yuan	32nd year of the Republic of China			City gate tower	Instructions			Vertical
	200 yuan								

(Continued)

Issuer	Denomination	Year		Size (length × width) (mm)	Main scene		Dominant color		Note
		Front	Back		Front	Back	Front	Back	
Third Sub-Branch of Jianghuai Bank in Central Jiangsu	100 yuan	May 18, 34th year of the Republic of China							
Southeast Office of Fourth Sub-Branch of Jianghuai Bank in Central Jiangsu	5 yuan	1945	August of the 34th year of the Republic of China	105 × 65	Gun bearer (right)	Liang Lingguang, the Fourth Administrative Commissioner of Central Jiangsu (seal), the President Ma Yihang (seal), the Vice President Jin Sun			
	5 yuan		September of the 34th year of the Republic of China			Nantong County Mayor (seal), Director of Finance and Economics (seal), Deputy Director (seal)			
East Zhejiang Bank	50 yuan	(Month Day), (Year) of the Republic of China		176 × 83	Fancy borders in printing	Instructions			
	50 yuan	(Month Day), 34th Year of the Republic of China		176 × 83	Fancy borders in printing	Instructions			
	100 yuan	(Month Day), 34th Year of the Republic of China		176 × 83	Fancy borders in printing	Instructions			

Source: Jia Zhangwang, *New Democratic Revolution Currency Chart* (Beijing: Communist Party History Publishing House, 2018), 136–269.

II. The Bill System in Base Areas During the War of Resistance Against Japanese Aggression

1. Bill System of Shandong Base Area

The Shandong Base Area, a significant component of the revolutionary base areas, actively promoted bill business. In March 1941, according to the *Group Share Brochure and Organizational Draft of Qinghe Branch of Beihai Bank in Shandong Province*, the Qinghe Branch of Beihai Bank considered discounting various bills of exchange and promissory notes, buying and selling securities related to bills of exchange, and all banking operations as its key business lines.[20]

In 1942, a bill exchange was organized in Qingdao by the Japanese puppet regime, but its operation was limited. Both the number and volume of bill exchanges were relatively small, and many banks and money houses, including Beihai Bank, struggled to maintain bill exchange operations.[21] Beihai Bank also managed bill exchanges and issued the *Beihai Bank Bill Exchange Measures*, detailing the types of bills that could be exchanged and the rules for doing so. In May 1949, to facilitate the flow of funds between various publicly-owned enterprises, Beihai Bank issued the *Measures for the Exchange and Settlement of Publicly-Owned Enterprise Bills*.[22]

The Shandong region conducted a significant amount of exchange business, and bills of exchange were an essential tool for this process. Beihai Bank's viewed bill exchanges as one of its important operations, and its articles of association contain comprehensive provisions on the handling fees, procedures, and remittance limits for remittance by demand draft and mail transfer. The bank established a business department to manage exchange shares and related matters.[23] Branches of Beihai Bank progressively took on foreign exchange operations. Notably, the central and east Shandong regions initiated bill exchange operations in August 1941, despite not yet engaging in actual exchange business. On October 14, 1942, the central and east Shandong region of the Shandong Base Area issued the *Measures for the Administration of Bill Exchange Business* to regulate and limit the buying and selling of bills within its jurisdiction, using bill exchange as a platform. The relevant regulations are as follows:

(1) Major municipalities should establish a bill exchange, centered around trade agencies and chambers of commerce. All buying and selling of bills must be conducted through this exchange.
(2) Anyone looking to sell a bill of exchange must first register with this exchange. The exchange will then negotiate the price based on market conditions. Monopolistic manipulation and price hikes are prohibited.
(3) Buyers of the bill of exchange must register with the government or trade authority. The bill number, amount, and pre-purchased items must be specified in the registration book. Additionally, a 10% reserve is required. However, cooperatives only need to pay a 5% reserve, which will be returned when the goods are received.
(4) Unauthorized activities that bypass the bill of exchange will lead to confiscation.[24]

In 1943, a bill of exchange was established in the central and east Shandong region of the Shandong Base Area. This exchange was managed by a trading company, with banks supervising its operations. The local chamber of commerce appointed an individual for registration. The procedures for purchasing a bill of exchange are as follows:

(1) When purchasing bills of exchange, a guarantor is required to ensure the return of essential goods within a specified period.
(2) Regional merchants are eligible to purchase bills of exchange if they can transport goods and obtain a tax bureau certificate.
(3) To purchase bills of exchange for debt repayment, certification from the Chamber of Commerce and approval from the government are required.
(4) The purchase of bills of exchange by government agencies must be approved by the trading company.[25]

In the first half of 1943, the Xihai Sub-Branch of Beihai Bank initiated bill acceptance and issued a draft payment of 58,000 yuan to the Qinghe Branch. The growth of bill acceptance facilitated civil and commercial activities, boosted trade, supported production, and played a crucial role in stabilizing the local currency and regulating cash circulation. According to records, in 1943, a total of 1,922,731 yuan was transferred to the Central Shandong region. Of this, 1,667,171 yuan was transacted through bills of exchange. A total of 409,995 yuan was transferred out, with 115,600 yuan executed through bills of exchange.

2. Bill System of Shanxi-Hebei-Shandong-Henan Base Area

On September 29, 1943, South Hebei Bank issued *A Notice on the Issuance of Promissory Notes*, explaining the nature of these notes, their advantages, credibility, and methods of identifying counterfeit notes. It also emphasized the need for widespread publicity and education on these aspects. The notice stated that promissory notes were to be treated as cash, to be recorded and stored following standard cash handling procedures. The notes were issued by the South Hebei Bank's head office and were in circulation from September 1, 1943, to June 30, 1944. Each promissory note included a counterfoil and a main note, with fixed denominations of 100, 200, 500, and 1,000 yuan. The notes were issued without a bearer's name and could be endorsed by the bearer on the back, with a signature and stamp in accordance with regulations. These notes were issued in the bill market in the Taihang Base Area (North Taihang Area, South Taihang Area, West Henan, and Central Shanxi), guerrilla zones, and Japanese-occupied regions. They could be freely transferred at the same value as local currency. To prevent credit inflation and stabilize prices, South Hebei Bank required that when issuing a promissory note, cash equal to the note's face value had to be collected. If other businesses needed to exchange for these notes, they had to withdraw cash and store it separately as a deposit. After a period of circulating these promissory notes, prices in the base areas stabilized to an extent. The local people and merchants appreciated the convenience of using these notes.[26]

In addition to the regulations on promissory notes, the Shanxi-Hebei-Shandong-Henan Border Region issued the *Interim Measures for the Administration of Foreign Exchange* in 1942. This document strictly governed the use of foreign exchange, including bills of exchange, promissory notes, checks, passbooks, and exchange notes. It implemented measures such as restrictions, registration, and licensing on the use of these notes. The goal was to compete for goods and materials with the enemy, protect the wealth of the base areas, and stabilize local prices. The interim measures specified that foreign exchange trading must take place at foreign exchange exchanges. It stated, "Unless otherwise authorized, all public, private, commercial, or civilian entities or individuals must first obtain import goods vouchers from the management bureau in accordance with the law when using foreign exchange bills. They can purchase foreign exchange from bill exchanges, or banks if there is no exchange. Bearer of foreign exchange must also sell it at the bill exchange."[27]

3. Bill System in Other Base Areas

In October 1942, the *Draft Regulations on the Shaanxi-Gansu-Ningxia Border Region Bank* included "handling various exchanges in the border region and other areas with exchange treaties," "managing the purchase, sale, and discounting of promissory notes and bills of exchange," and "overseeing the exchange and remittance of bills of exchange" into the scope of the bank's business operations. It also stipulated that the discount interest rate was to be determined by the bank, based on prices, financial conditions, and the nature and target of lending. The Shaanxi-Gansu-Ningxia Border Region Bank established a business department responsible for the deposit, lending, exchange, and discounting businesses.[28]

The East Zhejiang Bank Regulations promulgated on April 1, 1945 included "lending, discounting, and exchange" in its business scope.[29]

SECTION 3

Bills for Revolutionary Base Areas During the Liberation War

During the Liberation War, the revolutionary base areas used bills of exchange and promissory notes as financial weapons against the enemy. The issuance of bills in these areas aimed to alleviate deflation, replace currency with promissory notes in circulation, indirectly increase currency issuance, and stabilize the financial order.

I. Bills of Base Areas During the Liberation War

1. Beihai Bank Promissory Notes

During the Liberation War, as the liberated areas in Shandong expanded, the circulation scope of Beihai Bank's currency rapidly grew, leading to a surge in the money supply. To facilitate withdrawals and meet economic development needs, Beihai Bank issued a total of 4.9 billion yuan in fixed-amount promissory notes in December 1948, each with a face value of 100,000 yuan. The notes were vertically arranged in blue. "Beihai Bank" and "Promissory Note" were printed at the top, "ONE HUNDRED THOUSAND YUAN" on the lower floral symbol, and the face value of "ONE HUNDRED THOUSAND" at the four corners. The reverse side also had the face value of the arabic numeral "100,000" printed at the top and four corners. Usage instructions were as follows:

(1) The promissory note is limited to domestic circulation.
(2) The promissory note can only be used to exchange for Beihai dollars at the issuing bank.
(3) The promissory note cannot be replaced if lost.
(4) The amount stated on the promissory note does not include interest.
(5) Any alterations made to the promissory note are invalid.

There was also a section for "Issuing Bank." The promissory notes issued by the Xuzhou Sub-Branch of Beihai Bank had the word "Xuzhou" stamped in red in the first blank space of the instructions, indicating that the notes were only circulated within Xuzhou City. "Beihai Bank Xuzhou Sub-Branch" and "President Huang Yuming" were stamped in the "Issuing Bank" section in red. The issuance of these promissory notes was primarily to address the shortage of currency and meet the market demand for large banknotes. The market generally viewed these fixed-amount promissory notes as a form of large-denomination banknotes.[30]

2. Central China Bank Promissory Notes

Following its establishment, the Central China Ban issued Central China Bank bills that circulated throughout various liberated areas in Central China. Subsequently, the bank issued large-denomination promissory notes, with four instructions titled "Instructions for Using Promissory Notes" printed on the back.

In January 1948, the Central China Bank's head office issued a 2,000-yuan promissory note, which was vertically oriented and printed on yellow textured paper with a light blue hue. The bank's name and the words "Promissory Note" appeared at the top of the note, followed by a red number. "TWO THOUSAND YUAN" was written in the center. The President's small red seal was imprinted on the bottom right, while the Vice President's small red seal was imprinted on the bottom left. Below these seals, the phrase "All Applicable for Grain Tax Payments" was inscribed. The note was framed by various floral patterns, with the capital letters "TWO THOUSAND" printed in the four corners. As per regulations, this note could be exchanged for standard currency at banks at any time.

3. Bank of Chang Chung Promissory Notes

Following the establishment of the Bank of Chang Chung (Great Wall) in February 1948, the bank issued a unified Bank of Chang Chung currency and two types of promissory notes in denominations of 50,000 yuan and 100,000 yuan. The promissory notes featured a straight design, which is simple and elegant, with the name of the Bank of Chang Chung at the top of the front frame, an image of the ancient Great Wall in the center, and the denomination printed vertically below. These notes, printed in 1948, included an "endorsement" and explanation on the back.[31]

Figure 5-1 Bank of Chang Chung promissory notes

Source: Collected by Guo Kai.

Figure 5-2 Tung Pei Bank of China promissory notes

Source: Collected by Guo Kai.

4. Tung Pei Bank of China Promissory Notes

In March 1946, the Tung Pei (Northeast) Bank of China issued promissory notes in denominations of 50,000 yuan, 100,000 yuan, 500,000 yuan, and 1 million yuan, which circulated throughout Northeast China. Tung Pei Bank of China promissory notes are quite rare, with very few surviving examples. As depicted in figure 5-2, the words "Sample Note" is printed on the front of these notes, which are single-sided samples. The main image features the building of Tung Pei Bank of China, with the face value written directly below it. The signatures and seals of Cao Juru and Wang Qizhi are located on either side of the face value. The reverse side displays usage instructions, and the city of circulation is also specified.[32]

5. Bills of Other Base Areas

In January 1947, Fengmin Trading Company, Huaihai Trading Company, Central China Bank Suzhong Office, and Central China Bank successively issued promissory notes in central and northern Jiangsu. A year later, in January 1948, Tung Pei Bank of China issued promissory notes in denominations of 50,000 yuan and 100,000 yuan. With the expansion of the liberated areas, these promissory notes circulated in a larger scope. Banks and cooperatives in the Shaanxi-Gansu-Ningxia Border Region also began issuing bills of exchange, checks, and the like.

II. The Bill System in Base Areas During the Liberation War

1. Bill System of Central China Base Area

In February 1946, the Huangqiao Bill Exchange was established in the First Division of Central China to adjust finance, stabilize the currency system, and promote market prosperity. The exchange primarily dealt with the introduction and adjustment of foreign exchange bills, as well as the buying and selling of bills. Following the victory of the large-scale counterattack from the People's Liberation Army, the value of fiat currency dropped significantly. This led to people in various regions rejecting fiat currency in favor of Central China currency, resulting in an increased demand. Furthermore, with the cotton being brought to the market during autumn, there was a shortage of market chips. To address this shortage, facilitate the public's rejection of fiat currency, and protect the people's interests, the Central Jiangsu Office of Central China Bank requested the issuance of promissory notes in October 1947, and subsequently released a notice regarding the issuance.

(1) The face value of this promissory note is divided into three denominations for the time being: 1,000 yuan, 2,000 yuan, and 5,000 yuan.

(2) This promissory note is equivalent to Central China currency and is circulated within the first, second, and ninth administrative regions of central Jiangsu.

(3) This promissory note can be exchanged for smaller notes at any time at our branches, sub-branches, and county offices. It can also be used to offset bank debts or facilitate exchange. Additionally, it can be used to purchase goods from public stores in various administrative regions.

(4) The promissory note is issued by the Jiangsu-Anhui Border Region Government's Office in Central Jiangsu as a reserve for purchase of the public grain for this year. The reserve amount is greater than the total issuance amount. The note can be used to pay grain taxes, serve as cash for agricultural taxes paid-in grain, and pay for all government expenses.

(5) The note is printed on white glossy paper with "Central China Bank Suzhong Office" written horizontally across at the top. The number and amount of the note are in capital letters in the center. The phrase "Applicable for All Grain Taxes" is on the right and the director's signature is on the left, all set against a light-colored background.[33]

Promissory notes in the Central China Revolutionary Base were primarily issued by various regional trading companies and the Central China Bank. These notes were equivalent to Central China currency. However, they could not be exchanged for cash and were only used for paying grain taxes or purchasing goods from public stores.[34]

To facilitate the receipt and payment of a large number of bills by public and private enterprises, in May 1949, the head office of the Central China Bank submitted a request for approval to handle promissory note business. This standardized the basic information and circulation details of promissory notes. The main content is as follows:

(1) This promissory note is an interest-free sight note that can be exchanged with the original issuing authority for an amount equal to the face value at any time. However, banks in other regions that do not issue this promissory note are not obligated to redeem it.
(2) This promissory note has restricted circulation and cannot be used in places other than those specified on the face of the note.
(3) A promissory note shall be considered issued even if it does not bear the name of the circulation place, the issuing bank's name, and the signature of the person in charge.
(4) There are two types of bills: bills with fixed denominations and those with non-fixed denominations. Fixed-denomination Central China bills have two denominations: 50,000 yuan and 100,000 yuan. Those with non-fixed denominations can be issued at any time when needed.
(5) There are signed and unsigned notes. Both types can be freely transferred and circulated. The unsigned notes are payable on sight, while the signed notes require continuous endorsements from the designated party before payment can be made.
(6) This note has no time limit on circulation and can be collected by the issuing bank when necessary.
(7) If this note is lost, burned, or stolen, no replacement will be made.
(8) This note cannot be scraped or marked with a knife, nor can it be altered or written on. Otherwise, it will not be redeemed.
(9) If anyone forges promissory notes or uses forged ones, they will be strictly handled in accordance with the law by the government.[35]

2. Bill System in the Shanxi-Hebei-Shandong-Henan Base Area

Bill operations in central Hebei can be divided into two stages: direct bank throughput and foreign exchange operation. From May 1946 to August 1947, banks primarily conducted foreign exchange operations through bill buying and selling, export lending, regular exchanges, direct organization of mass exports, and controlling export warehouses. Bill buying and selling was the most common, accounting for about 95%, with the most effective method being the direct organization of mass exports. Starting from September 1947, bill operations in central Hebei switched to foreign exchange handling. Once these exchanges were established, the banks' exclusive bill operations transformed into mass operations. This new approach allowed the drawing of cadre funds to support rural production and minimized the losses from bill speculation[36] and depreciation. Bill exchanges also intensified their research on exporters. They aimed to collect and exchange bills through familiar exporter transactions and rewarded bills with good credit. If an exporter issued a large number of bills, payment might be deferred until the other party confirmed it. The bill of exchange business area was divided, and for those who issued bills in enemy-controlled areas, they were only allowed to return after the bills had been paid. Various methods were employed to combat bill speculation.[37]

To simplify withdrawals and minimize the inconvenience of advance payments, the East Hebei Sub-Branch of the Shanxi-Chahar-Hebei Border Region Bank introduced the *Interim Measures for Promissory Notes* in 1947, permitting the bearers to cash out at the issuing bank anytime.

(1) The promissory note is issued to simplify the withdrawal process for the drawer and reduce the inconvenience associated with advance payments.
(2) The East Hebei Sub-Branch and its subordinate offices are temporarily assigned as the issuing authority of these promissory notes.
(3) The individuals requesting the issuance of the promissory note can exchange their deposit receipt or cash for the note.
(4) The promissory note issued by this bank is valid for both public and private payments.
(5) The note is valid for 30 days from the date of issuance.
(6) The promissory note can be cashed at the original issuing bank at any time; other banks are not obligated to honor it.
(7) If the promissory note is lost, our bank is not responsible for tracking it unless the loss is promptly reported to our bank.
(8) The value of this promissory note must not exceed five million yuan per note.
(9) All required information and seals on the promissory note must be completed; none can be omitted.
(10) This document will be implemented starting from April 10, 1947.[38]

In August 1948, the Shanxi-Hebei-Shandong-Henan Border Region issued the *Interim Measures for the Administration of Foreign Exchange in the North China Region*. This document established stricter regulations on foreign exchange bills, which included fiat currency and instruments such as bills of exchange, checks, and promissory notes.

(1) The purchase and sale of foreign exchange bills should only be handled through the North China Bank or a foreign exchange bureau. Private transactions are prohibited to prevent financial disruption.
(2) Exporters must process their foreign exchange settlement with the designated Industrial and Commercial Bureau at the time of export, in accordance with the scope stipulated in the *Interim Measures for the Administration of Import and Export Trade in the North China Liberation Area*. The regulations are as follows: First, the foreign exchange bill issued by the exporter before export must be registered to the North China Bank or a foreign exchange bureau for sale along with the certificate of approval for foreign exchange settlement by the Administration for Industry and Commerce. The goods cannot be exported before the bills are certified by a bank or a foreign exchange bureau after a certain period following their sale. Second, during the settlement period, if the exporter exchanges foreign exchange bills, they must exchange them into the standard currency with the Export Bank. If they exchange for gold and silver, they must sell them to the North China Bank. All these procedures must be documented, and the export documents must be canceled at the Industrial and Commercial Bureau.
(3) Anyone who carries and sells foreign exchange bills will be fined 20% to 50% of the total foreign exchange value, in addition to the recovery of the foreign exchange. For first-time minor offenders, the fine may be reduced or waived. For those who commit more than three offenses, the foreign exchange will be recovered and a fine of more than twice the total foreign exchange value will be imposed. In addition, the offender will be disqualified from applying for the use of foreign exchange for six months.[39]

3. Bill Regulations of the Northeast Revolutionary Base Area

On January 28, 1948, Tung Pei Bank of China's head office decided to issue promissory notes in denominations of 50,000 yuan and 100,000 yuan. The specific regulations are as follows:

(1) The promissory note is intended for urban circulation. Each branch should stamp its name on the front and bottom of the note. If a note is to be used in two places (such as Tao'an and Taonan), the names of the two locations should be stamped.
(2) This promissory note is initially distributed in seven cities, including Harbin. These include the liberated areas of Heilongjiang: Harbin, Mudanjiang, Qiqihar, and Nenjiang, along with Yanji in Jilin and Tao'an and Taonan in northern Liaoning. (The actual circulation later expanded to eight locations: Harbin, Qiqihar, Mudanjiang, Andong, Yingkou, Jilin, Baichengzi, and Taonan.)
(3) The endorsement on the back of the promissory note must be personally signed by one of the branch managers or deputy managers.

(4) The accepted promissory note can be reissued and put back into circulation.
(5) Promissory notes issued outside of the local area are generally not accepted.[40]

As the Northeast Liberation Area expanded, Tung Pei Bank of China issued new versions of promissory notes in denominations of 50,000 yuan and 100,000 yuan. These notes were accepted in fifteen cities: Harbin, Mudanjiang, Bei'an, Jiamusi, Qiqihar, Jilin, Siping, Changchun, Shenyang, Fushun, Benxi, Anshan, Andong, Yingkou, and Wafangdian. This is to adjust urban circulation. The new version is identical to the old version in terms of front elements, and its back is printed with the names of the fifteen cities and usage instructions.

(1) Tung Pei Bank of China can only issue promissory notes if the recipient voluntarily requests them. They cannot be forcibly used.
(2) Those who need the notes can redeem them from Tung Pei Bank of China at any time, either in cash or by check. They must also acknowledge the following regulations: First, the note is only valid in the fifteen cities listed in the left side. Second, note bearers can exchange for locally circulated vouchers with branches of Tung Pei Bank of China in various places at any time. Third, note bearers can use the promissory notes to purchase goods from public stores and pay off debts at any time. However, private acceptance must be voluntary, and forcing rural people to accept them is prohibited.[41]

4. Bill System of Shandong Revolutionary Base Area

To facilitate fund flow among various publicly-owned enterprises, revive production, boost the economy, and simplify collection and payment procedures, Beihai Bank issued the *Measures for the Exchange and Settlement of Publicly-Owned Enterprise Bills* in May 1949. These measures mandated that bill exchanges should be centrally managed by the general settlement officer of Beihai Bank. Except for Beihai Bank, other banks and money houses were required to secure approval from the local government. All participating banks and money houses needed to make a deposit to Beihai Bank, equivalent to 10% of the total amount of funds involved. This deposit was not accessible until the bill exchange process concluded. The issued deposit could not be used as collateral or for other purposes. A monthly interest rate of 1.2% was also imposed.[42]

The types of exchange bills are currently limited to promissory notes issued by this bank. The terms and amount for these notes should be decided by both parties. Promissory notes issued by various public enterprises are not allowed to circulate in the market. These notes must reach their due date before they can be exchanged or settled. To facilitate collection and payments, publicly-owned enterprises involved in the exchange should open a deposit account with this bank. Each participating entity can submit their expired promissory notes to the bank at any time, and upon settlement, funds will be received and paid out separately into each entity's deposit account. The transfer of settlement differences is limited to the deposit balances of various publicly-owned enterprises participating in the exchange. For deposits that are insufficient to cover expenses, an overdraft limit must be agreed upon in advance with the bank, in line with the bank's interim measures for lending to publicly-owned enterprises. Any transfers exceeding the overdraft limit must be supplemented before the transfer can be made.[43]

5. Bill System in Other Base Areas

In June 1946, Ruihua Bank, the first privately-owned joint-stock commercial bank in Handan, Hebei Province, explicitly added "discounting" to its lending services in its articles of association. In addition to this, the bank conducted foreign exchange operations. With market growth and the booming development of various industries, Ruihua Bank's foreign exchange business also saw significant growth. In the first half of 1948, the bank transferred a total of 13.2 billion yuan.[44]

Summary

In the New Democratic Revolution era, the financial initiatives and bill development led by the CPC aimed to enhance credit and serve the economy. During the Agrarian Revolution, promissory notes acted as financial vouchers to aid rural economic development and as debt vouchers to ensure the Red Army's grain supply. During the War of Resistance Against Japanese Aggression, the bill business in revolutionary base areas helped resist enemy forces' invasion to some extent. Issuing promissory notes to replace currency in circulation mitigated deflation, supporting commercial circulation and production in the rear areas. The development of checks and bills of exchange fostered trade in the base areas. During the Liberation War, issuing promissory notes in revolutionary base areas facilitated enterprise withdrawals, quickened the flow of industrial and commercial funds, encouraged commodity transactions, and stabilized wartime production. Furthermore, issuing promissory notes with certificates of deposit or cash as collateral reduced bank credit risks.

NOTES

1. The People's Bank of China, *A Brief History of Financial Development Under the Leadership of the Communist Party China* (Beijing: China Financial Publishing House, 2021), 16–17.
2. Compiling Group of *A Brief History of the Communist Party China, A Brief History of the Communist Party China* (Beijing: People's Publishing House, Communist Party History Publishing House, 2021), 56.
3. Yin Jing, "A Brief Study on Millet-Purchasing Promissory Notes in Xiang-Gan Province of the Chinese Soviet Republic," *Literary Circles of CPC History*, no. 16 (2013): 11–13, 18.
4. Jiangxi Provincial Archives, *Selected Historical Materials of the Xiang-Gan Revolutionary Base Area (Volume 2)* (Nanchang: Jiangxi People's Publishing House, 1984), 715.
5. Financial Research Institute of the People's Bank of China and Financial Science Research Institute of the Ministry of Finance, *Currency of Chinese Revolutionary Base Areas (Part 2)* (Beijing: Cultural Relics Publishing House, 1982), 122.
6. Yin Jing, "A Brief Study on Millet-Purchasing Promissory Notes in Xiang-Gan Province of the Chinese Soviet Republic," *Literary Circles of CPC History*, no. 16 (2013): 11–13, 18.
7. Financial Research Institute of the People's Bank of China and Financial Science Research Institute of the Ministry of Finance, *Currency of Chinese Revolutionary Base Areas (Part 2)* (Beijing: Cultural Relics Publishing House, 1982), 122.
8. Hong Rongchang, "Promissory Notes During the Red Army Period," *Chinese Numismatics*, no. 2 (2009): 39–40.
9. "Provisional Regulations of the State Bank of the Chinese Soviet Republic," in *Currency of Chinese Revolutionary Base Areas (Part 2)*, ed. The Financial Research Institute of the People's Bank of China and the Financial Science Research Institute of the Ministry of Finance (Beijing: Cultural Relics Publishing House, 1982), 5–8.
10. Ibid.
11. Five Chinese characters in the original document are illegible.
12. Zhang Shufan, *A History of Currency in Huainan Resistance Base Area* (Beijing: China Financial Publishing House, 2004), 58.
13. Zhang Junli, *A History of Currency in the Revolutionary Base Areas of Eastern Zhejiang* (Ningbo: Ningbo Publishing House, 2002), 42–43.
14. Zhang Zhuanfang, "A History of Currency in the Shanxi-Hebei-Shandong-Henan Border Region (Volume 1)," in *History of Currency in the Revolutionary Base Areas of Southeast Shanxi* (Beijing: China Financial Publishing House, 1996), 81–85.
15. Financial Research Institute of the People's Bank of China, Shandong Branch and Financial Research Institute of the People's Bank of China, *Historical Materials of Beihai Bank in China's Revolutionary Base Areas* (Jinan: Shandong People's Publishing House, 1986), 557.
16. Ibid., 557–559.
17. Ibid., 562.
18. Ibid., 558.
19. *Bank Museum Treasure: Collection of Shanghai Bank Museum* (Shanghai Bank Museum, 2003), 155.
20. "Stock Brochure and Organizational Draft of Shandong Beihai Bank Qinghe Branch Group," in *Compilation of Chinese and Foreign Financial Regulations (Volume 3)*, ed. Financial Research Institute of the Head Office of the People's Bank of China (1988), 41–42.
21. Financial History Research Office, Financial Research Institute, Head Office of the People's Bank of China, *The Financial Market in Modern China* (Beijing: China Financial Publishing House, 1987), 306.
22. "Measures for Handling Bill Exchange at Beihai Bank," *Shandong Political Daily*, no. 1 (1949): 62–63.
23. "Business Brochure of Shandong Beihai Bank," in *Compilation of Chinese and Foreign Financial Regulations (Volume 3)*, ed. Financial Research Institute of the Head Office of the People's Bank of China (1988), 48–50.

24. Wan Liming, *A Study on the Institutional Changes of the Modern Chinese Bill Market* (Shanghai Far East Publishing House, 2014), 92.
25. Ibid.
26. Zhang Zhuanfang, "A History of Currency in the Shanxi-Hebei-Shandong-Henan Border Region (Volume 1)," in *History of Currency in the Revolutionary Base Areas of Southeast Shanxi* (Beijing: China Financial Publishing House, 1996), 85.
27. Deng Chenxi, "Interim Measures of the Shanxi-Hebei-Shandong-Henan Border Region Government for the Administration of Foreign Exchange in This Region," in *Financial and Economic Development*, vol. 1 and 2 (Taiyuan: Shanxi People's Publishing House, 1987), 765–766.
28. "Draft Regulations on Banks in the Shaanx-Gansu-Ningxia Border Region," in *Collected Works in Commemoration of Zhu Lizhi*, ed. the Party History Research Office of the Henan Provincial Committee of the Communist Party of China (Beijing: Communist Party History Publishing House, 2007).
29. "East Zhejiang Bank Regulations," in *Currency of Chinese Revolutionary Base Areas (Part 2)*, ed. The Financial Research Institute of the People's Bank of China and the Financial Science Research Institute of the Ministry of Finance (Beijing: Cultural Relics Publishing House, 1982), 122.
30. The Editorial Committee of *Collection of Xuzhou Paper Currency*, *Collection of Xuzhou Paper Currency* (Beijing: China Literature and History Publishing House, 2003), 127.
31. *Bank Museum Treasure: Collection of Shanghai Bank Museum* (Shanghai Bank Museum, 2003), 156.
32. Ibid., 159.
33. Gao Guancheng, *Selected Historical Materials of Central China Bank* (Beijing: China Radio and Television Press, 2003), 186–187.
34. Wan Liming, *A Study on the Institutional Changes of the Modern Chinese Bill Market* (Shanghai Far East Publishing House, 2014), 88.
35. Shang Ming and Bai Wenqing, et al., *The Financial Dictionary* (Chengdu: Sichuan People's Publishing House, 1992), 569.
36. "Top-tier trading" refers to unscrupulous merchants exploiting low banking technology and exporters' limited credit knowledge to engage in various speculative activities.
37. Hebei Provincial Institute of Finance, *Shanxi-Chahar-Hebei Border Region Bank* (Beijing: China Financial Publishing House, 1988), 128–132.
38. "Interim Measures for the Issuance of Promissory Notes by the East Hebei Sub-Branch of the Shanxi-Chahar-Hebei Border Region Bank," in *Selected Financial and Economic History Materials of the North China Liberation Area (Volume 2)*, ed. the Compilation and Editing Group for Financial and Economic History Materials of the North China Liberation Area (Beijing: China Financial and Economic Publishing House, 1996), 44–45.
39. Wan Liming, *A Study on the Institutional Changes of the Modern Chinese Bill Market* (Shanghai Far East Publishing House, 2014), 93.
40. Heilongjiang Financial Research Institute, *Financial Historical Materials of Heilongjiang Base Area (1945–1959)* (1984), 104–105.
41. Ibid., 105.
42. "Measures for Handling Bill Exchange at Beihai Bank," *Shandong Political Daily*, no. 1 (19491): 62–63.
43. Wan Liming, *A Study on the Institutional Changes of the Modern Chinese Bill Market* (Shanghai Far East Publishing House, 2014), 89.
44. Kong Xiangyi, *Historical Materials on Finance in Shanxi Province During the Republic of China Period* (Beijing: China Financial Publishing House, 2013), 687–688.

PART THREE

BILLS SINCE THE FOUNDING OF THE PEOPLE'S REPUBLIC OF CHINA

CHAPTER SIX

Bills from the Founding of PRC to the Issuance of Electronic Bills

At the founding of the PRC, finance and credit development were limited, regulated, and singular, leaving no room for commercial credit expansion. However, the beginning of the reform and opening up in 1978 marked a new phase characterized by the establishment of regulations and the testing of pilot projects. Economic development became the primary focus of China's growth, leading to effective reforms in the financial and economic sectors. The period saw the growth of the market economy and an improvement in commercial credit for enterprises. After China's entry into the World Trade Organization in 2001, the Chinese market, with its low labor costs and preferential policies, attracted substantial foreign investment. This influx spurred rapid economic growth, signifying a new stage in domestic economic development.

Following the founding of the People's Republic in 1949, the bill market struggled to grow due to an unfavorable environment. It wasn't until the reform and opening up began that bills re-emerged in the market economy's commodity circulation, payment, and settlement sectors. This resurgence was a result of the need to promote commercial development and tackle the "chain debt" issue that arose during the growth of commercial credit. Despite its growth, the bill market remained fragmented, small-scale, and disorganized due to the absence of nationwide laws and regulations. Most of the relevant measures were administrative regulations that lagged behind the increasingly open and active market economy. In 1995, *The Negotiable Instrument Law of the People's Republic of China* (hereafter referred to as *The Negotiable Instrument Law of the PRC*) was promulgated, providing the bill market with necessary legal support. Following this, a series of supporting laws were enacted, which improved the institutional structure of the bill market.

In the 21st century, the bill market expanded rapidly along with economic growth. Commercial banks began to prioritize bill businesses, and the decentralized operation model became unsuitable for the evolving market. The Industrial and Commercial Bank of China

(ICBC) was the first to set up a specialized Bill Business Department in 2000, and other commercial banks soon followed suit. Private intermediary institutions also entered the bill market, impacting it both positively and negatively. While they were responsible for the prevalence of bill brokers and forged bills, they also played a role in promoting the development of the bill market. Despite these developments, the bill market lacked a complete bill system and exhibited regional characteristics. To tackle the problem of information asymmetry, the China Foreign Exchange Trade System and National Interbank Funding Center launched the China Bill Network in 2003. This platform provides public quotations, historical quotation data queries, policy information sharing, and market research functions.

The business volume of the bill market has grown rapidly. From 1995 to 2008, the commercial bill acceptance amount increased from 242.4 billion yuan to 7.1 trillion yuan, and its share in GDP rose from 3.95% to 22.10%. The discount amount jumped from 141.2 billion yuan to 13.5 trillion yuan. Its share in GDP increased from 2.30% to 42.06%. The acceptance balance of commercial bills grew from 86.5 billion yuan to 3.2 trillion yuan, and its share in GDP rose from 1.71% to 10.56%. The discounted balance increased from 15 billion yuan to 3.2 trillion yuan, and its share in GDP rose from 0.30% to 6.27%. The bill market has significantly contributed to China's economic development by serving the real economy.

SECTION I

Relaunch of Bill Business and Its Role in Resolving "Chain Debt" Issue

When the PRC was founded in 1949, bills were briefly part of its financial system. However, with the start of the "First Five-Year Plan" in 1953, credit began to be centrally regulated. This led to the withdrawal of bills from the financial landscape. However, with the onset of the reform and opening up in 1978, the bill market was reintroduced to stimulate commercial credit growth and tackle the "chain debt" issue.

I. Commercial Credit and Bills in PRC's Early Days

On October 1, 1949, the PRC was founded, initiating a new socialist era for the Chinese people. Prior to this, China's social system and national economy were on the brink of collapse due to prolonged foreign aggression and war damage. After 1949, establishing the social system and reviving the national economy became urgent tasks.

In establishing New China's financial system, the state chose a unique approach that diverged from the one of dispossessing the bourgeoisie and nationalizing capitalist banks. During the early days of the PRC, the government allowed bank and commercial credit to continue while rectifying and transforming national capitalist financial institutions. The PBC, China's central bank, accepted deposits from private banks and offered bill acceptance services in an effort to promote economic development. During a period of financial difficulty for private factories in Shanghai, the PBC Shanghai Branch initiated the bill acceptance business in December 1949. Private factories in need of funds issued commercial bills, which the PBC reviewed and accepted before discounting them to private banks and money houses.[1] This strategic use of commercial bill acceptance and discounting adjusted funds, helped private enterprises restore and develop production, and directed national capital toward the right investments. From the start of this business until the end of the year, the PBC Shanghai Branch completed 95 transactions, amounting to about 5.76 million yuan, which aided a group of enterprises and revitalized them.

Following the founding of the PRC, centralized management and planned allocation of funds were needed for large-scale economic development. Commercial credit between state-owned enterprises, which accounted for 10% to 20% of their working capital, was seen by the government as an obstacle to this goal. As such, there was an urgent need to replace the commercial credit system with a national credit system. In September 1952, the PBC approved the *Draft Measures for the Preparation of Comprehensive Credit Plans*, which proposed a method of "unified deposit and lending." In May 1953, the Ministry of Commerce (MOC) and the PBC jointly issued the *Specific Provisions on Several Issues in the Interim Measures of the People's Bank of China for Handling Short-Term Loans to State-Owned Commercial Enterprises*. This document stated that commercial businesses could only have commercial credit relationships in rare circumstances.[2]

In March of the following year, the commercial credit within the state-owned commercial system was eliminated. It was mandated that all commodity purchase loans and fund transactions among state-owned commercial enterprises should be settled through the PBC. In September 1953, the Financial and Economic Affairs Commission of the Central People's Government issued the *Instructions on Strengthening the Work of Cash Cashier Plans*, requiring unified management of cash cashier plan work. In June 1954, the PBC dissolved its regional branches in major administrative regions and established branches in various provinces, autonomous regions, and municipalities directly under the central government. This move reinforced the vertical management of banks and strengthened the unified leadership and centralized management of financial activities by the PBC and other PBC-led financial institutions. Subsequently, China established a centralized and unified interest rate and foreign exchange management system.[3] In March 1955, following instructions from the State Council, the PBC and the Ministry of Finance reached a unanimous agreement to abolish credit after conducting joint research with relevant departments.[4]

During the Great Leap Forward (1958–1960), the PBC addressed its excessive and rigid credit management by reforming the system and delegating credit planning power. This was in line with the State Council's requirement to improve the banking management system and allowed all regions to fully utilize their enthusiasm in organizing and using credit funds. However, this reform led to a loss of credit control, resulting in fiscal and credit inflation. In response to the rapid increase in commercial credit during the Great Leap Forward, the country emphasized the basic policy of canceling commercial credit to maintain the fund operation mechanism of the planned economy. This resulted in a series of policies that required state-owned enterprises to neither collect nor pay for goods in advance and to refrain from selling goods on credit.

During the Cultural Revolution (1966–1976), financial operations were disrupted. After the campaign ended, as the country started adjusting its economic development layout, the issue of inter-company debts became increasingly serious. To solve the issue of "illegal" commercial credit, the PBC introduced relevant measures in 1977. These measures mandated that all entities must not default on each other, sell goods on credit, or make or receive advance payments, unless authorized by national regulations. However, during the era of the planned economy, commercial credit was necessary in some economic sectors due to practical needs. For example, in the production and circulation of agricultural products, commercial credit was legally allowed.

From 1953 to 1978, China's highly centralized management system under the planned economy impeded the growth of the commodity market. The country implemented centralized credit management, eliminated commercial credit, and primarily utilized bank transfers for settlements, occasionally resorting to check settlements. Bills of exchange and promissory notes, intended to act as carriers of commercial and bank credit, could not perform their roles in payment settlements and credit expansion under the planned economy.

II. Origin of Chain Debts

The Third Plenary Session of the Eleventh Central Committee of the CPC in 1978 marked the beginning of China's economic reform and opening up to the outside world. The central government clearly stated that China was still in the primary stage of socialism, and called on all officials and citizens to emancipate their minds. Economic development was prioritized, with planning and market mechanisms serving as tools to stimulate economic growth. This effectively removed the ideological barriers to reform and opening up. The report to the 12th CPC National Congress in 1982 affirmed that individual and private economies are necessary and beneficial supplements to socialist public ownership.

In April 1979, the Central Committee of the CPC held a working conference, proposing the policy of "adjusting, reforming, rectifying, and improving" the national economy. It was stressed that economic development must align with China's national conditions and economic and natural laws. During this period of adjustment, various sectors witnessed significant changes in industrial structure, product structure, capital structure, and sales channels. Some enterprises, particularly those in the electromechanical industry, struggled due to a decrease in infrastructure orders and difficulties in changing their service direction. These challenges significantly impacted product sales. To overcome these challenges, enterprises employed various strategies to clear inventory and promote product sales while adjusting production. The slower the product sales, the greater the commercial credit involved. Due to slow fund recovery under credit control, enterprises had limited access to necessary funds, impacting normal procurement processes. Consequently, they resorted to credit purchases to secure raw materials. As a result, in some enterprises, both credit sales and purchases developed concurrently.

In August 1980, a symposium was held, participated by the presidents of PBC branches. During the symposium, the opinions of the State Council leaders were shared and it was suggested that certain traditional banking practices conducive to socialist modernization drive could be implemented. Based on symposium discussions, the PBC head office pointed out as follows:

> The credit system need improvement in light of the new circumstances. While credit should be handled primarily in banks, certain commercial credit should be cautiously expanded under certain conditions. Previously, our policy was that credit must be exclusively handled in banks and commercial credit was not allowed, except for special cases approved by the State Council. However, with the implementation of market regulation, the situation has significantly changed. To stimulate economic growth, down payments and installment payments can be received for large-scale equipment with long production cycles and high capital requirements. Installment payments can also be made for enterprises with raw materials or semi-finished products but insufficient production tasks, if other entities need to purchase their equipment but are temporarily low on funds. Credit sales are allowed to manage product backlogs. Moreover, banks should support enterprises with surplus equipment and funds and the willingness to engage in domestic compensation trade, provided it is beneficial for both parties' production.

This symposium marked the beginning of a breakthrough in the traditionally restricted zone of the credit business, bringing the traditional bill credit business into the agenda of the socialist credit system.

In May 1981, the National Economic Commission, along with ten other departments, issued the *Interim Measures for Implementing the State Council's Relevant Power Relegation Documents and Consolidating and Improving Power Relegation Work.* The regulation stated, "To clear channels and revitalize the economy, enterprises lacking immediate funds can purchase necessary mechanical and electrical products through credit sales or installment payments. However, this can be done only after obtaining the bank's consent and ensuring that the payments can be made within one or two years without delaying infrastructure construction." As the power relegation work progressed and fund supply management improved, the types of commercial credit used in practice became more diverse than what was originally stipulated.

The year 1982 was a year of significant changes in market conditions. Successful national economic adjustment and a substantial increase in consumer goods transformed the market into a buyer's one overflowing with goods, which was a welcome development. To expand the market and boost sales, the MOC decided to introduce "advance payment and installment payment" for certain high-priced, slow-selling, and overstocked durable consumer goods in September 1982. These included televisions, cassette recorders, high-end radios, musical instruments, cameras, washing machines, and refrigerators. Other departments also implemented similar measures, leading to a rapid expansion of commercial credit. According to statistics from the PBC, sampled from cities like Beijing and Chongqing as well as 11 provinces including Inner Mongolia, Liaoning, Jilin, Shanghai, Fujian, Anhui, Henan, Hubei, Guizhou, and Shaanxi, 79.3% (4,320) of the 5,450 surveyed industrial and commercial enterprises had commercial credit. Among these enterprises, a total of 5.6 billion yuan of commercial credit occurred in 1982, accounting for 50% of all commercial credit that year. This total represented 13.6% of their total purchase and sales of 1.4 billion yuan, and the year-end balance was 147.7 billion yuan, accounting for 2.9% of the total commercial credit that year. The scope, scale, diversity, and influence of commercial credit were unprecedented in the history of the PRC.

The introduction of economic system reforms and the continuous incorporation of market factors had unleashed economic growth potential and significantly improved people's living standards. However, the transition from a traditional planned economy system was fraught with challenges. A new system was yet to be established and improved, and the serious friction between the old and new systems had created prominent contradictions in economic operations. These contradictions included an imbalance between total demand and supply, significant economic structure distortion, and a tendency for local governments and enterprises to prioritize output value and speed over quality and efficiency. These issues have, to some extent, resulted in an abnormal situation of increased production, backlog, and losses. As the economy entered a stage of governance and rectification, and a policy to tighten control over spending and credit was implemented in 1989, these contradictions began to emerge. A large number of overdue payments surfaced in various forms, and an increasing number of businesses found themselves caught in "chain debts." In 1989, mutual arrears between Chinese enterprises were approximately 50 billion yuan, which skyrocketed to over 200 billion yuan by early 1990, accounting for approximately 10.5% of the 1990 GDP. The substantial "chain debts" had interrupted normal business operations, significantly impacted social credit, and hindered the healthy development of the national economy.[5]

III. Measures Adopted by Financial Institutions to Settle Debts Through Bills

The PBC, along with governments at various levels, had sought to implement policy measures to promote paper-form commercial credit. This approach, using bills as the carrier, aimed to circumvent the drawbacks associated with credit purchases in the old commercial credit system.

In 1979, the PBC began planning a pilot program for the issuance of commercial acceptance bills by enterprises. In August 1980, a symposium attended by the presidents of the PBC branches was held, proposing to adapt the credit system to new circumstances. This meeting represented a significant shift in commercial credit restrictions and brought the traditional bill credit business into focus within the socialist credit system. Given the extensive range of commercial credit issues, the headquarters of the PBC approved an initial pilot project in Shanghai, with intentions to gradually expand the program after gathering experience.

The Shanghai Financial Society (SFS) responded proactively to the directives from the PBC headquarters by establishing the Bill Discounting Research Association. To combine theoretical knowledge with practical application, various symposiums were held in factories and stores. The purpose of these meetings was to explore and discuss the current state and management methods of commercial credit, and to evaluate the feasibility of using bill discounting as an economic stimulus. This educational and practical experience led to a shift in perspective, promoting a new understanding of the nature and role of bills.[6]

In 1981, Shanghai drafted measures for bill acceptance and discounting, and the PBC Shanghai Branch decided to pilot the program in two districts. The first local commercial bill acceptance and discount occurred in February 1981, in collaboration with the Yangpu and Huangpu district offices.[7] This pilot program converted a long overdue payment from a steel mill into a three-month commercial draft with the debtor as the payer. The acceptance of this draft put pressure on the debtor to clear their backlog, expand sales, and ultimately settle the bill on time. In October of the same year, the first inter-provincial and municipal bank bill acceptance and discount was attempted in collaboration with the Xuhui District Office in Shanghai and the Tianchang County Sub-Branch in Anhui Province. There were several cement shipments in Shanghai that needed immediate processing, and an entity in Tianchang wanted to purchase them but lacked the necessary funds. The local bank agreed to a loan, but the funds were insufficient. Consequently, the local bank accepted the loan, and the Shanghai Bank discounted it to facilitate the transaction. This was the first instance of the bill acceptance and discounting business crossing municipal and provincial boundaries, expanding from the same city to other regions. The successful handling of these two bill discounting businesses marks the restart of the bill market. This underscored the role of bills in supporting the development of the real economy and presented a solution to the problem of overdue payments. Similarly, in situations of tight bank credit limits, bill business can provide a new way to alleviate fund shortages.

The handling of these two bill businesses sent a signal to the market that bill businesses had reappeared on the historical stage, incentivizing both enterprises and banks to accept them. Enterprises started using bills for payment and settlement, while banks also began to launch their own bill businesses.

In May 1981, the PBC headquarters approved the Shanghai branch's request to resume bill acceptance and discount business. This was done to avoid mutual arrears caused by credit sales and prepayment behavior, which could disrupt the regular flow of funds. Shanghai pioneered the bills of exchange acceptance and discount business, and began piloting the transformation of commercial bank credit bills. The SFS compiled the results of their investigations, research, and pilot projects into a book titled *Bill Acceptance and Discounting*, which was widely distributed in the financial and business sectors. At SFS's first annual meeting in 1981, the initiative of "paper-form commercial credit bills" was proposed.

In May 1982, drawing from trials in Shanghai, the PBC began piloting the commercial bill acceptance and discount business in provinces such as Liaoning and Sichuan. However, due to the government's tendency to intervene in the financial market through administrative means under the planned economy system, bank credit was more often adopted during the process of commercial credit securitization. This, along with excessive restrictions imposed by the state and banks on bills and weak professional skills among many bank employees, hindered the successful promotion of paper-form commercial credit bills.

In August 1983, the Financial Administration Department of PBC headquarters organized a commercial credit investigation meeting, attended by representatives from eight branches in Shanghai, Tianjin, Chongqing, Fujian, Hubei, Shaanxi, Jilin, and Liaoning. During the meeting, several reports were delivered and discussions were held. The head of PBC headquarters concluded the meeting with a significant speech. He stressed that adopting various forms of credit with bank credit as the main body, and piloting commercial credit and commercial bills, had been a crucial part of bank reforms since the Third Plenary Session of the Eleventh Central Committee of the CPC in 1978. Banks needed to prioritize and execute this task well, making it one of their primary responsibilities. The head stressed the need to conduct research, gather experience, and implement reform measures, to gradually improve China's socialist credit system over time. This reform was crucial to meet the needs of the broader economic management system reform and modernization drive. He explained that commercial credit arose from the contradiction between goods and currency in the country's economic development process, a problem that bank credit could not resolve. Therefore, it was crucial to manage commercial credit according to capital circulation laws and new changes in institutional reform. He noted that bills of exchange were a representative form of commercial credit, and bills should be promoted in normal commercial activities.

In December 1984, the PBC issued the *Interim Measures for the Acceptance and Discount of Commercial Bills*, which decided that the acceptance and discount of commercial bills would be promoted nationwide starting from 1985. The Interim Measures was a unified bill procedure issued by the PBC, following a three-year trial in cities such as Shanghai and Chongqing. The introduction of these measures signaled a transition from disjoined regional bill systems to a unified national approach. Designed by the PBC, this top-level system provided a legal foundation for nationwide bill operations. This change had several benefits:

- It strengthened the guidance and management of commercial credit, enhancing its positive role.
- It facilitated the clearing of overdue payments among businesses.
- It fostered new credit relationships between banks and enterprises, spurring continuous economic system reform.
- It supported the development and expansion of the bill market, contributing to the goal of revitalizing the economy through bills.

In April 1986, the PBC and the ICBC jointly issued *A Notice on Clearing Overdue Payments Through Bill Acceptance and Discount*. Trials of this initiative were conducted in several cities, including Beijing, Shanghai, Tianjin, Guangzhou, Chongqing, Wuhan, Shenyang, Harbin, and Nanjing. To further stimulate the growth of the bill discount market, the PBC introduced the *Trial Measures for Rediscounting of the People's Bank of China* later that year.

On December 19, 1988, the PBC began a reform of the bank settlement system to address nationwide payment arrears. To promote the use of commercial bills, PBC issued *Measures for Bank Settlement* and *Bank Settlement Accounting Procedures*. Additionally, a notice was issued to strengthen the management of commercial bills and facilitate their growth. In the same year, the State Commission for Economic Restructuring proposed a comprehensive plan to deepen economic system reform. This plan emphasized the importance of vigorously promoting commercial bills and improving commercial bill discount and rediscount systems. As part of this plan, it was decided that the PBC should reduce its credit loans to specialized banks, and increase the proportion of central bank rediscounted mortgage loans and funds financed through bills and bonds. The PBC should be tasked with further promoting the use of commercial bills as a significant step in reforming the bank settlement system and improving the commodity circulation system.

In April 1989, *Measures for Bank Settlement* were officially implemented. This enabled the circulation, discount, interbank discount, and rediscount of bills, which facilitated settlement through bills. In the same year, the PBC launched the "three bills and one card" service, which included bills of exchange, promissory notes, checks, and credit cards.

On March 26, 1990, the State Council issued *A Notice on Nationwide Clearing of Chain Debts* and established a leading group for this purpose. The principle of "enterprises actively collecting payments, banks assisting in clearing, and multiple sources of funds combining commercial bills" was followed, setting in motion the nationwide chain debt clearance. During the clearance process, funds were sourced from various regions and specialized banks. The PBC also arranged over 30 billion yuan in special loans and 21 billion yuan in loan funds for debt clearance. This greatly assisted enterprises in their production. However, deep-seated issues related to finance, industry structure, and enterprise system, which contributed to the formation of chain debts, remained unsolved. The debt clearance was concentrated in enterprises for consumer goods production. Notably, the root causes of chain debts were not addressed, leading to the reemergence of chain debts after the clearance. This remained a serious problem.[8]

In 1991, the government decided to use commercial bills as a solution to the serious problem of payment arrears in commodity transactions. This applied to dual-protection enterprises (those protecting the rights and interests of both their employees and customers) under mandatory plans and those dealing in industrial products in the commercial, foreign trade, and material supply and marketing sectors. Banks were tasked with discounting and rediscounting these bills, and with organizing various resources to address chain debts. In September of the same year, the PBC issued *A Notice on Strengthening the Administration of Commercial Bills* to regulate the use of commercial bills and the behavior of the bank bill acceptance and discount market. The following year, the PBC issued the *Interim Measures for the Administration of Loans to Financial Institutions*, dividing its loans to financial institutions into credit mortgage loans and rediscount loans, based on different lending methods. It stipulated that rediscount could be used in specific operations at preferential interest rates. This laid a solid foundation for the further development of the commercial bill acceptance and discount market.

In 1994, the PBC implemented the new *Interim Measures for the Administration of Credit Funds*, introducing rediscount as a monetary policy tool. In July of the same year, the State Council approved the use of commercial bill settlement in the coal, electricity, metallurgy, chemical, and railway industries. Meanwhile, the PBC issued *Measures for Commercial Bills* and *Measures for Rediscount of Commercial Bills*, which stipulated that buyers without sufficient funds could make purchases with the accepted bill funds, and seller without sufficient funds could request a discount of the accepted bills from the bank. These bills could be endorsed and transferred. In October, the PBC earmarked a rediscount fund of ten billion yuan for the first time, exclusively for the rediscount of bills in the previously mentioned industries and four agricultural and sideline products: cotton, tobacco, swine, and sugar.[9]

IV. Causes for the Slow Development of Bill Business

Despite the issuance of policies by competent departments, the progress of bill business was relatively slow during this period, failing to match the rapid economic growth. There were multiple causes for this slow progress.

1. Insufficient Publicity Efforts, Lack of Expertise, and High Risk of Fake Bills

Effective promotion of the bill business required a team of specialized talents with expertise in bills, banking, and economics. This could not be achieved solely through the banks' efforts, but necessitated close collaboration across various sectors and enterprises. One reason for this was that society and banks had not given extensive publicity to the advantages of the bill business. As a result, enterprises often failed to fully recognize its benefits and continued to rely on traditional methods. In addition, there was a lack of necessary training for banks and enterprises to implement bill settlement. The accounting personnel were not adequately equipped to handle bill-related tasks. They were understaffed, lacked professional training, and had limited knowledge about the bill business. This resulted in their inability to handle bill business in a timely, accurate, quick, and safe manner. Errors and accidents occurred frequently, which hindered the development of the bill business. Moreover, commercial banks lacked operational and managerial experience, leading to widespread violations and fake bills in the bill market. The risk associated with bill-based discount loans was not lower than that of regular credit loans, making commercial banks hesitant to accept them.

2. Impact of the Hierarchical Intra-Bank Networks

Hierarchical networks within various specialized banks often resulted in systemic and local monopolies of settlement funds. The practice of "direct remittance within a bank and mutual transfer between banks" extended the operational procedure of interbank fund settlement and increased the time of funds in transit. Besides the settlement system established by the PBC, each specialized bank operated independently for the benefit of its own system using its own regulations. This resulted in inconsistent systems and disorderly settlements. For example, in the settlement of bills of exchange, a popular option among enterprises, specialized banks followed different practices. Some used steel seals and stamping machines, while others used intra-bank seals and encrypted documents. For high-value bills, some banks required additional counterfoils, and the starting points for the amounts were inconsistent. This often resulted in situations where customers and bills arrived, but the counterfoils did not, preventing timely securing of funds. This not only violated the requirement of bank bills of exchange that "funds should be secured upon the arrival of customers and bills," but also infringed on the interests of bill bearers and drawees, tarnishing the bank's reputation. Some banks, motivated by self-interest, misused funds to maintain credit scale and bridging funding gaps. They occupied the payable inter-bank balance difference, refused to honor bills from other places, and deliberately delayed payment or returned the bills under various pretexts. This resulted in blocked settlement and remittance channels, negatively impacting the promotion of the bill business.[10]

3. Weak Concept of Corporate Integrity and Subsequent Prominent Chain Debt Issue

During that period, China's credit control mechanism was unsound, the corporate credit ratings were low, and the concept of integrity was not firmly established. A widespread belief held that debtors were in an advantageous position and could profit from their debts. Many enterprises faced challenges with unsold inventory, insufficient funds, and an inability to pay bills when due. To address immediate production needs, some enterprises focused solely on signing bills to obtain raw materials, without considering whether they could make timely payments. This significant impairment of the credit system posed a significant obstacle to the development of China's commercial bill market. Bill stakeholders, cautious of financial issues such as chain debts, were hesitant to use bills as payment methods. This partially explains why the Chinese bill market had been dominated by bills of exchange, with bank acceptance bills significantly outnumbering commercial acceptance bills.

4. Poor Bill Regulation and Insufficient Legal Protection for Bill Circulation

A bill law is a legal norm that regulates the types, forms, and content of bill settlements, as well as the rights and obligations of all parties involved. It ensures safe and smooth bill circulation by providing a legal basis for their transfer and circulation. Additionally, it enforces legality, combats illegal activities, and protects the legitimate rights and interests of all entities involved in bill transactions. However, the absence of a bill law or legally binding regulations in China had led to inadequate legal protection for bills in the commodity market. When a bill dispute arose, the judicial branch might struggle to handle it fairly in accordance with the law, and, as a result, the legitimate rights and interests of relevant parties may not be guaranteed. This lack of assurance had deterred banks and enterprises from promoting bill business.

SECTION 2

The Negotiable Instrument Law of the PRC: Legal Foundation of the New China Bill Market

Before the promulgation of *The Negotiable Instrument Law of the PRC*, China's bill market was governed by scattered rules and regulations and lacked a fundamental law, which impeded the development of the market. The introduction of *The Negotiable Instrument Law of the PRC* provided the necessary legal framework for China's bill market, allowing it to progress beyond its previous state of uncertainty.

I. Background

Before *The Negotiable Instrument Law of the PRC* was promulgated, regulations varied across regions and departments, with the vast majority being administrative regulations. This lack of a unified guiding document for the bill market to refer to and implement hindered the development of the bill market. Moreover, the rapid growing economy imposed higher demands on the bill market, necessitating guiding rules and regulations. To address these issues, it became urgent to formulate laws to regulate bill activities. These laws would enhance the functionality of bills as tools for payment, settlement, exchange, and credit, protect the legitimate rights and interests of relevant parties, and deter and combat illegal activities in the bill market. This would help maintain social and economic order and foster the growth of a socialist market economy.

II. Birth

1. Commencement and Suspension of Bill Legislation Work

In September 1986, following the instructions of the State Council, the PBC organized a legislative meeting on negotiable instruments. They drafted the *Interim Regulations of the PRC on Negotiable Instruments* and solicited opinions from the financial and legal sectors. Despite increased activities in China's bill market, there was a lack of deep and unified understanding of bills, resulting in the work being put on hold.

2. Promulgation of *The Negotiable Instrument Law of the PRC*

Until 1990, at the National People's Congress, some delegates proposed to accelerate the creation of a negotiable instrument law. At the end of that year, the PBC officially established a drafting group for this law. After research and discussion, *The Negotiable Instrument Law of the PRC (Draft Version)* was prepared in November. In September 1991, the drafting group organized a symposium and created a revised draft. Based on in-depth research, practical experience, and opinions from various sectors, the revised draft underwent multiple changes before it was submitted to the State Council in 1993. The Legislative Affairs Office of the State Council then spent over a year modifying the draft, primarily deleting content with administrative management color and supplementing advanced foreign bill practices. On December 5, 1994, it was signed by the Premier of the State Council and submitted to the Standing Committee of the National People's Congress for review. The Legislative Committee of the National People's Congress, the Central Committee for Financial and Economic Affairs, and other competent departments conducted extensive and in-depth research and discussion on the draft from the State Council. Finally, on May 10, 1995, *The Negotiable Instrument Law of the PRC* was passed at the 13th session of the Standing Committee of the 8th National People's Congress and came into effect on January 1, 1996.[11]

III. Main Contents and Features

1. Main Contents

The Negotiable Instrument Law of the PRC is comprised of 7 chapters and 110 articles, including General Provisions, Bills of Exchange, Promissory Notes, Checks, and Application of Law to Negotiable Instruments Involving Foreign Elements. The first two chapters are the most crucial. The first chapter introduces the legislative purpose and scope of application, defines the types of bills of exchange, and explains the characteristics of promissory notes, checks, and bills of exchange. This chapter also details the recording items, the relationship and the basic relationship, the commission and agency, and the loss of bills of exchange. Chapter two is divided into six sub-sections. It provides detailed explanations on the issuance, endorsement, acceptance, guaranty, payment, and right of recourse of bills of exchange.

- Types of negotiable instruments and application scope of *The Negotiable Instrument Law of the PRC*. Article 2 of *The Negotiable Instrument Law of the PRC* stipulates, "This Law is enacted to regulate acts involving negotiable instruments, protect the lawful rights and interests of the parties engaged in activities involving negotiable instruments, maintain public and economic order, and promote the development of the socialist market economy."
- Authorization and agency relationship. Article 5 of *The Negotiable Instrument Law of the PRC* stipulates: "A party to a negotiable instrument may authorize his agent to sign the instrument and the agency relationship shall be indicated thereon. A person who without authorization signs a negotiable instrument in the name of an agent shall be liable for the instrument."
- The issue, acquisition, negotiation, and payment of consideration. Article 10 of *The Negotiable Instrument Law of the PRC* stipulates: "The issuance, acquisition, and negotiation of an instrument shall follow the principle of good faith and reflect the true relationship of transaction and between the creditor and the debtor. A negotiable instrument shall be acquired by payment of consideration, that is, the price corresponding to what is agreed upon by the two parties to the instrument." There is a great deal of controversy surrounding this article.

- Defenses of negotiable instruments. Article 13 of *The Negotiable Instrument Law of the PRC* stipulates: "A person liable for a negotiable instrument may not set up against the holder such defenses that are available as between himself and the drawer or between himself and the holder's prior party or parties, unless the current holder acquires the instrument with knowledge of the defenses. A person liable for a negotiable instrument may set up defenses against the holder who has a direct creditor-debtor relationship with him and does not perform the obligations agreed upon. 'Defense' as used in this Law means refusal by a person liable for a negotiable instrument to perform his obligations to the creditor in accordance with the provisions of this Law."

In addition, *The Negotiable Instrument Law of the PRC* regulates the negotiable instruments' liquidity, right to be paid, non-causality, independence, and strict adherence to formality.

2. Features

(1) Mandatory

Negotiable instruments are monetary debt securities that perform both payment and credit functions, and also circulate as commodities. If parties have complete discretion to issue, transfer, accept, and guarantee them these instruments, it could create ample opportunities for unscrupulous individuals to engage in fraudulent profit-seeking, deceive others, and disrupt the order of the financial market.

The Negotiable Instrument Law of the PRC upholds private law autonomy in creating rights and obligations, ensuring both safety and convenience. It mandates rules for behavior related to negotiable instruments, resulting in a mandatory regulatory system. Neither violation nor modification of its provisions by any party are allowed. Any improper actions or negligence during bill activities may not yield the desired legal outcome. It could lead to the bill's invalidity or adverse consequences for the perpetrator, with no scope for resolution through negotiation. For example, Article 8 of *The Negotiable Instrument Law of the PRC* stipulates that the sum on a negotiable instrument shall be specified in both capital Chinese characters and numerical figures. The two must be exactly the same; otherwise, the instrument shall be null and void.

(2) Technical

Legal norms can be divided into moral norms and technical ones depending on whether they are designed to uphold ethical principles or provide behavior guideline. The primary purpose of *The Negotiable Instrument Law of the PRC* is to regulate the bill execution methods, along with the exercise, preservation, and protection of bill rights. Its legislative intention focuses on regulating the use, circulation, and preservation of these rights. As it is specifically designed by legislators and does not primarily rely on general moral concepts or legal principles, it is considered a technical norm.

(3) Unified: "Strict Adherence to Formality"

The Negotiable Instrument Law of the PRC highlights the formality of bills and related behaviors, which are protected when aligned with regulations. However, bills and associated behaviors are deemed invalid if they do not comply with regulations, irrespective of the legality and validity of the reasons behind their creation.

IV. Judicial Practice

The Negotiable Instrument Law of the PRC regulates the rights and obligations of parties involved in bills of exchange, promissory notes, and checks. It has significantly contributed to the growth of the bill market. Following its promulgation, judicial organs have resolved various bill dispute cases in accordance with this law.

For example, a dispute over bill revery rights arose between the Bank of China Wenchang Sub-Branch and the Second Construction Engineering Company (SCEC) East China Branch. Yangzhou Yarong Materials Company (hereafter referred to as Yarong Company) pledged commercial bills related to this case to the Bank of China Wenchang Sub-Branch, guaranteeing a maximum debt amount of 20 million yuan. The bill of exchange, issued on September 18, 2012 and due on March 18, 2013, had a par value of 25 million yuan, with both the issuer and acceptor being the SCEC East China Branch. To meet its funding needs, Yarong Company pledged and endorsed these commercial bills on September 18, 2012, with Bank of China Wenchang Sub-Branch as the endorsee. After receiving the bill of exchange through endorsement, the sub-branch confirmed receipt and specified that "the bill will be invalidated upon factoring payment." On September 24, 2012, Bank of China Wenchang Sub-Branch, acting as a factoring agent, signed *Domestic Commercial Invoice Discount Agreement No. 2001* with Yarong Company, the seller. On the same day, Yarong Company submitted a domestic commercial invoice discount financing application to Bank of China Wenchang Sub-Branch. After deducting a transaction fee of 200,000 yuan, the sub-branch actually issued a discount payment of 19.8 million yuan to Yarong Company.

After the accounts receivable under the *Domestic Commercial Invoice Discount Agreement No. 2001* expired, BOC Wenchang Sub-Branch twice reminded SCEC East China Branch to make the payment. Despite these reminders, SCEC East China Branch refused payment on two occasions, April 22 and May 30, 2013, claiming that the supplier had failed to deliver. On June 6, 2013, the BOC Wenchang Sub-Branch issued a lawyer's letter to the SCEC East China Branch, demanding payment of 25 million yuan. Due to SCES East China Branch's refusal to honor its payment obligation, BOC Wenchang Sub-Branch filed a lawsuit, demanding SCEC East China Branch to take responsibility for the bill payment.

In this case, the court dismissed the debtor's claim. According to the reviewed documents, courts at all levels concurred that the instrument holder, when had no direct relationship with the debtor before or after obtaining the instrument, should have their rights reserved. This was in line with Article 14 of the *Provisions of the Supreme People's Court on Several Issues Concerning the Trial of Negotiable Instruments Dispute Cases.* It emphasized the independence of the bill relationship from the basic relationship, stating that the effectiveness of the bill relationship should remain unaffected even if the basic relationship was flawed. Therefore, unless legally specified otherwise, if the holder legally obtained the bill, the debtor's defense based on the basic relationship should not and would not be upheld.

V. Significance and Limitations

1. Significance

(1) Addressing the Critical Absence of a Negotiable Instrument Law

At that time, there were problems with the circulation of negotiable instruments, including haphazard use, lax oversight, lack of credibility, fraudulent activities, and inconsistent rules and regulations across regions and departments. The enactment of *The Negotiable Instrument Law of the PRC* helped address these issues. It provided a dedicated negotiable instrument law, bringing relevant behavior under the purview of national law. This legislation, with its authority and stability, safeguards the lawful rights and interests of parties involved in bill transactions and promotes the stable development of the bill market. *The Negotiable Instrument Law of the PRC* establishes a clear legal standard for regulating bill transactions. It defines the transaction parameters and effectiveness of various bills, sets the conditions and procedures for bill rights and transactions, and outlines the obligations and responsibilities of relevant parties. It helps regulate settlement procedures, safeguards bank settlement processes, enables financing expansion, maximize capital efficiency, and promote stable and coordinated economic development in China.[12]

(2) Boosting Enterprises' Confidence in Negotiable Instruments

The Negotiable Instrument Law of the PRC significantly impacts the growth of the financial industry and provides legal protection for enterprises' bill activities. It offers credit guarantees for enterprises' bills and security for their funds. Moreover, it expedites fund transfers and turnover for enterprises, promoting the use and circulation of funds through negotiable instruments. This law has been pivotal in regulating corporate credit and mitigating loan defaults.[13]

(3) Bridging the Gap in China's Civil and Commercial Laws

The enactment of *The Negotiable Instrument Law of the PRC* is crucial for improving China's civil and commercial laws. Bills, with their unique features and operational rules, require specific legal systems for regulation and adjustment. Many countries view bill law as vital for managing economic relationships. In the past, bill activities in China were conducted and disputes resolved using the general principles of civil law and other existing laws due to the lack of a dedicated legal framework. This often complicated the proper management of negotiable instrument relationships. Therefore, *The Negotiable Instrument Law of the PRC* marks a significant step in the evolution of China's legal system for the financial industry, heralding a new era for China's socialist financial industry. It signifies the progression of the financial industry toward standardized and lawful management.

2. Limitations

(1) Limitations of the Times

Generally speaking, economic development is the primary driving force behind legal amendments. *The Negotiable Instrument Law of the PRC* was enacted and implemented during China's transition from a planned economy to a market economy in the 1990s. For a period of time after its implementation, the law showed adaptability to China's economic development, particularly in bill practice. However, as China's economy and bill business evolved, the roles of bills had expanded far beyond the exchange and payment functions initially established by *The Negotiable Instrument Law of the PRC*. This law failed to address emerging electronic commercial drafts and digital bills, leaving a legislative gap. Some of its provisions lacked practicality, necessitating additional rules from departmental and industry regulations. As bill practice and judicial practice developed, the limitations of *The Negotiable Instrument Law of the PRC* had become increasingly apparent. While it was only revised in 2004 by removing Article 75, the current diversity of payment methods and the highly market-oriented nature of bill business had led to conflicts between some provisions of this law and bill market practices. This makes revising *The Negotiable Instrument Law of the PRC* an unavoidable trend.

(2) Value Orientation

Throughout the history of bill formation and development, circulation has been its fundamental value. This is evident in the bill laws of the Anglo-American legal system and *Convention on the Unification of the Law Relating to Bills of Ex-Change and Promissory Notes*, where bill negotiability is the primary goal. However, China's bill law focused on payment and exchange functions. This approach was not congruent with actual business practices, challenging the legislative purpose stated in Article 1 of *The Negotiable Instrument Law of the PRC*: promoting the development of the socialist market economy. Therefore, China should prioritize promoting bill circulation when legislating bills. This would involve addressing issues related to the on-causality, circulation mode, and medium of bills.[14]

(3) A Legislative Perspective

From a legislative perspective, the causal provisions outlined in Article 10 of *The Negotiable Instrument Law of the PRC* actually contradict the principle of promoting bill circulation and ensuring bill payment. From a policy perspective, restrictions on private bills of exchange and the exclusion of commercial promissory notes have impaired the functions of bills. From a technical perspective, there are numerous errors in the legislation's concepts, expressions, and logical relationships. The legislation is plagued by inappropriate imitation, unnecessary innovation, and overreach by formulating legal rules beyond its jurisdiction.

SECTION 3

Development of Bill Market: From the Beginning of Reform and Opening Up to the Electronic Bills

Over the thirty years from the beginning of the reform and opening up in 1978 to the enactment of *The Negotiable Instrument Law of the PRC*, the bill market had grown from non-existence to significant development. It had made significant progress in business volume, infrastructure construction, institutional development, market innovation, and risk prevention and control.

I. Overview

In 1979, China's financial sector began exploring the combination of bank and commercial credit, using bank credit to guide commercial credit. In 1981, the Shanghai Branch of the PBC trialed the first local commercial bill acceptance and discount business, along with the first inter-city and inter-provincial bank bill acceptance and discount transaction.

Despite the resumption of commercial bill acceptance and discount business in 1981, the volume of commercial bills used in commodity transactions remained limited. By the end of July 1983, only 552 bill acceptance transactions had been handled, totaling 40.92 million yuan, with an average of only 74,000 yuan per transaction. More branches of the PBC joined the pilot bill business program, and by 1984, branches in 23 provinces, autonomous regions, and municipalities directly under the central government had handled bill acceptance and discount businesses of varying scales. In June 1984, the number of bill acceptance transactions handled by the PBC Shanghai Branch increased to 2,668, totaling 203.7 million yuan, but the average transaction remained small, reaching only 76,000 yuan. Provinces like Liaoning, Sichuan, Hebei, Zhejiang, Fujian, Hubei, and Shaanxi successively launched bill acceptance and discount services, and by the first half of 1984, nationwide transactions totaled 260 million yuan.[15]

In 1986, Liaoning Province initiated a pilot program for commercial bill acceptance and discount in Shenyang City. In November, 1,927 bank bill acceptance transactions were handled in 13 cities, totaling 633.17 million yuan. Additionally, 3,331 bill discount transactions were handled, totaling 554.9 million yuan, along with 1,280 rediscount transactions, which amounted to 385.68 million yuan.[16]

By the end of 1990, 379,000 commercial bill acceptance transactions had been handled nationwide, totaling 50.7 billion yuan. 577,000 bank bill acceptance transactions had been handled, amounting to 171.6 billion yuan. Banks had handled 248,000 bill discount transactions, totaling 80.4 billion yuan. Specialized banks had handled 1,159 interbank transfers, totaling 270 million yuan. The PBC had handled 30,000 rediscount transactions for specialized banks, amounting to 18.7 billion yuan. The total financing of the bill acceptance and discount market reached approximately 32 billion yuan by the end of 1990, equivalent to 17% of the country's GDP that year.[17]

In 1991, the bill market entered a period of sluggish growth. For example, the total discount amount in Shanghai, a significant bill market in the country, was 23.2 billion yuan in 1991, but it decreased to 15 billion yuan in 1992, a decline of over 35%. The total rediscount amount was 7.3 billion yuan in 1991, but it decreased to 6.6 billion yuan in 1992, a decrease of 9.6%. By the end of 1993, the national rediscount balance was only about 4.8 billion yuan.[18] However, in 1994, China's commercial bill market saw significant development. The rediscount balance of the PBC reached approximately 20.3 billion yuan, representing an increase of 4.16 times.[19] It accounted for about 20% of the central bank's lending increase and 0.42% of the country's GDP that year.

From 1995 to 1999, the volume of acceptance and discount transactions in the entire market doubled, with acceptance transactions increasing from 242.4 billion yuan to 507.6 billion yuan. The proportion of acceptance transaction volume to GDP increased from 3.95% to 5.60%. The discount amount also increased from 141.2 billion yuan to 249.9 billion yuan, and its proportion to GDP increased from 2.30% to 2.76%. By the end of 1999, both the acceptance balance and the discount balance had more than doubled. Specifically, the discount balance increased by 268%, from 15 billion yuan at the end of 1995 to 55.2 billion yuan in 1999.[20] This growth pattern was highly consistent across acceptance and discount businesses, indicating steady overall growth. However, 1998 saw a significant contraction in business volume, primarily due to the issuance of the *Notice on Strengthening the Management and Promoting the Development of Commercial Bills* by the PBC. This notice highlighted issues in bank transactions and led to the first special inspection of commercial and bank bill business. In the five years following the enactment of *The Negotiable Instrument Law of the PRC*, the interbank discount business began to emerge. As the bill market initially scaled, bill rediscounts also increased. In 1999, the nationwide rediscount volume was 115 billion yuan, marking a 36% increase from 1995, while the rediscount balance was 50.2 billion yuan, up 56% from 1995.

From 2000 to 2008, both the acceptance and discount businesses in the market saw rapid growth. The acceptance amount rose from 744.5 billion yuan to 7,100 billion yuan, with its proportion in GDP increasing from 7.42% to 22.24%. The discount amount skyrocketed from 644.7 billion yuan to 13,500 billion yuan, with its proportion in GDP growing from 6.43% to 42.29%. By the end of 2008, both acceptance and discount balances had seen rapid and synchronous growth. The discount balance alone increased from 153.5 billion yuan to 1.9279 trillion yuan, an increase of 11.56 times, while its proportion in GDP grew from 1.53% to 6.04%.

In 2003, the PBC canceled the acceptance risk control indicator, which stated that the total amount of bank bill acceptance should not exceed 5% of the balance of various deposits at the end of the previous year. This led to a significant year-on-year increase in the growth rate of acceptance business. However, in 2004, the PBC raised the rediscount interest rate and deposit-reserve ratio, implemented a differential reserve system, and carried out targeted control of the rapid growth of currency and credit. This slowed down the growth rate of the bill businesses in the market significantly, with the discount amount growth rate decreasing to 1.35%, and the transaction volume growth rate falling to 9.57%.

After 2005, with the establishment of the ABC Bill Business Department and the official operation of the Shanghai Interbank Offered Rate (Shibor), the bill market resumed its high-speed growth trend. But the scale of the bill market continued to decline from 2006 to 2007. In 2006, the PBC raised the renminbi deposit-reserve ratio of deposit financial institutions three times, totaling 1.5 percentage points. It also raised the reserve requirement ratio ten times in 2007, totaling 5.5 percentage points, and raised the lending and deposit benchmark interest rates of financial institutions six times.

In 2008, the bill market resumed its growth. During the first half of the year, the reserve requirement ratio was raised five times, a cumulative increase of 3 percentage points, to hedge liquidity. However, in the second half of the year, in response to the international financial crisis, the PBC lowered the lending and deposit benchmark interest rates five times and decreased the reserve requirement ratio four times, effectively relaxing the hard constraints on the credit planning of financial institutions.

Table 6-1 Development of China's Bill Market (1995–2008) (unit: 100 million yuan)

	Total acceptance amount		Total discount amount		Transaction volume		Unmatured acceptance balance		Discount balance	
Year	Sum	Annual growth rate (%)	Sum	Annual growth rate (%)	Sum	Annual growth rate (%)	Sum	Annual growth rate (%)	Sum	Annual growth rate (%)
1995	2,424	278.75	1,412	200.43	3,836	245.59	865	—	150	—
1996	3,898	60.81	2,264	60.34	6,162	60.64	1285	48.55	505	236.67
1997	4,600	18.01	2,740	21.02	7,340	19.12	1335	3.89	581	15.05
1998	3,841	-16.50	2,400	-12.41	6,241	-14.97	1595	19.48	547	-5.85
1999	5,076	32.15	2,499	4.13	7,575	21.37	1,873	17.43	552	0.91
2000	7,445	46.67	6,447	157.98	13,892	83.39	3,676	96.26	1,535	178.08
2001	12,699	70.57	17,645	173.69	30,344	118.43	5,110	39.01	2,795	82.08
2002	16,139	27.09	23,073	30.76	39,212	29.22	7,347	43.78	5,200	86.05
2003	27,700	71.63	44,400	92.43	72,100	83.87	12,800	74.22	8,167	57.06
2004	34,000	22.74	45,000	1.35	79,000	9.57	15,000	17.19	10,000	22.44
2005	44,480	30.82	67,508	50.02	111,988	41.76	19,574	30.49	13,837	38.37
2006	54,300	22.08	84,900	25.76	139,200	24.30	22,100	12.90	17,200	24.30
2007	58,700	8.10	101,100	19.08	159,800	14.80	24,400	10.41	12,818	-25.58
2008	71,000	20.70	135,000	33.60	206,000	28.91	32,000	30.90	19,279	50.40

Source: Compiled based on data from the official website of the PBC.

II. Infrastructure Construction

During this period, *The Negotiable Instrument Law of the PRC* was enacted, and supporting laws and regulations were put in place, forming the basic legal framework for China's bill market. Additionally, improvements were made to the discount and rediscount rate formation mechanism, which further promoted the development of the bill market.

On May 10, 1995, the 13th session of the Standing Committee of the 8th National People's Congress deliberated and passed *The Negotiable Instrument Law of the PRC*, which came into effect on January 1, 1996. Following its enactment, the PBC introduced a series of relevant regulations. In 1996, the PBC issued *General Provisions on Lending*, which included bill discount in lending and credit scale management. In 1997, it issued more regulations such as the *Implementing Measures for the Administration of Negotiable Instruments*, *Measures for Payment and Settlement*, and *Interim Measures for the Administration of Acceptance, Discount, and Rediscount of Commercial Bills*. These regulations strengthened the macro-management and institutional construction of commercial bills, filling the legal gap in China's bill market. This led to the preliminary establishment of laws and regulations for commercial banks to conduct bill business.

The pricing mechanism for discount and rediscount services was refined and optimized. Before 1998, China's commercial bill discount rate was 5% lower than the lending rate, while the rediscount rate was 10% lower than the refinancing rate. In March 1998, a profit-driven mechanism for bill business was introduced, which fostered the development of a price formation mechanism. The PBC implemented a price mechanism based on the re-discount interest rate to guide the discount and interbank discount interest rates indirectly. Between 1998 and 1999, the PBC repeatedly cut the rediscount rate, reducing it from 6.03% at the beginning of 1998 to 2.16% in June 1999, a total reduction of 64%. This substantial drop prompted commercial banks to lower their corporate discount rates. The reduction in discount and rediscount rates gave bill business a more significant price advantage, driving its growth during that period. Moreover, rediscount became an essential tool for monetary policy operations, assigning a new role to the bill business in transmitting monetary policies and regulating the macro market.

After 2000, the number of participants in the bill market continued to grow. Some commercial banks, credit cooperatives, and foreign-funded banks in certain cities began to expand their bill businesses, using this opportunity to explore other credit markets. During that period, financial institutions capitalized on the advantages of the bill acceptance business to attract customers, encourage marginal deposits, and increase acceptance fees.

The operating model of the bill market was evolving toward intensification. The Bill Business Department of the ICBC led to intensive management of bill businesses. This change resulted in consolidation of scattered bill businesses at the head office, which strengthened overall management, improved resource utilization efficiency within the bank, and provided a new business model for market development. It also mitigated risks linked to weak professional capabilities in branch offices. In June 2003, the China Foreign Exchange Trading

Center established the "China Bill Quotation System," also known as the China Bill Network. This system provided quotation, matching, and inquiry services for bill interbank discounting and repurchase transactions between financial institutions. It resolved information blockage issues, changing the scenario where banks struggled to secure credit sources and funds, and enterprises struggled to reach banks.[21] To further increase transaction frequency, circulation rate, and utilization rate of commercial bank bill resources in the bill market, various commercial banks have started to establish specialized bill management departments to explore professional operation paths.

The interest rate pricing mechanism in the bill market was improving. In January 2007, the Shibor began operating, and, following this, the PBC urged major commercial banks to develop a bill discount rate pricing model based on Shibor. In April that year, the ICBC took the lead to introduce a bill interbank discounting and repurchase quotation rate based on Shibor. In November, it also launched a bill discount rate pricing mechanism pegged to Shibor, marking the shift in bill business pricing from fixed to floating interest rates.[22]

On January 18, 2008, Yi Gang, then Vice President of the PBC, stated that the existing pattern of deposit and loan interest rates would persist for a while. However, a significant breakthrough occurred in interest rate marketization, as seen in the correlation between discount rates and Shibor. In 2008, the Shanghai Branch of the PBC instructed city financial institutions to standardize and unify the *Bill Interbank Discounting Contract*. This contract stipulated that the interbank discount interest rate should be based on the Shibor on the agreed date, and it was piloted in the Yangtze River Delta region.[23] Concurrently, numerous financial institutions in the bill market collectively signed the *Standard Contract for Bank Bill Acceptance and Interbank Discounting*, the *Standard Contract for Commercial Bill Acceptance and Interbank Discounting*, and the *Convention on the Acceptance of Negotiable Instruments*. These documents indicated a move toward standardization and self-regulation in bill transactions, reflecting the market's demand for uniform and standardized rules.

III. Institutional Development

In May 1981, the head office of the PBC approved the *Request to Resume Bill Acceptance and Discount Business* submitted by its Shanghai Branch. In December 1984, it issued the *Interim Measures for the Acceptance and Discount of Commercial Bills*, announcing the nationwide promotion of commercial bill acceptance and discount business, starting from 1985.

In April 1986, the PBC and the ICBC jointly issued *A Notice on Implementing Measures for Commercial Bill Acceptance and Discount to Clear Payments in Arrears*. That same year, the PBC introduced *Trial Measures for Rediscounting of the People's Bank of China*.

On December 19, 1988, the PBC released *Measures for Bank Settlement* and *Accounting Procedures for Bank Settlement*. Additionally, they issued *A Notice on Strengthening the Administration of Commercial Bills and Promoting Their Development*. In that same year, the National Commission for Economic Reform proposed a comprehensive plan to deepen economic system reform. This plan stressed the importance of promoting commercial bills and improving the commercial bill discount and rediscount system. Also in 1988, the Shanghai Municipal People's Government issued the *Interim Provisions on Negotiable Instruments*, which was the first comprehensive local regulation on negotiable instruments in China.

In 1989, the PBC introduced the "three negotiable instruments and one card" service, encompassing bills of exchange, promissory notes, checks, and credit cards.

On March 26, 1990, the State Council issued *A Notice on Nationwide Campaign to Clear Chain Debts*.[24]

In 1991, the government, recognizing the serious problem of payments in arrears in commodity transactions, decided to promote commercial bills for double-guarantee businesses executing mandatory plans, and for commercial, foreign trade, and material supply and marketing businesses to buy and sell industrial products that satisfy their own needs. Banks processed the discount and rediscount of these bills, and enlisted various resources to clear chain debts. In September of that year, the PBC issued *A Notice on Strengthening the Administration of Commercial Bills*. The following year, in the *Interim Measures of the People's Bank of China for the Administration of Loans to Financial Institutions*, the central bank divided its loans to financial institutions into credit mortgage loans and rediscount, based on different issuance methods. It declared that rediscount should be handled on a limited scale at preferential interest rates under certain circumstances. This laid a solid foundation for the development of the commercial bill acceptance and discount market.

In 1994, the PBC introduced the new *Interim Measures for the Administration of Credit Funds*, using rediscount as a monetary policy tool. In July of that year, with the State Council's approval, the central bank promoted commercial bill settlements in five industries: coal, electricity, metallurgy, chemical, and railway; it also released *Measures for the Administration of Commercial Bills* and *Methods for Rediscount of Commercial Bills*.[25]

On May 10, 1995, the 13th session of the Standing Committee of the 8th National People's Congress deliberated and passed *The Negotiable Instrument Law of the PRC*, which came into effect on January 1, 1996. In the same year, the PBC issued *General Provisions on Lending*. The document stipulated that bill discounts should be included in lending and credit scale management.

In March 1997, the PBC released the *Interim Measures for the People's Bank of China to Handle Rediscount Business for the Head Office of State-Owned Commercial Banks*. In September, the central bank issued *Measures for Payment and Settlement*, which came into force on December 1, 1997, replacing *Measures for Bank Settlement* introduced in December 1988. This laid the preliminary legal groundwork for commercial banks to conduct bill business.

In March 1998, the PBC undertook decided to improve and optimize the rediscount and discount rate formation mechanisms. The rediscount rate was established as a statutory benchmark interest rate of the central bank, separate from the refinancing interest rate. The discount rate was determined by adding points to the rediscount rate and was made independent from the loan rate of the same period, thereby widening the fluctuation range of the discount rate. This policy positively influenced the subsequent development of the bill market and laid the groundwork for interest rate marketization in the bill market. In June of the same year, the PBC issued *A Notice on Strengthening the Administration of Commercial Bills to Promote Their Development*. The notice identified issues encountered by banks in their handling of bill business. A specific inspection of commercial bank bill business was initiated for the first time, urging commercial banks to focus on discounting business, impose strict control over discounting business at bank branches, and promote the sale of bills to higher-level banks for interbank discounting to finance funds. Priority was given to rediscount bills issued by enterprises that complied with policy requirements, to guide the flow of credit funds and promote structural adjustment.

Since June 1999, the PBC has progressively lowered the rediscount rate and expanded the rediscount quota for various branches. In September of the same year, the bank issued *A Notice on Improving the Administration of Rediscount Business*. This notice proposed to selectively support enterprises with good credit status and stable production, supply, and sales relationships. It promoted the issuance and use of commercial acceptance bills, supported enterprises to expand financing through bills, and advocated for the use of commercial credit bills.

As we entered the 21st century, the liquidity of the bill business has increased, bringing with it a surge in bill disputes. In February 2000, the Supreme People's Court of the PRC enacted the *Provisions of the Supreme People's Court on Several Issues Concerning the Trial of Negotiable Instruments Dispute Cases*. This document supplemented aspects of bill preservation, endorsement, and legal liability from a judicial perspective, while also introducing new provisions such as public notice and reminders for bills.

In July 2001, the PBC issued *A Notice on Effectively Strengthening the Administration of Commercial Bill Acceptance, Discount, and Rediscount Business*. The notice required commercial banks to establish separate accounting subjects to accurately reflect these transactions. Additionally, it suggested that central cities should consolidate the operation and administration of the commercial bill business to improve efficiency and scale effect, mitigate bill risks, and provide a policy basis for future reforms regarding the concentrated operation and administration of the bill business.

In November 2002, the PBC issued *A Notice on Issues Related to Bank Bills and Bank Bill Acceptance Business*, deciding to remove the previously set acceptance risk control indicator, which stated "the total amount of bank acceptance bill business shall be controlled, and the total acceptance amount should not exceed 5% of the balance from various deposits at the end of the previous year."

In September 2005, the PBC released *A Notice on Issues Related to Improving Bill Business System*, stating that the background materials would no longer be necessary for interbank discount and rediscount of negotiable instruments. This change significantly improved the efficiency of business processing for these operations.

In November 2006, the PBC issued the *Guiding Opinions on Promoting the Development of Commercial Bill Acceptance Business*. This document proposed measures such as establishing efficient mechanisms to promote commercial bill acceptance business, leveraging enterprise information databases, boosting enterprise confidence in accepting commercial bills, implementing effective penalty mechanisms for payment breaches, preventing and controlling risks in commodity transactions, and strengthening publicity and training, to guide and encourage the orderly development of commercial credit.

In December 2008, amid the escalating international financial crisis, the PBC issued *A Notice on Improving the Administration of Rediscount Business to Expand Financing for Agriculture, Rural Areas, and Farmers as Well as Small and Medium-Sized Enterprises.* The central bank emphasized the role of rediscount in guiding the development of financing through negotiable instruments. It aimed to steer credit investment through rediscounts to boost financing for industries related to agriculture, rural areas, and farmers, as well as SMEs. Thus, rediscounts began to serve a policy role in targeted regulation.

IV. Innovation

The enactment of *The Negotiable Instrument Law of the PRC* marked a significant turning point in the growth of the bill market. It addressed the primary issue of the absence of a bill law, attracted more participants, spurred market innovation, and facilitated breakthroughs in bill functions, pricing mechanisms, and urban and regional markets.

The rise of the interbank discount business disrupted the traditional structure of bill business. Following the enactment of *The Negotiable Instrument Law of the PRC*, regulatory bodies implemented various relevant legislation, ensuring that bill business operations were legal and compliant. For instance, the Huaxin Sub-Branch of the ICBC, located in Zhengzhou City, Henan Province, was one of the pioneers in focusing on bill business. It generated financing and profit through the interbank discounting market. Its services included bank bill acceptance and interbank discounting, and commercial bill acceptance and interbank discounting (commercial bill business is typically avoided due to risk considerations by many commercial banks in China, but actively pursued by the Huaxin Sub-Branch with proper risk prevention and control), bill custody, short-term financing, and investment management. The branch also established a member client service system, creating a comprehensive business system.[26] Within just two years, by 1999, the sub-branch's bill discount and interbank discount had reached 13.7 billion yuan and 1.3 billion yuan, respectively, which accounted for over a third of the bill business volume in Henan Province.

Regional bill platforms were gradually taking shape. The ICBC Huaxin Sub-Branch expanded its business scope to surrounding provinces and across the country, leveraging its advantages in bill business. At that point, the Huaxin Sub-Branch had over 1,500 regular clients, including large state-owned enterprises like Anshan Iron and Steel Group, Shougang Group, and Tianjin Automotive Industry Group. Its successful model led many commercial banks to shift their focus from exclusive credit lending to exploring bill discount, interbank discount, and related businesses. By the end of the 20th century, a regional bill market encompassing central cities such as Chongqing, Guangzhou, Zhengzhou, and Nanjing had essentially formed. The rise of regional bill markets, commercial bill business sub-branches, and bill centers has provided valuable experience and laid a solid groundwork for the concentrated administration of the bill market in later stages.

Private bill intermediaries started to emerge due to the gradual standardization of bill businesses. Due to the control of corporate bill financing, scale restrictions and complex procedures involving bank discount, private bill transactions increased, which led to a relatively large private bill market. Individuals or enterprises established bill intermediaries to meet the market demand for bill transactions. For example, in the late 20th century, private enterprises and operators with idle funds set up bill trading intermediaries for arbitrage in Yongkang, Zhejiang Province. In the early 21st century, private bill intermediaries grew rapidly, resulting in increased activity in the bill market. Numerous specialized and innovative bill intermediaries emerged, notably Shanghai Purang Investment Co., Ltd., established in May 2002. Its business scope includes bill brokering, bill consulting, and other services, fostering a more specialized division of labor in the bill business. These intermediaries continually strengthened their business competitiveness and routinely innovated bill financing forms to adapt to changing market demands. Commercial banks introduced services such as bill discount, bill investment, and bill asset management.

Product innovation contributed to a more dynamic market. This was evident in the emergence of electronic bill products. In the 20th century, the bill market was dominated by paper-form bills, with the national market divided into multiple relatively independent sectors. Information inquiry and retrieval methods were outdated and there was no unified information platform. The launch of the China Bill Network in 2003 improved this situation by enabling information query for bill transactions, thus enhancing the timeliness of market information. From 2005 onwards, commercial banks such as China Merchants Bank (CMB), China Minsheng Bank, and ICBC, introduced new transaction methods to boost their competitiveness. These banks launched electronic bill products based on their internal systems. Notable products included the "Bill Pass" online bill service by CMB and the "YeePay" electronic credit bill service by ICBC.[27] Additionally, commercial banks created personalized bill service models and products tailored to their customers' needs. For instance, ICBC introduced the "discount business for partial abandonment of commercial bills"; China Minsheng Bank developed "Manufacturers' All-in-One Bill Service" and "Bill Package Purchase Service." China CITIC Bank launched a "commercial invoice discount plan" to help large enterprises with significant accounts receivable; and Shenzhen Development Bank marketed "short-term financing solutions for enterprises," with bills as the core, to customers like Lenovo Group. To keep up with the rapid growth of domestic and international logistics business for large enterprise groups, domestic financial institutions introduced characteristic bill products such as chattel pledge (warehouse receipt), bill exchange (bill splitting), commercial bill guaranteed discount, entrusted agent bill discount, buyer interest payment bill discount, and accounts receivable bill securitization.[28] Regarding service content, besides meeting the financing needs of enterprises, some financial institutions now offered comprehensive bill services including bill custody, appraisal, inquiry, and due collection.

V. Risk Prevention and Control

The increasing use of bill payments in payment settlement led to the increase of bill-related risks, primarily credit and fraud risks. Credit risk surfaced when the acceptor of a commercial bill failed to meet the bill amount at maturity, resulting in financial losses for the beneficiary.[29] Fraud risk typically involved counterfeiting or impersonating others to generate bills, or manipulating bill elements, to defraud others of money or property. Common methods included altering bank bill applications, forging bill settlement notices, altering or "cloning" bills. When *The Negotiable Instrument Law of the PRC* was first enacted, the bill market was dominated by paper-form bills, without a nationwide platform for bill information inquiries. Coupled with outdated domestic communication methods, information inquiries and retrieval were often conducted through mail or landline telephones, which made fraud risks a major threat.

As risks in the bill market began to accumulate, instances of bill fraud became more common, making the healthy development of the bill market an essential task for all participants. To mitigate these fraud risks, commercial banks began to redefine their business procedures and signed cooperation agreements with enterprises to clearly establish the rights and obligations of both parties. Banks also set up dedicated positions for information inquiry and bill verification to improve their capabilities of risk resistance. These roles were equipped with advanced equipment and verification tools under a two-person cross-verification mechanism. To minimize credit risk, banks implemented stricter qualification reviews, conducting comprehensive, timely investigations into their clients' actual business conditions. The introduction of these risk prevention measures significantly decreased the likelihood of risk incidents, effectively supporting the bill market's healthy development.

At the beginning of the 21st century, the infrastructure of the bill market struggled to keep pace with bill business development. Some commercial banks involuntarily engaged in bill acceptance business against regulations and non-standard margin management. Certain banks adopted a model of granting loans first, followed by requiring enterprises to deposit these loans as margins for bill issuance. This method enabled banks to meet loan deposit targets and earn acceptance fees as intermediary business income. However, this practice led to a large number of counterfeit and financing bills in the market, posing significant risks. Furthermore, enterprises issued financing bills to each other through collusion, created false trading background for bill discount, and implemented a continuous acceptance and discount strategy. Funds from bill discount were flowing into high-risk areas such as the stock, real estate, and futures markets at a concerning scale.

According to data, there were 8,000 suspected cases of fraudulent financial bills and illegal acceptance of bills in 2001, involving a total of 5.2 billion yuan. In 2002, a major bill fraud case involving 300 million yuan occurred at the Shanghai Branch of a certain bank, and another significant bill fraud case was reported in Heyuan, Guangdong Province. In 2003, Dingxing County Sub-Branch, Hebei Province, was involved in a bill fraud case worth 1.7 billion yuan. In 2005, a financial fraud case occurred in a certain province, where bills were misused to embezzle 700 million yuan from bank funds.

The frequent involvement of illegal bill intermediaries was a significant factor leading to recurring risk cases in the bill market. These intermediaries leveraged their information acquisition capabilities to be highly active in the market. Initially, they focused on matching private transactions. However, to gain larger profit margins, they progressed from creating fraudulent interbank accounts to using the same bills multiple times and collaborating with bank employees for illicit gain. This excessive participation of non-compliant bill intermediaries in the bill market weakened the internal controls of banks, thereby escalating moral and operational risks.

SECTION 4

Specialized Bill Institutions: Attempt of Bill Business Marketization

As commercial banks saw increased growth in their bill business volume, they began to recognize its contribution to their profits. The ICBC was ahead of the curve, establishing a Bill Business Department as early as 2000. This department, a directly affiliated institution of the head office, implemented independent settlement. Since then, commercial bank bill business has been evolving toward intensive, specialized, and scaled development.

I. ICBC Bill Business Department

1. Background

Since 1989, the PBC has increased its use of rediscount policies to combat the impact of the Asian financial crisis and drive domestic economic growth. It lowered rediscount rates four times, which significantly encouraged commercial banks to engage in bill discounting business, leading to the rapid growth of the bill market. Against this backdrop, the ICBC leveraged its close ties with domestic industrial and commercial enterprises and its service provision advantages to carry out specialized, intensive, and large-scale reform of its bill business, with a strong emphasis on risk prevention. The bank initiated the pilot reform of the bill management system and established China's first head office-level specialized bill institution. This establishment became a significant symbol of the rise of specialized bill institutions.[30]

2. Preparations

The Huaxin Sub-Branch of ICBC Henan Branch was established in 1997, evolving from the Huaxin capital market. Over time, the Huaxin Sub-Branch realized that the bill business, with its rapid circulation, high credibility, and strong profitability, was a viable financing product. As a result, it became the first specialized sub-branch of a commercial bank in China to primarily deal with bills. Its exploration and practices have since spurred the creation of several commercial bank bill centers.[31]

By 2000, the robust growth of the bill business had rendered the decentralized operational model of commercial banks' bill operations inadequate for the evolving market environment. The initial practices of bill operation and specialized institutions provided valuable experience for establishing head office-level specialized bill institutions. On November 9, 2000, the ICBC Bill Business Department, China's first bill trading institution approved by the PBC, was officially established in Shanghai. This department is a first-level branch directly under the head office, implementing relatively independent accounting. Approved by the PBC, its business scope included: handling the discount, interbank discount, rediscount, and repurchase business of both bank and commercial bills; providing commercial bill custody services; offering intermediary services such as bill consultation and witnessing; and handling other business approved by the PBC.[32]

3. Development

On November 9, 2000, the ICBC Bill Business Department, China's first bill trading institution approved by the PBC, was officially established in Shanghai.

In 2002, the ICBC Bill Business Department initiated the establishment of the China Urban Finance Society Bill Research Association (now known as the China Urban Finance Society Bill Professional Committee) in Shanghai. It also established China's first professional bill research journal: *Negotiable Instrument Research.*

In November 2002, the ICBC Bill Business Department officially initiated the ISO9001 quality management system certification process. By 2003, it had successfully obtained the certification, becoming the first specialized bill institution in China to succeed in doing so. This achievement underscored the department's commitment to creating a professional bill "processing bank."

At the end of 2002, the IICBC Bill Business Department established eight directly affiliated branches in major cities including Shenyang, Guangzhou, Xi'an, Chongqing, Tianjin, Zhengzhou, Beijing, and Shanghai. This nationwide network, with its headquarters in Shanghai, solidified a business operation model that integrated both headquarters and branches. This step laid a solid foundation for the bank's further penetration into the domestic bill market.

In 2003, the first national bill price index, the ICBC Bill Price Index, was officially published in national economic and financial professional newspapers. Its compilation drew from domestic and foreign index theories, using the compilation methods of stock, bond, and fund market indices. By incorporating the actual situation of China's bill market, it achieved high representativeness.

In 2004, the ICBC Bill Business Department consolidated various risk control systems and introduced China's first *Standard for Handling Commercial Bill Purchase Business.*

In 2005, the ICBC set up four bill salons in key economic regions: the Yangtze River Delta, the Pearl River Delta, the Bohai Rim, and the three eastern provinces. These salons serve as communication and exchange platforms, attracting the active participation of local commercial banks, financial companies, and other financial institutions and experts. They have become an essential channel for the local PBC and the China Banking Regulatory Commission to stay updated on the local bill market's operations and understand market trends.

In 2007, the ICBC Bill Business Department took the lead in launching a bill trading quotation system based on Shibor on the China Bill Network. This system aimed to guide participants in the bill market to quote according to the trends in money market prices, thereby improving the efficiency of bill transactions.

Since 2008, the ICBC Bill Business Department has been holding joint meetings on business involving bills of exchange, promissory notes, and checks. It introduced the country's first authoritative regional bill market price index—the "Yangtze River Delta Bill Discount Price Index." This index served as a "weathervane" that reflected the dynamic changes in the bill market price in the Yangtze River Delta region. Over eight years, the annual average bill trading volume expanded rapidly from 100 billion yuan at its inception to around 600 billion yuan in 2008. Nearly 1.1 million transactions had been made, totaling over 4.2 trillion yuan.

The profit centers pilot reform launched in early 2010 accelerated the development of a business model tailored to profit centers. It also fostered integrated management mechanisms such as risk, internal control, technology, and information, thereby significantly improving the bank's profitability. During the 15 months from the start of the reform to the end of the first quarter of 2011, the ICBC Bill Business Department achieved a cumulative profit of 1.327 billion yuan. In 2010, a profit of 1.037 billion yuan was achieved, with a per capita profit of over 4 million yuan. In the first quarter of 2011, a profit of 290 million yuan was achieved, a year-on-year increase of over 30%. In the same year, ICBC initiated a joint conference on commercial bank bill business with bill business operation (management) institutions of national commercial bank head offices. This led to the development of bank bill business standards to promote product innovation in the bill market.

In 2016, the ICBC vigorously advanced the reform of its bill business management system. This involved strengthening the management system and business operation mechanism, as well as evolving the Bill Business Department into an operation center, innovation center, risk control center, and profit center for the bank's bill product lines. The focus was on expanding the bank's bill business operation positioning and bolstering the development of bill product lines. Since the reform in 2016, the Bill Business Department has achieved an average annual bill discount volume exceeding 1 trillion yuan. This has directly or indirectly served over 90,000 various enterprises, securing a leading position in the discount business market.

Since 2018, the ICBC Bill Business Department, using the concept of "large bills," has been promoting the integration of the complete bill product chain and the coordinated development of all product lines. It has improved the overall service level of the bill business for its customers. This has played a significant role in serving the development of the real economy and leveraging the advantages of "ONEICBC," thereby improving the bank's market competitiveness.[33]

Additionally, the ICBC Bill Business Department has independently developed and launched China's first supply chain-based integrated bill combination product, "Payment Bill Pass," and the first self-service discount product of state-owned banks, "ICBC e-Ties." It has also timely launched its innovative sub-product, "Inclusive Exclusive Ties," which accurately aligns with inclusive policies, significantly improving the market competitiveness of "ICBC bills." At the same time, in the era of the Shanghai Commercial Paper Exchange Company Ltd., the ICBC Bill Business Department has cooperated with the head office to spearhead the support for the construction of national financial infrastructure. It has invested a substantial number of talents and technical forces and completed the commissioned development, operation, and maintenance project of the Shanghai Commercial Paper Exchange Company Ltd. trading system, becoming the first large bank in the country to fully integrate with this system.

In 2020, the ICBC Bill Business Department achieved a cumulative bill trading volume of over 30 trillion yuan. The number of direct trading customers increased from 87 at its inception to over 2,000. By the end of 2021, the balance of ICBC bank bill acceptance was 449.1 billion yuan, a year-on-year increase of 86%. In 2021, the volume of bill discounting business was 2.3 trillion yuan, a year-on-year increase of 80%, ranking first in the bill market.

4. Significance

(1) Promoting and Regulating the Development of the Bill Market

In the face of fierce market competition, specialized bill institutions constantly seek change, becoming key players in the bill market and major national interbank discounting centers. They serve as crucial contact points for the PBC and the China Banking and Insurance Regulatory Commission to provide guidance and regulation. Leveraging their professional advantages, these institutions actively propagate risk prevention and control measures as well as business processing standards in the bill market. They have played a leading role in standardizing the bill market, contributing significantly to its stable development.

(2) Driving the Bill Business of Commercial Banks

Specialized institutions have demonstrated unique and vital roles in aiding and supporting commercial banks' stable development of their bill businesses. They also facilitate effective credit structure adjustments. For instance, amid its rapid development, the ICBC Bill Business Department has groomed a batch of bill business backbone for the bank through bill financing courses, touring lectures, and other methods. Simultaneously, it has played a positive exemplary role, assisting branches in establishing bill centers, building a bank-wide bill operation network, promoting bill product innovation, and improving risk prevention and control technology, thereby propelling the development of the bank-wide bill business.[34]

(3) Actively Participating In and Promoting China's Financial Reform

The bill market is a key component of the financial market and an essential channel for monetary policy transmission. In China's currency market, it is the only sub-market directly linked to corporate financing. Under the guidance of specialized bill institutions and the combined efforts of various bill market practitioners, the bill market has evolved into a significant part of China's financial market and a major sector in the currency market. Moreover, specialized bill institutions have proven to be a successful experiment in reforming commercial banks' operating mechanisms. They have gained valuable experience in implementing business line-based departmental reforms.

(4) Leading Innovation in the Bill Market

Since its inception, the ICBC Bill Business Department has consistently led innovation in the bill market. In 2002, it launched the "China Urban Finance Society Bill Research Association" (now the "China Urban Finance Society Bill Professional Committee") in Shanghai, and published *Negotiable Instrument Research*, the first professional bill research journal in China. The following year, the department introduced ICBC Bill Price Index, the first bill price index in China's financial industry. In 2007, it launched the first bill trading quotation system based on Shibor on the China Bill Network. This guided market participants to quote according to currency market trends, thereby improving bill market trading efficiency. From 2008 onwards, the department established negotiable instrument joint conference. It also released the first authoritative regional bill market price index in the country, the Yangtze River Delta Discount Price Index. This index serves as a "weathervane" reflecting the dynamic evolution of the Yangtze River Delta bill market prices. The ICBC has achieved multiple industry firsts, including the handling of Shanghai's first bill transaction in a bill trading venue and the first blockchain digital bill business. It also independently developed and launched the first supply chain-based integrated bill combination product in China's banking industry, "Payment Bill Pass," and the first self-service discount product of state-owned banks, "ICBC e-Ties." Additionally, it timely launched the innovative subproduct, "Inclusive Exclusive Ties," which accurately aligns with inclusive policies, thereby significantly improving the market competitiveness of "ICBC bills."

II. Other Major Specialized Bill Institutions

1. ABC Bill Business Department

The ABC Bill Business Department was officially established in Shanghai in May 2005, with the approval of the China Banking Regulatory Commission. It is the second bank, following ICBC, to establish a Bill Business Department directly under its head office.

The ABC's bill business encompasses acceptance, discount, interbank discount, repurchase, and rediscount of commercial bills, credit asset repurchases, interbank deposits, and other bill-related ventures. In 2011, the proportion of interbank trading volume rose by 12 percentage points, amounting to 151.9 billion yuan, which represented 81% of total trading volume. The contribution of interbank income grew by 4 percentage points, with interest income from the interbank business reaching 33.3 billion yuan, making up 79% of all interest income. The Bill Business Department processed a total of 185.5 billion yuan (including 300 million yuan for electronic bills), which included 55.1 billion yuan for buyouts and 130.4 billion yuan for reverse repurchases or reverse repos. As of the end of December, the balance of bill assets stood at 63.2 billion yuan, with the buyout balance at 19.9 billion yuan and the reverse repurchase balance at 43.3 billion yuan. The bank realized an annual interest income of 42.40 billion yuan, of which the bill business alone contributed 42.04 billion yuan. The post-provision operating profit (PPOP) amounted to 18.39 billion yuan.

By the end of the third quarter of 2016, the ABC Bill Business Department had accomplished a cumulative transaction volume of 3.7 trillion yuan. The PPOP reached 13.6 billion yuan, and the total assets exceeded 180 billion yuan. The department also established business relationships with over 500 financial institutions nationwide. In recent years, to adapt to market development trends, it has launched several new products and models, such as the "Bill Forward Trading," a product for interbank discount business, the "bill asset package transfer and custody business," and the "interbank discount and buyout business based on abandoned recourse."

As of the end of the third quarter of 2020, the ABC Bill Business Department recorded a cumulative transaction volume of 9.4 trillion yuan, yielding a business revenue of 64.4 billion yuan. The department has also established business relationships with over 600 financial institutions nationwide. In 2020, the bank's repurchase transaction volume exceeded 1 trillion yuan, and the bill transaction volume surpassed 2 trillion yuan. In 2021, the bank's bill discounting business volume reached 424.329 billion yuan, marking a year-on-year increase of 8.95%.

The ABC Bill Business Department is one of the first institution to quote bill business based on Shibor on the China Bill Network. It accomplished the first Shibor-based interbank discounting in the bill market and has actively promoted interest rate marketization. As the deputy director unit of the Bill Professional Committee of the China Banking Association (CBA), it has taken on and participated in numerous significant projects. It actively organizes and partakes in national and regional meetings on bill business, discussing key issues with peer institutions. The department also collaborates with regulatory authorities to research bill business and market development work. Following the establishment of the Shanghai Commercial Paper Exchange Company Ltd., the department handled the first bill trading in the market, and it has been leading in bill business volume. The ABC became the first of the four major banks to access CPES through a full direct connection. It initiated the founding of the China Bill Research Center, becoming one of its first council members and actively undertaking annual research projects to explore market trends. From 2017 to 2021, the bank received accolades such as "Excellent Member Unit" and "Excellent Bank Trader" from Shanghai Commercial Paper Exchange Company Ltd.

2. CMB Bill Business Department

From 2002 to 2008, CMB set up several regional bill centers, creating institutional advantages while continually advancing the reform of the bill business management system. In 2005, the bank pioneered the "Bill Pass" online bill service. In collaboration with TCL, the bank issued China's first electronic bank bill at the end of 2005.

In 2009, the PBC launched the ECDS, with CMB playing a significant role in its research and development. The bank achieved three major milestones: issuing China's first electronic bank bill, the first electronic commercial bill, and discounting the first electronic bank bill. These achievements garnered multiple honors from the PBC, allowing the bank to secure a leading position in China's banking industry. In 2010, the bank pioneered a reform in the accounting system for bill business, becoming the first to account for the spreads of bill buying and selling as non-interest income. This accurately reflected the attribute of bill trading spreads, which significantly boosted the customer managers' enthusiasm in marketing their bill business.

In 2013, CMB's independently developed electronic bill tracking image system was widely recognized and promoted by member units of the National Commercial Bank Bill Business Joint Conference, making the bank a leader in innovative electronic bill trading.

In 2016, the bank ranked first in the market in terms of cumulative direct subsidy business volume, with its bill business volume accounting for up to 20% of the banks' total. In the same year, CMB became a shareholder of the Shanghai Commercial Paper Exchange Company Ltd. and one of the first council members of the China Bill Research Center.

In 2017, CMB ranked among the top in the industry for six consecutive years in terms of bill trading, risk control, and profitability. That same year, they led the way in innovation by launching the "Grand Bill Manager" unified platform, which provides businesses with one-stop bill settlement, financing, risk control, management, and other full life cycle services. It has become a comprehensive bill service platform with online, intelligent, and personalized features through continuous product innovation, process optimization, and system iteration. Services offered include online discount, online acceptance, bill pooling, Discount Pass, and bill management reports.

In 2018, private enterprises made up 86% of the discount customers and contributed to 75% of the discount volume, which totaled 1.0255 trillion yuan. SMEs comprised 91% of the discount customers and accounted for 76% of the discount volume.

In 2020, CMB's direct bill discount volume was 1,178.48 billion yuan, a year-on-year decrease of 4.67%. However, it still ranked second in the industry in terms of business volume. The scale of on-balance-sheet bills soared to 330.7 billion yuan, an increase of 104 billion yuan from the previous year. The proportion of on-balance-sheet bill assets also rose to 6.58%, a year-on-year increase of 158 basis points. At the end of 2020, the acceptance balance of CMB's bank drafts was 267.2 billion yuan, a year-on-year decrease of 2%, while the discount balance stood at 330.7 billion yuan, a year-on-year increase of 46.3%.

At the end of 2021, the acceptance balance of CMB's bank bills was 345.62 billion yuan, marking a year-on-year increase of 29.36%, while the discount balance was 429.10 billion yuan, a year-on-year increase of 31.03%. In 2021, the volume of direct bill discounting business reached 1,250.78 billion yuan, a year-on-year increase of 6.14%, securing the second position in the market. The volume of the interbank discount buyout business reached 1,248.31 billion yuan, a year-on-year increase of 28.07%, also ranking second in the market. However, the discounting business volume decreased by 8.17% to 177.18 billion yuan. At the end of 2021, the rediscount balance was 65.41 billion yuan, ranking first in the market.

3. China Minsheng Bank Bill Business Department

Since 2000, China Minsheng Bank has specialized in bill business, no longer delegating it to every branch or business outlet. Instead, they established a bill business center in each sub-branch for centralized management.

In October 2003, the bank's bill business attained the ISO9002 quality management system certification.

Starting with the bill business with interest paid by the buyer in 2001, followed by the bill business by agreed interest in 2002, the package buying business in 2003, the agency bill discounting business in 2004, and the enterprise bill management business in 2005, China Minsheng Bank has consistently introduced new products to meet customers' comprehensive needs for risk control and financing. In 2005, the bank launched a bill management system specifically for major clients, transforming itself from a "bill dealer" attracting deposits through bills into a high-end comprehensive bill manager in the competitive field of bill business.

As of November 2005, China Minsheng Bank's bill business recorded a gross profit exceeding 700 million yuan. The total income amounted to 1.48 billion yuan, accounting for 12% of the national market share. The bank developed 5 business models for its 1,900 bill customers. In 2005, the interest spread income doubled, and the business scale was 1.2 times of that in the previous year. Its collaboration with the Midea Group in 2006 marked the beginning of commercial bank involvement in bill pooling business in China. On August 8, 2016, the bank successfully launched CITIC-CMB Yield Right Supporting Program No. 1, the first bank-guaranteed bill asset securitization product.

In 2012, China Minsheng Bank's direct bill discounting business volume reached 1.005692 trillion yuan, with commercial bill discounting business volume reaching 190.8 billion yuan, representing a year-on-year increase of 140.37% and 47.92%, respectively. In the first half of 2013, despite a lower growth rate compared to 2012, the direct bill discounting business volume still reached 700 billion yuan. However, a significant change occurred in the third quarter of 2013 when the bank's interbank assets and liabilities began to decline sharply. The bank initiated new plans for its bill business and started reducing the scale of bills in the second half of 2013.

On October 16, 2020, the China Minsheng Bank Guangzhou Branch successfully handled China's first online supply chain bill discount service. China Minsheng Bank is also one of the first financial institutions in the market to directly connect with the supply chain bill platform system of the Shanghai Commercial Paper Exchange Company Ltd. Corporation. By the end of 2020, the acceptance balance of the bank's bill business was 403.5 billion yuan, a year-on-year decrease of 25.6%, while the discount balance reached 227.9 billion yuan, a year-on-year increase of 37%. By the end of 2021, the discount balance increased to 280.65 billion yuan, 52.796 billion yuan more than that in the previous year, representing an increase of 23.18%.

4. Shanghai Pudong Development Bank Bill Business Department

On December 9, 2005, the Shanghai Pudong Development (SPD) Bank Bill Business Department, as a first-level branch directly under the headquarters, was established in Shanghai with the approval of the PBC. From September to December 2014, the SPD established seven business branches across the nation, in cities such as Beijing, Tianjin, Chongqing, Guangzhou, Xi'an, Zhengzhou, and Shenyang, marking the start of their cross-regional bill business operations.

In late 2013, the Shanghai Municipal Commission of Economy and Information authorized the SPD to establish the Shanghai Small Bill Discount Center to handle small bill discounting business for small and micro businesses. During the first nine months of 2014, the bank's Shanghai Branch saw a 72% year-on-year increase in the discount amount of small bills valued at less than 1 million yuan. The number of bill discount transactions also grew by 135% compared to the previous year. However, as the business volume rapidly grew, the average discount amount for small bills saw slight decrease. Single bills with a par value less than 1 million yuan had an average discount amount of 300,000 yuan, while it was 410,000 yuan during the same period the previous year. These statistics reflect the bank's long-standing commitment and success in serving small and micro businesses, and in contributing to the well-being of the people.

By the end of 2019, the bank's bill discount assets had increased to 415.1 billion yuan, a 66% increase from the previous year. This was the fastest growth rate among the top ten banks. The bank's bill discount balance, recorded on its balance sheet, constituted approximately 10.45% of its credit amount. This was the largest percentage among Chinese banks with assets exceeding 500 billion yuan.

As of the end of 2020, the bank had an acceptance balance of 553.5 billion yuan, which represented a year-on-year increase of 16.9%. The discount balance was 435.9 billion yuan, marking a year-on-year increase of 5.0%. The total annual business volume reached 4.52 trillion yuan, a year-on-year increase of 7.52%, with the interbank discount business volume reaching 3.51 trillion yuan, a year-on-year increase of 16.55%. The repurchase business volume amounted to 1.02 trillion yuan, positioning the bank among the top institutions in the industry.

At the end of 2021, the bank's acceptance balance was 617.735 billion yuan, a year-on-year increase of 11.60%; The discount balance is 487.692 billion yuan, marking a year-on-year increase of 11.88% and accounting for 10.19% of the bank's credit.

5. Industrial Bank Bill Center

In 2018, the Industrial Bank reformed the organizational structure of its bill operation, and established the bill center directly under its headquarters, integrating the management and operation of discount and interbank discount businesses into this center.

In 2019, the Industrial Bank's bill business development indicators ranked top among its peers. The bank handled bill acceptance business exceeding 1 trillion yuan, serving over 20,000 enterprises. It handled bill-pool financing exceeding 100 billion yuan for over 5,000 enterprises, and processed bill discounting business of 570 billion yuan for over 10,000 enterprises. Additionally, the bank undertook the role of secondary market maker, handling various types of businesses totaling 2.4 trillion yuan. It achieved a year-end rediscount balance of 48 billion yuan. In August 2019, the bank launched the "IB e-Ties," an instant discount product, which replaces manual reviews with automatic system reviews. This allows for an entirely online discount process and real-time receipt of discount funds. In 2019, the bank received eight awards from the Shanghai Commercial Paper Exchange Company Ltd., including Excellent Acceptance Institution, Excellent Discount Institution, Excellent Banking Trader, and Excellent Technology Application Institution.

In 2020, the bank's bill business volume reached 5.8 trillion yuan, an increase of 270% compared to that in 2017, the year before the bill center was established. The spread income accounted for over 50% of the net operating income of its bill business.

At the end of 2021, the bank bill acceptance balance was 835.418 billion yuan, marking a year-on-year increase of 1.59%. The discount balance reached 324.356 billion yuan, a significant year-on-year increase of 56.16%. In 2021, the Industrial Bank's average bill discount yield rate was 2.64%, a decrease of 16 basis points from 2020, and slightly lower than the 2021 market-wide discount weighted average interest rate of 2.85%.

6. BOCOM Bill Center

In 2013, BOCOM underwent a business department reform, leading to the official establishment of the Bill Business Center. From the bill discounting business, the bank accrued an interest income of 3.741 billion yuan. On July 13, 2017, BOCOM Guangdong Branch officially set up the "Small Bill Discount Center."

By the end of 2019, BOCOM had used commercial acceptance bills to assist over 6,000 enterprises, primarily inclusive customers, in activating more than 25,200 accounts receivable, totaling approximately 40 billion yuan. On November 13, 2019, the Commercial Paper Summit Forum themed Pooling Wisdom for Financing and Coexisting in Harmony was held in Nanjing, attracting over 100 representatives from consumers like Yueda Group, HBIS Group, XCMG Group, and Zhejiang Juhua Group. They witnessed the official launch of the "Yuntong Bill Manager," a one-stop bill service platform developed by BOCOM. In 2020, the bank handled close to 900 billion yuan in bill acceptance and discount, serving nearly 30,000 enterprises.

BOCOM is one of the first institutions in the market to specialize in repurchase business. In recent years, it has stepped up its efforts to expand this business. As of October 2021, the volume of bill repurchase business was close to 1 trillion yuan, a 25-fold increase from 2016, serving the diverse bill financing needs of interbank customers. By the end of 2021, the bank's discount balance was 136.722 billion yuan, a decrease of 23.349 billion yuan or 14.59% compared with the year-end balance in the previous year. The bill repurchase trading volume stood at 13.512 billion yuan, a year-on-year increase of 268%, while the income from bill discounting business was 4.481 billion yuan, a year-on-year decrease of 18.27%.

SECTION 5

Bill Intermediaries: Exploration by Private Bill Institutions

The bill market consists of two sectors: the official bill market represented by banks and the private bill market represented by bill intermediaries. Institutions like Shanghai Purang Financial Services (SPFS) have notably contributed to the growth of the Chinese bill market as part of the private sector.

I. Introduction to SPFS

SPFS, originally known as Shanghai Purang Investment Co., Ltd., was established in 2002. Over the past two decades, it has played a significant role in driving the extremely rapid development of the Chinese bill market. It is a primary creator of China's private bill market and continues to exert a substantial influence, providing positive guidance on the mainstream business model of the private bill market. After many years of development, SPFS Co., Ltd. was established in May 2012. It was approved by the Shanghai Municipal Government and the Pudong New Area Government due to its standardization and professionalism. It has become China's first innovative financial services company with the business scope of "bill intermediaries."

SPFS currently employs over a thousand individuals, with 35 branches across the country, serving more than 80,000 enterprises and over 5,000 commercial banks and other financial institutions. In the transfer discount intermediary market, it can achieve a daily business volume of over ten billion yuan at its peak. The company's operations extend beyond its initial bill business. It now offers market participants a wide range of financial services, including matchmaking, consulting, data, software, and knowledge process outsourcing. These services cover trading varieties such as bills, bonds, funds, interbank business, and technology, with ongoing efforts to expand into foreign exchange, derivatives, and other fields.[35]

II. Transformation of SPFS

1. Standardized Services

The direct involvement of bill intermediaries in transactions had not been acknowledged by relevant parties. This was primarily due to the legal ambiguities involved and the need for further legal clarification of many actions. Moreover, private bill intermediaries often engaged in transactions seeking short-term, high profits, relying on aggressive trading methods and lacking risk resistance capabilities. This direct involvement could easily lead to financial risks, harm the economic interests of parties involved, and impede the standardized development of the bill market. Initially, SPFS also briefly dabbled in bill trading. However, the company officials quickly recognized that while this model could deliver significant short-term profits, it was not sustainable for long-term operation. To ensure consistent stability, the company needed to undergo transformation and adopt a business model that complied with legal and regulatory requirements. Considering the market situation, SPFS quickly decided on the model of bill trading matching. They successfully obtained the bill intermediary operating license in 2012, becoming China's first innovative financial service company to do so. Following this standardized transformation, and due to the booming bill market and the correct choice of business model, the company's bill trading brokerage volume has grown rapidly. Their matching model has become an industry benchmark and a leading example for the transformation of private bill intermediaries.

2. Diversified Services

Diversifying enterprise services helps tap into the enterprise's full potential, optimize resource allocation, form economies of scope, minimize operational risks, and ultimately improve the enterprise's core competitiveness. Transformation toward diversified services can be seen as a necessary path for enterprises to grow in scale and strength. This was the case for SPFS. In 2012, the company embarked on this path of transformation.

SPFS, in addition to its bill brokerage business, has applied its practical experience to other fields of the money market. The company has expanded to include various financial product brokerage businesses such as bonds, funds, certificates of deposit, assets, and deposits. This was made possible by releasing timely transaction information on trading platforms and carrying out efficient matching. As a result, the company was gradually transitioning into a currency brokerage company. With the bill market becoming increasingly competitive and the spread between direct and transfer discounts continuing to shrink, more specialized operations were required and the demand for third-party professional services was also growing. Consequently, SPFS has expanded to offer currency market consulting, data, technology, training, and other services. In terms of consulting, the company offers integrated solutions for policy analysis, risk assessment, strategy recommendations, and currency market business operations in various financial markets through specialized institutions such as research institutes, bill advisory departments, bond advisory departments, and investment camps.

3. The Third Transformation Under New Market Landscapes

In 2009, the PBC led the launching of the ECDS, marking a significant milestone in the digitization process of China's financial industry. Since then, electronic bills have emerged as a new trading variety in the bill market. In August 2016, the PBC issued *A Notice on Regulating and Promoting the Development of Electronic Commercial Bill Business* (No. 224 [2016] of the PBC). This further boosted the widespread use of electronic bills through official regulations. As a result, the Chinese bill market has now fully transitioned to electronic processing.

In the era of electronic bills and the growing field of rural finance, SPFS has actively adapted to market changes. It has implemented the "Internet Plus" model and transformed itself into a "service provider for banks serving agriculture, rural areas, and farmers." Under the "Internet Plus" transformation, the company launched the "Financial Village" electronic brokerage platform in 2015, shifting its previous off-line matchmaking service to online. Online matchmaking is more efficient and has a simpler procedure than the off-line model. Customers can directly contact their counterparties through the platform, reducing the risk of arbitrage by brokers. In the transformation toward service provider for banks serving "agriculture, rural areas, and farmers," SPFS launched the "Bright Sunny Skies" service platform in November 2017. This platform is a green ecological platform integrating county economy, finance, and culture under the "Internet Plus" model. It is a processing banking system that integrates planning, risk control, marketing, operation, and assessment, aiming to serve the development of rural banks and foster the growth of county economy.

III. Problems

1. Lack of Unified Institutional Norms

The bill intermediary industry lacks clearly defined entry barriers. Currently, there are no unified entry standards, business processes, or regulatory systems in place. This results in varying skill levels among bill intermediary agencies and uneven personnel quality. Many individuals joined the industry with the intention of making fast money, often disregarding legal norms, moral constraints, and lacking risk awareness. These problems resulted in numerous risk events, impeding the standardized development of the bill market.

2. Lack of Internal and External Supervision

First, some bill intermediaries have ulterior motives, seeking to arbitrage through exploiting loopholes in the banks' internal control systems. Second, financial institutions collaborating with these intermediaries are typically small and medium-sized banks, such as local commercial banks and rural credit cooperatives. These institutions might not have robust internal control mechanisms and could possess inadequate risk control capabilities. Third, some bill intermediaries might exploit institutional loopholes in bank interbank discounting to trade the same bill multiple times. If they use the excess discount funds for investment and incur losses, they may not be able to repurchase the bills when due. This could lead to significant financial losses for the related financial institutions. Fourth, there are no clear regulations or self-discipline organizations for private bill intermediary institutions. Their bill trading behavior is largely self-controlled. Without the constraints of regulatory departments, any behavioral deviations may not be regulated and corrected in a timely and effective manner. Over time, this could lead to industry chaos and frequent risk events.

3. Lack of Legal Support

Many actions taken by bill intermediaries are currently in a legal gray zone and need more legal clarification. To comply with Article 10 of *The Negotiable Instrument Law of the PRC*, which requires true background of transactions, bill intermediaries often register shell companies, fabricate trade relationships, and forge value-added tax invoices. They then transfer the endorsement of bills from enterprises to these shell companies before banks discount these bills, which poses significant risks. Additionally, bill intermediaries have been known to manipulate smaller financial institutions, such as rural credit cooperatives, to engage in interbank discounting for profit. They are also suspected of overselling a single bill during the interbank discounting process. Both practices may violate regulations and pose major risks to the smooth operation of the financial system.[36]

SECTION 6

China Bill Network: First Official Bill Quotation Internet Platform

Before the launch of China Bill Network, the bill market was fragmented and lacked access to information. The introduction of network significantly reduced the issue of information asymmetry in the market, making it a key infrastructure in the Chinese bill market.

I. Introduction

China Bill Network was a specialized website launched with the approval of the PBC. It was managed by the China Foreign Exchange Trading Center and the National Interbank Funding Center, providing trading quotes, information queries, and regulatory services for the bill market. The platform employed a membership system, offering features such as an open quotation platform, historical quotation data query, policy and regulation check, bill loss information sharing, and member market research and exchange. The website was officially launched on June 30, 2003. As of May 2017, the China Bill Network had 2,890 member institutions. That month, 184 financial institutions published bill interbank discounting quotes, totaling 1,025 quotations, a month-on-month increase of 6.22%. The accumulated amount was 372.24 billion yuan, a decrease of 3.17% from the previous month. As the China Bill Network was managed by the China Foreign Exchange Trading Center and the National Interbank Funding Center, its members were exclusively banking and financial institutions. The network served various regions and the vast majority of banking and financial institutions across the country, making it highly representative and credible in the market.[37]

II. Significance

1. Improving Market Efficiency

In the past, specialized bill institutions could only exchange and request bill information through methods such as phone calls, faxes, and physical document transfer. This resulted in limited information access, time-consuming processes, and low efficiency. Now, all network members could directly obtain and send information online, enabling them to choose suitable trading partners, bill types, and trading methods. By doing so, financial institutions had broadened their business scopes, achieved information resource sharing, reduced operating costs, and resolved the long-standing issues of fragmentation and information scarcity in the bill market. As an official platform, China Bill Network had received widespread market recognition, effectively bringing the era of fragmented bill market to an end.

2. Preventing Market Risks

Information asymmetry poses a significant threat to the security of the bill market, especially in bill interbank discount businesses where financial institutions have difficulty verifying their counterparts' credibility. With the introduction of the bill market service platform, prospective network members must provide genuine and reliable documents such as a business license, a financial institution business certificate, and a bill business authorization letter. An applicant could only become a member after these documents are verified and certified. This process bolstered the credibility and transparency of trading partners, thus serving as a "firewall" for the bill market.

3. Accelerating Bill Interest Rates Marketization

The bill interest rate is a sensitive indicator of market fund supply and demand, as well as business creditworthiness. It reflects the varying relationships and changes in the money market. The launch of the China Bill Network established a comprehensive price index system for the bill market, with regular publication and analysis of interest rate trends. This guided commercial banks in business operations and provided the central bank with signals and a basis for macroeconomic regulation. As a result, the bill interest rate had become a key factor in short-term interest rate marketization and had positively influenced China's interest rate marketization reform.

4. Improving Market Efficiency and Regulatory Measures

The launch of the China Bill Network improved the technological content of market operation methods. This change had completely transformed the manual operations of acceptance, transfer, discount, interbank discount, and rediscount in China's bill business, helping to prevent fraudulent activities such as forgery and alteration of paper bills. The information and statistics analysis capabilities of the China Bill Network allowed management to conduct real-time analysis and monitoring of bill sources and flows, fund utilization, and risk levels.[38]

5. Sending an Important Signal: The PBC Attaches Great Importance to the Bill Market

The bill market, a significant subdivision of the money market, plays a role in transmitting the monetary policy of the PBC. The rediscount rate, one of the three key monetary policy tools, is specifically designed for bills. The China Bill Network, approved by the PBC, sent a signal that could instill confidence in the bill market, reflecting the PBC's attention and support for this market.

III. Closure

1. Flaws in the Network

The China Bill Network, while rich in information, lacked key features. It did not offer negotiation, matchmaking, or integration with the PBC's credit reporting, clearing, and electronic bill systems. It also lacked commercial banks' payment and transaction functions, resulting in some incompleteness. The network, primarily composed of banking members, didn't include quotation information from new market participants such as funds, securities, and financial companies. Moreover, it lacked market research and forecasting information. These limitations impeded comprehensive research on the bill market's overall status and price trends. Due to these shortcomings, users could only gather minimal information from the platform, which hindered data integration and led to fragmented information throughout the process.[39]

2. Historical Tasks Accomplished

On June 20, 2017, China Bill Network announced that it would cease operations on June 30, 2017, marking the end of its 14-year run. While the specific reasons for its discontinuation were not disclosed, it's believed to have fulfilled its purpose, giving way to the Shanghai Commercial Paper Exchange Company Ltd. and electronic commercial draft. In 2016, several major cases shook the bill market, prompting efforts to develop electronic commercial draft as a key risk prevention measure. In August 2016, the PBC issued *A Notice on Regulating and Promoting the Development of Electronic Commercial Draft Business*, setting the course for digitization in the bill industry. The Shanghai Commercial Paper Exchange Company Ltd., a nationwide unified bill trading platform, was established in accordance with the State Council's decisions and arrangements, led by the PBC. It began operations on December 8, 2016. The platform offers various services, including bill trading, registration and custody, clearing and settlement, and information services. Its online presence paved the way for the development of electronic commercial draft, marking the beginning of the bill exchange era.

Summary

Resolving the "chain debt" issue and fostering the growth of commercial credit were key factors in the resurgence of bills. The practice of substituting bill acceptance for creditor-debtor relationships and the securitization of commercial credit spurred the development of bill acceptance business. Therefore, the origin of bills lies in credit development, and their primary function is also credit-based. As the commodity economy rapidly expanded, the volume of payments and settlements increased, making sole reliance on cash impractical. Consequently, bills played an increasingly vital role in payments and settlements. As the bill market evolved, commercial bills gained prominence. Enterprises no longer depended solely on bank bills, thus enabling new financing methods through their own credit and capital. This made the financing function of bills more evident. The introduction of *Interim Measures for the Administration of Acceptance, Discount, and Rediscount of Commercial Bills* further reinforced the role of rediscount as a monetary policy tool, allowing bills to play a more significant regulatory role.

The importance of bills in economic development is demonstrated in several ways. First, they effectively address the "chain debt" issue during periods of economic transition. Second, bills strongly support the growth of the real economy and the reform and opening up process, with their supportive role steadily increasing. Last, bills serve as a useful tool for improving business operations, with bill financing emerging as a significant short-term financing channel.

Bills also play multiple roles in driving financial development. Rediscount has become a crucial regulatory tool for the central bank, acting as a lender of last resort and offering rediscount support for specific regions or industries. In addition, due to their low risk and high liquidity, bills have become highly favored by China's commercial banks, significantly enhancing the asset quality of these banks.

NOTES

1. Wang Hanqiang, *Commercial Credit and Commercial Bills of Exchange* (Beijing: China Finance and Economics Publishing House, 1986).
2. Yao Sui, *A History of Chinese Finance* (Beijing: Higher Education Press, 2007), 453.
3. Joint Institute for Commercial Paper of JUFE and BOJJ, *A History of Bills* (Beijing: China Financial Publishing House, 2020).
4. Yao Sui, *A History of Chinese Finance* (Beijing: Higher Education Press, 2007), 453.
5. Fan Xiaozhong, "The Investigation and Inspiration of Resolving 'Chain Debt' Issue in the Early 1990s," *Journal of Hubei University of Economics*, no. 11 (2019): 29–31.
6. Wang Hanqiang, *Commercial Credit and Commercial Bills of Exchange* (Beijing: China Finance and Economics Publishing House, 1986), 3.
7. Zhao Xuejun, *The Evolution of Commercial Credit in China* (Beijing: Fangzhi Publishing House, 2008), 179.

8. Wang Hanqiang, *Commercial Credit and Commercial Bills of Exchange* (Beijing: China Finance and Economics Publishing House, 1986), 3.
9. Joint Institute for Commercial Paper of JUFE and BOJJ, *A History of Bills* (Beijing: China Financial Publishing House, 2020).
10. Zhang Yingxue, Xiao Yun, and Jia Yongshen, "It Is Necessary to Promote the Method of Bill Settlement," *Economic Work Communication*, no. 6 (1992): 13–15.
11. Wang Xiaoneng, *A Textbook on Negotiable Instrument Law* (Beijing: Peking University Press, 2001), 7.
12. Luo Yong, "Know, Understand, and Abide by the Law to Ensure Effective Implementation of the 'Two Laws,'" *Finance and Economics*, no. 6 (1995): 9, 18.
13. Du Deqing, "The Negotiable Instrument: Law-Legal Protection for Promoting the Development of Bills," *China Industry and Commerce*, no. 7 (1995): 42–43.
14. Zuo Zhifang, Wang Chengtao, and Zhong Jun, "Revision of the Bill Law: Logic and Suggestions," *Financial Horizons*, no. 11 (2015): 92–98.
15. Joint Institute for Commercial Paper of JUFE and BOJJ, *A History of Bills* (Beijing: China Financial Publishing House, 2020).
16. People's Bank of China, and Industrial and Commercial Bank of China Liaoning Branch, "Several Practices for Organizing the Acceptance and Discounting of Commercial Bills," *China Finance*, no. 5 (1987): 38–39.
17. Que Fangping, *The Institutional Evolution in China's Bill Market* (Beijing: China Financial Publishing House, 2005).
18. "Rediscount Business," in *China Financial Yearbook (1995)*, ed. Editorial Department of China Financial Yearbook (Beijing: China Printing Corporation, 1996), 34.
19. Li Yang, *Six Decades of Finance in New China* (Beijing: China Finance and Economics Publishing House, 2009).
20. Joint Institute for Commercial Paper of JUFE and BOJJ, *A History of Bills* (Beijing: China Financial Publishing House, 2020).
21. Lin Yuli, "Establish a Modern Electronic Service System for the Bill Market," *China Finance*, no. 18 (2003): 19.
22. Jing Hailong, "Empirical Analysis of the Effect of Interest Rate Policy Regulation in Qinghai Province in 2009," *Qinghai Finance*, no. 8 (2010): 14.
23. Yu Xuepeng, "Research on the Concentrated and Differentiated Competitive Strategy of Industrial Bank's Bill Business" (Master's thesis, Fudan University, 2009).
24. Wang Hanqiang, *Commercial Credit and Commercial Bills of Exchange* (Beijing: China Finance and Economics Publishing House, 1986).
25. Joint Institute for Commercial Paper of JUFE and BOJJ, *A History of Bills* (Beijing: China Financial Publishing House, 2020).
26. Wang Guitang and Li Yinghui, "The Development Orientation of China's Bill Market: Insights from a Financial Institution's Perspective," *Financial Theory and Practice*, no. 5 (2000): 11–15.
27. Shu Xiong, "The Current State, Limiting Factors, and Future Development of China's Electronic Bill Market," *Guangxi Financial Research*, no. 6 (2008): 37.
28. Yu Xuepeng, "Research on the Concentrated and Differentiated Competitive Strategy of Industrial Bank's Bill Business" (Master's thesis, Fudan University, 2009).
29. Lu Baojiang, "On Bill-Related Risks and Prevention," *Research on Rural Finance in Guangxi (Semi-Monthly)*, no. 3 (2001): 63.
30. Industrial and Commercial Bank of China Bill Business Department and Financial Market Management Department of the Shanghai Headquarters of the People's Bank of China, *Report on the Development of China's Bill Market (2008)* (Beijing: China Financial Publishing House, 2009), 109.
31. Zhang Lizhou, *The Revolution of Negotiable Instruments* (Beijing: CITIC Publishing Group, 2019).
32. Please refer to the official website of ICBC for details.
33. Ibid.

34. Industrial and Commercial Bank of China Bill Business Department and Financial Market Management Department of the Shanghai Headquarters of the People's Bank of China, *Report on the Development of China's Bill Market (2008)* (Beijing: China Financial Publishing House, 2009), 113.
35. Please refer to the official website of SPFS.
36. Xiao Xiaohe, "Standardizing Bill Brokerage Behavior to Promote Bill Market Development," *Shanghai Securities Journal*, November 25, 2016 (009).
37. Industrial and Commercial Bank of China Limited Bill Business Department and Financial Market Management Department of the Shanghai Headquarters of the People's Bank of China, *Report on the Development of China's Bill Market in the New Century (2000–2011)* (Beijing: China Financial Publishing House, 2013), 5.
38. Li Jun, "Steadily Building a Unified Chinese Bill Market," *China Money Market*, no. 9 (2003): 46–47.
39. Xiao Xiaohe and Yu Bei, "Accelerate the establishment of a nationwide unified and standardized bill information platform," *Shanghai Securities Journal*, April 11, 2015 (006).

CHAPTER SEVEN

Bills from Electronic Notes to the Establishment of the Shanghai Commercial Paper Exchange Company Ltd.

The development of the bill market is intricately linked to the economic and financial landscapes. From 2009 to 2015, influenced by factors such as the international financial crisis and China's economic transformation, China's monetary policy became both relaxed and prudent, creating a relatively favorable financial environment. As a result, bill acceptance and discount businesses flourished during this period. This era saw unprecedented prosperity for paper bills, marking their final golden period. However, significant risks and drawbacks lurked in the paper commercial draft business process. Issues such as forgery and alteration of bills, violation of bill business regulations, unreasonable refusal to honor accepted bills, disruption of normal bill circulation, and collusion to defraud bank funds were prevalent. These issues obstructed the formation of a unified national bill market and hindered the healthy development of the bill business. Market participants needed a safer and more efficient medium for bill circulation, which led to the initial exploration of electronic bills. With the continuous electronification of China's financial industry and improvements in financial infrastructure, the national check image clearing system was established in 2007, realizing partial electronification of paper check processing. On October 28, 2009, the ECDS, built and managed by the PBC, was completed and officially launched.

On October 16, 2009, the PBC issued the *Measures for the Administration of Electronic Commercial Draft Business*, marking 2009 as the beginning of electronic commercial draft in China. These bills have significantly impacted the development of enterprises, commercial banks, the central bank, and the bill market. Compared to paper commercial drafts, electronic ones improve safety, efficiency, and risk control, facilitate transactions, and promote innovative business development. However, in the early years, electronic commercial draft saw relatively slow development. It wasn't until 2016, amid market chaos and frequent major bill cases, that the PBC started to promote electronic bills more vigorously. Commercial banks also started preferring electronic bills to maintain stable operations, which provided a significant boost to the development of electronic bills. Simultaneously, the bill market entered a period of prosperity in the broader macroeconomic context. In 2009, the cumulative bill acceptance volume exceeded 10 trillion yuan, and the cumulative discount volume expanded to over 20 trillion yuan. The bill market has experienced rapid growth ever since.

Over the past decade, as the bill market rapidly grew in an environment driven by excessive pursuit of idle arbitrage, risks also accumulated quickly. Market issues, such as overselling the same bill and exchanging counterfeit bills for genuine ones, have started to arise. Some bank employees and intermediaries even colluded to embezzle large bill assets. In 2016, major risk events occurred frequently in the bill market, such as N Bank's 3.9-billion-yuan bill case, X Bank's 1-billion-yuan bill case, T Bank's 7.8-billion-yuan bill case, a certain bank's 500-million-yuan cross-regional interbank investment fraud case in Anhui Province, the 400-million-yuan bill fraud case in Fushun, Liaoning Province, and J Bank's 1.3-billion-yuan electronic bill fraud case. These events seriously disrupted the stability of the financial market. As a result, regulatory departments took decisive action to rectify the chaos. In April 2016, the PBC and the China Banking Regulatory Commission jointly issued *A Notice on Strengthening the Supervision of Bill Business to Promote the Healthy Development of the Bill Market*. A few months later, the China Banking Regulatory Commission released several policy documents on financial market governance, including *A Notice of the General Office of the China Banking Regulatory Commission on Carrying Out Special Governance Work for "Illegal, Non-Compliant, and Irregular" Behaviors in the Banking Industry*, *A Notice of the General Office of the China Banking Regulatory Commission on Carrying Out Special Governance Work for "Regulatory Arbitrage, Idle Arbitrage, and Related Arbitrage" in the Banking Industry*, and *A Notice of the General Office of the China Banking Regulatory Commission on Carrying Out Special Governance Work for Improper Innovation, Trading, Incentives, and Fees in the Banking Industry*. These policy documents imposed unprecedented regulatory pressure on the bill market, leading it into a period of stagnation.

SECTION I

Coexistence of Paper and Electronic Bills: Final Golden Period of Paper Bills

Since the 21st century, the development of the bill market has been closely tied to China's economic landscape, becoming a significant part of the money and broader financial market. The advent and evolution of electronic bills have led to a rapid expansion of the bill market, continuously enlarging its scale.

I. China's Economic and Financial Landscapes

In 2009, following the decisions and deployments of the Central Committee of the CPC and the State Council, China adopted a moderately loose monetary policy, providing strong financial support to counter the downward trend in economic growth. As a result, the financial environment became more relaxed, leading to a rapid growth in the money supply.

In 2010, the global economy was in a state of recovery, but the European sovereign debt crisis brought additional uncertainty. Amid the complex domestic and international economic environment, China continued its comprehensive crisis management plan, maintaining a relatively relaxed financial market environment. However, the PBC strengthened liquidity management and raised the deposit-reserve ratio six times that year. With the notable improvements in the flexibility and relevance of China's monetary policy, the financial market underwent substantial fluctuations, resulting in a step-like increase in the bill market's interest rates.

Starting from 2011, China's monetary policy became increasingly prudent. However, the structure of the supply stock underwent significant changes, with the proportion of credit products steadily increasing. Medium-term bills showed the largest increase in scale. To improve the sustainability of direct debt financing for SMEs, collective bills were first issued under the regional optimization model. In 2012, China made significant progress in interest rate marketization. The PBC allowed financial institutions to adjust their deposit and lending interest rates. This granted them more freedom in pricing and encouraged rapid improvement in their pricing mechanisms.

In 2013, the financial market strengthened its core role in supporting the real economy, with a significant increase in the number of financial bonds issued by commercial banks for small and micro enterprises. By 2014, the banking system maintained reasonable and moderate liquidity, experienced rapid growth in overall credit volume, optimized loan structures, and saw a slowdown in the growth rate of total currency volume. From 2009 to 2015, the proportion of direct financing in China increased significantly, effectively meeting the financing needs of enterprises.

II. Great Development of Paper Bills

From 2009 to 2016, the bill market emerged as a significant player in the money market, offering a convenient financing channel for the real economy. Bills can inject working capital into enterprises through direct discounts and provide additional financing through interbank discounting. These bills serve as a bridge between the money market and the real economy, playing a regulatory role in the operation and management of commercial banks. They have also become a tool to strengthen macroeconomic regulation and increase the effectiveness of monetary policy.

In terms of bill transactions, the cumulative volume of bills issued by financial institutions nationwide increased from 23.2 trillion yuan in 2009 to 102.1 trillion yuan in 2016. Meanwhile, the cumulative bill discount volumes issued by these institutions rose from 8.49 trillion yuan in 2009 to 84.5 trillion yuan in 2016. The bill acceptance balance of financial institutions nationwide increased from 2.21 trillion yuan at the end of 2009 to 9 trillion yuan at the end of 2016. However, the discount balance fluctuated due to credit scale regulation, ending with an increase to 5.5 trillion yuan at the end of 2016. At the same time, the proportion of bill discount volume to GDP increased from 29.55% in 2009 to 34.34% in 2014. It decreased slightly in 2015, and dropped to 24.25% in 2016. The proportion of bill discount volume to GDP increased from 66.57% in 2009 to 113.21% in 2016, indicating a constant expansion of bill scale in the money market. The proportion of bill issuance volume to the financial loan balance increased from 25.77% in 2009 to 28.24% in 2013, before gradually decreasing to 16.98% in 2016. The proportion of bill discount volume to the financial loan balance fluctuated between 2009 and 2012, and then increased from 63.56% in 2013 to 79.27% in 2016.

Table 7-1 Overview of national bill business development (2009-2016)

Year	Proportion of bill issuance volume to GDP (%)	Proportion of bill discount volume to GDP (%)	Proportion of bill issuance volume to loan balance (%)	Proportion of bill discount volume to loan balance (%)
2009	29.55	66.57	25.77	58.05
2010	29.60	63.09	25.46	54.26
2011	30.95	51.24	27.56	45.62
2012	33.24	58.67	28.42	50.17
2013	34.23	77.07	28.24	63.56
2014	34.34	94.32	27.06	74.32
2015	32.52	148.22	23.84	108.67
2016	24.25	113.21	16.98	79.27

Source: Compiled based on data from the official website of the PBC.

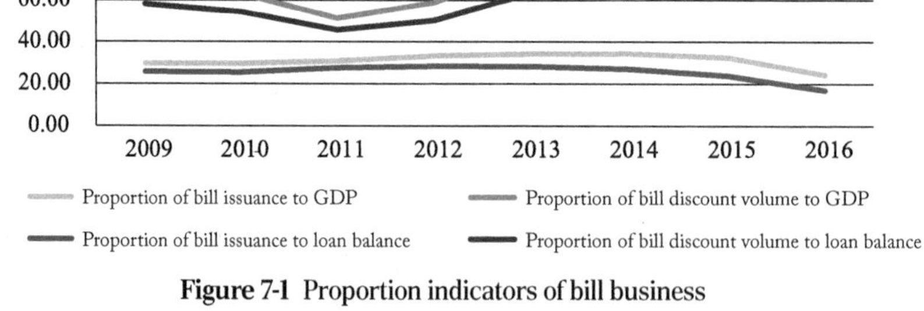

Figure 7-1 Proportion indicators of bill business

While the paper bill business volume continued to grow, this growth rate began to slow down and its share in all commercial bill business was decreasing due to economic growth and rising popularity of electronic bills. In 2010, paper bills accounted for 97.7% of all acceptance bill, totaling 11.9 trillion yuan, representing 28.9% of the GDP. The cumulative discount volume of paper bills was 25.8 trillion yuan, accounting for 99.2% of all bill discounts and 62.6% of the GDP. Over the next four years, bill discount and acceptance volume continued to increase. By 2014, the acceptance volume of paper bills peaked at 19 trillion yuan, accounting for 29.6% of the GDP, marking a year-on-year increase of 0.8%. Despite this, the annual growth rate sharply dropped from 22% in 2011 to 1.9% in 2014. The proportion of paper bills in all bill transactions decreased from 97.7% in 2010 to 86.1% in 2017. The discount volume of paper bills reached 54.4 trillion yuan, 1.2 times the amount in 2010, representing 89.6% of the market share, a decrease of 9.6 percentage points since 2010. Its proportion to GDP was 84.5%, an increase of 11.9 percentage points compared to 2010. In 2016, factors such as economic downturn, rising corporate credit risk, and stricter regulation led to frequent paper bill risk cases, causing a sharp decline in the acceptance and discount volume of paper bills. The annual acceptance volume of paper bills fell by 42.7% from the previous year to 9.5 trillion yuan, and the discount volume decreased by 61.2% to 29.5 trillion yuan. The acceptance and discount volume accounted for 52.6% and 42.9% of the market share respectively, a decrease of 45.1 percentage points and 64.3 percentage points compared to 2010. Their proportion to GDP was 12.8% and 39.6%, a year-on-year decrease of 11.3 percentage points and 70.9 percentage points, respectively.

Table 7-2 Overview of the development of paper bill business (2010–2016) (unit: 100 million yuan)

Year	Acceptance amount	Year-on-Year increase (%)	Market share (%)	Proportion to GDP (%)	Discount volume	Year-on-Year increase (%)	Market share (%)	Proportion to GDP (%)
2010	119,226		97.7	28.9	257,845		99.2	62.6
2011	145,512	22	96.4	29.8	246,133	-4.5	98.5	50.4
2012	169,272	16.3	94.6	31.4	305,998	24.3	96.7	56.8
2013	186,702	10.3	92	31.5	430,936	40.8	94.3	72.7
2014	190,280	1.9	86.1	29.6	543,926	26.2	89.6	84.5
2015	166,127	-12.7	74.2	24.1	761,377	40.0	74.7	110.5
2016	95,200	-42.7	52.6	12.8	295,300	-61.2	34.9	39.6

Source: Compiled based on data from the official website of the PBC.

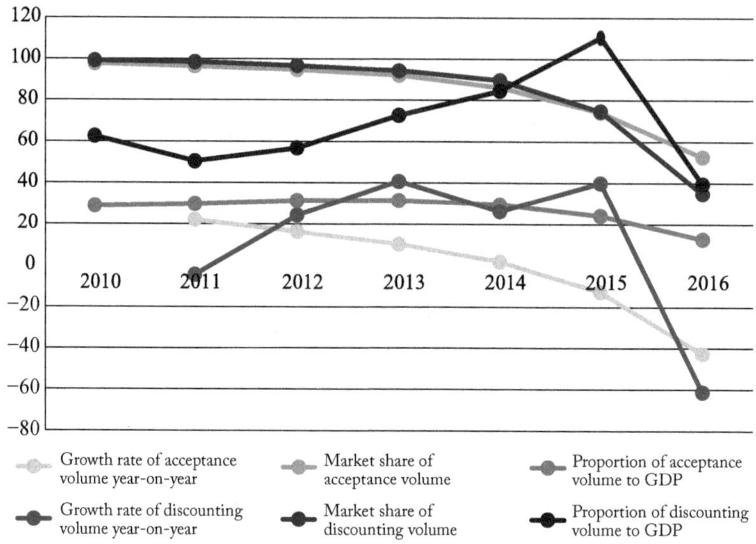

Figure 7-2 Growth rate and proportion indicators of paper bill business

Paper bill operations carried numerous risks, with security issues becoming increasingly prominent as the bill market developed. Many banks perceived interbank bill businesses such as interbank discounting as "low risk," assuming that the risks were absorbed by the accepting bank, which often led to lax management. Banks employed various methods such as drawer protocols, proxy holding, and asset management transfers to divert funds, inflate the deposit and loan scale, and reduce capital possession. For instance, they used bill interbank discounting services to reduce credit scale and capital possession. Commercial banks often converted the credit business into a fund management business for arbitrage, a method known as "bill proxy holding."

Repurchase and buyout were common practices in bill discounting businesses among financial institutions. The payee, due to their business needs, first signed a repurchase agreement with the seller and then a buyout agreement upon the expiration of the repurchase. This buyout and resale business dual-listed credit assets. In the transfer discount of bank bills, violations such as "one bill with two mortgages" and list forging were prevalent, with the first scenario also common in purchase and resale businesses, as well as bill proxy holding businesses. During the custody process of proxy holding, there were incidents where safe-stored bills were replaced with newspapers and then given to an intermediary for discount. Some rural and local financial institutions may even transfer discount the bills they held on behalf of others, forge lists, and use the funds for other purposes. From 2014 to 2015, the non-standard business of most urban commercial banks, including bill purchase and resale, grew rapidly.

In early 2016, several financial institutions experienced bill risk incidents, resulting in significant financial losses. This accelerated the development of electronic commercial draft as a key measure against bill risks. In August 2016, the PBC issued *A Notice on Regulating and Promoting the Development of Electronic Commercial Draft Business*, encouraging the use of electronic bills. The Shanghai Commercial Paper Exchange Company Ltd.'s online operation expedited the transition from paper bills to electronic bills. On December 8, 2016, the Shanghai Commercial Paper Exchange Company Ltd., a unified national bill trading platform, was officially launched. As the bill market's infrastructure, the platform handles the registration, custody, quotation, trading, clearing, and collection of all paper and electronic bills. Through the ECDS, information related to issuance, acceptance, pledge, guarantee, and discount of electronic commercial draft can be transmitted real-time to the Shanghai Commercial Paper Exchange Company Ltd. trading system, which significantly improves bill circulation efficiency. However, paper bills must be converted into electronic form before they can be included in the Shanghai Commercial Paper Exchange Company Ltd. In its initial phase, the Shanghai Commercial Paper Exchange Company Ltd. primarily focused on paper bills, resulting in inactive trading. But with the launch of its second phase, the benefits of electronic commercial draft over paper bills became more apparent. It's expected that electronic commercial draft will become the standard method for bill trading.

III. Preliminary Exploration of Electronic Bills

From 2009 to 2015, influenced by the international financial crisis and China's economic transformation, China's monetary policy eased before shifting to a more prudent approach. This led to abundant liquidity in the financial market, sparking an unprecedented boom in the bill market. Consequently, acceptance and discount businesses underwent a period of rapid growth.

Commercial bills, as financial tools with payment, settlement, and short-term financing functions, are essential in satisfying enterprises' payment needs, broadening financing avenues, and decreasing financial expenses. They also play a crucial role in improving commercial banks' payment service quality, bolstering asset liability management, and diversifying the central bank's monetary policy tools. However, paper commercial draft presented substantial risks and drawbacks, including forgery and alteration of bills, non-compliant handling of bill transactions, unreasonable refusal to honor accepted bills, and disruption of normal bill circulation. Fraudulent activities involving collusion could also lead to the misappropriation of bank funds, resulting in frequent incidents that hindered the formation of a unified national bill market. These problems impeded the healthy growth of the bill business, leading market participants to advocate for safer and more efficient bill circulation mechanisms.

The progress in financial electronification provided technical support for the electronic transformation of commercial bills. As China's financial electronification level and infrastructure continued to improve, bank services related to bills like bank bills of exchange, promissory notes, and checks had been partially electronic, significantly enhancing security and efficiency. In 2007, the National Check Image Clearing System was established, allowing for partial electronic processing of paper checks. In 2008, the bank promissory note and bills of exchange transactions in East China's three provinces and one city were handled through a micro payment system, achieving electronic processing. Despite these advancements, the electronification of commercial bills had been slower. The ongoing processing methods were mostly traditional, manual, and paper-based, resulting in low efficiency and high risk. However, starting from 2005, China's commercial banks, such as CMB, China Minsheng Bank, and CITIC Bank, began to explore the use of electronic bills. Their experiences provided valuable practical insights. Moreover, numerous experts and scholars conducted extensive research on electronic bills, yielding significant findings. The introduction and enforcement of the *Electronic Signature Law of the PRC* (hereafter referred to as *Electronic Signature Law*) also offered crucial legal safeguards for the progress of electronic bills. All these factors provided the PBC with the necessary theoretical, legal, technical support, and practical experience to establish the ECDS.

SECTION 2

Electronic Commercial Draft: Innovation in the Bill Market

On October 16, 2009, the PBC issued the *Measures for the Administration of Electronic Commercial Draft Business*. Later that year, on October 28, the ECDS, developed and managed by the PBC, was completed and officially launched, marking 2009 as the beginning of electronic commercial draft in China. The establishment and operation of the ECDS is a significant milestone in the electronic transition of the bill market. Compared to their paper counterparts, electronic commercial drafts offer improved security, efficiency, and risk management.

I. System Construction

In light of the domestic economic circumstances and the evolution of the bill market at the time, the PBC decided to establish the ECDS in January 2008. This decision followed a thorough investigation, research, and ample deliberation. The ECDS commenced trial operations in Beijing, Shanghai, Shandong, and Shenzhen on October 28, 2009, and was launched nationwide on June 28, 2010.

On June 9, 2014, according to the unified deployment of the PBC, seven pilot finance companies, including Baosteel Finance Company and SAIC Finance Company, successfully integrated into the high-value payment system. They completed the transformation of their internal electronic bill system and became among the first finance companies to facilitate direct electronic bill settlement business with various commercial banks.

On April 20, 2015, the ECDS underwent an upgrade and transformation, joining the high-value payment system as a second-generation platform. The successful launch of this system marked the nationwide promotion of the payment system. This upgrade improved the business processing capability of the ECDS, as well as the security and stability of electronic commercial draft.

The ECDS comprises a core functional module for electronic commercial draft business processing and two auxiliary modules for paper commercial draft registration query and commercial bill interbank discounting public quotation. Initially, only the first two functions were activated. The core functional module registers and stores electronic commercial draft issued by various banks' customers in one place. It provides an interconnected platform for circulation and transfer, digitizing processes like bill issuance, acceptance, endorsement, guarantee, prompt payment, and recourse. The module also connects with the modern payment systems of banks, financial companies, and the PBC. It enables real-time transfer and settlement of financing transactions such as bill discount, interbank discount, rediscount, and prompt payment. It can accomplish the delivery of bill financing transactions and delivery versus payment (DVP) simultaneously. The paper commercial draft registration query module is mandatory for system participants. It offers registration and query services for paper commercial draft processes like acceptance, discount, interbank discount, rediscount, pledge, pledge release, loss reporting, and payment suspension. This module enables centralized registration and storage of paper commercial draft information, thus facilitating the discount and pledge business query of paper commercial draft.

In October 2009, to meet the processing needs of electronic commercial draft, promote their circulation, and protect the rights of all involved parties, the PBC issued *A Notice on Issuing Relevant Systems of Electronic Commercial Draft* (No. 328 [2009] of the PBC). This document includes *Measures for the Administration of ECDS*, *Electronic Commercial Draft Business Processing Procedures*, *Measures for Paper Commercial Draft Registration and Query Management*, *Electronic Commercial Draft Rediscount Business Processing Procedures*, *Measures for the Administration of ECDS Operations*, *Measurement for the Administration of ECDS Digital Certificates*, *ECDS Crisis Response Plan*, and *Electronic Commercial Draft Business Service Agreement Guidelines*. These eight normative systems provide institutional safeguards to encourage the healthy development of China's electronic commercial draft business and promote widespread use and circulation of electronic commercial draft.

II. Creation

On October 16, 2009, the PBC issued the *Measures for the Administration of Electronic Commercial Draft Business* (No. 2 [2009] of the PBC). When designing electronic commercial draft-related systems, the PBC adhered to the definitions of bill issuance, acceptance, discount, endorsement, payment, and recourse established by *The Negotiable Instrument Law of the PRC*. This was done based on relevant laws and regulations which include *Law of the PRC on the People's Bank of China*, *The Negotiable Instrument Law of the PRC*, *Electronic Signature Law*, and *Implementing Measures for the Administration of Negotiable Instruments*. With the formal introduction of the *Measures for the Administration of Electronic Commercial Draft Business*, the PBC has effectively facilitated the use of electronic commercial draft as a financial tool.

In August 2016, the PBC issued *A Notice on Regulating and Promoting the Development of Electronic Commercial Draft Business* (No. 224 [2016] of the PBC). The notice eliminated the need for background review for electronic bill discount transactions, meaning businesses no longer need to present contracts, invoices, or other materials when applying for electronic bill discounts. Financial institutions are no longer required to sign contracts for interbank discounting operations. If a contract is necessary, only online electronic contracts are required. From January 1, 2017, all commercial bills with a single issuance amount exceeding 3 million yuan must be processed through electronic bills. From January 1, 2018, in principle, all commercial bills with a single issuance amount over 1 million yuan should also be processed electronically. Financial institutions other than banks can join the electronic commercial remittance system via banking financial institutions to carry out prescribed services. These services include electronic bill interbank discounting (including buyout and repurchase) and prompt payment, but with limited business permissions like acceptance, discount, and rediscount.

The primary innovations of electronic commercial draft involve five key aspects: First, it revolutionizes the operation of commercial bills by replacing paper vouchers with data messages and physical signatures with electronic ones. This transforms the bill business from a manual, traditional approach to a modern one that leverages computer network technology for issuance, circulation, and settlement. Second, financial companies are now direct participants in the bill market. This increases the number of market participants, encourages financial companies to engage in the development of the bill market, and provides electronic commercial draft services. It helps reduce the financial costs for enterprise groups, improves their overall competitiveness, and stimulates the bill market. Third, the maximum payment term for electronic commercial draft is set to one year. This encourages enterprises to opt for electronic commercial draft as payment and financing tools, promotes the development of bill business by financial institutions, facilitates the formation of market interest rates for various grades of bills within a year, and diversifies bill market transactions. Fourth, the concepts of discount, interbank discount, and rediscount are clarified, along with redemption operating methods, thereby significantly reducing the risk of bill transactions. Finally, the DVP method is introduced in bill financing transactions and bill settlement businesses. This links the ECDS with the high-value payment system in real-time, ensuring funds are delivered concurrently with bill rights, thus eliminating potential credit and liquidity risks in bill transactions.

III. Significance

The introduction of electronic commercial draft, as well as the establishment and operation of ECDS, marked another significant milestone in China's financial digitalization process. It indicated the near completion of China's modern payment system and marked the transition of China's commercial bill business into the electronic age. This shift would greatly impact the development of e-commerce and the bill market.

The introduction of electronic commercial draft holds significant implications for the growth of businesses, commercial banks, the central bank, and the bill market. For businesses, electronic commercial drafts offer all the functionalities of paper bills while eliminating their physical constraints. This reduces the transit time of transaction funds, significantly enhancing efficiency. For commercial banks, these electronic bills allow for real-time, cross-regional circulation and usage, reducing costs related to labor, printing, and bill custody. They also mitigate the risk of bill loss, enhance business security, accelerate settlement speed, and effectively improve the banks' financial service efficiency. For the PBC, electronic commercial draft can establish it as a regular trading entity in the electronic commercial draft market. In the future, they will become a major medium for the central bank's open market operations, enhancing the flexibility and strength of its monetary policy actions. These bills can also improve the central bank's ability to regulate the money market and facilitate monetary policy transmission mechanisms.

The ECDS offers a secure, efficient, interconnected, standardized, and convenient platform for bill transactions. Unlike paper commercial drafts, electronic commercial drafts are issued and circulated via data messages. This system addresses the problems of low efficiency, information asymmetry, and high risk in paper commercial draft transactions. Moreover, it allows the central bank to effectively monitor bill activities, understand fund flows accurately, and provide a crucial reference for macroeconomic decision-making.

IV. Development

From 2009 to 2015, the bill market saw significant growth. In terms of transaction volume, the acceptance volume of financial institutions nationwide increased from 10.3 trillion yuan in 2009 to 22.4 trillion yuan in 2015. This represented an average annual growth rate of 13.8%. The discount volume of financial institutions nationwide increased from 23.2 trillion yuan in 2009 to 102 trillion yuan in 2015, with an average annual growth rate of 28%. The bill acceptance balance of financial institutions nationwide increased from 4 trillion yuan at the end of 2009 to 10.4 trillion yuan at the end of 2015. The discount balance fluctuated due to the regulation of credit scale, but by the end of 2015, it had grown to 4.6 trillion yuan.

In 2009, the total acceptance volume in the bill market exceeded 10 trillion yuan, and the cumulative discount volume expanded to more than 20 trillion yuan. Since then, the bill market has seen rapid growth. Commercial banks actively conduct bill acceptance businesses, with small and medium-sized joint-stock commercial banks, urban commercial banks, and rural commercial banks as the primary acceptors in the bill market.

During a period of high prosperity in the bill market, a clear differentiation was observed between the total amount and growth rate of acceptance transactions. While the total amount of transactions consistently hit new highs, the growth rate slowed down significantly. It dropped from 45% in 2009 to a mere 1.36% in 2015, a performance weaker than the GDP in the same period. The growth rate of discount illustrated a distinct trend. After dropping to -3.85% in 2011, it rebounded swiftly to 68.04% in 2015. This represented an increase in both total amount and growth rate, significantly outpacing the GDP trend during the same period.

Table 7-3 Development of bill market business (2009–2015) (unit: 100 million yuan)

	Annual acceptance amount		Annual discount volume		Acceptance balance		Discount balance	
Year	Sum	Annual growth rate (%)	Sum	Annual growth rate (%)	Sum	Annual growth rate (%)	Sum	Annual growth rate (%)
2009	103,000	45.07	232,000	71.85	40,387	26.21	24,000	26.32
2010	122,000	18.45	260,000	12.07	56,000	38.66	15,000	-37.50
2011	151,000	23.77	250,000	-3.85	67,000	19.64	15,000	0.00
2012	178,900	18.48	316,400	26.56	83,000	23.88	20,400	36.00
2013	203,000	13.47	457,000	44.44	90,000	8.43	20,000	-1.96
2014	221,000	8.87	607,000	32.82	99,000	10.00	29,000	45.00
2015	224,000	1.36	1,020,000	68.04	104,000	5.05	46,000	58.62

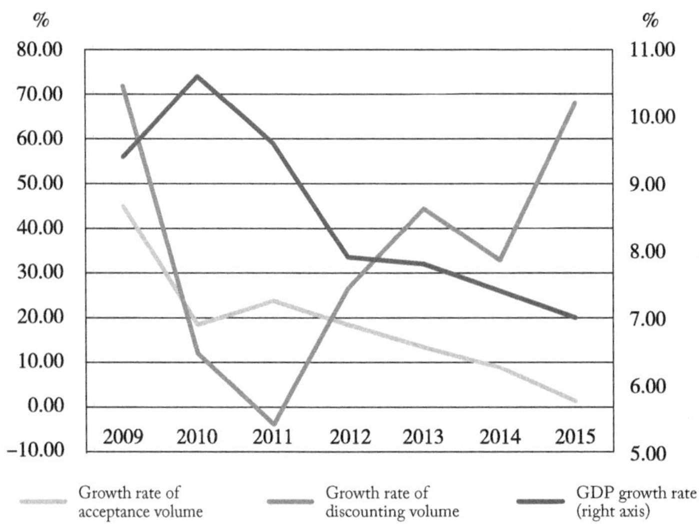

Figure 7-3 Indicators of the bill market and annual GDP growth rate from 2009 to 2015

Since 2010, due to the PBC's shift from a moderately loose to a prudent monetary policy, commercial banks have increasingly favored repurchase transactions. These transactions do not affect their credit size, leading to a tightening of credit scale and an abundance of funds. This change has effectively regulated credit business and released credit scale. In 2011, the bill market was stable with active bill acceptance and discounting businesses. Regulatory impact on bill transactions declined to some extent. With the central bank's shift toward prudent execution in 2011, major commercial banks balanced credit funds and bill assets by actively conducting bill repurchase transactions. The market particularly favored reverse repurchases. In 2014, regulatory authorities issued several documents targeting the financial industry, which dampened financial institutions' enthusiasm for engaging in bill repurchase business. With the advancement of information technology, some financial institutions began combining electronic services with differentiated services, marking the start of "Internet Plus Bills" financial innovation.

In the initial years, electronic commercial draft saw slow development. By the end of 2013, four years into their development, there were 359 participants in the ECDS. In 2013, this system issued bills totaling 1.5864 trillion yuan, with an acceptance amount of 1.6298 trillion yuan, a discount amount of 640.5 billion yuan, and a cash interbank discounting amount of 1.951 trillion yuan. The acceptance amount of electronic bills represented only 8% of the total bill acceptance, and the transaction amount accounted for only 7% of the total bill transactions. It wasn't until 2016, when major incidents in the bill market became frequent, that the PBC intensified its efforts to promote electronic bills. Commercial banks also actively adopted electronic bills to ensure stable operations. This period marked the true opportunity for the development of electronic bills.

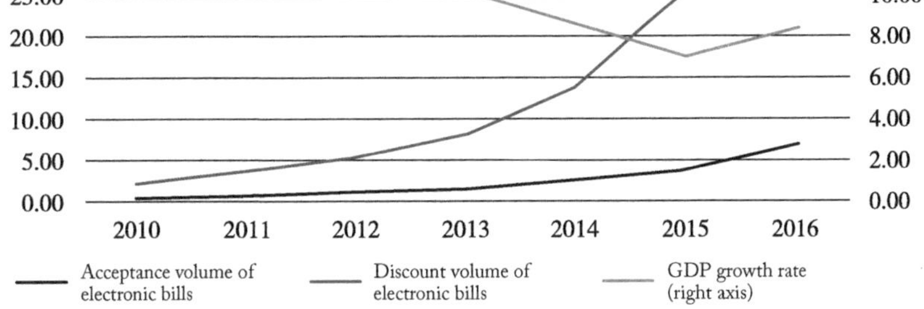

Figure 7-4 Electronic bill indicators and annual GDP growth rate from 2010 to 2016

From 2010 to 2016, both the bill market and electronic bills saw rapid growth. The acceptance and discount volume of electronic bills rose yearly, with a significant increase in 2015. The proportion of accepted electronic bills surged from 25% in 2015 to 47% in 2016, outpacing the GDP trend during the same period. The growth rate of the discount volume for electronic bills displayed a distinct upward trend.

Table 7-4 Market size changes of electronic bills (2010–2016) (unit: 100 million yuan)

Year	Acceptance amount	Annual growth rate (%)	Discount volume	Annual growth rate (%)
2010	2,774		2,155	
2011	5,488	97.84	3,867	79.44
2012	9,628	75.44	10,402	168.99
2013	16,298	69.28	26,064	150.57
2014	30,720	88.49	63,074	142.00
2015	57,873	88.39	258,623	310.03
2016	85,800	48.26	549,700	112.55

In 2009, China introduced electronic bills for the first time. Initially, the electronic bill market didn't immediately scale due to inadequate infrastructure and lagging institutional development. In 2010, the total amount of electronic bills in China was only 277.4 billion yuan, with the cumulative discount volume (including both discounts and interbank discounting amounts) of 215.5 billion yuan, representing only a small share of the overall bill market. However, the market started to evolve and electronic bills began to gain favor due to their safety and efficiency. Since 2010, the electronic bill market has seen rapid growth. By 2016, after six years of development, it began to take form. The acceptance volume of electronic bills reached 8.58 trillion yuan in 2016, representing an average annual growth rate of 77.17% from 2010 to 2016. Meanwhile, the discount volume of electronic bills was 54.97 trillion yuan in 2016, with an average annual growth rate of 151.83% from 2010 to 2016.

V. Problems

1. Inadequate Legal Guarantee

The Negotiable Instrument Law of the PRC, introduced in 1995, played a crucial role in stabilizing the early development of the bill market. However, since it was enacted in the era of paper bills, it fails to include provisions for electronic bills, resulting in an absence of core legislation for their development. While China's *Electronic Signature Law* has been in effect since 2005, electronic signatures still lack legal status in *The Negotiable Instrument Law of the PRC*. Furthermore, beyond signatures, there is an absence of rules for circulating electronic bills, leading to a lack of standardization. Certain provisions in *The Negotiable Instrument Law of the PRC* can impede the development of electronic bills. For instance, the law mandates, "When making a negotiable instrument, the drawer shall sign it pursuant to the requirements prescribed by law and shall be liable according to its tenor." Electronic bills, however, do not carry a physical signature; instead, they transmit payment instructions electronically. This means that the current *Negotiable Instrument Law* doesn't recognize the payment and settlement methods of electronic bills authenticated by digital signatures. Consequently, there is no unified understanding among relevant laws and regulations.

2. Practical Problems

First, the processing mode of electronic bill business restricts the liquidity of electronic bills, as demonstrated by the operation of the ECDS. Second, Business management lacks unified and standardized practices. While bill digitization has simplified financing, banks don't have specific guidelines for electronic bill discounts. They must rely on the guide for paper bill discounts. Despite enterprises applying for discounts through online banking, they are still required to provide paper discount vouchers, application forms, and agreements. This red tape limits the convenience and broader application of electronic bills. Third, Enterprises often lack a comprehensive understanding of electronic commercial draft operations. Online banking systems vary across financial institutions, and bank operators rarely access other banks' online systems. This leads to unfamiliarity with procedures like issuing and accepting bills with other banks. Consequently, enterprises are hesitant to promote electronic draft services, hindering the growth of this business segment. Finally, the electronic commercial draft business is fraught with risks. Deliberate attacks and unintentional errors can significantly damage the electronic bill network system, increasing operational risks for enterprises and banks. The integration of three major electronic systems—the ECDS, enterprise online banking system, and financial institutions' internal bill electronic systems—means that instability in any one system can affect the timeliness and accuracy of electronic bill processing, leading to security risks. Furthermore, the underdeveloped legal framework for e-commerce and electronic bills results in high legal risks and litigation costs due to various electronic information security issues.

SECTION 3

Bill Wealth Management and Bill ABS: Initial Realization of Investment Function

The advent of electronic bills has streamlined trading for market participants, spurring the development of diverse and innovative business practices. This evolution has led to the creation of sophisticated products with complex trading models and extended chains. Two notable examples are bill wealth management and bill ABS.

I. Bill Wealth Management

Bill-based financial products emerged rapidly during this period. Initially, most were developed through a cooperative model between commercial banks and trust companies. Banks issued financial products to investors, and the raised funds were invested in trust plans to purchase bill assets. However, regulatory changes from late 2009 to early 2011 made this model more challenging. Documents issued by the China Banking Regulatory Commission clarified that off-balance-sheet assets of bank-trust cooperation needed to be transferred to on-balance-sheet assets and could not be invested in bill assets. In February 2012, the Commission issued a document, banning trust companies from conducting any bill asset acquisition business with commercial banks, effectively ending the bill trust business model. Despite this setback, the bill wealth management business evolved, shifting to the burgeoning field of internet finance. By early 2014, various entities, from P2P platforms and off-line bill service companies to e-commerce giants and traditional banking institutions, began adopting the online bill financing model, following the "Internet Plus" trend.

Internet bill financing links bill financing enterprises with general investors via digital platforms using big data and cloud computing. The process works as follows: Enterprises pledge their bills to these platforms, which then create and offer wealth management products based on these pledges. Investors buy these products online, and their investment becomes the enterprise's financing. From a financing standpoint, internet bill financing is a form of pledge financing. As a product, it's classified as a loan-type financial instrument. In essence, it is private lending facilitated through internet platforms.

Enterprises operating internet bill and wealth management platforms fall into three main categories:

- The first category comprises enterprises primarily selling internet bill and wealth management products. Examples include Shanghai Fortune Cat Financial Services (SFCFS), PJ.com, Yinpiao.com, and Touchu.cn. SFCFS offers products like "Bank-Enterprise Financing" and "Commercial Bill Loans." PJ.com focuses on "Bill Management" products, while Yinpiao.com specializes in "Bank Bill Wealth Management" products. Touchu.cn mainly deals in "Bill Wealth Management" products.
- The second category comprises banking platforms offering online wealth management products. These include bill-based products from institutions such as China Minsheng Bank, CMB, and Ping An Bank. Minsheng Easy Loan, a China Minsheng e-commerce subsidiary, mainly offers products like "Smart e-Bill." CMB's "Small Enterprise e-Home" features products from the "e + Stable Profit Financing" series. Ping An Bank's Lu.com provides bill wealth management products such as "ANCHOR Bill."
- The third category includes internet or e-commerce enterprise platforms that sell wealth management products online, such as bill wealth management products. These platforms typically operate in collaboration with the first two categories of institutions. Key players include Alibaba, Sina, JD.com, and Suning. Alibaba's Zhaocaibao platform used to sell "bill loan" products, while Sina Micro Fortune mainly offers "Bank Bill Wealth Management," "Piaojinsuo," "Bill Customers," "Bill Smart," "Collaborative Bill Profit," and "Money-Generating Bill." JD Finance offers the "Small Silver Bill" series, and Suning e-commerce primarily offers products such as "Enterprise Bill Loans," "Fortune Cat Bills," and "Golden Bill Pass."[1]

The rise of internet bill wealth management business can be attributed to three main factors: First, there is a demand for financing. This fills the need for small-denomination bill financing for small and micro enterprises. These businesses primarily use internet bill financial products for financing, often with small-denomination bills. As they frequently struggle to obtain funds through bank discounts, the emergence of internet bill wealth management products provides a new financing channel. Second, there is a demand for investment. Internet bill wealth management offers low-threshold, high-return investment channels perceived as "low risk." The "1-yuan minimum purchase" model attracts individual investors and their "idle funds," contrasting with the traditional 50,000-yuan threshold for bank wealth management products. Returns on investment typically exceed those of common monetary fund products and mainstream bank wealth management products. While the claim of "zero risk" can be misleading, it has attracted numerous investors. Finally, there is a relative lack of a regulatory framework. As an innovative product, internet bill wealth management has not yet been fully regulated, with measures still being formulated. Internet finance currently operates within a regulatory vacuum. Internet platform enterprises exploit this regulatory imbalance, bypassing commercial banks' discount process and connecting directly with investors, thus addressing enterprises' financing issues.

Internet-based wealth management business is significant for several reasons: First, it offers new solutions for bill discounting to small and micro enterprises. Internet platforms use technology to connect investor fund supply with financing enterprises. These enterprises can secure funds simply by having reliable guarantees and bills, creating a direct link between funding sources and the real economy. This approach bypasses many steps in the traditional bank discount process, providing a viable financing method for bills with real trade backgrounds but incomplete documentation. Second, these platforms reduce enterprise bill financing costs. By leveraging their data and platform advantages, they match a large volume of individual investor data with the financing needs of small and micro enterprises. Using big data and cloud computing, they quickly pair these enterprises with suitable "partners," increasing transparency between investment and financing parties. This reduces information search costs and, indirectly, decreases financing costs for enterprises.

Internet bill wealth management products face both common internet finance issues and unique risks due to the virtual nature of internet finance and the specific features of bill business. These risks fall into three categories: platform, product, and legal risks. Platform risks stem from the companies themselves. Many are small, newly established entities that may lack credibility, qualifications, or standard operating procedures. They might misuse pledged bills for secondary financing, misappropriate funds, or even disappear with investors' money. Product risks primarily involve redemption issues. Bills carry a higher risk of chargebacks or delayed payments compared to instruments used in money market funds. There's also the risk of forgery—fake or cloned bills. Even legitimate bills may face redemption delays or rejections from accepting banks due to their business needs. Legal risks arise from the nascent state of these platforms. Their systems, processes, and risk control measures are often underdeveloped. Coupled with weak regulations and insufficient investor protections, this can lead to significant losses for investors in case of disputes. These risks are exacerbated by the early stage of development of internet bill wealth management platforms, highlighting the need for improved oversight and investor safeguards in this emerging financial sector.

II. Bill ABS

The Negotiable Instrument Law of the PRC stipulates that bill issuance, acquisition, and transfer must adhere to the principles of good faith and genuine transaction and debt relationships. Consequently, bills cannot serve as underlying assets in bill asset securitization or be directly transferred. The process we observe today is more accurately described as the securitization of bill yield rights assets. Since 2015, asset securitization has experienced explosive growth, making bill asset securitization a promising field. However, despite initial attempts in 2016, widespread adoption has been hindered by various factors. The scale of bill asset securitization remains relatively small compared to the scale of bill assets themselves. Notable bill asset securitization products include Rongyin No. 1 2016-1, Chengxin Orange No. e1 2016-1, Minsheng Bill No. 1 2016-1, and Rongyuan No. 1 2016-1.[2]

Several issues may arise during the securitization of bill assets. First, the effectiveness of bankruptcy remoteness is questionable. Despite measures like bill pledge guarantees and full margins, securitization, which involves pooling the income rights of bill assets as the underlying asset, cannot fully achieve bankruptcy remoteness. As Tu Sheng (2017) noted, this transfer is defined from a financial or accounting perspective, not a strict legal one. Second, substantial rigid redemption clauses are included. Initial market credit enhancement measures, such as pledging the full margin of the drawer, bank credit, and providing an unconditional joint guarantee for the bill acceptor, are overly simplistic. These measures could significantly violate the rigid redemption requirements in the new asset management regulations. Last, the business model may not be sustainable. While bill assets are not standardized debt assets under the new asset management regulations, they are among the most liquid of bank non-standard assets. The liquidity of bill assets exceeds that of ABS. Therefore, if the purpose of asset securitization is to turn illiquid assets into highly liquid securities, bill asset securitization seems to achieve the opposite. There's no need for asset securitization for bank bills or commercial bills guaranteed by banks through methods such as guaranteed discount, guarantees, and letters of guarantee.

III. Innovation and Regulation

As the bill market expanded, products and business models among participants became increasingly homogeneous. During this period, entities prioritized potential profits from bill business innovations, often outpacing market supervision. It wasn't until 2016, following a series of risk incidents in the bill market, that participants began reevaluating their development models. Subsequently, regulatory changes have started reshaping the market through measures such as infrastructure development and the establishment of legal frameworks.

Starting from 2010, regulatory authorities began to intensify their oversight of the particularly focusing on the emerging bill wealth management and bill trusts. They released

Table 7-5 Basic information of bill asset securitization products

Product	Features	Launcher	Launch date	Initial owners	Total amount (100 million yuan)	Asset pool face value (ten thousand yuan)	Number of bill holders	Number of bills transactions	Issuing rate (%)
Rongyuan No. 1	First bill yield asset securitization product	Huatai Securities (Shanghai) Asset Management Co., Ltd.	2016.03.29	14 companies	6.44	6.56	14	14	3.6
Chengxincheng No. e1	The first bill asset securitization product issued in shelf storage mode	Boshi Capital Management Co., Ltd.	2016.03.30	Ping An Bank Co., Ltd.	5.33	5.50	3	3	3.6
Rongyin No. 1	First Bank Bill Yield Rights Asset Securitization Product	Huatai Securities (Shanghai) Asset Management Co., Ltd.	2016.07.27	12 companies	4.96	5.82			2.8
Minsheng Bill No. 1	The first approved and issued bank-guaranteed bond asset securitization product	CITIC Securities Co., Ltd.	2016.08.08	China Minsheng Banking Corp	4.7				2.6

regulatory documents such as *Notice of the China Banking Regulatory Commission on Further Regulating the Credit Asset Transfer Business of Banking and Financial Institutions* and *Notice of the China Banking Regulatory Commission on Further Regulating Matters Related to Bank Credit Cooperation Wealth Management.* These directives mandated prudent credit asset transfer practices and prohibited banks from investing cooperative wealth management funds in their own credit or bill assets. This preemptive action effectively curtailed regulatory arbitrage in bill wealth management. Subsequently, regulators conducted targeted inspections on illegal operations, interbank activities, and buyback and sell transactions in the bill market. They issued numerous regulatory documents to address the rising systemic risk from regulatory arbitrage and the exposure of internal control weaknesses in commercial banks' bill operations. The China Banking Regulatory Commission and similar bodies continuously enhanced their regulatory measures, imposing severe penalties on financial institutions violating bill business rules. In 2015 alone, banking regulatory bureaus nationwide issued hundreds of fines for illegal bill practices. These concerted efforts successfully curbed illicit bill activities among financial institutions and brought much-needed regulation to the bill market's operations.

SECTION 4

Frequent Bill Cases: "Era of Strict Supervision"

In 2016, the bill market was rocked by a series of major cases. These incidents typically involved multiple institutions, large sums of money, and significant moral hazard issues, causing a stir in the domestic market. Over the past decade, the aggressive growth of the bill market often led to conflicts between profit pursuit and professional integrity among practitioners. Market participants, driven by profit and innovation, gradually strayed from regulatory risk prevention and control requirements. Consequently, a large-scale risk event unfolded in 2016. This, coupled with frequent market disruptions, prompted unprecedented regulatory tightening in the bill market, ushering in an era of strict supervision.

I. Major Bill Cases

On January 25, 2016, a significant risk event involving Bank N's bill purchase and resale business resulted in a staggering loss of 39.15 billion yuan. Public security organs investigated two bank employees for allegedly diverting transaction funds into the stock market. Media reports revealed that Bank N and Bank A were engaged in a bank acceptance bill interbank discount business. The bank bills associated with this transaction were meant to remain in Bank N's safe until the repurchase agreement expired and should not have been transferred. However, a Chongqing bill intermediary illicitly removed these banknotes from the safe, replacing them with newspapers. Using the stolen bills, the intermediary conducted a repurchase and discount transaction with Bank B. Instead of returning to Bank N's account, the funds were illegally invested in the stock market. The subsequent unsuccessful investments led to financial losses, preventing the bills from being repurchased and ultimately exposing the case.

On January 28, 2016, Bank X faced a significant risk event in its bill business, involving 969 million yuan. Public security organs launched an investigation into the case. From May to July 2015, a suspect allegedly colluded with Bank X's staff to manipulate bank deposit receipts and other documents for handling bank acceptance bills. They pledged these bills using false guarantees and subsequently discounted them. The funds obtained through this process were primarily used for capital allocation and stock market speculation. The scheme came to light in the fourth quarter of 2015 due to fluctuations in the capital market.

Bank T's 786-million-yuan bill case unfolded in January 2016. Bank T and Bank C initiated a 986-million-yuan bank bill repurchase transaction. However, on the business expiration date of April 6, 2016, Bank T received only 200 million yuan from a Zhangjiagang trading company controlled by Huitong Finance, a bill intermediary. The remaining 786 million yuan was not received, and the bill package was prematurely released. Zhang, a T Bank employee, conspired with several bill intermediaries. On January 13, 2016, despite knowing the package contained no bills, Zhang handed it over to an intermediary at an unauthorized location without inspection. Zhang then instructed the bill review staff to sign the package, complete documentation, and manage warehousing procedures, all without verifying the bills' existence. On April 6, 2016, Zhang falsely claimed that the opposing bank requested an early withdrawal of bills. He directed the review staff to process this withdrawal and handed the supposed bills over to a bill intermediary.

In a cross-regional inter-bank investment fraud worth 500 million yuan, Ding and accomplices posed as staff from Bank A's branch. They approached Bank B's branch, recommending high-yield financial products. Both banks agreed to purchase 500 million yuan of Bank A's wealth management products through C Asset Management Company, a subsidiary of Bank B's interbank business (Company C). Ding's group fraudulently obtained account opening information and forged Company C's seal. They used these to open and control an interbank current account at Bank A, tricking Bank B into transferring 500 million yuan. Later, Bank B discovered a mismatch between the account on the investment receipts and Company C's actual account. Bank B promptly reported the incident to authorities and froze Company C's account, effectively ending the fraud attempt.

In March 2016, police in Fushun City, Liaoning Province, investigated a 400-million-yuan bill fraud case. The suspect, Chen, forged bank bills and sold them to various parties. These bills had a face value of 5 million yuan but were initially sold for only 20,000–30,000 yuan. The price was gradually inflated until suspect Mei bought them for over 200,000 yuan each. Between January and February, Mei acquired four forged bank bills totaling 19 million yuan in face value. Using these, he fraudulently obtained 3,200 tons of steel worth 6.2 million yuan from a Fushun company. Mei then sold the steel at a discounted rate of 1,500–1,600 yuan per ton, netting 4.47 million yuan in illicit gains. The scheme unraveled when the defrauded company tried to endorse one of the 4-million-yuan bills to another enterprise for bank discount, revealing the forgery. Further investigation by public security organs uncovered a larger network of forged bookkeeping treasury bonds and bank bills traded among the suspects, with a total face value exceeding 400 million yuan.

Bank J fell victim to a 1.3-billion-yuan electronic bill fraud orchestrated by a former employee. The perpetrator forged the bank's information and seal, established an electronic bill proxy acceptance service at Bank G, and created a fraudulent electronic bank bill. This bill was then discounted and sold through Bank H. The fraud came to light in August 2016 when Bank H uncovered the deception.

II. Causes for Frequent Cases

In a rapidly growing market, motivated by the desire to avoid regulatory objectives, the innovative bill business started to stray from its original attributes. The credit features of these bills became less prominent, if not entirely disregarded, as capital business traits—fueled by market arbitrage goals—took center stage. As the pursuit of idle arbitrage intensified, funds chasing social profits flooded the bill market. This influx not only caused the bill market to expand rapidly but also led to a swift accumulation of risks.

First, the primary source of risk lies in the compliance and quality of basic bill asset creation. Since 2012, China's economic growth has slowed significantly. As financial market funds shifted away from the real economy, it suffered from capital depletion, leading to weak demand for effective funding. Consequently, the growth potential for compliant bills backed by genuine transactions declined. This resulted in sluggish growth in bank acceptance business, with volume growth dropping markedly since 2015. According to the PBC, in 2015, enterprises issued 22.4 trillion yuan in commercial bills, a year-on-year increase of only 13%, down 7.6 percentage points from the previous year's growth rate. The value of outstanding commercial drafts at year-end was 10.4 trillion yuan, up 5.4% year-on-year, but with a growth rate 3.9 percentage points lower than the previous year. In this environment, many bills with financing characteristics emerged, fueled by the growth of bill intermediaries. These intermediaries became the primary creators of bill assets. Some shell companies, with registered capital under ten million yuan, issued substantial bills. The authenticity of trade backgrounds and basic transaction relationships mandated by bill regulatory rules became mere formalities. This situation echoes the lead-up to the 2008 US subprime mortgage crisis, where financial institutions lent to borrowers unable to repay. Indeed, in finance, regardless of innovation, when widespread violations or "falsification" occur on the underlying asset side, a crisis often looms.

Second, the abundance of liquidity in a relaxed monetary policy environment facilitated the evolution of the bill business into a quick arbitrage operation capitalizing on idle assets. This expansion of underlying assets was driven by a trading logic and business model that prioritized short-term gains, which led to a continuous increase in the bill market's trading volume. Data shows that as financial institutions shifted their bill business models toward faster bill creation, increased circulation, and trading arbitrage, the interbank discounting amounts in the secondary market continually hit new highs. Consequently, bill circulation accelerated. The bill market, propelled by its own momentum, snowballed into an increasingly large entity.

Third, intense market competition drove business innovation in the bill market away from serving the real economy. Instead, it focused on manipulating regulations, evading rules, and exploiting loopholes. This shift intensified the trend of "reducing scale, conserving capital, and promoting idle interbank transactions." The complex trading structure and non-standard arbitrage significantly increased the operational risk associated with bill business. Furthermore, disorganized trading processes and the continuous influx of various participants amplified risks related to hidden trading chains and counterparties.

As the bill market underwent rapid expansion, homogeneous products and interest rate liberalization led to narrowing interest rate spreads. This put considerable performance pressure on commercial banks. To circumvent regulations and increase their bill scale, some commercial banks partnered with rural credit cooperatives, entities often hampered by weak internal controls and outdated accounting systems. Together, they devised innovative business models and introduced new transaction schemes characterized by reduced scale and interbank dealings. These developments lengthened the overall transaction chain and complicated the transaction model. Lured by the promise of high profits, private capital and new market entrants flooded in, significantly elevating the industry's moral hazard. Alarming market irregularities emerged, such as multiple sales of single bills and swapping counterfeit bills for genuine ones. In some cases, bank employees even colluded with intermediaries to accumulate bill assets. These practices severely undermined the financial market's stable growth.

Finally, bill intermediaries played a significant negative role in the rise of bill-related cases. As previously discussed, collusion was a key factor in bank-related incidents, with non-bank personnel, particularly those from bill intermediaries, emerging as crucial perpetrators. As a result, these intermediaries came under intense scrutiny.

According to *The Negotiable Instrument Law of the PRC*, the issuance, acquisition, and negotiation of an instrument must adhere to the principle of good faith and accurately reflect the true relationship between the creditor and debtor. Ideally, the main participants in the bill market should be enterprises and financial institutions engaged in actual business operations. However, as the bill market evolved, formal financial institutions, particularly banks, failed to expand their bill businesses sufficiently to meet the timely financing needs of private enterprises. This shortfall led to the emergence of numerous private intermediary institutions. These intermediaries effectively leverage their information advantages to broker transactions and earn commissions, serving as a bridge between those needing funds and those holding them, with bills as the medium of exchange. Consequently, private bill intermediaries have become an inevitable result of the growing tension between enterprises' increasing demand for funds and the limited supply from formal financial institutions like banks.

Private bill intermediaries often operate for extended periods without regulatory recognition. This persistence stems from two factors: the current bill system's inadequacy in meeting enterprise financing needs and the intermediaries' unique, growth-enabling business models. These intermediaries primarily function in two ways. The first and most prevalent model, accounting for over 90% of operations, involves direct participation in bill transactions. Here, intermediaries profit from bill price spreads by introducing bill sources to banks and actively engaging in buying and selling. The second model focuses on providing consultation and trading information. In this approach, intermediaries earn commissions without directly participating in transactions. Instead, they offer valuable transaction information and matching services for direct and transfer discounts.

The bill market's ongoing evolution has enhanced operational flexibility in bill businesses. However, regulatory loopholes in various laws have allowed private intermediary institutions to generate profits and foreign exchange, encouraging risk-taking behaviors that disrupt the normal financial order. This was particularly evident in bill forgery and alteration, as well as the practice of overselling single bills. While the Shanghai Commercial Paper Exchange Company Ltd. has mitigated these risks, the primary concern in the private bill intermediary market now lies in fund embezzlement. This occurs when intermediaries misappropriate funds or abscond with money during bill transactions.

Private bill intermediaries, while serving various market entities, can engage in misconduct under certain circumstances. However, in China's steadily improving market economy, the benefits of the demand-driven market should always outweigh its drawbacks. Rather than ignoring or fearing these intermediaries, regulatory authorities and commercial banks should adopt a positive, standardized, and mutually beneficial approach. They ought to respond proactively to innovative businesses and products in the financial market, thereby fostering its long-term development.

III. "Era of Strict Supervision"

Following a series of risk events, significant fluctuations occurred in the bill market. Regulatory authorities responded swiftly, implementing stringent measures to address the instability.

In April 2016, the PBC and the China Banking Regulatory Commission jointly issued *A Notice on Strengthening the Supervision of Bill Businesses to Promote the Healthy Development of the Bill Market*. This notice mandated rigorous examination of trade background authenticity and strict management of interbank accounts. A few months later, the China Banking Regulatory Commission released several policy documents on financial market governance, including *A Notice of the General Office of the China Banking Regulatory Commission on Carrying Out Special Governance Work for "Illegal, Non-Compliant, and Irregular" Behaviors in the Banking Industry*, *A Notice of the General Office of the China Banking Regulatory Commission on Carrying Out Special Governance Work for "Regulatory Arbitrage, Idle Arbitrage, and Related Arbitrage" in the Banking Industry*, and *A Notice of the General Office of the China Banking Regulatory Commission on Carrying Out Special Governance Work for Improper Innovation, Trading, Incentives, and Fees in the Banking Industry*. The Commission took special measures to tackle high leverage, excessive nesting, long chains, and excessive arbitrage in cross-market and cross-industry financial services. These measures encompassed interbank, investment, and wealth management businesses of banking and financial institutions. The bill business became a key area of inspection and governance. Consequently, stricter regulation, improved internal control systems, and changes in business models led to a rapid cooling of the bill market, ushering in an era of strict regulation.

Summary

The paper bill business experienced significant growth from 2009 to 2016. However, its high operational risks and rising security issues led to frequent bill-related incidents. As such, electronic commercial draft emerged as an important tool to mitigate these risks. The introduction of the ECDS was a pivotal event that sparked innovation in the bill industry, leading to the rapid emergence of products such as internet bill wealth management and bill asset management. This progress laid the groundwork for a thriving bill market. However, the pursuit of excessive profits led to accumulating social risks, triggering large-scale risk events. This dilemma prompted the establishment of the Shanghai Commercial Paper Exchange Company Ltd., marking the transition of the bill market from chaos to order. In this context, 2016 marked the beginning of a new era in the Chinese bill market.

NOTES

1. Wang Hongxia, Zeng Yicun, and Wang Wuchao, "Current Situation and Development Suggestions of Internet Bill Financing Business," *Journal of Shanghai University of Finance*, no. 3 (2015).
2. Xiao Xiaohe and Hu Jun, "Exploration of China's Bill Asset Securitization Business Under the New Asset Management Regulations," *Finance and Economics*, no. 3 (2019).

CHAPTER EIGHT

Bills After the Establishment of Shanghai Commercial Paper Exchange Company Ltd. (I)

In 2016, the rapid growth of China's bill industry led to an accumulation of risks, leading to significant market fluctuations when these risks surfaced. This scenario underscored the urgent need for comprehensive reform and regulation. Amid a sluggish bill market, managing and preventing bill-related risks became the primary goal and mission of the Shanghai Commercial Paper Exchange Company Ltd. This chapter delves into the establishment of the Shanghai Commercial Paper Exchange Company Ltd. and its achievements since its inception. It outlines the background, development process, and key responsibilities associated with the exchange's creation, and provides an overview of its innovative bill products.

China's bill market faced several challenges: a lack of unified organization, inadequate top-level design, delayed infrastructure development, and insufficient legal and regulatory systems. These issues led to frequent risk events. However, since its inception, the Shanghai Commercial Paper Exchange Company Ltd. has effectively served as the risk prevention and control center for the bill market. The exchange has made significant strides in institutional development by formulating and implementing regulations such as the *Negotiable Instrument Trading Rules*. These measures have helped regulate trading behavior and improve market efficiency. As the largest infrastructure in the bill market, the exchange has continuously advanced its system development, achieving integration and digitization of paper and electronic bill trading. This progress has minimized operational risks and incorporated risk prevention measures into the system design to curb illicit activities. In terms of long-term mechanism construction, the Shanghai Commercial Paper Exchange Company Ltd., under the guidance of the PBC, has introduced a commercial bill information disclosure platform. This platform enhances enterprise information transparency and establishes a market-oriented constraint mechanism for credit risk prevention.

After five years of persistent efforts, risks in China's bill market have been effectively mitigated and controlled. A safe, efficient, and unified bill market infrastructure, along with an advanced bill trading system, has been established across the country. This has improved the efficiency and transparency of bill trading, cleansed the market environment, increased institutional involvement, and steadily expanded bill trading volume. From 2017 to 2021, following the establishment of the Shanghai Commercial Paper Exchange Company Ltd., the bill market returned to rational development. China's stable and relatively relaxed policy environment fostered a favorable atmosphere for both fund and credit scale. As a result, the price index of Chinese bills gradually declined, enterprises' bill financing costs decreased, and bills' ability to support the real economy was strengthened. The development index of Chinese bills continued to rise, reaching 17,011 points at the end of 2021, a 24% increase compared to 2018. According to Shanghai Commercial Paper Exchange Company Ltd. statistics, the bill market business saw an average annual growth of 14.98% from 2017 to 2021. In 2021, the total business volume of the bill market exceeded 167 trillion yuan, with acceptance, endorsement, discount, interbank discount, and repurchase amounts being 24.15 trillion yuan, 56.56 trillion yuan, 15.02 trillion yuan, 46.94 trillion yuan, and 22.98 trillion yuan respectively. The establishment of the Shanghai Commercial Paper Exchange Company Ltd. has revitalized the once-tumultuous bill market by addressing numerous unstable factors accumulated over the years. This has given the market new vitality after periods of irrational surges and rapid decline.

In this era of dynamic exchanges, the Shanghai Commercial Paper Exchange Company Ltd. has evolved beyond its role as an infrastructure builder and top-level designer of the bill market. It now serves as a beacon for innovation, spearheading the bill market's innovative development. The bill market is a crucial bridge linking the money market and the real economy, with product innovation providing a channel for the former to better serve the latter. Since its establishment five years ago, the Shanghai Commercial Paper Exchange Company Ltd. has offered fundamental business services while adapting to the real economy's needs and the trend toward electronic bill payments and online financing. It has developed an innovative product system that spans the entire life cycle of bills, continuously enhancing the functional role of bill services in the real economy. At the issuance end, the Shanghai Commercial Paper Exchange Company Ltd. has developed an online supply chain bill platform, handling the entire life cycle of supply chain bills and transforming accounts receivable into bills. On the payment end, it has launched the "Bill Payment Pass" product, offering online payment functions for bills in B2B e-commerce and supply chain scenarios. In discounting, it has launched products, Discount Pass, providing independent discounting inquiry, system matching, and online clearing services, aiming to break down information barriers in the discounting market. On the financing front, it has introduced standardized bills to facilitate services related to creating beneficiary securities. These utilize the cash flow generated by bills as repayment support, effectively bridging the bill market and the bond market.

SECTION I

Shanghai Commercial Paper Exchange Company Ltd.: Milestones in the Development of China's Bill Market

On December 8, 2016, the PBC led the establishment of the Shanghai Commercial Paper Exchange Company Ltd. This platform ushered in a new bill system, model, and set of participating entities to China's bill market. The event marked a pivotal moment in the history of China's bill market, heralding the era of the bill exchange.

I. Background

Since the turn of the 21st century, China's rapid economic development has fueled swift growth in the bill market. The international financial crisis of September 2008 prompted China to implement a 4-trillion-yuan macroeconomic stimulus policy. This initiative led to unprecedented bill trading activity, causing significant expansion in the bill market from 2009 to 2015. However, this rapid growth set the stage for a surge in bill-related risk events in 2016, resulting in a severe downturn and significant contraction in the bill market. The establishment of the Shanghai Commercial Paper Exchange Company Ltd. was not merely a response to these risk events but also a major reform addressing issues such as low trading efficiency and obstructed information channels in the bill market. Prior to its establishment, China's bill market grappled with three major problems.

1. Insufficient Infrastructure Construction

Although regional bill centers existed in some economically advanced areas, China lacked a nationally unified, transparent, and electronically processed bill trading platform. The bill market remained fragmented, with divisions between regions and financial institutions hindering information flow and resource allocation. This fragmentation increased trading and supervision costs while heightening risks for market participants. Moreover, the lagging infrastructure of China's bill market resulted in a lack of consolidated organizational management and top-level design. Consequently, participants struggled to access information, conduct trades, and perform other bill-related activities efficiently. The establishment of a unified national bill trading platform was therefore crucial to address the disjointed and fragmented nature of bill trading in China.

2. Absence of Robust Laws and Regulations

The Negotiable Instrument Law of the PRC, enacted over two decades ago, was fundamentally legislated around the payment and exchange functions of bills. However, its relevance has diminished with 21st-century technological advancements, particularly electronic payments, which have significantly propelled bill digitization. Certain sections of the law, which were out of sync with market practices, had impeded further advancement of the bill market.

Specifically, *The Negotiable Instrument Law of the PRC*, constrained by its era of creation, did not provide for electronic bills, a glaring omission given the surge in electronic commercial acceptance bills. Its rules for recovering lost bills were not applicable to electronic commercial draft, and it lacked provisions for electronic signatures on such bills. Moreover, as China's economy grew rapidly, the circulation and trading functions of bills had gained importance, with their financial characteristics continually strengthening. The law's emphasis on "real transactions" had stymied the expansion of financing bills, posing a legal barrier to their progress. This exclusion of financing bills from China's financial market has significantly limited the bill market's ability to provide short-term direct financing for businesses. Moreover, *The Negotiable Instrument Law of the PRC* continues to be plagued by several controversies and shortcomings, including the issue of the non-causation principle of bills. These disputes extend beyond legal terms, affecting market practices and bill operations as well.

3. Insufficient Internal Control Management in Financial Institutions

Financial institutions, driven by profit and explosive bill market growth, often grappled with disorganized internal control management. This is primarily evident in two ways. First, banking and financial institutions had deficient internal control systems. The low-interest rate spread in bill trading necessitated high transaction volumes for profitability. However, banks' unregulated management of physical bills increased the risk of violations like overselling and holding unverified proxies. The lack of a unified bill discounting venue led to scattered business across branches and sub-branches, complicating centralized risk control. This, coupled with varying risk control levels among different branches, increased overall bill risks. Furthermore, some rural banks and credit cooperatives continued to use outdated accounting methods, blurring the line between sold-out bills and repurchase transactions. This allowed commercial banks to use the rural credit cooperative model to reduce the credit scale of bill discounting on their balance sheets. Second, private bill intermediaries often lacked compliance and risk control awareness. Frequent incidents caused by ethical and operational risks disrupted market order. Without a unified, standardized bill trading platform, these intermediaries, who should facilitate bill issuance and circulation due to their information advantages, often fell short. The booming bill market attracted a wide range of intermediaries, including many non-compliant ones taking risks for profit, which increased the risk in the bill market.

II. Establishment

In January 2016, a significant bill fraud case involving 3.9 billion yuan came to light at N Bank's Beijing Branch. This incident exposed the risks that had been building up in China's bill market after years of unchecked growth. As a result, numerous bill-related risk cases made headlines. Given the nation's focus on enhancing financial governance and mitigating financial risks, the bill market was poised for substantial reforms.

In March 2016, the Payment and Settlement Department of the PBC issued *A Letter Regarding Research on Promoting the Development of Electronic Commercial Draft Business*. This document addressed issues like the measures for the administration of electronic bills, the improvement of the ECDS, and the potential necessity of mandatory measures to encourage electronic bill adoption. On March 9, 2016, Pan Gongsheng, a member of the National Committee of the Chinese People's Political Consultative Conference and Vice President of the PBC, reviewed in a *Shanghai Securities News* interview that the central bank was actively working the creation of a unified national bill market. This initiative was a crucial component of the central bank's forthcoming work plan. Pan Gongsheng expressed his belief that an electronic bill trading system would improve the bill market's trading efficiency while reducing transaction costs and risks.

After the PBC publicly announced its plans to establish a unified national bill trading market for the first time, it began increasing communication with commercial banks. The central bank organized meetings with various banks to discuss the construction plan of the Shanghai Commercial Paper Exchange Company Ltd. On May 25, 2016, the PBC spearheaded the formation of a preparatory group for the establishment of a national unified bill market platform (Shanghai Commercial Paper Exchange Company Ltd.). This group was led by the Financial Market Department and Payment and Settlement Department of the PBC, with members comprising experts in commercial bank bills. With this, the construction of a national unified bill market officially commenced.

In September 2016, to accelerate the adoption of electronic bills and support the launch of the Shanghai Commercial Paper Exchange Company Ltd., the PBC issued *A Notice on Regulating and Promoting the Development of Electronic Commercial Draft Business*. This notice helped promote electronic commercial draft, laying a solid groundwork for the official operation of the Shanghai Commercial Paper Exchange Company Ltd.

On November 2, 2016, the General Office of the PBC issued *A Notice on Preparing for the Integration of Bill Trading Platform* to various central bank branches, commercial banks, and other institutions. This notice aimed to promote the digitization of paper bills and announced plans to launch the first phase of the bill exchange trading system on December 8. The initiative's goals were to prevent market risks and improve trading efficiency in the bill market. The notice outlined a two-phase construction plan for the Shanghai Commercial Paper Exchange Company Ltd., differentiated by access methods and implementation functions. In the first phase, members would access the trading system through a client to trade paper commercial draft. In the second phase, technically advanced members could directly access the system to trade both paper and electronic commercial drafts. The pilot program's initial batch of participants comprised 35 commercial banks, 2 financial companies, 3 securities companies, and 3 fund companies.

On December 6, 2016, just before the official trial operation of the Shanghai Commercial Paper Exchange Company Ltd., the PBC issued the *Measures for the Administration of Bill*

Trading. This document outlines the functions of the Shanghai Commercial Paper Exchange Company Ltd. and provides regulations for bill market participants. It covers various aspects, including bill market infrastructure, bill information registration, digitalization, registration and custody, trading, settlement, and maturity processing. As such, this document serves as a significant institutional framework from the PBC for developing the infrastructure of the bill market.

On December 8, 2016, the Shanghai Commercial Paper Exchange Company Ltd. Co., Ltd., established over the course of a year under the guidance of the PBC, officially opened. In a congratulatory letter, Zhou Xiaochuan, then President of the PBC, urged the Shanghai Commercial Paper Exchange Company Ltd. to

- deeply understand its mission,
- learn from mature international markets,
- focus on real economy demands,
- innovate bill products and trading methods,
- enhance bill market functions,
- optimize financial resource allocation,
- strengthen trading systems and internal management,
- improve business rules and risk prevention,
- bolster investor education,
- conduct thorough research and monitoring, and
- elevate the bill market's professionalism.

At the opening ceremony, Pan Gongsheng, Vice President of the PBC, emphasized that the Shanghai Commercial Paper Exchange Company Ltd. should

- improve central bank financial regulation;
- enhance monetary policy transmission;
- prevent financial risks;
- serve the development of the real economy;
- foster awareness of the overall situation, service, and risk;
- improve corporate governance;
- strengthen the bill talent team;
- enhance standardization, marketization, and specialization; and
- boost the bill market's ability to serve real economic development.

III. Main Responsibilities

1. Standardizing Bill Business Development

The Shanghai Commercial Paper Exchange Company Ltd. provides a comprehensive suite of services, including bill processing, registration and custody, clearing and settlement, and information services. These apply to various tradable bills, both paper and electronic, such as bank acceptance bills, commercial acceptance bills, and other negotiable instruments. By utilizing its ECDS and CPES, the exchange supports the entire life cycle of electronic commercial draft. This encompasses issuance, endorsement, pledge, guarantee, discount, payment confirmation, credit enhancement, interbank discount, repurchase agreements (both pledge and buyout), presentment for payment, and recourse actions.

Table 8-1 Overview of Shanghai Commercial Paper Exchange Company Ltd.'s business

Business type		Content	
Bill business processing	Bill transaction	Type	Interbank discount, pledged repurchase, buyout repurchase
		Methods	Transaction inquiry, divided into dialogue quotation and intention quotation; click to complete the transaction; anonymous click
	Rediscount	The issuer, a financial institution, applies for rediscounting through the CPES to the PBC or one of its branches. Once the rediscounting window of the PBC approves the application, the rediscounting transaction is completed and the bill pledge registration is finalized.	
	Presentment for payment	Within the prescribed time limit for presentment for payment, typically within ten days of the bill's due date, the bearer may present the bill to the accepting bank or the bank holding their account for payment. The accepting bank must respond on the same day, either agreeing to pay or declining payment. Failure to respond is considered a refusal to pay.	
	Course and recourse	If the bill is dishonored by non-acceptance, the bearer can exercise the right of recourse only in a specific order: first, the guarantor credit bank (if any), then the discounting party, and finally the discounting guarantor (if any). The bearer waives the right of recourse against previous parties in the secondary bill trading market. On the first working day after the bill's expiry date, the bearer can initiate online recovery through the Shanghai Commercial Paper Exchange Company Ltd.'s trading system. The system will automatically deduct the payment in the specified order, with the recourse operation adapting to the specific situation.	
		For undiscounted bills, the bearer can exercise the right of recourse against the drawer, acceptor, prior endorser, and other bill debtors off-line. They can target any one, several, or all of them without following a specific order. If the person against whom the right of recourse is exercised has settled the debt, the bearer can continue to exercise the right of recourse against other bill debtors off-line.	

(Continued)

Business type		Content
Registration and custody	Initial registration of ownership	Participants record bill ownership in the electronic bookkeeping system of the Shanghai Commercial Paper Exchange Company Ltd., thereby increasing their bill custody account balance.
	Registration change	When changes in bill rights occur among system participants, whether due to trading, non-trading, or other reasons, the Shanghai Commercial Paper Exchange Company Ltd. manages these changes within its bill custody account.
	Registration cancellation	When a bill is settled through presentment for payment, recourse, or invalidated by judicial decision, the Shanghai Commercial Paper Exchange Company Ltd. cancels the bill and reduces the bill custody account balance accordingly.
Clearing and settlement	Clearing pathways	When the high-value payment system is inactive, funds for bill transactions are settled through the Shanghai Commercial Paper Exchange Company Ltd.'s non-bank fund account and its clearing account with the PBC.
	Type	Gross settlement. When both parties agree on a transaction, the Shanghai Commercial Paper Exchange Company Ltd.'s trading system settles funds in real-time for each individual transaction. The trading system (Phase I) only supports this type of full settlement. Netting settlement. After a transaction is agreed upon, the Shanghai Commercial Paper Exchange Company Ltd.'s trading system processes real-time fund netting. It settles funds at a designated time using the net accounts receivable or payable.
	Speed	Bill clearing typically occurs on T+0 (same day) or T+1 (next day), with T+0 being more common. Trading parties negotiate which option to use. This clearing schedule applies exclusively to bill trading transactions.
	Settlement methods	DVP is a settlement method wherein the transfer of bills and payment of funds occur simultaneously and are mutually dependent. Free of payment (FOP) is a settlement method wherein the transfer of bills and payment of funds are handled independently by the two parties.
	Finance company online clearing	Clearing is conducted online through either the fund account of the Shanghai Commercial Paper Exchange Company Ltd. or the clearing account of the PBC.
Information business	Information registration	The CPES provides information registration services for paper bills that go beyond simple transactions. These services include acceptance, pledging and guaranteeing of undiscounted bills, discounting, inventory transfer, credit enhancement, payment confirmation, payment suspension, and settlement. This comprehensive approach enables the digital and online processing of paper bills.
	Information disclosure	The commercial bill information disclosure platform offers daily updates on essential details for each accepted bill. These include the issuance and acceptance dates, bill number, names of the issuer and acceptor, acceptor's bank name, face amount, and bill maturity date. Additionally, acceptance credit information is released monthly, providing data on acceptance amount, acceptance balance, cumulative overdue amount, and overdue balance.

(Continued)

Business type	Content	
	Market monitoring	Market data includes a market overview, daily statistical reports, and monthly statistical reports. These reports provide data on acceptance volume, discount volume, and transaction volume. The monthly reports further break down data into commercial acceptance bills and bank acceptance bills. Currently, two yield curves are available: the State-Owned and Joint-Stock Bank Note Interbank Discount (BAEX-1) yield curve, released on December 6, 2018, and the City Commercial Bank Note Interbank Discount (BAEX-2) yield curve, released on December 6, 2019. The public can inquire about the status of bills registered and entrusted on the Shanghai Commercial Paper Exchange Company Ltd. through the bill status inquiry feature. Market analysis reports, issued monthly, quarterly, and annually, offer a multi-dimensional perspective on trends in acceptance, discount, and trading business development.
Fee pricing	The Shanghai Commercial Paper Exchange Company Ltd. has formulated the *Measures for Shanghai Commercial Paper Exchange Company Ltd. Paid Bill Services* and *Shanghai Commercial Paper Exchange Company Ltd. Bill Service Price List*, which have been implemented since January 1, 2019.	

Electronic bill transactions before discounting are typically conducted online through the ECDS. In contrast, paper bill transactions primarily occur off-line between enterprises, though they require online information registration via the opening bank within the CPES. After discounting, both paper and electronic bills are registered for ownership and entered into the CPES for online electronic bill operations.

2. Unifying Bill Trading Platform

The establishment of the Shanghai Commercial Paper Exchange Company Ltd. marks the beginning of a modern, unified, nationwide bill market featuring transparent information and electronic processing. Since 2016, the PBC has accelerated the development of this unified national bill market. The creation of the Shanghai Commercial Paper Exchange Company Ltd. represents a significant milestone in the development of China's bill market infrastructure, paving the way for the future expansion of the country's bill business. Following its inception, the Shanghai Commercial Paper Exchange Company Ltd. has actively promoted various electronic commercial draft businesses. In its first year alone, the volume of electronic bill acceptance surged to 1.302 billion yuan, representing a year-on-year increase of 51.75%.

As the facilities of the bill market, the Shanghai Commercial Paper Exchange Company Ltd. is designated by the PBC as an institution providing services such as bill trading, registration, custody, clearing, settlement, and information inquiry. It also performs policy functions such as central bank monetary policy rediscounting operations. Since its inception, the Shanghai Commercial Paper Exchange Company Ltd. has continually optimized its trading system architecture. It has integrated distributed technology into its trading system, improving information transmission performance and direct business availability. Furthermore, it has developed a standardized API interface specification that covers the entire business process from registration and custody to trading, clearing, settlement, and member management.

Under the guidance of the PBC, the Shanghai Commercial Paper Exchange Company Ltd. is currently focusing on enhancing its core system functions. It is setting industry standards and accelerating system integration, with the goal of completing this integration within the next 2–3 years. This effort will result in a more comprehensive and robust bill market infrastructure. The CPES, serving as the exchange's core business system, has been recognized with the Special Prize of the 2016 Shanghai Financial Innovation Achievement Award and the First Prize of the 2017 Bank Technology Development Award. To meet evolving market demands, the exchange regularly updates and expands its system functions. By the end of 2018, the system had undergone nine upgrades, introducing new trading varieties and methods, optimizing trading and non-trading functional modules, and launching a custody accounting subsystem and special scenario business processing functions, among other improvements.

3. Fostering Bill System Development

The Shanghai Commercial Paper Exchange Company Ltd. adopts a goal-oriented and problem-oriented platform. It conducts a comprehensive and systematic review of the bill business chain, aligning with the business logic of "centralized registration, independent custody, over-the-counter trading, and bill payment settlement." This approach has led to the issuance of several business regulations, which ensure uniqueness of credit entities, diversified trading entities, standardization of trading objectives, synchronization of bill settlements, and standardization of contract texts. This system innovation for paperless bill collection has established an electronic business processing model that effectively curbs non-standard behavior in bill business.

Following the establishment of the Shanghai Commercial Paper Exchange Company Ltd., various supporting management rules and regulations have been successively launched. These include the *Measures for the Administration of Bill Trading*, *Bill Trading Master Agreement*, *Regulations for Paper Commercial Draft Business Operations*, and *Rules for Bill Registration, Custody, Clearing, and Settlement Business*. These documents have effectively supported the growth of innovative businesses and enriched the existing legal and regulatory framework for bills. Notably, the *Measures for the Administration of Bill Trading*, as the top-level design of the bill market, supplements *The Negotiable Instrument Law of the PRC* by providing clarifications on bill trading.

The establishment of the Shanghai Commercial Paper Exchange Company Ltd. has spurred continuous institutional innovation, addressing challenges in the bill market's development and fostering a favorable environment for its growth. First, the promotion of bill business' electronification has reduced operational risks through the further integration of the ECDS, unification of rules for paper and electronic bill business, and improvement of electronic commercial draft regulations. Second, the clearing system has been innovated. The Shanghai Commercial Paper Exchange Company Ltd. now uses a unified electronic platform for direct processing and DVP settlement. This eliminates time and space asymmetry, boosts settlement efficiency, and mitigates ethical and operational risks. Third, the trading system has been revamped, introducing transaction types like interbank discounting, pledge-style repurchases, and buyout-style repurchases. Various trading methods such as inquiry trading, click trading, and anonymous click trading have been introduced. These aid in counterparty and price discovery in the bill market, thereby improving bill trading efficiency. Fourth, a credit subject system has been established. Under *The Negotiable Instrument Law of the PRC*, *Measures for the Administration of Bill Trading* and *Bill Trading Master Agreement*, the Shanghai Commercial Paper Exchange Company Ltd. identifies the credit subject of discounted bills as the highest credit rating subject among the acceptance bank, discount bank, and guarantee credit enhancement bank. This ensures the uniqueness of "bill credit subject" and aids bill pricing, facilitating traders' judgement and decision-making. Last, a system of rules for bill trading has been established. The Shanghai Commercial Paper Exchange Company Ltd. has issued several business operation standards, outlining requirements for participant admission, registration, custody, settlement, and other market behaviors. Additionally, a monitoring indicator system and management framework for the bill market have been introduced.

4. Accelerating Bill Market Innovation

The Shanghai Commercial Paper Exchange Company Ltd. is embarking on a new journey amid the gradual shift toward a unified, secure, and efficient bill market with transparent information and electronic operations. Guided by directives from the Party Central Committee and the State Council, the exchange aims to serve the real economy, prevent and control financial risks, and deepen financial reforms. To promote high-quality development in the bill market, it's launching innovative products and services, including digital bill trading platforms, bill yield curves, and Bill Payment Pass products. These innovations address the real economy's needs and meet new demands from businesses and financial institutions for payment, financing, and trading in the rapidly evolving landscape of internet technology, financial technology, and big data. The exchange is also proactively aligning with future trends toward more standardized, online, and transparent bill businesses, leading the way in market standardization and innovation.

The first innovation involved establishing an experimental production system for digital bill trading platforms, aiming to achieve breakthroughs in the application of financial technology in the bill market. As a crucial part of China's financial market, the Shanghai Commercial Paper Exchange Company Ltd. has been actively monitoring the evolution of financial technologies like blockchain, and exploring their potential applications since its inception. Starting in 2016, under the guidance of the PBC, the Shanghai Commercial Paper Exchange Company Ltd. and the Digital Currency Research Institute of the PBC spearheaded the effort to build a digital bill trading platform in collaboration with the Hangzhou Blockchain Technology Research Institute of China Bank Credit Card Industry Development Co., Ltd., the ICBC, Bank of China, SPD Bank, and Hangzhou Bank. Following the completion of the prototype system for the digital bill trading platform in late 2016, the experimental production system was officially launched and started operating in January 2018. This system realized the full process business functions of bills. It combined cutting-edge blockchain technology with the practical needs of bill business, creating a system with comprehensive business functions, enhanced performance, improved security and privacy protection, real-time monitoring and management, and production application services. This marked a significant breakthrough in the application of blockchain technology in financial market infrastructure.

The second innovation involved analyzing and introducing the yield curve of bills, a valuable reference for bill asset evaluation. As a part of the bill market's infrastructure, the Shanghai Commercial Paper Exchange Company Ltd. is responsible for providing high-quality data and information services to the market. This improves market transparency, optimizes price formation mechanisms, and increases operational efficiency. Ever since its inception, the Shanghai Commercial Paper Exchange Company Ltd. has incorporated data and information services into its work plan and initiated research on the bill yield curve. In May 2018, the first yield curve developed by the Shanghai Commercial Paper Exchange Company Ltd. underwent trial operation in ten major institutions in the bill market. This curve, the interbank discount yield curve of electronic bank acceptance bills, uses state-owned and joint-stock banks as credit subjects. After the trial, the pilot institutions consistently reported a strong alignment between the curve and real market price trends. The curve satisfied all application requirements in terms of accuracy, stability, smoothness, and applicability. On December 6, 2018, the exchange officially released the yield curve. The introduction of this yield curve filled a void in bill asset pricing and valuation, providing market participants with fair and transparent trading price references and risk management tools. It contributed to the standardization of bill assets and laid a solid foundation for the development of the bill market.

The third innovation involved launching innovative products like the Bill Payment Pass, designed to enhance bill payment services' support for the real economy. *The Notice on Pilot Implementation of Supply Chain Innovation and Application* encourages the prudent use of financial infrastructures, such as the Shanghai Commercial Paper Exchange Company Ltd., for supply chain finance. It emphasizes effective risk prevention to create a safe channel for funds entering the real economy, enabling low-cost, efficient, and fast financial services for eligible SMEs. In response to this directive and based on thorough research, the Shanghai Commercial Paper Exchange Company Ltd. officially launched the Bill Payment Pass in January 2019. This product offers an efficient, cost-effective online bill payment model for eligible SMEs. By integrating bill payment into the supply chain platform, it shifted the process from off-line to online, creating a symbiotic relationship between bill payments and B2B platform transactions. Bill Payment Pass addresses the issue of non-payments, enhances enterprise payment efficiency, facilitates bill stock flow for small, medium-sized, and private enterprises, and further improves bill payment's service to the real economy. One year after its launch, five financial institutions, including CMB, China CITIC Bank, Ping An Bank, Bank of Jiangsu, and Ningbo Bank, along with over 20 platforms, have piloted the integration of Bill Payment Pass. Consequently, 700 enterprises have initiated 6,500 bill payments, totaling approximately 6 billion yuan.

The fourth innovation involved introducing innovative discounting products to tackle the prevalent issue of information asymmetry in the discounting market. In May 2019, the Shanghai Commercial Paper Exchange Company Ltd. launched Discount Pass to address this challenge and uneven resource distribution. Discount Pass is a service mechanism where a bill brokerage institution, commissioned by a discounting applicant, registers discounting information, publishes inquiries, and matches transactions in the CPES. The discounting applicant and institution then complete bill discounting through the ECDS. This system includes four functional modules: information registration, inquiry and transaction, clearing and settlement, and parameter management. Operations such as discounting information registration, inquiry publishing, and transaction matching are managed through the discount subsystem. The discounting service for small and micro enterprises will be improved through the construction of a bank-enterprise interoperability platform. The introduction of Discount Pass will mitigate information asymmetry in the discount market. This innovation bridges the "last mile" of discount services, improving discount financing efficiency and reducing discount financing costs.

The fifth innovation involved launching a supply chain bill platform to promote the innovative development of China's supply chain. The platform commenced its trial operation on April 24, 2020. Supply chain bills, an innovative product launched by the Shanghai Commercial Paper Exchange Company Ltd., enable enterprises to manage issuance, acceptance, endorsement, expiration processing, and information services. This is achieved by directly connecting to the exchange's supply chain platforms, such as Simple Exchange and China Enterprise Cloud Chain. By integrating technology, Bill Pass seamlessly fits into supply chain scenarios, offering benefits like swift issuance, real-world applicability, and divisible circulation. This greatly improves the ease of enterprise bill financing. The supply chain bill platform is a key measure to standardize accounts receivable between enterprises, optimize their structure, and boost the turnover rate and financing options for SMEs.

The sixth innovation involved introducing innovative standardized bill products to support SMEs with financing and to develop supply chain finance. These standardized bills, with similar core credit elements and terms (such as acceptors), are pooled by entrusted institutions to create a basic asset pool. The cash flow is then restructured into evenly differentiated, tradable beneficiary vouchers in the interbank market, backed by the redemption cash flow from the pooled bills. This innovation has addressed the previous low standardization of bill transaction targets and the issue of small, indivisible bill amounts. By making bill transactions as standardized as bonds, it has expanded financing options for SMEs.

The seventh innovation involved establishing a cross-border renminbi trade financing and transfer service platform to boost renminbi cross-border financing and trade. On February 14, 2020, the PBC, along with three other departments and the Shanghai Municipal Government, collectively released the *Opinions on Further Accelerating the Construction of Shanghai International Financial Center and Financial Support for the Integrated Development of the Yangtze River Delta* ("30 Opinions"). This document explicitly recommended leveraging the Shanghai Commercial Paper Exchange Company Ltd. to build a platform fostering renminbi cross-border trade and financing business. Construction of cross-border platforms officially began on July 6, 2020. Under the guidance of the PBC and its Shanghai headquarters, the Shanghai Commercial Paper Exchange Company Ltd. successfully completed the cross-border platform's construction and institutional access. The platform began online operations on November 3, 2020. The cross-border platform features business parameter control, permission management, trade and financing information registration, interbank payment transactions, and forfaiting transfers. It enables a fully online process for renminbi cross-border trade, financing, and transfer business, enhancing information centralization and transaction efficiency. By setting business parameters, it effectively manages the scale of renminbi cross-border trade, financing, and transfer business, as well as the direction of fund flow. This platform assists the PBC in monitoring the direction and scale of renminbi cross-border flow at a macro level.

The eighth innovation involved creating a commercial bill information disclosure platform to standardize the disclosure of commercial acceptance bill information. This effort aimed to facilitate the development of the credit system in the bill market, aligning with the PBC's requirements on piloting commercial bill information disclosure. On January 16, 2020, the Shanghai Commercial Paper Exchange Company Ltd. initiated a trial operation of the commercial bill information disclosure platform. Allowing commercial bill acceptance institutions to release relevant bill information. Enterprises and institutions could disclose their daily bill acceptance information and monthly acceptance credit details, which market institutions could then access. To strengthen the credit system for commercial acceptance bills, improve the market-oriented constraint mechanism, and protect bill bearers' rights, the PBC issued *A Notice on Regulating Information Disclosure on Commercial Acceptance Bills* on December 23, 2020. Subsequently, on December 30, the Shanghai Commercial Paper Exchange Company Ltd. introduced *Operating Rules for Information Disclosure of Commercial Acceptance Drafts*, set to be implemented on August 1, 2021. The document encouraged commercial acceptance enterprises and finance companies to proactively disclose information during the transition period between the announcement and implementation dates.

The ninth innovation involved activating the active account management service for bills. Provided by the Shanghai Commercial Paper Exchange Company Ltd., this service mitigates the risk of counterfeit bills and improves bill business quality. Legal entities and organizations, excluding financial institutions, entrust the exchange to register all their eligible settlement account information for bill business. This registration is performed in the exchange's system by the institution (bank or affiliated group financial company) that opens a settlement account with electronic bill functionality. By utilizing this proactive service, enterprises significantly reduce their exposure to counterfeit bill risks. Even if fraudsters forge documents and open accounts at other banks under an enterprise's name, they cannot conduct bill-related activities such as issuance, endorsement, or discounting. This approach effectively eliminates the threat of counterfeit electronic bills at its root.

The tenth involved the continuous invigoration of the innovative energy of various market participants following the establishment of the Shanghai Commercial Paper Exchange Company Ltd., leading to the flourishing of innovative bill-related products. The "Military Industry Bills" project, launched on October 31, 2016, was a notable innovation by central enterprises to reduce and manage costs, improve payment efficiency within the group's industrial chain, and promote the development of the military industry chain. In bill discounting, various financial institutions are striving to reduce financing costs and improve efficiency. They are accelerating their digitalization efforts and introducing products and services such as ICBC's "e-Ties" and JD's "Beijing Bill Instant Ties," triggering a shift toward online and self-service bill discounting. In terms of bill platform building, the emergence of commercial bill circulation platforms, like Enterprise Bill Pass, opens new avenues for bill innovation. Enterprise Bill Pass brings together central enterprises, commercial banks, and SMEs in the supply chain to build a central enterprise commercial acceptance bill circulation platform. This platform helps reduce accounts receivable and payable for central enterprises, optimizes asset liability structures, and facilitates credit transmission through the industrial chain, thereby alleviating financing difficulties for SMEs.

5. Improving Risk Prevention and Control

Since its inception, the Shanghai Commercial Paper Exchange Company Ltd., under the guidance of the PBC, has developed a variety of rules. These rules help foster standardization of business practices, ensure effective fulfillment of responsibilities and rights by all market participants, and further mitigate overall market risks. The platform has strived to improve risk prevention and control in the bill market, bolstering the foundation for long-term development. It has also prioritized institutional development, system function optimization, integration of paper and electronic bills, direct interface project development, and rediscount system development. This approach has effectively achieved the goal of controlling market risks, and aided the transformation of the bill market from a traditionally segmented and opaque region, dominated by paper bills and off-line operations, into a unified, secure, efficient, transparent, and nationwide electronic market.

Specifically, the Shanghai Commercial Paper Exchange Company Ltd. has implemented several measures for risk prevention and control. First, it has improved the electronic handling of bill business, achieving the digitization of paper bills. All transactions, clearing, custody, and recourse of discounted paper bills are now completed online. This eliminates non-standard operations like overselling, list buying and selling, and mismatched terms, effectively mitigating the risks associated with paper bills. Second, it has implemented unified electronic platform transactions. Centralizing off-line bill transactions on a single electronic trading platform improves information transparency, eliminates information asymmetry between institutions and regions, and curbs non-standard behavior. Third, it has explored the establishment of a frontline monitoring mechanism for bill market risks. This involves creating and continuously improving risk monitoring and early warning indicators, as well as analysis mechanisms in the bill market, which plays an increasingly important role in maintaining market order and stability. Fourth, it has built a bill information disclosure platform. This is a significant step toward establishing and improving the bill information disclosure mechanism, enhancing the transparency of bill business and effectively revealing the risks of the business. It helps promote the circulation of commercial bills and enhance the vitality of the market. Last, it has activated the active management function of bill accounts, which prevents the risk of counterfeit bills and improves service quality by addressing forgery at its source.

IV. Historical Significance

1. Promoting the Further Development of the Bill Market

Before the Shanghai Commercial Paper Exchange Company Ltd. was established, China's bill market lacked a nationwide trading platform, resulting in severe fragmentation. This led to irregular activities, opaque information, and significant credit, operational, and compliance risks for market participants. The Shanghai Commercial Paper Exchange Company Ltd. was created to address these challenges and the shortcomings of previous reforms in meeting the market's long-term needs. A unified national bill trading platform was crucial for advancing China's bill market, and the Shanghai Commercial Paper Exchange Company Ltd. fulfilled this role. As a key piece of financial infrastructure, it has improved the market's structure by filling gaps, increasing circulation efficiency, and facilitating risk prevention and control through unified systems, rules, standards, and platforms. Moreover, the exchange has streamlined the financing chain by minimizing intermediate trading links. This has reduced the complexity and cost of issuing and discounting bills for enterprises, helping small and medium-sized businesses overcome financing difficulties through more affordable options.

2. Enhancing the Ability to Serve the Real Economy

The bill market is a crucial part of China's financial market. It bolsters market liquidity, provides financing for private as well as SMEs, and aids in implementing monetary policy tools. First, bills have become a significant liquidity management tool for financial institutions. In 2018, the average turnover rate of discounted bank bills was 2.62%, while that of spot bond trading in the bond market was 0.83%. This high liquidity underscored the important role of discounted bank bills as a money market tool. Second, bill financing offers a simpler alternative to traditional loans. For bank acceptance bills, businesses need only deposit a margin percentage and pay a small fee to secure a bank credit guarantee for a set period. This streamlined process serves as a key financing channel for private enterprises and SMEs. The Shanghai Commercial Paper Exchange Company Ltd. reported that in 2020, 2,705,800 enterprises used bills, an 11.22% year-on-year increase. These enterprises utilized bills valued at 82.7 trillion yuan, up 4.27% from the previous year. Notably, SMEs, comprising 92.5% of all enterprises using bills, accounted for 53.24% of the total bill value, amounting to 44.03 trillion yuan. Last, bill rediscounting, a traditional monetary policy tool, helps guide market interest rates and promotes interest rate marketization through rediscount rates. By selectively rediscounting different types of bills, credit funds can be directed to various industries, effectively optimizing credit resource allocation.

3. Facilitating Bill Price Discovery

The bill price, or bill interest rate, is a crucial short-term base rate in the credit market. It guides fund allocation by financial institutions and businesses. Bill assets, with their financial and credit features, reflect both real economy fund demand and financial institutions' credit provision. Market-oriented centralized bidding exchanges determine the bill interest rate. Bills are attractive due to their high liquidity, profitability, low risk, and high trade volume. Since the Shanghai Commercial Paper Exchange Company Ltd.'s establishment, bill trading has become centralized, transparent, and more popular. The streamlined trading process now allows factors like fund prices, supply and demand, and time windows to fully influence bill prices. This transparency aids in determining bill prices that accurately reflect the market price of funds. As a result, it establishes a fair benchmark interest rate for bills, enhancing the marketization of discount rates.

4. Building a Strong Credit Environment for Chinese Enterprises

China's corporate credit environment was previously underdeveloped, marked by a low awareness of corporate credit. Bills, as credit-based financial instruments, played a crucial role in this scenario. The Shanghai Commercial Paper Exchange Company Ltd.'s establishment contributes significantly to creating a robust corporate credit environment and effectively promotes the evolution of commercial credit value. The exchange, known for its high information transparency and integrated processing, leverages big data technology to aggregate trading data from all bill holders. This aggregation provides the bill transferee with ample, objective credit information about the payment performance of commercial bill acceptors, issuers, and guarantors. By partnering with social credit service agencies, the exchange offers valuable resources for enterprise credit evaluation and analysis, fostering a healthy interaction between bill credit and enterprise credit. Moreover, the establishment of the Shanghai Commercial Paper Exchange Company Ltd. paves the way for developing commercial acceptance bills based on commercial credit, promoting the growth of commercial credit value. Commercial acceptance, offering lower costs and higher efficiency than bank acceptance, appeals to enterprises aiming to establish their own commercial credit. With the launch of the Shanghai Commercial Paper Exchange Company Ltd. trading system, more enterprises are participating in bill trading. To gain a foothold in the bill market, enterprises must actively contribute to improving China's commercial credit environment.

5. Promoting Bill Product Innovation

Before the Shanghai Commercial Paper Exchange Company Ltd. was established, bill business innovations mainly focused on regulatory arbitrage and trading methods. The market was hesitant to embrace substantial product innovation, and integration with the capital market progressed slowly. However, the creation of the exchange laid a conceptual foundation for innovative bill products. In the future, the Shanghai Commercial Paper Exchange Company Ltd. can list and trade money market products like letters of credit and factoring certificates of deposit. It can also establish a leveling fund system to regulate the supply and demand of the bill market during special circumstances. In term of business variety, the Shanghai Commercial Paper Exchange Company Ltd. can enhance cross-industry and cross-border innovation, and explore linkage innovation with subsidiary markets like the money market, insurance investment asset management market, trust securities asset management market, and bill asset securitization market. It can also innovate capital market derivatives like swaps, futures, and options.

The establishment of the Shanghai Commercial Paper Exchange Company Ltd. not only modernizes the traditional philosophy of bank bill business but also diversifies the participants in the bill market. This significant institutional innovation has allowed non-bank financial institutions to participate and fostered the development of commercial acceptance bills. The product chain of the bill business has extended to upstream enterprise bill credit enhancement markets and downstream bill asset management markets. As a result, banks are now planning innovative transformations of bill business with a broader perspective on asset business. The improved bill market system promotes financial innovation, with market participants becoming more diverse and non-bank financial institutions increasingly participating in bill innovation businesses and products. Cross-border, cross-market, and cross-regional development trends are becoming more pronounced. New market entities like enterprises, banks, trusts, funds, securities companies, and financial companies are expected to increase their participation in the bill market. This provides a platform and market space for the innovative development of a diversified and comprehensive bill business in banks.

6. Enhancing the Transmission Effect of Monetary Policies

The bill market serves as a platform for the central bank to conduct open market operations, facilitating the implementation of their monetary policies. Its close ties with the real economy make the bill market highly responsive to monetary policies, aiding in achieving policy objectives set by monetary authorities. The establishment of the Shanghai Commercial Paper Exchange Company Ltd. will assist the central bank in implementing rediscount policies more effectively. It broadens the operational scope of rediscounting policy tools. As mentioned earlier, the exchange will substantially increase the range, depth, and transaction efficiency of the bill market. This expansion provides the central bank with a wider array of bill types and trading entities to choose from when implementing rediscount policies.

Implementing rediscounting operations through the Shanghai Commercial Paper Exchange Company Ltd. allows the central bank, as a key participant, to efficiently screen bills that align with market policies. This transparent approach more effectively guides the flow of social funds and optimizes resource allocation. Moreover, the exchange enhances the flexibility and effectiveness of rediscounting policy regulation. The electronic handling of bills enables overnight rediscounting operations, increasing monetary policy flexibility. Bills play a crucial role in transmitting monetary policies, improving policy execution efficiency, promoting adjustments in credit institutions, and guiding the expansion of financing for SMEs. This helps achieve core macroeconomic regulation objectives and ensures a stable money supply. The central bank can regulate the financial market using the rediscounted interest rate as a monetary policy tool. It can also directly buy and sell bills in the market, guiding interest rate trends and adjusting funding conditions to meet policy goals. The establishment of the Shanghai Commercial Paper Exchange Company Ltd. has led to a more standardized and unified bill market, making it an important platform for the PBC to implement its policies. The exchange provides a convenient and effective channel for transmitting the central bank's monetary policies, facilitating the execution of central government policies to boost the real economy. Through big data analysis of complex financial market information, more precise and effective macroeconomic policy decisions and implementations can be made.

SECTION 2

Shanghai Commercial Paper Exchange Company Ltd. Trading System: Infrastructure of Bill Market

The bill market, a vital short-term financing sector intricately linked to China's real economy, credit market, and capital market, plays a pivotal role in adjusting credit structures and directing fund flows. Historically, paper bills dominated this market, with transactions conducted via traditional methods like phone calls, faxes, and face-to-face meetings. These manual processes and the physical nature of the bills posed significant operational risks, severely impeding market development. The introduction of the ECDS in 2009 partially mitigated paper bill-related risks. However, technological constraints, regional limitations, transaction peculiarities, and entrenched habits prevented electronic bills from fully supplanting paper bills quickly. Consequently, both formats persisted side by side. Prior to the establishment of the Shanghai Commercial Paper Exchange Company Ltd., the bill market lacked transparent top-level design, a unified business platform, and clear operational rules, resulting in a non-standardized, opaque market prone to frequent bill-related incidents. To tackle these challenges, the newly formed Shanghai Commercial Paper Exchange Company Ltd. aimed to centralize and unify quotation, trading, registration, custody, clearing, settlement, and data information services in the bill market. This endeavor to boost market operational efficiency culminated in the launch of an innovative bill trading system—the CPES.

I. Development and Online Operation

On November 2, 2016, the General Office of the PBC issued *A Notice on Preparing for the Access of Bill Trading Platform* to its branches, commercial banks, and other affiliated institutions, in an effort to promote the transition from paper bills to electronic bills. It emphasized that this shift was necessary to prevent market risks in the bill market and improve trading efficiency. The notice stated that the Shanghai Commercial Paper Exchange Company Ltd. trading system (phase I) was scheduled to begin its trial operation on December 8. It broke down the development of the Shanghai Commercial Paper Exchange Company Ltd. into two phases, based on functions and access methods. In the first phase, members would access the trading system via a client to trade paper commercial draft. In the second phase, technically proficient members would have direct access, enabling them to trade both paper and electronic commercial drafts. The pilot program initially included 35 commercial banks, 2 finance companies, 3 securities companies, and 3 fund companies.

The system underwent a trial operation from December 8, 2016, to February 26, 2017, followed by a promotion phase from February 27 to July 31, 2017. Participants began joining the platform in stages starting from February 27. All participating legal entities were online by the end of May, marking the completion of the first phase. The promotion phase concluded successfully at the end of July, with all members fully integrated into the system.

On March 27, 2017, the PBC issued Notice Yin Fa [2017] No. 73 to establish a unified national bill market. They decided to transfer the ECDS to the Shanghai Commercial Paper Exchange Company Ltd. for operation. Under the guidance of the PBC, the Shanghai Commercial Paper Exchange Company Ltd. managed the ECDS transfer and switch, scheduled from October 1 to 7, 2017. On October 9, the exchange successfully completed the ECDS transition, incorporating all 310 ECDS access point institutions, consisting of 2,722 legal entities and 90,038 system participants. All electronic commercial draft operations, such as issuance, acceptance, discount, and interbank discount, transitioned smoothly.

In July 2017, the PBC announced a crucial policy to integrate paper and electronic commercial drafts, set for implementation in October 2018. Under the central bank's guidance, the Shanghai Commercial Paper Exchange Company Ltd. cooperated with the Clearing Center of the PBC to launch the first phase of this integration in August 2017. They utilized the CPES and ECDS, replacing off-line bilateral contracts with a *Bill Transaction Master Agreement* and transaction notes. This shift introduced buyout repurchase, pledge repurchase, and interbank discount as new transaction types, unifying the rules for both paper and electronic bills. From October 1 to 5, 2018, the Shanghai Commercial Paper Exchange Company Ltd., in cooperation with 369 access point institutions, successfully completed the integration of paper and electronic bill trading. This achievement enabled simultaneous trading of both bill types, effectively establishing a nationally unified, secure, and efficient electronic bill trading platform, which was a significant leap forward in modernizing China's bill market.

Under the guidance of the PBC, the Shanghai Bill Trading System has undergone continuous upgrades and optimization since its inception. This has led to progressive advancements in both the system's first and second phases. The system has not only successfully migrated the electronic bill system and integrated paper and electronic forms but has also developed a discounting business module. Created in accordance with the PBC's requirements and based on the exchange's trading system, this module provides robust support for the central bank to implement rediscount policies with precision.

II. Introduction

The CPES, developed and managed by the Shanghai Commercial Paper Exchange Company Ltd., is a computer business processing system and data communication network. It leverages advanced network and computer technology to offer trading members a comprehensive suite of services, including inquiry, quotation, transaction, registration, custody, clearing, and paperless collection. The first phase of the project, primarily serving members and system participants in a client mode, consisted of seven subsystems: institutional management, paper bill registration, bill trading, registration and custody, clearing and settlement, billing and payment, and U-shield management. Through continuous upgrades and enhancements, the current system has expanded to include ten subsystems: institutional management, paper bill registration, bill trading, registration and custody, clearing and settlement, rediscounting, general inquiry, electronic bill business, custody accounting, and U-shield management. Each subsystem within the CPES serves a distinct purpose. In the following sections, we will briefly introduce the main functions of several key subsystems.

The institutional management subsystem oversees members, system participants, venues, and parameters, providing essential data and parameter support for other subsystems. The paper bill registration subsystem digitizes paper bills, forming the foundation for paper bill trading on the Shanghai Commercial Paper Exchange Company Ltd. At the core, the bill trading subsystem manages inquiries, quotations, and transactions of tradable bills. It interacts with the registration and custody subsystem and the clearing and settlement subsystem to complete transactions. This subsystem encourages market participation through various trading methods, including inquiries, click-through transactions, and anonymous clicks, facilitating real-time online transactions of paper and electronic commercial drafts, such as interbank discounts, pledging repurchases, and buyout repurchases. The registration and custody subsystem manages bills' lifecycles and ownership, handling changes in ownership, status, circulation stage, risk status, and bookkeeping based on transaction and non-transaction behaviors. The clearing and settlement subsystem processes various settlement instructions, including bill interbank discount, pledging repurchase, buyout repurchase, repurchase expiration, rediscount, prompt payment, recourse, and fee collection. It uses clearing methods like FOP and DVP to complete fund clearing. The rediscount subsystem comprises five business modules: rediscount, institutional management, registration and custody, clearing and settlement, and general query.

PBC branches serve as rediscount acceptance windows, electronically processing rediscount applications and managing quota control and parameters. Financial institutions can access business information such as rediscount handling and credit limit usage. Last, the electronic bill business subsystem manages pre-discount processing of electronic bills, supplying tradable electronic bills to the Shanghai Commercial Paper Exchange Company Ltd. and ensuring comprehensive coverage of the exchange's bill subject matter.

III. Significance and Prospects

The Shanghai Commercial Paper Exchange Company Ltd. trading system holds significance in two major areas. First, it eliminates market segmentation and improves trading efficiency. After the successfully migrating the ECDS from the Clearing Center of the PBC to the Shanghai Commercial Paper Exchange Company Ltd. in October 2017, the exchange achieved the integration of paper and electronic bill trading by October 2018. This integration allows simultaneous trading of both bill types and migrates various transactions such as discounted transactions, custody, clearing, and settlement, from the ECDS to the CPES. As a result, both paper and electronic bills now follow the same business rules and use the same trading platforms, thereby improving trading efficiency, transparency, and risk prevention capabilities. This, in turn, stimulates market activity and increases the business volume of the bill market. Data from the Shanghai Commercial Paper Exchange Company Ltd. shows a 15.5% total annual growth rate of the bill market business from 2017 to 2020. In 2020, the total business volume of the bill market exceeded 148 trillion yuan, with a trading volume of 64.09 trillion yuan, marking a 22.83% increase compared to 2017. Second, it promotes bill digitization and supports real economy development. ECDS, along with CPES, forms a comprehensive electronic bill trading system, catalyzing the transformation and upgrade of electronic trading in China's bill market. While traditional paper bills are prone to fraud, loss, damage, and delayed fund settlement, electronic bills use data messages and electronic signatures to enhance security and efficiency in enterprise fund turnover. This provides new financing channels and robust support for the development of the real economy.

Despite the integration of paper and electronic trading systems in the Shanghai Commercial Paper Exchange Company Ltd.'s trading system, members must still differentiate between pre- and post-discounting when managing the complete life cycle of electronic bills. This results in separate handling within the ECDS and the CPES. Historical constraints have led to differences in rules, functional architectures, interface specifications, and operation and maintenance mechanisms between these two systems. This complicates business processing and increases costs for system development and operation. Looking ahead, the Shanghai Commercial Paper Exchange Company Ltd. plans to develop a new generation of bill business systems. The goal is to create a more robust, efficient, and stable platform for managing the complete life cycle of bills by integrating a business system with interfaces compatible for both paper and electronic bills. This integration will resolve issues of repeated investment and system fragmentation caused by the current dual-system setup.

This new system will further improve the efficiency of bill market operations, strengthen comprehensive prevention and control of bill-related risks, paving the way for high-quality development in the real economy.

SECTION 3

Bill Information Disclosure Platform: Establishing a Bill Information Disclosure Mechanism

The bill information disclosure platform, recognized by the PBC, is developed and operated by the Shanghai Commercial Paper Exchange Company Ltd. This platform serves to disclose bill-related information, supporting acceptors in revealing commercial bill acceptance and credit information. Additionally, it provides query services for financial institutions, bill-holding enterprises, and the public to access this relevant information.

Since its inception, the Shanghai Commercial Paper Exchange Company Ltd. has focused on building a credit system in the bill market, continuously optimizing the market environment and mitigating credit risks. Through joint efforts with the PBC, the exchange launched a bill information disclosure platform on January 16, 2020. The exchange's promotion efforts led to active participation from businesses and finance companies in bill information disclosure. After more than a year of pilot testing, full implementation of bill information disclosure began on August 1, 2021. This initiative laid a solid foundation for advancing China's bill market credit system and significantly contributed to the standardized development of the country's bill market.

I. Background

Since the inception of the Shanghai Commercial Paper Exchange Company Ltd., China's bill market has seen significant improvements in management efficiency, trading efficiency, information registration, and risk prevention. These advancements have fostered a conducive environment for the growth of commercial acceptance bills, which are continually expanding. According to the Shanghai Commercial Paper Exchange Company Ltd., the total acceptance volume of commercial bills in 2020 reached 3.62 trillion yuan, an increase of 19.77% from the previous year. This amount accounted for 16.39% of the total market volume, an increase of 1.55 percentage points. The total discount volume of commercial acceptance bills during the same period was 1.03 trillion yuan, a year-on-year increase of 9.85%, accounting for 7.70% of the total market discount volume. While bank acceptance bills still dominated payment and financing transactions, commercial acceptance bills, with their unique characteristics, have exhibited higher growth rates in both acceptance and discount sectors. The acceptance and discount scale of commercial acceptance bills continued to expand, accompanied by a significant increase in the secondary market trading volume. Moreover, the proportion of interbank discounting of commercial bills to the total interbank discounting was steadily rising.

The expansion of supply chain and the securitization of accounts receivable are key factors propelling the rapid growth of China's commercial acceptance bill market. Currently, the large scale of accounts receivable in China significantly hinders the growth of SMEs and supply chains. Converting these receivables into commercial bills offers an effective solution. Accounts receivable, often characterized by poor liquidity and opaque information, can be transformed into commercial bills. This transformation not only improves liquidity but also provides stronger legal protection for enterprises. The benefits of commercial bills, such as legal validation, fixed payment terms, easy issuance, straightforward financing, and low costs, make them popular for business settlements and financing. These advantages significantly contribute to the growth of SMEs and supply chains.

Despite the rapid expansion of commercial bills, they remain less effective than bank bills for payment and financing. This is due to China's underdeveloped commercial credit system and slow-growing commercial bill market. Commercial bills, relying on corporate credit, lack the liquidity and market acceptance of bank bills, hindering their circulation among businesses and financial institutions. The low discount ratio of commercial bills also makes it challenging for companies to use them as a financing tool. Moreover, the commercial bill market's lack of transparency exposes holders to significant credit risks and complicates the protection of their rights. These issues stem primarily from the underdeveloped commercial credit system, where economic entities often engage in dishonest practices like mutual arrears and defaults. The lack of corporate credit awareness and transparency in commercial credit information further exacerbates these problems. Ultimately, the shortcomings in China's commercial credit system directly hamper the growth of commercial bills.

The development of commercial acceptance bills is shaped by the supply chain dynamics and the securitization of accounts receivable. However, an underdeveloped commercial credit system hinders this growth. Despite factors promoting its growth, challenges persist. To address these issues, it's crucial to establish and improve the information disclosure mechanism for commercial acceptance bills. This would enhance market transparency, reduce information asymmetry, mitigate risks, strengthen market constraints, promote bill circulation, and ultimately provide better support for the real economy.

II. Progress

1. Institutional Construction

On January 15, 2020, following the directives of the PBC, the Shanghai Commercial Paper Exchange Company Ltd. issued *A Notice on the Trial Operation of the Commercial Bill Information Disclosure System* to guide pilot institutions in disclosing commercial bill information. On June 5, 2020, the PBC released the *Announcement on Standardizing the Disclosure of Commercial Bill Information (Draft)*. Two days later, the Shanghai Commercial Paper Exchange Company Ltd. sought public opinions on the draft of the *Rules for the Operation of Com-*

mercial Bill Information Disclosure. On December 23, 2020, the PBC issued Announcement No. 19 [2020] of PBC (*Regulating Information Disclosure of Commercial Acceptance Drafts*), which was slated for official implementation on August 1, 2021. This notice also detailed the constraint mechanism for bill information disclosure. On December 30, 2020, the Shanghai Commercial Paper Exchange Company Ltd. issued *Operating Rules for Information Disclosure of Commercial Acceptance Drafts*, which provided specific operational guidance for information disclosure.

2. Operation

Since its launch, the bill information disclosure platform has continually refined its system and optimized its features. It has actively promoted its use and encouraged enterprises and institutions to participate in bill information disclosure.

On February 28, 2020, the Shanghai Commercial Paper Exchange Company Ltd. issued *A Notice on the Online Operation of Self-Registration Function of the Commercial Bill Information Disclosure Platform* (Bill Exchange Document [2020] No. 21). This was done to streamline the process of disclosing bill-related information by commercial bill acceptors. The pilot program's scope was gradually expanded. Subsequently, on April 30, 2020, the Shanghai Commercial Paper Exchange Company Ltd. issued *A notice on the Upgrade of the Commercial Bill Information Disclosure System to the May 2020 Version* (Bill Exchange Document [2020] No. 63). This system upgrade enhanced several functions, including authentication of financial company bill business accounts, public display of user-disclosed information, presentation of basic enterprise information, real-time disclosure of user-uploaded information, and improved disclosure and query capabilities for bill acceptance and credit information.

The Shanghai Commercial Paper Exchange Company Ltd. continually refines its system processes, monitors business operations, and improves the user experience for enterprises. Simultaneously, it actively promotes its bill information disclosure platform. Working closely with various branches of the PBC, the exchange provides training and promotes bill information disclosure services across numerous regions, including cities such as Shenzhen, Chongqing, Tianjin, and Beijing, as well as provinces like Shandong, Guangdong, Heilongjiang, Shanxi, Fujian, Shaanxi, and Henan. This comprehensive effort encompasses background data analysis, information disclosure service training, and technical support for the platform.

The training and promotional activities have enabled financial institutions and businesses to better understand the bill information disclosure systems and processes. These efforts have yielded initial success in guiding commercial bill acceptance enterprises to register on the platform and disclose information. By December 31, 2020, the bill information disclosure platform had registered 418 users, including 387 businesses and 31 financial companies, from 24 provinces across China. Approximately 150,000 bills had been disclosed, with their total value exceeding 100 billion yuan. Moreover, the platform had processed about 280,000 queries.

III. Significance

The development and operation of the bill information disclosure platform marked an important stride toward establishing and improving the commercial bill information disclosure mechanism. With the ongoing upgrade of the platform, it discloses and displays more bill-related information, thereby increasing the transparency of bill business. This increased transparency allows for effective disclosure of bill business risks, promoting commercial bill circulation and invigorating the bill market to support the real economy. The significance of the platform is evident in two main ways. First, disclosing commercial bill information can significantly mitigate operational risks, such as creating accounts for bogus businesses, recording false electronic commercial draft information, and forging bills. The bill information disclosure system dramatically reduces these operational risks in the bill market. Second, the platform provides credit information for acceptors, including the most recent and historical commercial bill business volumes and overdue situations. This information allows for a basic evaluation of whether the enterprise has misused commercial bills, thereby revealing risks for acceptors and aiding in credit risk management of commercial bill business.

SECTION 4

Bill Payment Pass: Innovation in Payment and Collection Scenarios

Bill Payment Pass is an online bill payment service used on the B2B platform. It allows parties to use electronic commercial acceptance bills as a payment method. The payer initiates bill payment instructions through their partnered financial institution. This institution then works with the payee's account-holding institution to complete various online processes, including bill issuance, submission, locking, unlocking, and signing, via the Shanghai Commercial Paper Exchange Company Ltd.'s interface service. The Shanghai Commercial Paper Exchange Company Ltd. has developed and operates an online bill payment system using its ECDS. This system integrates Bill Payment Pass functionalities and manages all aspects of online bill transactions, including issuance, submission, locking, unlocking, signing, and information notification, through a single interface.

Bill Payment Pass offers two primary functions: First, its bill payment witness function addresses the issue of non-receipt of bills upon payment through bill locking and unlocking services. This fosters a secure credit environment for transactions between unfamiliar enterprises on internet platforms, effectively bridging the security gap in bill payments. Second, it enables online processing, allowing for complete, one-stop handling of bill issuance and enterprise endorsement via the internet. This feature significantly enhances the convenience of bill payment.

I. Background

As the internet evolved, traditional businesses began moving their supply chains online, shifting purchasing, production, and sales activities to digital platforms. This rapid growth of the platform economy led to an increase in online transactions between businesses. However, as online procurement expanded, the limitations of cash-based settlements became more apparent. The common practice of paying suppliers after receiving goods resulted in extended transaction accounting periods and delayed payment collection for platform suppliers. Additionally, purchasers often had to monetize their accounts receivable before making payments, significantly increasing their financing costs. B2B platforms faced several challenges: improving fund utilization efficiency, activating existing financial assets, and building trust in unfamiliar trading scenarios. Despite advancements in internet payment methods, these B2B payment pain points remained largely unresolved. In response to the *A Notice on Launching Pilot Projects for Supply Chain Innovation and Application* (Shang Jian Han [2018] No. 142) issued by eight departments, including the MOC and the PBC, efforts were made to foster supply chain innovation. The goal was to meet online bill payment needs for supply chain platforms and B2B e-commerce platforms, and achieve DVP. On January 26, 2019, the Shanghai Commercial Paper Exchange Company Ltd. successfully launched its Bill Payment Pass. The first batch of online institutions to adopt this system included CMB in partnership with www.yzw.cn and Petrochemical e-commerce, CITIC Bank with www.Inc086.com, and Bank of Jiangsu with www.esgcc.com.cn.

II. Development

On the launch day of Bill Payment Pass, the system processed 24 transactions involving 30 bills, with a total value of approximately 71.9 million yuan. The first transaction, facilitated by www.yzw.cn, was a 10 million yuan payment from the Second Construction Limited Company of China Construction Eighth Engineering Division to China Minerals Corporation Xiamen Co., Ltd. The highest cumulative bill payment volume of the day was achieved by www.ynl086.com, which processed 15 bill payments totaling about 54.7 million yuan. Meanwhile, www.esgcc.com.cn completed the first bill package payment service, enabling its contracted user, Linggu Chemical Co., Ltd., to pay a package of six bills amounting to 5.5878 million yuan.

Following a six-month pilot, the Shanghai Commercial Paper Exchange Company Ltd. expanded the scope of financial institutions in the Bill Payment Pass platform to better serve the real economy while keeping risks under control. As participation grew and operations scaled up, the Bill Payment Pass introduced new features such as "support for multiple platforms under the same legal entity" and an "information service interface." To ensure standardized operations and enhanced effectiveness, the Shanghai Commercial Paper Exchange Company Ltd., with approval from the PBC, formulated several key documents, including the *Rules for Shanghai Commercial Paper Exchange Company Ltd.'s Bill Payment Pass Business (Provisional), Requirements for Access to Shanghai Commercial Paper Exchange Company Ltd.'s Bill Payment Pass Business (Provisional)*, and *Bill Payment Pass Business Direct Connection System Participant Interconnection Specification v2.1*, and *Bill Payment Pass Business Integration Testing and Acceptance Standards v1.0.*

By December 2021, 44 B2B platforms had launched bill payment pass services in partnership with major financial institutions, including BOCOM, CMB, CITIC Bank, SPD Bank, Ping An Bank, Bank of Jiangsu, Industrial Bank, Ningbo Bank, Sinopec Finance, Baosteel Finance, Haier Finance, and other financial institutions, processing over 21,000 transactions totaling nearly 61 billion yuan from 3,025 signed enterprises. This marked a 283% increase compared to the end of 2020. The services spanned various sectors, including manufacturing, transportation, energy, wholesale and retail, as well as scientific research and technology services.

III. Practical Significance

1. Supporting the Development of SMEs and Private Enterprises

The Bill Payment Pass aligns with the country's efforts to support supply chains and foster the growth of private, small, and micro enterprises. It expands bill payment scenarios, addressing a portion of enterprise financing needs. Currently, over 5 trillion yuan in undiscounted bills and more than 6 trillion yuan in discounted bills exist in the market. The low liquidity of undiscounted bills forces businesses to rely on bill pledging and bill pools for payments. Meanwhile, a significant portion of discounted bills is used for operational payments. By activating bill stock, the Bill Payment Pass can ease financing challenges for small, micro, and private enterprises while reducing unnecessary financing costs.

2. Boosting the Development of Supply Chains and B2B Platforms

The supply chain is pivotal to modern business development, with B2B e-commerce emerging as a potential future trend in business transformation. However, the absence of online payment tools on supply chains and B2B platforms impedes this progress. Bill Payment Pass can address this deficiency and accelerate supply chain development.

3. Promoting Bill Monetization

At the most advanced stage, bills become equivalent to monetary funds, enabling businesses to make substantial cash payments using bills. This bill monetization can significantly reduce credit disbursement and financial leverage, meeting enterprises' regular operational needs at virtually no cost. Widespread use of Bill Payment Pass is an essential prerequisite for this development. The Shanghai Commercial Paper Exchange Company Ltd. will continually explore improved and more advanced avenues for bill development to support the real economy.

SECTION 5

Discount Pass: Facilitating Official Bill Discounting

The Discount Pass is a platform where bill brokerage institutions act on behalf of discounting applicants to register discount information, post inquiries, and match transactions within the CPES. Applicants and institutions complete the bill discounting process through the ECDS. Three main parties participate in the Discount Pass: applicants, bill brokers, and discounting institutions. Applicants are legally recognized entities or economic organizations that hold bills and are registered, operational, and effectively existing within China. Pilot bill brokerage institutions include the ICBC, CMB, SPD Bank, Zhejiang Commercial Bank, and Bank of Jiangsu. Discounting institutions are those authorized by the CPES to participate in the process.

The Discount Pass offers two primary functions: First, it matches discounting business information. By creating a nationwide discount service platform, it allows discount applicants and institutions to publish, search, and match discount intentions. This expands discount business options and addresses information asymmetry in the market. Second, it facilitates online discounting business. The platform digitizes and automates discount application materials, contracts, and vouchers. By standardizing and moving discount business processes online, the platform reduces price parity costs for discount businesses, leading to cost savings and improved efficiency.

I. Background

The discount market has long suffered from a lack of uniform national standards. Traditional discount practices restricted enterprises to obtaining price information and financing from a few partner banks, leading to significant information asymmetry between banks and enterprises. This asymmetry resulted in inefficient supply and demand matching in the bill discount market. In this setting, some companies monopolized enterprise bill sources and exploited asymmetrical discount information to profit from financing spreads. This practice not only inflated enterprise financing costs but also posed risks to the development of the bill market. Moreover, financial institutions had inconsistent requirements for discount application materials and reviews. Enterprises had to repeatedly submit application materials, sign discount agreements, and even consent to on-site investigations and open settlement accounts when processing discounts through different financial institutions. This led to inefficient business operations. The outdated and inefficient bill discount market severely restricted small and micro enterprises at the end of the industrial chain, preventing bills from effectively serving the real economy.

On February 14, 2019, the General Office of the CPC Central Committee and the General Office of the State Council issued *Several Opinions on Strengthening Financial Services for Private Enterprises*. This document called for increased support for private enterprise bill financing, simplification of discount business procedures, and improvement of discount financing efficiency. Under the guidance of the PBC, the Shanghai Commercial Paper Exchange Company Ltd. launched the Discount Pass in May 2019, aiming to create a unified national discount service platform. The Discount Pass allows bill-holding enterprises to authorize bill brokerage agencies to register discount information and post discount intentions. Consequently, these enterprises can more easily locate suitable discount banks across the country and secure funds through discounting.

II. Development

On May 27, 2019, the Shanghai Commercial Paper Exchange Company Ltd. successfully launched its Discount Pass. The first day saw 86 discounting inquiries published, totaling about 95 million yuan. Of these, 47 intended transactions emerged, involving 49 bills and amounting to roughly 44.8 million yuan, an average of 914,000 yuan per bill. The Shanghai Commercial Paper Exchange Company Ltd. continues to foster the development of the Discount Pass market mechanism, sparking enthusiasm among discount enterprises, institutions, and bill brokers.

The Discounting Pass business saw rapid growth in 2020 amid the COVID-19 outbreak, largely due to its online and contact-free process. It allowed enterprises to secure essential funds for production and operations remotely, significantly contributing to economic recovery. In 2020, the Discount Pass attracted an additional 5,100 enterprise applicants, bringing the total registered enterprises to nearly 8,000. The financing business volume exceeded 40 billion yuan. Over 40 discounting institutions participated as legal entities, processing 21,512 commissioned quotation bills with a total face value of approximately 37.5 billion yuan, a 2.8-fold increase from the previous year. Of these, 17,604 bills reached a discount agreement, with the face value totaling around 32.3 billion yuan, tripling the previous year's figure.

III. Significance

1. Improving the Infrastructure of the Bill Market

The introduction of the Discount Pass service has improved the bill market infrastructure. The Shanghai Commercial Paper Exchange Company Ltd. has developed a robust system for its operation, creating a convenient and efficient platform that significantly enhances the financing capabilities of bills. Previously, the discounting service relied on point-to-point communication between enterprises and banks. Now, a streamlined communication system opens up information channels, breaking down the asymmetry of discounting information and boosting market efficiency. For enterprises, the Discount Pass helps access the market for "three small and one short" bills (small bills with short overdue period, which are held by small enterprises and accepted by small banks), which are often difficult to discount, thereby increasing the chances of bill financing. Small and medium-sized banks benefit by attracting more clients and business while lowering customer acquisition costs. Pilot banks of bill brokerage institutions gain valuable experience in the bill brokerage business. This innovative platform lays a solid groundwork for future operations and improves the overall functionality of the bill market's infrastructure.

2. Facilitating Small Businesses to Finance at Lower Costs

SMEs often hold bills that are small in amount and low in credit rating, making discounting difficult and costly. The Discount Pass addresses this issue in two ways: First, it consolidates resources from financial institutions across the country, expanding the discounting options for enterprises from cooperative banks to all market institutions. This breaks down information barriers between supply and demand, institutions, and regions, effectively activating and settling bill assets and improving discount market efficiency. Second, through public inquiry and negotiation, bill brokerage firms can secure better interest rate discounts for these enterprises, reducing their financing costs. As of the end of 2020, 7,243 enterprises applying for discount services through the Discount Pass were private enterprises or small and micro enterprises, accounting for 93% of the total. The entrusted bills were primarily small, with an average face value of 1.68 million yuan. The Discount Pass has significantly facilitated financing through bill discounting for small and micro enterprises.

3. Preventing Bill Market Risks

The Minutes from the National Conference on Civil and Commercial Trial Work of Courts highlights that bill discounting is a state-sanctioned business. Discounting bills to a party without the necessary legal qualifications is considered invalid. The growth of discount services relies not only on the comprehensive business system of the Shanghai Commercial Paper Exchange Company Ltd. and various bill brokerage and discounting institutions but also on the safety and reliability of the CPES. By addressing enterprises' financing needs, this system can regulate, clarify, and promote orderly market development, playing a crucial role in mitigating risks in the bill market.

4. Supporting Coordinated Development of Regional Economy

In June 2019, at the 11th Lujiazui Forum, Yi Gang, the President of the PBC, expressed his support for the Shanghai Commercial Paper Exchange Company Ltd.'s initiative to pilot and promote the Discount Pass services in the Yangtze River Delta region. This initiative has garnered substantial backing from local government and financial supervision departments in the area. As a result, the pilot promotion of the Discount Pass has been incorporated into key strategic documents, including the *Three-Year Action Plan for Integrated Development of the Yangtze River Delta Region (2021–2023)*, the *14th Five-Year Plan for the Development of Shanghai International Financial Center*, *Key Points for the Development of Shanghai International Financial Center in 2021*, and the *Overall Plan for the Development of Hongqiao International Open Hub*. This collective support aims to boost both the integrated development of the Yangtze River Delta region and the construction of the Shanghai International Financial

Center. Notably, in terms of Discount Pass business volume, the Yangtze River Delta region accounts for 46%, a percentage significantly above the discount market average.

SECTION 6

Standardized Bills: Attempt to Build Open Market Financing Channels

I. Background

Bills serve as a crucial financing channel for SMEs and a vital tool for financial institutions to manage assets and trade funds. However, constraints in China's bill market development have hindered the availability and efficiency of bill financing for SMEs. From the perspective of asset trading by financial institutions, bills possess distinct characteristics, complex price formation mechanisms, and lower standardization levels. The primary goal of creating standardized bills, as stated in both the *Announcement on Applying for the Creation of the First Batch of Standardized Bills in 2019* and the *Measures for the Administration of Standardized Bills*, is to increase liquidity support for small and medium-sized financial institutions and facilitate financing for SMEs and supply chains. The need for standardized bills is primarily evident in two areas.

First, there was a growing need to transition from non-standard to standard bills in bill asset management. In the context of financial deleveraging and efforts to prevent idle fund operations, regulatory authorities increasingly restricted bill asset management, which was classified as a "non-standard" business due to its large scale, control challenges, evasion of credit requirements, and weakened regulation. Since the *Guiding Opinions on Regulating the Asset Management Business of Financial Institutions* was issued on April 27, 2018, non-standard asset investment entities had faced significant restrictions, casting a shadow over the future of bill asset management business. Consequently, practitioners began exploring ways to shift from non-standard to standard management of bill assets. Furthermore, the "non-standard" business, which operated over longer time frames and required liquidity support, posed risks in the tight market funding environment and amid rising non-performing assets in the banking industry. To address high financing costs for small and medium-sized financial institutions, a consequence of Baoshang Bank's takeover due to credit risk premiums, and to bridge the liquidity gap in the bill discount and interbank discount markets, the Shanghai Commercial Paper Exchange Company Ltd. announced the creation of the first batch of standardized bills on August 15, 2019. This marked a significant step toward standardizing bill asset management.

Second, it ensures that bills are used to support the real economy, particularly by addressing financing challenges faced by SMEs. This approach was crucial given the mounting pressure on large industrial enterprises due to increasing accounts receivable. Consequently, many small businesses at the end of the supply chain often struggled with financing. Integrating bills into supply chain scenarios allowed for the creation of bills for accounts receivable at the source. Standardizing these supply chain bills effectively bridges the gap between the supply chains and the broader capital market. Supply chain bills, issued against real trading backgrounds and backed by core enterprises' credit, reduce the credit risk associated with standardized bills that form the basic asset. Furthermore, the expansive trading market for standardized bills greatly improves the liquidity of supply chain bills, offering a substantial funding source for supply chain financing. This, in turn, promotes the creation of more supply chain bills.

II. Development

On April 27, 2018, new regulations on asset management were introduced. These greatly restricted investment in non-standard assets, casting shadow over the future of bill asset management business. Amid financial deleveraging and the efforts to prevent idle fund operations, restrictions on "non-standard" assets increased. This prompted commercial banks to transition from non-standard to standard bill asset management.

To address high financing costs for small and medium-sized financial institutions following Baoshang Bank takeover and bridge the liquidity gap in the bill discount and interbank discount market caused by credit risk premiums, the Shanghai Commercial Paper Exchange Company Ltd. launched a pilot project for standardized bill innovation business from August to September 2019. Approved by the PBC, this project provided crucial support for financial institutions under severe liquidity pressure. Four standardized bills were issued, totaling approximately 1.38 billion yuan. The first three bills, based on bank acceptance bills discounted by Jinzhou Bank, had 2–3-month terms with subscription interest rates of 4.9%, 4.6%, and 3.6% respectively. The fourth, based on undiscounted bank bills accepted by Bank of Jiangsu, had a 349-day term and a 3.02% subscription rate. This initiative has drawn significant market attention and positive feedback, seen as effectively easing liquidity challenges for smaller banks and improving financing access for small, medium-sized, and private enterprises.

On January 26, 2020, the National Interbank Funding Center, Shanghai Commercial Paper Exchange Company Ltd., and Interbank Market Clearing House (Shanghai Clearing House) jointly released the *Standardized Bill Depository Agreement (2020 Edition).*

Following a review of the initial pilot work, the PBC issued the *Measures for the Administration of Standardized Bills (Draft for Comments)* on February 14, 2020. The central bank sought public opinions from February 14 to March 14. By the deadline, they had received 17 unique valid responses from 47 institutions and individuals. After the consultation period, the PBC meticulously examined each response and sought input from legal experts and market institutions on controversial issues. Ultimately, they fully incorporated 9 suggestions, partially adopted 3, and declined to implement 5.

On June 29, 2020, the PBC officially issued the *Measures for the Administration of Standardized Bills*, which were implemented from July 28, 2020. The document provides clear guidelines for standardized bills, covering their definition, participating institutions, basic assets, creation process, information disclosure requirements, investor protection measures, and regulatory framework. The goal was to regulate the development of the standardized bill business.

During the first week following the implementation of the *Measures for the Administration of Standardized Bills*, a total of 12 depository financial institutions conducted standardized bill business, creating 27 standardized bills. By August 3, 2020, all these bills had been successfully issued, totaling approximately 2.5 billion yuan. The successful creation of these standardized bills was expected to strengthen the link between the bill and bond markets, providing fresh impetus for financial support to keep business and employment stable.

On July 3, 2020, the PBC, the China Banking and Insurance Regulatory Commission, the China Securities Regulatory Commission, and the State Administration of Foreign Exchange jointly issued the *Rules for the Recognition of Standardized Debt Assets*. This document clearly defines the differences between standard and non-standard debt assets, along with their recognition criteria and regulatory frameworks. For standardized bills to be classified as standard debt assets, they must undergo an application and approval process.

On July 28, 2020, the Shanghai Commercial Paper Exchange Company Ltd., along with the National Interbank Funding Center and the Interbank Market Clearing House, issued the *Rules for Information Disclosure of Standardized Bills* with the approval of the PBC. The document, comprising 23 articles and 5 chapters, delineates the obligations, platforms, and methods for the disclosure of information on standardized bills. It establishes requirements for information disclosure before, during, and after the bills' existence. The document also includes eight appendices, providing templates for information disclosure materials and operational guidelines. On the same day, the Shanghai Commercial Paper Exchange Company Ltd. released the *Rules for Custody and Settlement of Standardized Bill Basic Assets* to standardize the custody and settlement processes for these assets. Also approved by the PBC, this document sets regulations for the admission of depository institutions, registration and custody of basic assets, settlement, and other related businesses in standardized bill transactions.

On October 9, 2020, the Interbank Market Clearing House officially released the standardized bill index series. This was an effort to enrich China's credit bond index product system and provide market participants with price indicators for standardized bills.

Following the implementation of the *Measures for the Administration of Standardized Bills* in July 2020, a total of 57 standardized bill products were launched that year, with a total value of approximately 6.12 billion yuan. By the end of 2020, 31 of these products had been redeemed, amounting to about 3.23 billion yuan. However, this momentum did not carry into 2021, as no new standardized bills were issued during that year.

In the first quarter of 2021, the issuance of standardized bills was suspended for three consecutive months, during which nine standardized bill products expired concurrently. This suspension was due to stricter regulatory standards and ongoing rectification processes within depository institutions' management systems. Regulatory authorities issued a model deposit agreement, indicating that issuance might resume once the standard debt recognition process was finalized. Throughout this period, products with a total value of about 1.3 billion yuan matured, leading to a steady decrease in stock size. The primary bills to mature in the first quarter of 2021 were nine standardized bills established in July and September 2020, with 4–6-month maturities. Following the expiration of the first batch of standardized bills, which were based on undiscounted commercial bills, the fundamental asset types of the stock products were primarily discounted commercial and bank bills, accounting for 45.36% and 26.88% respectively.

III. Operation Modes

1. Early Stage

Depository institutions, such as commercial banks or securities companies with expertise in the bill and bond markets, have initially established the fundamental elements of standardized bills.

2. Basic Asset (Bills) Collection Stage

- Depository institutions collect bills either directly from the original holders or indirectly via bill brokers.
- The original bill holders must possess genuine, legal, and valid bills. They should submit declaration documents, provide a list of basic assets, and fully transfer the rights of the basic assets through endorsement during the deposit process. This endorsement transfer is entrusted to the depository institution, and the Shanghai Commercial Paper Exchange Company Ltd. secures the listed bills.

3. Issuance and Subscription of Standardized Bills Stage

- Depository institutions should disclose information to investors at least one business day before creating standardized bills. This disclosure includes deposit agreements, lists of underlying assets, credit entity credit ratings, and subscription announcements.
- Depository institutions can either organize standardized bill subscriptions or entrust them to financial institutions for underwriting. Investors can directly subscribe or do so through underwriting institutions. Subscription funds are deposited into the standardized bill asset pool, and original holders receive financing funds.
- Depository institutions must disclose the results of the standardized bill creation within one business day after the subscription period ends.
- On the business day following a successful subscription, the underlying assets must be registered and maintained by the bill market infrastructure (Shanghai Commercial Paper Exchange Company Ltd.). Likewise, the standardized bills must be registered and maintained by the standardized bill registration and custody institution (Interbank Market Clearing House).

4. Standardized Bills Trading Stage

- Standardized bills are tradable and circulate in both the interbank bond market and bill market. They can be used in various transaction types, including spot trading, repurchase agreements, and forward contracts.
- Depository institutions must promptly disclose information about underlying asset redemption, major operational issues, or litigation matters related to credit entities. The depository institution should inform investors of any significant events affecting the underlying assets' value within three business days of obtaining such information.
- A standardized bill holder meeting must be convened to review and decide upon any changes or dismissals of the depository institution, alterations to the deposit agreement, overdue recovery of underlying assets, court litigation, or other circumstances as stipulated in the deposit agreement that require a resolution.

5. Standardized Bills Maturity Stage

Upon maturity of the standardized bills, the Shanghai Commercial Paper Exchange Company Ltd. distributes the final collection and recovery funds to the respective investor's custody account in the Interbank Market Clearing House.

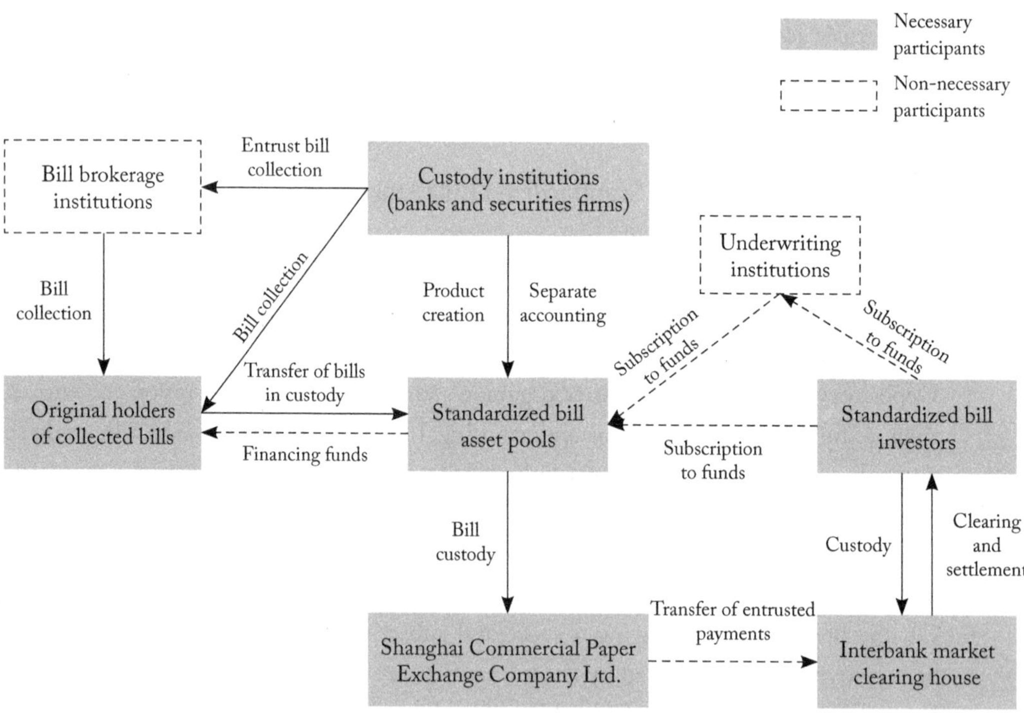

Figure 8-1 Flow chart of standardized bill operation

IV. Significance

1. Expanding the scope of Bill Investors

China's bill market had limited financing capabilities due to the non-standardized nature of bill debt assets, which restricted the participation of financial institutions in bill asset investment. Standardized bills can help address this issue, exhibiting five key characteristics:

- adequate information disclosure
- differentiation and tradability
- centralized registration with independent custody
- fair pricing facilitated by an improved liquidity mechanism
- compliance with trading regulations in interbank markets, securities exchange markets, and other trading venues as per the new asset management regulations on standardized debt assets

Standardized bill investment institutions participate in the interbank bond market. The inclusion of non-bank financial institutions and various asset management products expands the investor base. Recognition of standardized bills as standardized debt assets is likely to attract further investment from wealth management funds, public funds, and other asset management products.

2. Addressing the Liquidity Problem in the Bill Market

Bills backed by high-quality underlying assets possess strong liquidity, making them unlikely to become the primary component of the standardized bill market. Instead, standardized bills with potential credit risks in their underlying assets may emerge as the market's mainstay. The development of a standardized bill business could activate notable online assets such as bank, commercial, and financial bills, which typically have poor liquidity and higher credit risks. This could expand their application scenarios, introducing them to a money market with a wider range of participants and diverse investor risk preferences, effectively bridging the current liquidity gap in the bill market.

3. Improving the Risk Resilience of the Bill Market

Before the introduction of standardized bills, bills were circulated exclusively in the bill market, with banks and licensed securities firms as the main investors. This concentration led to a narrow pool of risk-bearing entities. The advent of standardized bills, however, expanded trading into the interbank bond market, fostering stronger correlations with various bond types. As a result, the influence of the bond market on standardized bill interest rate volatility increased. Concurrently, the broader investor base brought diverse trading strategies and richer market structures, which helped stabilize bill market volatility. These changes enhanced the bill market's resilience to risk and strengthened connections among the bill, capital, and bond markets.

4. Creating Conditions for Supply Chain Financial Services

The Shanghai Commercial Paper Exchange Company Ltd. has established a supply chain bill platform, simplifying the issuance of commercial acceptance bills for supply chain enterprises. Standardized bills offer a new financing avenue in addition to discount financing for supply chain commercial bills held by bill holders. Commercial acceptance bills issued in supply chain scenarios have more attractive interest rates than bank bills. These commercial bills, as standardized bill-based assets, hold advantages over bank bills. Moreover, the "supply chain bill plus standardized bill" model offers lower financing rates than commercial bill discounting, effectively reducing enterprises' financing costs. The standardized bill market is poised to become a crucial tool in supply chain financing, addressing the financial challenges faced by small and micro businesses.

SECTION 7

Supply Chain Bills: New Directions for Bill Development

The supply chain bill platform is the ECDS that interfaces with various supply chain finance platforms. It provides enterprises with a range of functions, including the issuance, acceptance, endorsement, and maturity management of electronic commercial draft. The platform also provides information services.

I. Background

In October 2017, the General Office of the State Council issued the *Guiding Opinions on Actively Promoting Supply Chain Innovation and Application*, emphasizing the need for active and steady development of supply chain finance. Following this, the PBC, the MOC, and other departments issued additional documents outlining specific requirements for standardizing, developing, and innovating supply chain finance. Since its inception, the Shanghai Commercial Paper Exchange Company Ltd. has transformed the bill market through institutional and systematic improvements. This transition has transformed what was once a traditional market, characterized by regional segmentation, lack of transparency, and paper-based offline operations, into a unified, secure, efficient, and nationwide electronic modern market. This change has laid a solid foundation for expanding the application of bills in supply chain finance.

In recent years, slowing economic growth and intensified market competition have led large corporations, leveraging their advantageous supply chain positions, to accrue debts from SMEs both upstream and downstream. This has significantly increased inter-enterprise accounts receivable. At the Lujiazui Forum in June 2019, Yi Gang, President of the PBC, emphasized the importance of "supporting the Shanghai Commercial Paper Exchange Company Ltd. in promoting the securitization of accounts receivable in the Yangtze River Delta region." This was a crucial step toward developing the Shanghai International Financial Center. Keeping this in view, the Shanghai Commercial Paper Exchange Company Ltd., under the guidance of the PBC, was actively exploring the creation of a supply chain bill platform. The goal was to enhance the role of bills in supply chain finance, improve the efficiency of bill services in the real economy, tackle payment and financing issues for SMEs, and encourage standardized growth in supply chain finance.

II. Construction

On April 24, 2020, the supply chain bill platform began its trial operation. The Shanghai Commercial Paper Exchange Company Ltd. issued *A Notice on the Trial Operation of the Supply Chain Bill Platform* (Shanghai Commercial Paper Exchange Company Ltd. Document [2020] No. 58) on the same day, announcing the access standards for the trial phase. The first four supply chain finance platforms participating in the trial operated across industries like manufacturing, software and information technology services, electricity and thermal power production and supply, wholesale and retail services. On the launch day, 17 enterprises issued 17 bills totaling approximately 1 million yuan, while 2 enterprises endorsed and circulated 3 bills totaling 51,000 yuan.

On June 18, 2020, the first batch of supply chain bill discounting business was successfully processed. Nine enterprises completed ten transactions totaling approximately five million yuan through supply chain bill discounting. The participating companies included two from China Enterprise Cloud Chain, four from Ouyeel, and three from JDH. Discount interest rates ranged from 2.85% to 3.8%, with all discounted bills being commercial in nature. The applicants were small and medium-sized suppliers from various sectors such as manufacturing, wholesale, and metal processing, spread across Shanghai and provinces such as Guangdong, Anhui, Jiangsu, Fujian, Shaanxi, and Liaoning. Five financial institutions, including CITIC Bank, CMB, Ma'anshan Rural Commercial Bank, Baosteel Finance Company, and TCL Finance Company, provided the discount services.

On July 30, 2020, the Supply Chain Bill Platform of the Shanghai Commercial Paper Exchange Company Ltd. was included into the tenth batch of financial innovation cases in the Shanghai Pilot Free Trade Zone. Then, in September 2020, the PBC, along with eight other departments, issued the *Opinions on Standardizing the Development of Supply Chain Finance to Support the Stable Circulation, Optimization and Upgrade of Supply and Industry Chains* (Yin Fa [2020] No. 226). This document established clear guidelines for the development of supply chain bill platforms.

To standardize the development of supply chain finance in line with national decisions and deployments, and to enhance its supporting infrastructure, the Shanghai Commercial Paper Exchange Company Ltd. formulated the *Rules for Admission of Supply Chain Bill Platforms (Trial)* on January 28, 2021, with the approval of the PBC. These rules clarify access thresholds and processes, significantly raising standards for supply chain finance platforms. The rules increase the operation platform's required registered capital to 300 million yuan and establish specific regulations regarding shareholder background and credit ratings to promote integration with industrial backgrounds. The document also outlines requirements for monitoring and evaluating the supply chain platforms and provides measures for handling abnormal situations. These rules are crucial for promoting the healthy development of the supply chain bill business.

III. Advantages

1. Promoting the Invoicing of Accounts Receivable

Bills, as a standardized form of accounts receivable governed by *The Negotiable Instrument Law of the PRC*, offer convenience in issuance and circulation. They improve financing channels and enjoy higher market acceptance due to their connection with real trade backgrounds. The launch of the supply chain bill platform is expected to expedite the promotion of accounts receivable invoicing. This platform offers enterprises an alternative way to handle bill business, eliminating the need for bank online banking. Enterprises can directly manage the issuance, acceptance, endorsement, circulation, and financing of supply chain bills through the platform. This simplifies the conversion of accounts receivable into bills and promotes invoicing at the source, offering significant convenience for enterprises.

2. Addressing Mismatched Bill Holding and Payment Amounts

The supply chain bill platform introduces an innovative solution: equal differentiation and issuance of bills, with a minimum amount of one cent. This new approach significantly increases flexibility for enterprises. Companies can now endorse and transfer any amount without incurring additional fees. This enhancement greatly improves the adaptability of bill usage, accelerates enterprise fund turnover, and resolves the issue of mismatched bill holding and payment amounts. By fully utilizing the payment and financing functions of these bills, the platform opens up broader operational possibilities for enterprise fund management.

3. Reducing Financing Costs and Improving Financing Efficiency

Supply chain bills allow the credit of high-quality enterprises to be extended to all enterprises on the supply chain, including small and medium-sized businesses at the end. The issuance of these bills relies on transaction data from the supply chain platform, enhancing the authenticity and transparency of the trade background. This transparency facilitates easier access to credit or preferential financing rates from financial institutions. Typically, the discount rate is 100–150 basis points lower than the loan rate for the same period, significantly reducing financing costs for enterprises. Additionally, the supply chain bill platform enables swift issuance, circulation, and acceptance of bills. SMEs can now discount or standardize bill financing online, markedly improving their financing efficiency.

4. Promoting the Development of the Commercial Bill Market

Commercial acceptance bills offer an effective solution to the financing challenges faced by SMEs. However, their liquidity and acceptance are currently constrained by information asymmetry. Bill Pass, integrated with supply chain platforms, have developed a unique operational mechanism and business model. These bills leverage the creditworthiness of core enterprises and the service advantages of third-party logistics companies. By combining technological solutions with financial services, they significantly reduce information asymmetry. This enhancement greatly increases the acceptance of issued commercial bills, thereby fostering the growth of the commercial bill market.

Summary

The establishment of the Shanghai Commercial Paper Exchange Company Ltd. marks a significant milestone in China's bill market, signaling its transition into the bill exchange era. This platform provides a robust, standardized foundation for the market, introducing new systems, entities, and models. Since its inception, the exchange has fostered steady growth, with rapid expansion in bill payment and discount scales, leading to diversified transactions and increased innovation. The platform plays a crucial role in promoting China's high-quality economic development by enhancing the payment, trading, and financing functions of bills. It offers a nationwide trading platform, improving efficiency and encouraging bill issuance and payment through innovations like Bill Payment Pass and supply chain bills. These have become vital tools for everyday payment and settlement among Chinese enterprises. Moreover, the exchange serves as a platform for implementing the PBC's rediscounting policies. Bill-based monetary policy tools cater to private and small businesses, guide credit structure optimization, support key economic areas, and assist small and medium-sized financial institutions with liquidity. Standardized bills and Discount Pass have emerged as significant financing methods, enhancing bills' financing attributes, reducing financing costs for holders, and improving financing efficiency. All these developments contribute to the high-quality growth of China's real economy.

CHAPTER NINE

Bills After the Establishment of Shanghai Commercial Paper Exchange Company Ltd. (II)

The establishment and development of the Shanghai Commercial Paper Exchange Company Ltd. have profoundly impacted the bill market, transforming it from a fragmented, opaque, and paper-based system into a unified, secure, efficient, and electronic nationwide platform. This transformation has reshaped the market's ecosystem, fortifying its foundation for further development, steadily increasing business volume, and spurring innovation. Bills now serve multiple purposes, including payment, settlement, investment, financing, and credit, with a life cycle encompassing issuance, acceptance, endorsement, pledge, and discounting. Each function and stage must comply with laws and regulations, and align with infrastructure and participating entities. The Shanghai Commercial Paper Exchange Company Ltd. has made significant strides in enhancing laws and regulations, developing infrastructure, and diversifying market participants. Consequently, the bill market continues to innovate and evolve after the establishment of the platform. This chapter delves into bill business innovations led by various market players, set against the backdrop of widespread adoption of financial technology and ongoing development of supply chain finance.

Innovation in the bill market, spearheaded by participating entities, primarily focuses on discount and financing segments. This includes various online "instant discount" products. These innovations not only streamline business operations for enterprises but also promote the widespread adoption of bill transactions. The ease of bill financing encourages more companies to use bills for payments and settlements, thereby attracting additional participants to the market. Bills, being compatible with supply chain finance, are increasingly utilized within supply chains, helping enterprises convert accounts receivable into invoices and enhancing the overall competitiveness of supply chains. For example, military industry and enterprise bills are used to leverage the credit of military and central enterprises, thus improving supply chain efficiency.

The Shanghai Commercial Paper Exchange Company Ltd. was established in response to China's national strategy to develop supply chains. However, the slow growth of China's bill market has impeded the widespread use of bills in supply chains. As financial technology advances, numerous supply chain service enterprises are developing their own platforms. They create bill-like financial products and manage issuance, circulation, trade, and finance on these platforms. This has led to the introduction of bill products such as "Golden Order," "Cloud Credit," and "Tongbao," and the emergence of supply chain service enterprises like JDH, Cloud Chain, and Ouyeel. Their innovative efforts in supply chain finance have encouraged the application of bills in this sector, fostering the development of supply chain bills. Bill innovation involves optimizing functions and various aspects of the entire bill life cycle, enabled by financial technology. Recently, blockchain technology, which shares many characteristics with bills, has been applied to bill transactions, offering solutions to various risks and challenges in bill operations.

The Shanghai Commercial Paper Exchange Company Ltd. has ushered in a new era for the development of the bill market, and the integration of financial technology has unlocked immense potential to the market. However, the market has also seen significant risk changes, resulting in a major shift. This transformation has attracted more research institutions to study the bill market theoretically. The growth of this market is inextricably linked to the exploration of bill theory, and any reform must be firmly grounded in theoretical insights. As the bill market thrives in the new era, research efforts are intensifying in tandem.

SECTION I

Instant Discount, Military Industry Bills, and Enterprise Bills: Financial Technology-Empowered Bills Serving the Real Economy

The establishment of the Shanghai Commercial Paper Exchange Company Ltd. has continually stimulated the innovative vitality of various market participants. This surge in creativity has led to the development of novel bill products, indicating a thriving environment for bill innovation.

I. Instant Bill Discount Products

Previously, enterprises grappled with several issues in traditional bill discounting: lengthy inquiry processes, complex procedures, extended payment collection periods, and high financial costs. To secure favorable discount rates, companies had to engage with multiple banks. The entire process, from credit inquiries and document submissions to account openings and loan approvals, was time-consuming and labor-intensive. As such, discount financing was a challenging task for enterprises.

Financial technology has revolutionized the banking industry, particularly in bill discounting. The advent of instant bill discounting offers corporate customers an unparalleled experience, featuring no-account-opening requirements, same-day fund receipt, and extensive internet scalability. This high-tech product of the internet era enables customers to initiate discounts through online self-service, with the banking system automatically disbursing loans. It primarily caters to SMEs and commercial bill discounting. In instant discount transactions, customers can initiate applications and receive funds in less than a minute, effectively achieving financing within seconds. This lending method is transparent, user-friendly, safe, and reliable. It offers unique advantages in supporting inclusive finance, promoting green credit, and assisting small and micro enterprises. The automated operation of instant bill discounting represents a paradigm shift from traditional business processes. By enhancing financing efficiency and reducing costs for small and micro enterprises, it serves as a powerful tool for advancing inclusive finance.

Since China's first instant discount system was launched in 2018, hundreds of such platforms have emerged, creating a unique dynamic in the bill discount market. A notable example is the self-service discount platform, "CITIC Instant Discount," launched by CITIC Bank in September 2018. This service offers intelligent pricing, online inquiries, one-click transactions, instant receipts, and real-time processing. It effectively overcomes the drawbacks of traditional bill discount services, such as lengthy inquiry procedures, multiple operational steps, delayed receipt times, and high financial costs. With CITIC Instant Discount, discounted funds are credited to an account in just two minutes, enabling customers to secure financing from the comfort of their homes—no bank visit required.

II. Military Industry Bills and Enterprise Bill Pass

In 2015, the Central Economic Work Conference outlined five priority tasks: cutting overcapacity, reducing excess inventory, deleveraging, lowering costs, and strengthening areas of weakness. From 2016, China shifted its focus to supply chain development. Relevant departments introduced special policies to promote supply chain finance, facilitating a "transition from serving the virtual economy to serving the real economy." Bills, as financial tools with multiple functions such as payment settlement and financing, are well-suited for use in the supply chain due to their high compatibility with enterprise needs and supply chain financing characteristics. First, they can meet the payment and settlement needs arising from daily operations. Second, they offer credit and financing functions, ensuring financial support for enterprises. Last, the rights associated with bills are legally protected. *The Negotiable Instrument Law of the PRC* mandates that bills must be paid when due, thus providing legal assurance. With the joint efforts of relevant national departments and central enterprises, a military industry and enterprise bill platform based on commercial acceptance bills has been established. This platform aims to reduce accounts receivable and payable in the supply chain using commercial acceptance bills, optimize the financial management of central enterprises, and leverage the overall benefits of the industrial supply chain, for the healthy development of the supply chain.

Military industry bills are commercial acceptance bills issued by financial companies affiliated with the top ten military industrial groups. Available in both paper and electronic formats, these bills are built on key principles: unified signing, standardized risk control, credit enhancement channels, and coordination centers. They operate on a system of mutual recognition among member units, facilitating easier circulation and realization. Military financial companies partner with banks to sign credit enhancement agreements, boosting the creditworthiness of bills and enabling holders to conduct discounting and other transactions at cooperating banks. This mutual recognition and credit enhancement significantly improve the payment, settlement, and financing functions of military industry bills. Consequently, these bills enhance the efficiency of the industrial chain operations of the military industrial group companies, promote the development of financial companies' bill business, and foster a military industry bill ecosystem that supports overall bill market growth.

Enterprise Bill Pass, established by the China Reform Holdings Corporation (CRHC), is a central enterprise commercial bill circulation platform. It operates on the principle of "joint contribution and responsibility sharing for mutual benefits." This platform leverages central enterprises as its core to manage enterprise credit, optimize accounts receivable and payable, and provide customers with a one-stop information service solution using commercial acceptance bills. The platform integrates central enterprises, commercial banks, and SMEs in the industrial chain to create a central enterprise commercial acceptance bill circulation platform and establish a "credit sharing and risk sharing" mechanism. It connects central enterprises at one end and commercial banks at the other, while also linking to the PBC's ECDS through commercial banks. This setup offers one-stop operational services for commercial bills, including issuance, acceptance, endorsement, pledge, splitting, discount, and payment. Enterprise Bill Pass, with its credit mutual recognition and enhancement mechanisms, is pioneering the diversification of payment methods among central enterprises. It effectively utilizes the commercial credit value of central enterprises and reduces overall financing costs in their industrial chain.

SECTION 2

Rise of Bill-Like Instruments on the Supply Chain: Transferable Electronic Vouchers

Narrowly defined bills, including promissory notes, bills of exchange, and checks, are financial instruments signed by the drawer. These securities signify an unconditional agreement to pay a specific sum to the drawer or another party. They can be circulated and transferred, serving various functions such as payment, settlement, financing, investment, and trading. Bill-like instruments, as the name suggests, resemble traditional bills but have additional features. They also facilitate payment settlement and financing. The emergence of bill-like instruments overcomes the limitations of traditional bills, such as indivisibility and difficult access. They are, to some extent, a product of internet finance growth in China. By leveraging advanced information technology, bill-like instruments address traditional bills' shortcomings in everyday payment and financing activities. Currently, well-established bill-like instrument platforms in China include supply chain financial technology service companies like JDH, China Enterprise Cloud Chain, and Ouyeel.

I. Background

1. Financing Difficulties for SMEs

SMEs play a crucial role in China's economy. The National Bureau of Statistics reported that in 2017, SMEs accounted for over 97% of all industrial enterprises in China. For China's economic upgrade and transformation, the healthy growth of SMEs is crucial. However, these businesses often lack efficient financial support, which hinders their development. SMEs face several challenges in securing financing. First, due to their small size and limited assets, SMEs struggle to secure financing and guarantees. This issue is particularly common among startup small and micro enterprises. Their modest size, strength, and limited assets often prevent them from obtaining bank loans, and finding guarantors is challenging. Second, when SMEs do secure loans, they face high costs. Banks typically charge high-interest rates, and some even require additional guarantee and fund usage fees. Last, the procedures for securing bank loans are complex and time-consuming. Loan approval can take up to half a month or longer in some banks. This is particularly problematic for SMEs, which often need small amounts of financing with short cycles and high frequency. Many orders require immediate financing, making long-term approval processes unfeasible, which creates a complex and challenging financing landscape for SMEs.

2. Difficulty in Leveraging Bill Functions

China's underdeveloped credit system and the operational risks associated with bills have made it difficult for enterprises to meet daily settlement and financing needs. The financial system in China revolves primarily around the banking sector, with bank credit dominating the market. SMEs, due to their limited scale and assets, often struggle to have their bills accepted by banks, preventing them from financing directly through bank acceptance bills. Additionally, the slow development of commercial credit in China has resulted in a significantly smaller market for commercial bills compared to bank bills. The market acceptance of commercial bills issued by SMEs is low, and even those issued and accepted by large enterprises sometimes struggle to find endorsement and circulation. Traditional paper bills also come with substantial operational risks such as susceptibility to forgery and alterations, leading to the emergence of cloned, altered, and defective bills. These risks can cause financial losses and reputational damage to enterprises. Moreover, the use of paper bills for payment settlement is less convenient than electronic payment methods, further reducing the appeal of bill usage for enterprises.

3. Rise of Supply Chain Finance

The evolution of supply chain finance greatly supports cost reduction, efficiency improvement, supply-demand matching, and industrial upgrading. It plays a crucial role in the structural reform of the financial supply side. Relevant government departments have introduced policies to bolster supply chain innovation and application. For example, in October 2017, the General Office of the State Council issued the *Guiding Opinions on Actively Promoting Supply Chain Innovation and Application*. In 2018, the MOC, the Ministry of Industry and Information Technology, and eight other departments jointly issued the *A Notice on Launching Pilot Projects for Supply Chain Innovation and Application*. Both documents encouraged core supply chain enterprises to cooperate with commercial banks and other enterprises to innovate supply chain financial service models. These policies, along with nationwide pilot demonstrations, have fostered a favorable environment for supply chain innovation. Universities are also encouraged to cultivate supply chain finance talent, further boosting the sector. This has created an unprecedented favorable political, social, and economic environment for the development of supply chain finance, providing opportunities for the leapfrog development of China's supply chain. SMEs are the mainstay of China's supply chain system. Therefore, resolving their financing problems is vital for the development of supply chain finance. Since traditional bills cannot fully serve this purpose, a similar credit tool could serve as a substitute. This context led to the emergence of bill-like instruments. Amid the vigorous development of supply chain finance, the "industrial chain + fintech" model has enabled the rapid growth of bill-like instruments on various supply chain fintech platforms. These tools help address challenges such as low capital turnover and difficult risk control in supply chain finance.

II. Development

1. JDH's Golden Order

In 2015, TCL set up à JDH supply chain financial information technology platform. This platform was designed to reduce financing costs for cooperative businesses within the industrial ecosystem, improve the financing environment, and foster mutually beneficial partnerships. In June of that year, the first electronic accounts receivable ownership certificate, known as the "gold order," was issued nationwide. This online-operated voucher, based on real transaction orders, represents accounts receivable rights. It can be divided, repurchased, and used for financing purposes.

The "Golden Order" created by JDH supply chain financing platform overcomes the drawbacks of traditional bills in two ways. First, it improves on traditional commercial bills by removing the limitations of paper bills, which can't be divided. SMEs can generate "golden orders" online and sell them to any fund provider, significantly improving financing efficiency and activating accounts receivable. These "golden orders" facilitate financing; enabling enterprises to increase their capital turnover rate, improve operational efficiency, and reduce operating costs. Second, the electronic "golden orders" eliminate the issues of complicated commercial bill verification and susceptibility to falsification. Core enterprises can obtain unique electronic credentials online. The use of blockchain technology in TCL's online supply chain finance application greatly enhances security. For financing enterprises, "golden orders" boost capital turnover efficiency. For banks and other fund providers, they reduce verification time and operational risks. By enhancing the entire supply chain's financing efficiency, JDH has also expanded the scope of banking services. The accumulated financing information helps improve core enterprises' supply chain management capabilities. As of September 2021, JDH has formed a comprehensive service system backed by "supply chain + technological innovation," with "golden orders" (electronic debt vouchers for multi-level circulation of accounts receivable) as the foundation, and intelligent credit and risk control as extensions. This system integrates supply chain digital management, intelligent risk control, and online operation. It provides supply chain financing services to over 25,000 supply chain enterprises, with small and micro enterprises constituting more than 90%.

2. "Cloud Credit" of Chinese Enterprise Cloud Chain

Established in 2015, China Enterprise Cloud Chain (Beijing) Financial Information Service Co., Ltd. is a state-owned, mixed-ownership internet finance company. It's jointly funded by CRRC Group, 11 central manufacturing enterprises (including China Railway Construction Corporation), 2 financial institutions (including the ICBC), 6 local state-owned enterprises (including Beijing Shougang and Zijin Mining), and 4 private enterprises (including Kingdee Software). The company aims to establish an industrial internet finance platform, providing supply chain financial management services for both large and small-to-medium-sized enterprises on the supply chain. These services also extend to financial institutions such as banks and factoring companies.

"Cloud Credit" is a financial information service operating on the Chinese Enterprise Cloud Chain platform. It enables large enterprise groups to convert their high-quality enterprise credit into transferable, financeable, and flexibly configurable assets. This secure, efficient, and real-time service has a specific validity period. SMEs can transfer, finance, or hold their received "cloud credit" through the Cloud Chain platform during this period. "Cloud Credit" breathes new life into idle "chain debt" by offering a novel debt clearance tool. It harnesses the premium credit resources of large enterprises to boost fund circulation throughout the industrial chain. This approach enhances both quality and efficiency in enterprise development, fostering shared prosperity among supply chain businesses. Beyond significantly improving debt clearance efficiency, "Cloud Credit" provides SMEs with a new, convenient avenue for low-cost financing. Since its launch in 2015, the Cloud Chain has attracted 50,623 enterprise users. "Cloud Credit" has confirmed rights of 119.3 billion yuan, facilitated 63.2 billion yuan in factored financing, and managed transactions totaling 349.4 billion yuan. Notably, over 86% of these transactions have supported SME financing.

3. "Tongbao" of Ouyeel

Shanghai Ouyeel Financial Information Service Co., Ltd. is a supply chain financial service platform under China Baowu Iron and Steel Group Co., Ltd. (China Baowu). Founded in February 2015, it comprises four subsidiaries: Ouyeel Factoring, Ouyeel Pawnshop, Ouyeel Guarantee, and Chengrong Real Estate. Ouyeel Service was established to provide supply chain finance solutions to participants in the steel ecosystem. By harnessing modern technology and the synergy of "industrial finance + financial technology," it aims to create a comprehensive financial service platform that integrates financial technology research and development, ecosystem financial services, and financial data and risk information management.

"Tongbao" is an electronic debt voucher issued by a buyer (core enterprise) to its seller (supplier) based on accounts payable. It offers differential circulation and easy financing. Developed by Ouyeel Services, the "Tongbao" platform provides comprehensive online services for issuance, acceptance, transfer, maturity collection, and financing applications to financial institutions. The product benefits suppliers through flexible splitting, non-recourse circulation, and online operations. Upon receiving "Tongbao," suppliers can engage in differential circulation, finance according to their needs, and agree to circulate in a non-recourse form, all through a simple and straightforward process. For core enterprises, "Tongbao" is separable, financeable, and easy to circulate, allowing their credit to extend to their superior suppliers. By leveraging finance and technology, it visualizes its own ecosystem. While offering new financing channels for SMEs in the iron and steel industry supply chain, it also enhances procurement and transaction conditions. As of January 25, 2021, following two years of development, the Ouyeel "Tongbao business" has expanded to cover 28 cities and provinces nationwide. With cumulative transactions exceeding 100 billion yuan, it promotes the digital transformation of supply chain finance and fosters the integration of financial innovation and technological services.

III. Advantages

1. Divisibility and Ease of Circulation

Bill-like instruments such as "Golden Order," "Cloud Credit," and "Tongbao" are known for their divisibility and ease of circulation. These features address the limitations of traditional bills, which are indivisible and difficult to circulate, while also providing superior payment and settlement functions. The divisibility of these instruments allows enterprises to tailor financing to their specific needs in terms of quantity and amount. This flexibility meets the funding requirements of SMEs, which often need small, frequent, and urgent funding, serving as an excellent complement to existing credit products. Bill-like products issued on supply chain finance platforms offer financing amounts ranging from a few hundred yuan to several hundred thousand yuan. This range fully accommodates SMEs' needs for small, low-interest, and convenient financing. Upon receiving these instruments, enterprises can divide them to meet various payment and financing needs. These products can be circulated between enterprises registered on the supply chain platform, reducing information asymmetry and enhancing liquidity. Data from the JDH platform demonstrates the strong liquidity of such bills in the supply chain: "golden orders" have reached the ninth level of suppliers, involving up to 126 suppliers.

2. Easy Financing and Cost Reduction

First, bill-like instruments are divisible, which allows businesses to raise funds precisely matching their needs, preventing waste. Second, supply chain platforms provide various financing models, including direct investment from partner banks, accounts receivable factoring, and supply chain ABS. This variety enables enterprises to choose the most suitable financing method, optimizing fund management and reducing costs. Finally, bill-like product financing can be completed online, eliminating the need for complex off-line loan procedures. This T+0 receiving experience is superior to traditional credit, saving enterprises significant time. Efficient grant of loans also improves cash management for enterprises. For example, Ouyeel's "Tongbao" platform connects directly with financial institutions like Baowu Finance Company, ICBC, ABC, Construction Bank, CMB, CITIC Bank, China Everbright Bank, and Huishang Bank. This connection provides full online, T+0 fast financing services for supply chain customers. Additionally, Ouyeel has established the "Factoring Pass" platform to offer more financing solutions for accounts receivable in the supply chain. This reduces capital management and operational costs for iron and steel enterprises.

3. Credit Transfer and Chain Debt Resolution

Bill-like instruments facilitate credit transfer and sharing among supply chain enterprises through their circulation. By enabling division and distribution, these Bill Pass-like products overcome the tracking, discount, and circulation challenges faced by traditional commercial bills. The divisibility of bill-like instruments allows for the quantification, fragmentation, and circulation of credit from high-quality enterprises that issue them. This results in a significant reduction in overall financial costs for all participants in the industry chain and effectively decreases bank financing risks. Moreover, it extends high-quality financing services to SMEs in urgent need of funds.

Much like traditional bills, bill-like products also have the function of offsetting debts. On supply chain platforms, enterprises can issue these products to suppliers to offset accounts payable, and accept them to balance accounts receivable. This process transforms accounts payable and receivable on the supply chain into more liquid bill-like instruments. As a result, it aids enterprises in clearing "chain debts," improving debt clearance efficiency, and optimizing corporate financial management.

IV. Lessons from Bill-Like Instruments

Bill-like instruments emerged as a response to challenges enterprises faced with traditional bills. While the indivisibility and difficulty in circulation of traditional bills was no longer a problem with the introduction of the Shanghai Commercial Paper Exchange Company Ltd.'s supply chain bill platform, the financing problems of bills still requires attention. Moreover, it's crucial to address non-interoperability of bill-like instrument platforms and strengthen system and regulatory frameworks. First, efforts should be made to propel the development of the Shanghai Commercial Paper Exchange Company Ltd.'s supply chain bill platform to a new phase. This platform can encourage eligible large core enterprises to establish their own supply chain platforms and integrate third-party services with the Shanghai Commercial Paper Exchange Company Ltd. system. Services like bill pledge financing, discount, interbank discount, rediscount, and cross-platform circulation of supply chain bills can enhance bill liquidity. Second, efforts should be made to promote the use of bills in the industrial, supply, and trade chains, to increase the willingness of enterprises to use bills for daily economic activities like payment, settlement, exchange, financing, and trading. Providing financing guarantees can alleviate financing difficulties for on-chain enterprises and foster commercial credit development within these chains. Finally, for rule creation and risk prevention, the Shanghai Commercial Paper Exchange Company Ltd. should lead efforts to refine supply chain bill practices, improve risk prevention mechanisms, ensure proper information disclosure, and learn from risk management experiences of platforms like JDH and Cloud Chain. Open dialogues should be encouraged to incorporate market suggestions and understand needs.

SECTION 3

Blockchain Bills: Application of Blockchain Technology

Since their inception, bill forms have continually evolved to keep pace with the times. Different historical periods and technological environments have spawned various bill formats. For example, China's recovered bill market, following the start of reform and opening up, has transitioned from paper to electronic bills over several decades. This progression mirrors the development and popularization of information technology in China. Technology continues to drive the evolution of bill forms. As the internet has developed, electronic bills have adapted to meet its requirements, leading to format changes. With the advancement of modern technologies like big data and artificial intelligence, bill digitization has become inevitable. In recent years, the emergence of blockchain-based financial applications such as Bitcoin has spurred exploration and practice of blockchain-based digital bills.

I. Adaptability of Blockchain and Bills

Despite the gradual improvement and growth of the Chinese bill market, SMEs in China still face difficulties using bills for financing. These enterprises generally hold bills with smaller amounts, shorter maturities, and acceptance by smaller banks, making it challenging to secure effective financing. Traditional financial institutions typically offer insufficient support to SMEs due to the high risks and transaction costs associated with these bills. In recent years, bill-related risks have frequently occurred, with several banks penalized by regulatory authorities for violating bill business regulations. To mitigate these risks, improve efficiency, and foster innovation, major commercial banks have started leveraging blockchain financial technology.

A bill is a transferable instrument that serves as a value voucher with both payment and financing functions. It carries high value and is backed by bank or commercial credit. Once issued, crucial details like the face amount and date cannot be changed. Bills are circulatory in nature, allowing for acceptance, endorsement, discount, interbank discount, and collection within a specific life cycle. Completed transactions are irrevocable, often necessitating a third party to ensure transaction security for participants. The nature of bills demands that their face information and transaction details be complete and tamper-proof. Due to the typically large transaction amounts involved, bills require higher security standards than general financial transactions.

Blockchain refers to a distributed, shareable public ledger maintained through consensus mechanisms and accessible to all participants. No centralized entity controls it, and revisions are only possible through strict rules and public protocols. This technology enables a decentralized, trust-free credit system and collectively maintains a reliable database, a Distributed Shared Ledger that's virtually unchangeable. From a data perspective, blockchain allows for distributed recording (maintained collectively by participants) and storage (where all nodes can save data). It creates an immutable, trustworthy database arranged chronologically, not stored on a central server. Blockchain maintains this distributed database through decentralization, trustworthiness, and encryption algorithms. Blockchain differs from traditional centralized technology in several key ways: First, it uses a decentralized trust mechanism, enabling secure transactions without fear of counterfeits or identity denial. Second, it ensures data security, integrity, and immutability through cryptographic algorithms. Third, it employs various privacy protection strategies to achieve participant anonymity. Finally, it offers programmable smart contracts, simplifying contract viewing and publishing for participants.

These characteristics make blockchain highly compatible with bill business. It uses asymmetric encryption algorithms and consensus mechanisms to build trust between network nodes, relying on algorithms rather than third-party financial institutions. Blockchain's capabilities to enable smart contract and automatic transactions can streamline the bill business process and enhance the efficiency of bill market operations. Each blockchain transaction is timestamped upon completion, with the bookkeeper sending transaction data to all other network nodes. These timestamps accurately indicate the order of transactions, providing traceability and transparency, which can mitigate risk in the bill market. The public ledger's distributed dissemination and recording can aid regulatory authorities in accessing bill transaction information, offering a novel approach to financial regulation. Consequently, blockchain technology has the potential to significantly improve the bill market. This potential was demonstrated when Ganzhou Bank and Shenzhen Blockchain Financial Services jointly launched a blockchain product on March 15, 2017. Subsequently, on January 25, 2018, the Shanghai Commercial Paper Exchange Company Ltd. successfully experimented with blockchain digital bills.

II. Digital Bill Blockchain Platform

In 2016, the PBC's head office led an initiative involving the Shanghai Commercial Paper Exchange Company Ltd., its Digital Currency Research Institute, Zhongchao Credit Card Industry Development Co., Ltd., and pilot commercial banks. Their goal was to research blockchain-based full life cycle registration and circulation of digital bills. On December 15 of that year, they successfully tested a prototype system in a simulated operating environment. Building on this success, the Shanghai Commercial Paper Exchange Company Ltd. and the Digital Currency Research Institute spearheaded further development in 2017. They focused on researching, developing, and launching an experimental production system for a digital bill trading platform. This system was launched on January 25, 2018, and has been operating successfully since its launch.

Blockchain digital bills are a novel form of bills developed using blockchain technology, combined with existing bill attributes, regulatory environments, and market realities. Unlike current electronic bills, blockchain digital bills have a distinct technological architecture. They retain all the features and functionalities of existing electronic bills, while adding the unique advantages of blockchain technology, making them more secure, intelligent, convenient, and promising. While bills align well with blockchain, bill transactions differ from Bitcoin transactions. They can't heavily emphasize decentralization and anonymity, as financial assets like bills require identity management and business supervision. As a result, Bitcoin's trading mechanism can't be directly applied to bill transactions. In developing digital bill platforms, the traits of blockchain and bills have been carefully considered. A digital bill technology infrastructure has been created using blockchain technology and smart contracts. Each digital bill is a program code containing the bill's business logic and relevant data. These digital bills, operating on the blockchain, have independent lifecycles and self-maintenance capabilities. They support core business types such as acceptance, endorsement, transfer, discount, interbank discount, and redemption. Various business rules can be executed through smart contract programming.

Blockchain digital bills offer several key advantages over electronic bills: First, they eliminate the need for central servers and applications in system construction and data storage. This reduces development costs, lowers maintenance and optimization expenses, and mitigates centralization risks. Second, blockchain technology ensures data integrity, transparency, and verifiability through timestamps, enabling tracking and querying of all value exchanges. It also protects trade secrets, such as issuer and acceptor identities. Third, blockchain's smart contracts allow for programmable and controllable bills throughout their life cycle. This enables diverse transaction control methods, like a bill-holding model where the buyback date is coded into the smart contract, triggering automatic redemption at maturity. Smart contracts, implemented through code, eliminate the need for off-line contracts and prevent execution defaults. The pilot operation of the new digital bill platform showcases these benefits, enhancing business transparency and regulatory efficiency. It also opens doors for bill business innovation. Within the bounds of *The Negotiable Instrument Law of the PRC*, new services such as bill pledges, bill pools, and bill splitting can be explored and developed.

The digital bill trading platform is a crucial initiative for incorporating blockchain technology into financial market infrastructure. The successful launch and trial run of the experimental production system represents a significant breakthrough in digital bills, marking a milestone in bill market development. First, this successful launch and trial in a real production environment demonstrates the first practical application of blockchain technology in bill business, proving its viability in real-world scenarios. Second, through the creation of this system, the Shanghai Commercial Paper Exchange Company Ltd. has gained valuable experience in blockchain development and application, fostered a professional team, and laid a solid foundation for future blockchain applications in the bill market. Finally, the development of this experimental production system offers the Shanghai Commercial Paper Exchange Company Ltd. an opportunity to further drive innovation in its development and services. By harnessing blockchain technology, the exchange can continuously innovate its services and products, foster standardized and efficient digital bill operations, and infuse new vitality into the bill market.

III. Problems

1. Capacity and Efficiency Issues

Capacity and efficiency challenges have long hindered the widespread adoption of blockchain technology in finance. Every transaction within the blockchain system is recorded, requiring each participant node to download, store, and update data blocks in real-time. Full data synchronization across all nodes can create significant network pressure, while the storage capacity requirements of each node could limit development potential. The transaction volume in the bill market is enormous, demanding high-speed transaction processing. If transactions per second exceed the system's design capacity or the capacity of the weakest node, transactions will queue, negatively impacting user experience. To address this, it's necessary to enhance single-chain performance through engineering optimization and algorithmic innovation, and to rethink the overall system architecture.

2. Lack of Encryption Mechanism

Public blockchains use a "pseudonym" system for anonymity, but their transaction records remain visible to all participants, compromising privacy. Real-world commercial applications demand varied and strict privacy measures, making robust cryptographic solutions essential for large-scale implementation. While blockchain technology itself lacks built-in encryption, custom functions can be added to blockchain nodes. However, this approach carries risks: if malicious code is introduced, it could potentially compromise the entire network, leading to system-wide failure.

3. Technical Risks

Implementing decentralized smart contracts using blockchain technology presents significant technical challenges and requires complex programming. Even with expert teams and thorough code reviews, absolute security remains elusive. Inherent operational risks in the technology may expose vulnerabilities to potential hacking. Moreover, as smart contracts are still in their infancy, future risks are difficult to anticipate. Legal and regulatory uncertainties further compound the application risks associated with blockchain and smart contracts.

SECTION 4

Green Bill: Facilitating Green Development

In August 2016, seven departments, including the PBC and the Ministry of Finance, jointly issued the *Guiding Opinions on Building a Green Finance System* with the State Council's approval. This document defines green finance and initiates the development of a green finance system, emphasizing the importance of a green finance policy system. While China's green finance products are diversifying and the scale of green credit and green bonds is growing rapidly, inconsistencies persist. Products such as green insurance and green funds are expanding quickly. However, the overall product structure remains uneven, with significant variations in the development speed of different products and some showing limited growth.

Green bills remain an evolving concept without a clear definition domestically or internationally. The *Guiding Opinions on Building a Green Finance System* describes them as bill business products and services that support green projects. These projects span areas like climate action, environmental protection, resource optimization, and green enterprise development. Green bills are typically issued or discounted by qualifying green enterprises and may include green bank acceptance bills and green commercial acceptance bills. Government bodies, including the PBC and the China Banking and Insurance Regulatory Commission, along with other regulatory departments and financial institutions, are actively exploring both practical and theoretical approaches to support the green industry through bills. China's green bill practices fall into three main categories: those in Karamay, Xinjiang; the Industrial Bank's "green bill" business; and the "green bill" operations of the PBC's Shenzhen Central Sub-Branch.

I. Background

China's green finance journey began in 2006 with the launch of the 11th Five-Year Plan. This plan introduced binding targets for reducing energy consumption and pollution, paving the way for green finance initiatives. In 2008, a significant milestone was reached when the China

Banking Regulatory Commission, the China Insurance Regulatory Commission, and the National Environmental Protection Administration jointly issued guidance on environmental protection, energy conservation, and emission reduction. These directives laid the groundwork for green credit, green insurance, and green securities, establishing the fundamental rules for these emerging financial products.

During the 12th Five-Year Plan period (2011–2015), green finance saw rapid development. The 18th National Congress of the CPC, for the first time, incorporated ecological civilization development into the five-sphere integrated plan, China's overall plan for building socialism with Chinese characteristics, that is, to promote coordinated progress in the economic, political, cultural, social, and eco-environmental fields. They proposed the idea that "lucid waters and lush mountains are invaluable assets." Green finance systems like the *Green Credit Guidelines* and the *Green Credit Statistical System* were introduced, creating a comprehensive policy framework encompassing business guidelines, recognition standards, statistical systems, and assessment and evaluation procedures.

In August 2016, seven departments, including the PBC and the Ministry of Finance, jointly issued the *Guiding Opinions on Building a Green Finance System*. This document comprehensively outlines the requirements for establishing a green finance system and provides a top-level design for its development. This marked the start of a deep implementation phase of green finance and green finance was constantly supporting the development of "Beautiful China." The size of green credit and green bonds grew rapidly, and green bills began to emerge.

II. Development

In June 2018, the Industrial Bank Beijing Branch successfully launched its "Green Bill Pass" initiative. This marked innovative breakthroughs in addressing the financing challenges and high costs faced by small and medium-sized green enterprises. The first enterprises using the "Green Bill Pass" service secured green bill discounts at rates below prevailing market rates, enabling them to achieve daily capital turnover with reduced financial costs. This initiative earned widespread acclaim. In the same month, the Karamay Central Sub-Branch of the PBC successfully processed the first green bill rediscount in Xinjiang. This marked a significant advance in the green financial reform and innovation pilot zone, backed by monetary policy tools. The funds from the green bills were primarily invested in the green upgrade of traditional petroleum and petrochemical industries in Karamay, the harmless treatment of pollutants like ground crude oil, and other transformation projects.

In October 2018, the Shenzhen Central Sub-Branch of the PBC launched its inaugural "Green Bill Pass" special rediscount quota, totaling 1 billion yuan. This initiative gave priority to rediscount operations for enterprises listed on the "Green Enterprise List," a roster jointly approved by the Shenzhen Central Sub-Branch and the Shenzhen Green Finance Committee. The program provided green small and micro enterprises with an accessible, cost-effective financing channel.

From 2018 to 2020, branches and sub-branches of commercial banks and sub-branches of the PBC nationwide successively implemented green bill discount and rediscount services. This move benefitted an increasing number of green enterprises. The precise allocation of green funds to these enterprises and projects led to the continuous expansion of the green bill market and a steady rise in market activity. Concurrently, some regions began developing guidelines and regulations to standardize green bills, while market research on this financial instrument continued to deepen.

In 2019, the Guangdong Interbank Association and the International Research Institute of Green Finance at the Central University of Finance and Economics published the *Research on Green Bill Standards.* They proposed that green bill standards should be identifiable, operable, measurable, and promotable. This approach would require a unified "standard setting process" and "standard setting elements," while considering green-related catalogs and clarifying boundaries between green industries and projects. On October 22, 2019, at a green finance government-bank-enterprise conference hosted by Bank of Jiujiang, the International Research Institute of Green Finance presented the nation's first research findings on green bill standards. Bank of Jiujiang had jointly initiated this groundbreaking research.

On March 25, 2020, the Nanchang Branch of the PBC issued the *Jiangxi Province Green Bill Recognition and Management Guidelines (Trial)* to standardize green bill recognition criteria. A month later, on April 27, the branch released *A Notice on Using Rediscounting Tools to Support the Development of Green Bills.* This notice established a proportion limit specifically to guarantee green bill rediscounting, creating a "green channel" for the process. Notably, this approach isn't constrained by individual bill amounts and provides exclusive services to ensure bills can be processed immediately.

On September 19, 2020, at the 2020 Annual Meeting of the Green Finance Professional Committee of the Chinese Financial Society and the China Green Finance Forum, the International Research Institute of Green Finance at the Central University of Finance and Economics unveiled the country's first green bill identification and certification system. This innovative system helps commercial banks accurately identify green bills, streamlining the application process. It also enhances traceability in business processing for third-party certification agencies, reducing the risk of "greenwashing." For regulatory authorities, the system simplifies green bill statistical work and provides valuable data to support future decision-making.

III. Significance

1. Implementing the National Green Development Strategy

The report to the 19th National Congress of the CPC proposed, "Building an ecological civilization is vital to sustain the Chinese nation's development ... What we are doing today to build an ecological civilization will benefit generations to come." Fostering innovation in green finance and developing green bills can incentivize financial institutions to allocate resources more effectively. This approach can bolster credit support for green industries and projects, promoting a harmonious balance between economic growth and environmental protection. Ultimately, it accelerates the development of an ecological civilization and aligns with national strategic policies.

2. Supporting Green Financing for SMEs

A significant issue currently plaguing the green finance system is its low penetration rate among various non-financial market entities, particularly SMEs. However, the bill market has seen significant growth in recent years, providing substantial support for SMEs. Currently, SMEs make up over 60% of bill financing. Bills offer easy issuance, high liquidity, and standardized transactions, meeting SMEs' needs for quick, frequent, and urgent financing. Green bills, in particular, can offer targeted support to green SMEs in line with monetary policy standards.

3. Enhancing the Commercial Credit System

Bills, particularly commercial acceptance bills, play a crucial role in establishing a commercial credit system. They function as settlement and financing tools for enterprises while serving as key instruments for commercial banks to manage their assets and liabilities. The rise of green bills, particularly green commercial acceptance bills, can expand the pool of bill issuers and diversify their application scenarios. This expansion fosters the development of a more sophisticated bill credit rating system, ultimately creating an ideal commercial credit environment within the domestic market.

4. Improving Monetary Policy Transmission Efficiency

Green bills directly impact the real economy through their trade, settlement, investment, and financing functions. Moreover, the PBC can fine-tune various factors such as total rediscount amount, price, industry, type, and target, to guide market expectations and precisely control currency release. This approach significantly enhances the effectiveness and flexibility of monetary policies.

IV. Difficulties

1. Inadequate Bill Infrastructure

The development of green bills in China is closely tied to infrastructure construction, which needs improvement. First, the regulations and systems concerning green bills in China are incomplete. Current rules fail to clearly define the characteristics and processes of green bills, or clarify the basic requirements for green project evaluation. This ambiguity hinders institutional support for green bills. Second, China lacks a comprehensive green information platform. The low level of digitization in green finance and projects makes information sharing difficult, reducing the efficiency of green bill financing. Last, China lacks clear assessment indicators and regulatory requirements for green bills. There's no specific plan for promoting and supervising the green bill business, which remains in the experimental and exploration stage.

2. Lack of Incentivization

Applying existing green bond standards to green bill certification poses significant challenges, impeding market growth. The frequent endorsement and circulation of bills further complicate the certification process. Operational complexities in certification and supervision make green bill certification more intricate than its green bond counterpart, demanding heightened risk prevention and control measures. Without targeted incentive policies, the green bills market struggles to reach its full potential.

3. Difficulty in Balancing Profitability and Risk Control in Bank-Enterprise Relationships

Compared to conventional bill business, green bill business requires commercial banks to establish their own recognition standards. This increases the internal management burden and business pressure on these banks, making it more costly than traditional bill business. Furthermore, account managers from various bank branches might intentionally "go greenwashing" to meet performance targets, or collude with enterprises to fabricate "green credentials" to secure green fund support. These practices could potentially introduce risks and hidden dangers. In the current green bill development landscape, banks and enterprises face a delicate balancing act between profitability and risk control.

SECTION 5

Theoretical Research: A Hundred Flowers Bloom

I. ICBC Bill Business Department

On November 9, 2000, the ICBC established its Bill Business Department in Shanghai. This department, approved by the PBC, became the country's first national, professional bill operating institution. From its inception, the department embraced the social responsibility of "serving the real economy for public good." Staying true to ICBC's stature as a major bank, it has prioritized "specialization, professionalism, and expertise." The department's achievements are impressive: Its cumulative bill trading volume has exceeded 30 trillion yuan, while its direct trading customer base has expanded from an initial 87 to over 2,000. The department's professional services have steadily grown to encompass various areas, including bill asset holding, trading operations, asset services, and product innovation.

1. Building Think Tanks and Establishing Journals

The ICBC established its Bill Business Department to foster the development of bill theory and business practices. Subsequently, the Bill Professional Committee of the China Urban Financial Society was formed, the first academic group and research think tank in China's bill industry. Supported by the China Urban Finance Society, the PBC, banking and insurance regulatory authorities, as well as external media, universities, and financial peers, the Bill Professional Committee has played a crucial role in strategic planning. It has organized high-level academic seminars, promoted collaboration in the bill market, and conducted research activities. On March 28, 2002, the ICBC's Bill Business Department and the Bill Professional Committee jointly launched *Bill Research*, the only professional journal in China's bill industry at the time. This publication served bill business operations and promoted the development of China's bill market. *Bill Research* has since actively promoted bill business policies, explored theoretical aspects, conducted practical research, exchanged advanced experiences, and disseminated knowledge of bill business. It has become an important platform for showcasing China's bill industry's academic contributions and research results while facilitating industry peer exchanges. In 2008 and 2012, the ICBC Bill Business Department and the Financial Market Department of the PBC's Shanghai head office collaborated to publish the *China Bill Market Development Report 2008* and the *Report on China Bill Market Development in the New Century (2000–2011)* respectively. As of September 2020, *Bill Research* has published 72 issues, consistently showcasing new theoretical and practical research achievements in bill business and contributing positively to the development of China's bill industry.

2. ICBC Bill Price Index: China's Financial Industry's First Bill Index

In May 2003, the ICBC Bill Business Department pioneered the ICBC Bill Price Index, the first of its kind in China's financial industry. This groundbreaking index was officially unveiled on November 9 of the same year, coinciding with the department's third anniversary. The ICBC Bill Price Index is divided into two categories: the bill interbank discount price index and the bill repurchase price index. It's published weekly in *International Financial News* and *Financial News*, as well as on the ICBC website for internal distribution. This index serves as an objective barometer of the bill market's overall trends, offering crucial insights for analyzing interest rate fluctuations in China's bill market. The information it provides on the trends of bill interest rates proves invaluable for the PBC, various commercial banks, and bill business institutions. Moreover, it represents a significant stride toward achieving centralized trading in the bill market.

3. China's First Authoritative Regional Bill Market Price Index

Since 2008, the ICBC Bill Business Department has spearheaded the creation of three joint conferences on bill business in Shanghai, the Yangtze River Delta region, and nationwide. It introduced China's first authoritative regional bill market price index—the Yangtze River

Delta Bill Discount Price Index. This index is a specialized tool that reflects the average price level and overall trend of the bill discount market in the Yangtze River Delta region over specific periods. Scientific, representative, and credible, it serves as a "weather vane" for dynamic changes in the region's bill market prices.

II. China Bill Research Center

In December 2017, the Shanghai Commercial Paper Exchange Company Ltd. and Shanghai University of Finance and Economics partnered with six major banks, including ICBC, ABC, CMB, SPD Bank, Industrial Bank, and China Minsheng Bank, to establish the China Bill Research Center. Since its inception, the center has adhered to the principles of "leveraging complementary advantages and resource sharing for mutual benefit." It has fostered communication among market participants, enhanced their collaborative innovation in theoretical research and talent cultivation, and driven the reform and development of China's bill market. The center functions as both an academic hub and a platform for translating research findings into practical applications for the reform and development of the bill market.

1. Hub for Experts and Scholars and Platform for Exchanges

The Shanghai Commercial Paper Exchange Company Ltd. hosts annual summit forums for the bill market, bringing together participants from regulatory departments, local governments, financial institutions, enterprises, and universities. Examples of these forums include the Bill Market Reform and Development Summit Forum, Bill Market Support for High-Quality Economic Development Summit Forum, and Summit Forum on Bill Market Development Under the Dual-Circulation New Development Pattern. These forums discussed key financial market topics in relation to the year's macroeconomic situation and policies. Additionally, the exchange hosted multiple "flowing water forums," where industry experts and scholars explore macroeconomics, market dynamics, and business aspects. These gatherings aim to harness collective wisdom, learn from domestic and foreign financial market experiences, and better guide the bill market in serving the real economy. Furthermore, the exchange launched "On Bills," a seminar series focusing on a specific theme in each issue. It addresses key issues in the development of the bill market, facilitates in-depth and problem-oriented discussions, and promotes industry exchanges to build consensus through thematic debates.

2. Research on the Bill Market and Essay Solicitation

Since its inception, the China Bill Research Center has collaborated with council members and universities to carry out annual key research projects. These initiatives have focused on improving the bill market's operational mechanism, revising bill laws and regulations, and developing innovative supply chain financial service models. This work has not only provided robust theoretical support and practical insights for policy formulation and market development but has also offered valuable recommendations for the reform, innovation, and growth of the bill market.

Each year, the China Bill Research Center organizes an essay solicitation for the bill market. The number of submissions has been growing, and their quality has steadily improved. This activity encourages market entities to reflect on and exchange ideas about bill business, garnering greater attention from various sectors of society. In 2021, the research center plans to launch a working paper series, which will be published periodically through new media channels to further promote market exchanges.

3. Writing Books and Publishing Publications

The Shanghai Commercial Paper Exchange Company Ltd., leveraging its extensive network of national bill market participants and centralized bill information data, has proactively assumed responsibility for industry knowledge dissemination. To date, it has published more than ten books, totaling over 2.2 million words.

The Shanghai Commercial Paper Exchange Company Ltd. has compiled and published *The Chinese Bill Market: A Historical Review and Future Prospects*, which thoroughly reviews the development of the bill market over the past three decades. It deeply contemplates the necessity and inevitability of the market's transformation and development, explores future directions, and provides practical reference materials for bill practitioners. Additionally, the Shanghai Commercial Paper Exchange Company Ltd. collaborates annually with key financial institutions to produce the *China Bill Market Development Report*. This joint effort not only sparks enthusiasm among market participants but also continues to drive the growth of China's bill market.

In 2019, the Shanghai Commercial Paper Exchange Company Ltd., through the China Bill Research Center, launched the quarterly magazine *Research on China's Bill Market*. This publication aims to showcase and share new trends and dynamics in China's bill market. The magazine welcomes submissions from all market participants and features outstanding theoretical work, creating a professional, authoritative, and open platform for academic exchange among bill market participants.

III. Joint Institute for Commercial Paper of JUFE and BOJJ

In the early stages of the 13th Five-Year Plan (2016–2020), China's first domestic bill research institute, Joint Institute for Commercial Paper of JUFE and BOJJ, was officially established. This non-profit bill research institution, co-founded by Jiangxi University of Finance and Economics and Bank of Jiujiang on November 6, 2016, emerged during a pivotal period marked by a booming bill market, frequent risk events, and the creation of the Shanghai Commercial Paper Exchange Company Ltd. As China's first deep collaboration between academia and industry in this field, the institute carries significant implications for the nation's bill market development. Its mission is threefold: to guide the standardized and orderly growth of the bill market, to foster integration between bills and the real economy, and to establish both a high-end think tank and a national platform for exchanges and cooperation in the bill sector. Since its inception over five years ago, the bill research institute has successfully fulfilled its mission and achieved notable accomplishments, thanks to the guidance of Jiangxi University of Finance and Economics and Bank of Jiujiang, the joint efforts of experts and the Secretariat staff from the institute, and the support from various sectors of society.

1. Organizing a Strong Team to Conduct New Research on Bill Business

Joint Institute for Commercial Paper of JUFE and BOJJ, as China's first bill research institute, is committed to expanding its research team and establishing a high-end think tank in the field of bills. For five consecutive years, the institute has recruited esteemed domestic financial scholars, as well as experts and professors from universities like the Chinese Academy of Social Sciences, Renmin University of China, Fudan University, East China University of Political Science and Law, Shanghai University of Finance and Economics, Tongji University, Jiangxi University of Finance and Economics, and Jiangxi Normal University. It has also appointed leaders and key personnel from state-owned banks, joint-stock banks, urban commercial banks, and rural commercial banks as think tank experts. Currently, the institute boasts a diverse team of 3 senior researchers, 40 researcher fellows, 22 researchers, and 1 research expert. The leadership structure comprises one dean, one executive dean, three advisers, two vice deans, and one secretary-general.

The bill research institute focuses on applied theoretical research, continuously intensifying its efforts to enhance both content and quality of research outcomes. Through the collective efforts of its researchers, the institute's academic achievements have shown a positive trajectory. Notably, over 300 research articles have been disseminated via the institute's WeChat official account. Over 100 research results, including articles like "Research on Building a Framework System for China's Bill Market," "On Utilizing Bill Price Index to Guide the Sound Development of the Bill Market," "Building Shanghai International Bill Trading Center with a Focus on Science and Technology," and "Six Inspirations for the Development of Revolutionary Bills," have been published in respected outlets. These include *Financial News*, *Shanghai Securities News*, *China Securities Journal*, *The Bankers of Today*, *The Money Market*, *International Financial Journal*, *Modern Finance Guide*, *Financial Management and Research*, *Journal of Shanghai Lixin University of Accounting and Finance*, *Credit Reference*, China Financial Information Network, and China Economic Network. Some of these research results have achieved a click-through rate exceeding one million. Furthermore, the institute holds the distinction of being the sole organization in China to annually release both the China Bill Development Index and China Bill Price Index.

The bill research institute not only conducts independent research but also actively engages in industry-wide research activities. In 2018, the institute won the first and third prizes in the "Reform and Development of China's Bill Market" essay competition held by the Shanghai Commercial Paper Exchange Company Ltd. It also received recognition in the "China Bill Market and Small and Micro Enterprise Financing" essay competition organized by the CBA. In 2019, the institute won first, second, and third prizes in two essay competitions, namely, the "High-Quality Development of the Bill Market" and the "Bill Market Development and

Innovation," hosted by the China Bill Research Center and the Jiangxi Financial Society respectively. In 2020, the institute achieved excellent results in the essay competitions organized by the China Bill Research Center and the Jiangxi Financial Society.

The bill research institute fully leverages the power of think tanks, and actively participates in research projects and the compilation of bill books. Over the past five years, the institute has published eight books on bills, totaling over three million words. In 2018, the institute participated in compiling the book *China's Bill Market: A Historical Review and Future Prospects*, led by the Shanghai Commercial Paper Exchange Company Ltd. The same year saw the publication of China's first graduate textbook on bills, *Basic Theory and Innovation of Bills*. In 2019, some researchers collaborated to compile the book *Research on Innovation in China's Bill Market*. The following year, *The History of Commercial Bills*, the first historical work on commercial bills, was published, outlining the historical progression of domestic and foreign commercial bills. In 2021, the book *Bill Studies* was released, exploring the basic theory and knowledge of bills, their operation and mechanism, and their development and laws. Notably, *The History of Bills* was selected as one of the top 100 economic books in 2020. In 2019, institute researchers participated in the significant project "Building an International Bill Trading Center in Shanghai Based on Science and Technology Centers." This project received official approval, and the center became a high-level academic institution and high-end think tank, jointly established by the Development Research Center of the Shanghai Municipal Government, Fudan University, Shanghai University of Finance and Economics, and Shanghai Jiao Tong University.

2. Building an Academic Platform for New Development in the Bill Market

In the past five years, the bill research institute has organized several well-targeted and multi-level academic conferences. These events have focused on new changes and trends in the bill market, and provided a platform to share innovative ideas on its development. The research institute, in collaboration with the Jiangxi Financial Society, held an academic exchange conference on "Bill Business Services for High-Quality Economic Development" in the Chinese bill market. It also organized a seminar on the development of the bill service industry chain and supply chain in Nanchang, Jiangxi Province. In collaboration with the Shanghai Finance and Development Laboratory, the institute held a seminar in Shanghai on bill development and innovation. Working with the Second Civil Division of the Higher People's Court of Jiangxi Province, it hosted a special seminar on "China's Bill Market and Rules for Judgment of Bill Dispute Cases" and a seminar on the revision of the *Rules for Judgment of Bill Dispute Cases (Draft)* in the cities of Nanchang and Gongqingcheng respectively. Together with East China University of Political Science and Law, Jiangxi University of Finance and Economics, and other universities, the institute held seminars themed "China Bill Forum—Bill Laws and Regulations," "Standardization of Bills and the Development of Bill Market in the Pos-Pandemic Era," and the ceremony to celebrate the first publication of *The History of Bills* in cities like Shanghai and Nanchang. The institute also partnered with several banks including United Postal Savings Bank, China Zheshang Bank, Bank of Jiujiang, Hankou Bank, Zhengzhou Bank, Liuzhou Bank, Xiamen Rural Commercial Bank, and others to hold seminars in cities like Beijing, Hangzhou, Wuhan, Zhengzhou, Liuzhou, and Xiamen. These seminars included Development and Innovation of Bill Business in the New Era, China Bill Forum and Review of Bill Market in the Past 40 Years of Reform and Opening Up, China Small and Medium-Sized Banks' Coordinated Development of Bills, Transformation and Risk Management of Small and Medium-Sized Banks' Bill Operations, China Small and Medium-Sized Banks and Bill Associations' Development Forum, and Opportunities and Challenges Faced by Small and Medium-Sized Bank Bill Business After the Integration of Paper and Electronic Bills. These conferences have stimulated lively discussions and facilitated rich resource sharing. The conference materials have received extensive coverage from various media outlets, generating a significant societal impact.

3. Serving the Bill Market and Supporting Growth of the Real Economy

The bill research institute is committed not only to academic research but also to serving the bill market and the real economy. It established the "China Bill Forum" to track market trends, unite academia and industry, foster cooperation, and gather talent to innovate and transform the bill market. The forum aims to encourage high-quality development of the bill market and promote bills that better serve the real economy. On August 29, 2020, the institute founded the China Commercial Bill Research Center at the Xinhua News Agency's China Financial Information Center (Shanghai). This center aims to consolidate various resources and expertise, conduct research, leverage the role of bill think tanks, expedite research output, cultivate professionals, and promote the bill market's service to the real economy on a larger scale. The bill research institute has also initiated the *China Small and Medium Bank Bill Collaborative Development Forum* for smaller banks, advocating for "resource sharing and development for win-win results." The forum encourages all member units to adhere to the *Self-Discipline Declaration on Small and Medium Bank Bill Business* to collectively boost the development of the bill business. The institute is committed to promoting integration among industry, academia, and research. They prioritize providing think tank support to member units of small and medium-sized banks and applying research outcomes to these banks. Each member unit prioritizes interbank credit work for bills, strengthens communication and cooperation through forum platforms, establishes information exchange and sharing mechanisms, and fosters mutually beneficial cooperation.

4. Leveraging Educational Resources to Cultivate Talent for the Bill Market

The bill research institute, in partnership with Bank of Jiujiang, has pioneered the nation's first postgraduate program in bill studies. Harnessing Jiangxi University's expertise in financial education, the program enlists bill experts as off-campus mentors and utilizes the bill research institute as a practical training ground. To date, the program has nurtured four cohorts, totaling 32 postgraduate students in bill studies. This initiative is committed to developing specialized professionals in the field, continually infusing the bill market with fresh talent to propel innovative growth.

Currently, the first cohort of bill specialists has secured positions in the PBC, commercial banks, and finance companies. The second and third cohorts have found roles in banks, universities, and other sectors, while the fourth cohort is studying bill theory in preparation for employment. For years, the bill research institute has been offering theoretical and practical bill-related courses to finance and accounting graduate students at Shanghai University of Finance and Economics and Jiangxi Normal University. Beyond educating college students, the institute actively trains industry professionals. In November 2018 and November 2020, it conducted two training courses on financial institution bill business operations and management, featuring lectures by respected domestic experts. These comprehensive learning experiences, which included specialized lectures, site visits, and interactive exchanges, benefited nearly 140 senior managers and bill business personnel from across the country.

5. Organizing Essay Competitions to Promote Industry-Wide Bill Research

The bill research institute regularly hosts public paper solicitation activities. Over the last five years, it has conducted five rounds of these activities, garnering enthusiastic participation from individuals across various fields. From the first call for papers on November 6, 2016, to the conclusion of the activity on July 15, 2021, the institute received over 380 submissions. Contributors ranged from academia and the banking sectors to non-banking financial institutions. Authors shared their insights and visions for the bill industry, drawing on their professional experience and understanding of the current bill market, adhering to the institute's submission guidelines. To ensure fair evaluation, the institute assembled a panel of judges comprising representatives from the PBC, commercial banks, universities, and industry experts. These judges evaluated the submissions anonymously. Based on their comprehensive assessments, the institute awarded 6 special prizes, 12 first prizes, 26 second prizes, 52 third prizes, and 75 encouragement prizes across the five essay competitions.

IV. Other Bill Research Institutions

The Bill Working Committee of the Payment and Clearing Association of China, established on September 27, 2013, aims to enhance the bill industry's self-discipline management system, standardize bill payment services, and promote sustainable, healthy growth in the sector. Since its establishment, the committee has conducted extensive research on the bill market. First, it has studied relevant laws and regulations, collaborated with business regulatory departments to introduce and revise these laws, and developed self-discipline norms and guidelines. These efforts have been made to guide member units to strengthen their internal control systems, improve risk management mechanisms, and develop a robust self-discipline management system for the bill industry. Second, it has explored measures and strategies to promote bill digitization and the use of payment passwords, thereby advancing the application and innovative development of electronic bills. Last, the committee has actively sought industry opinions and formed a bill business expert group to conduct research and consulting activities. It has established a training mechanism for practitioners in laws, regulations, business, and skills. It has also promoted general bill business education to the public and engaged in business exchanges with regulatory agencies or other relevant departments to explore the development of the bill market.

To improve communication between the banking industry and various stakeholders in the bill market, the Bill Professional Committee of the CBA was established. This move aimed to disseminate bill regulatory policies, regulate bill business practices, improve the bill market environment, and protect the rights and interests of the banking industry. The inaugural meeting and the first plenary session were held in Beijing on November 18, 2014. The establishment of this committee marked a new level of standardization and self-regulation in China's bill business development. Since its inception, the committee has actively researched the bill market, proposing legislative, administrative, and judicial suggestions based on industry needs and member demands. It has also assisted regulatory authorities in issuing and revising relevant laws, regulations, and normative documents. Moreover, the committee has organized industry experts to conduct project research and practical surveys, while exploring mechanisms for resolving interbank disputes in the bill business.

Regarding bill training, the CBA organized its first national advanced training course on bill business for the banking industry in Beijing from November 18 to 19, 2014. For project development, the association actively engages office directors, deputy directors of the bill committee's standing units, and member units' bill business leaders. They have been consistently researching and reporting on the development of the Chinese bill market for several years. As for essay solicitation activities, in 2018, the committee and *China Banking* jointly launched an essay solicitation activity themed "China's Bill Market and Small and Micro Enterprise Financing." This provided a professional platform for showcasing new research achievements in the practical and theoretical fields of the bill market.

The bill market has experienced rapid growth, with its size expanding and trading volume increasing nationwide. Bills have become a crucial financial tool for short-term financing of enterprises in various provinces and cities. To enhance the role of bills in regional economic development, some provinces and cities have established bill associations and professional committees. On August 16, 2013, the Hebei Financial Bill Association was officially established, led by the Shijiazhuang Central Sub-Branch of the PBC. The association, which was later renamed the Hebei Financial Market Association, serves as a communication channel for bill business within the Beijing-Tianjin-Hebei and Bohai Rim economic regions.

On January 15, 2015, the Bill Professional Committee of the SFS was officially established, during a conference hosted by the SFS and the Bill Professional Committee of the China Urban Financial Society, and organized by the Bill Business Department of the ICBC. This committee has worked toward promoting innovative and standard development of bill business in Shanghai, conducting high-level academic discussions, policy research, and bill business training. It has provided strong decision-making support for the development of the bill market in Shanghai and played a crucial role in advancing the development of the Shanghai International Financial Center and the Shanghai Free Trade Zone.

On September 14, 2017, the Bill Professional Committee of Jiangxi Financial Society was established during a meeting held at Jiangxi Qianhu State House. This committee has been conducting theoretical and practical research on bill services for the real economy and organizing bill-themed essay solicitations. Collaborating with the PBC and other market regulatory agencies, it holds seminars on bill business development, guiding bills to serve the real economy and promote high-quality economic growth.

In recent years, the application of financial technology to the financial market has spurred continuous innovation in and development of financial products. Advanced technologies such as big data, cloud computing, artificial intelligence, and blockchain have revolutionized the field of bills, opening up myriad possibilities for future development. As digitization progresses, the coordinated evolution of bill theory and practice, risk management and control, and innovation and growth is vital for guiding the bill market's standardized and orderly advancement. On June 3, 2017, the Central University of Finance and Economics Cloud Bill Research Center First Bill Summit was successfully held at the Beijing National Convention Center. This event, co-organized by the Central University of Finance and Economics Collaborative Cloud Bill (Shenzhen) Financial Services Co., Ltd., Beijing Jingshi Law Firm, and Shanghai-based CIB Fintech, marked the establishment of the Central University of Finance and Economics Cloud Bill Research Center. This initiative created a high-end think tank in the field of bills and a platform for national exchanges and cooperation.

Summary

Amid the ongoing support for supply chain finance development and the continuous application of financial technology, the bill market is witnessing the emergence of innovative businesses and products. Since its inception, the Shanghai Commercial Paper Exchange Company Ltd. has consistently leveraged cutting-edge technologies to drive business innovation and enhance the efficiency and quality of the bill market. These innovations amplify the payment, settlement, financing, transaction, and credit functionalities of bills. They streamline the issuance, circulation, and financing of bills, making them more efficient and convenient. This, in turn, reduces financing costs for SMEs and improves the real economy's ability to acquire funds from the financial system, thereby strengthening the role of bills in serving the real economy. Furthermore, extensive bill research provides valuable insights for the development of bill market systems and business optimization, adding momentum to bill market reform. Under the leadership of the Shanghai Commercial Paper Exchange Company Ltd. and research institutions such as Joint Institute for Commercial Paper of JUFE and BOJJ, innovation and theoretical research in China's bill market are flourishing. With innovation as its driving force, China's bill market is poised for a long and promising journey.

CHAPTER TEN

Reflections on the History of Bills

SECTION I

Evolution of Bill Functions and Services for Economy and Finance

I. Evolution of Bill Functions

The functions of bills have evolved and improved over centuries, paralleling the development of commercial economy and credit. This continual adaptation is key to their enduring relevance. The Zhou Dynasty's *zhiji*, *fubie*, and *shuqi*, which emerged from lending activities, were the precursors of modern bills. Their use continued into the Tang Dynasty when they were replaced by *feiqian*, serving as withdrawal vouchers. During the Tang Dynasty, as commercial trade grew, so did the demand for exchange across different regions. The establishment of credit institutions across regions provided robust support for the use of bills. The emergence of deposit concepts and a nascent commercial credit environment laid the foundation for the exchange function of bills. *Feiqian* facilitated the development of cross-region trade.

In the Song Dynasty, the use of *jiaozi* and *huizi* became more widespread in commodity transactions, eventually evolving into credit currency and pioneering the use of paper currency. This period saw the strengthening of the payment and settlement functions of bills. By the early and middle Qing Dynasty, the use of bills became more standardized and deeply ingrained in commerce. Banks, bill offices, and other institutions utilized bills widely in their operations, enhancing the influence of bills. Money house bills, money bills, money shop bills, bills of exchange, and bill shop bills were widely circulated. Bill shops, in particular, promoted progress in the exchange industry. During this period, the payment, settlement, and exchange functions of bills were significantly enhanced. Financial institutions such as money houses and bill shops supported bill discounting businesses, manifesting the financing function of bills.

Discovered Qing Dynasty bills reveal that they circulated not only in developed cities but also in rural markets. They primarily facilitated land transactions and agricultural trades, providing credit guarantees for these transactions. Rural bill credit often required mortgages, guarantees, and other credit enhancement measures, indicating a mature and complete bill credit system. In the late Qing Dynasty, traditional bills in China began to integrate with Western bills due to Western influence. The establishment of the remittance system initiated the era of centralized clearing of bills, improving clearing efficiency and promoting their widespread circulation.

During the Republic of China period, the bill market evolved from a chaotic coexistence of Chinese and Western systems to a more structured framework. This transition began in the late Qing Dynasty, laying the groundwork for formal commercial and bill regulations. A significant milestone was reached in 1929 with the introduction of *The Negotiable Instrument Law*, which unified Chinese and Western bill systems, marking China's first bill law and a pivotal moment in its bill market development. Following this, the government began to actively promote bill acceptance and discounting. Institutions like the Shanghai Bank Bill Acceptance Office and Chongqing United Bill Acceptance Office were established. The central bank gradually established a rediscount system, with some financial institutions also supporting interbank discount business. While the bill market's framework began to take shape, the full development of the bill market was hampered by political instability, disorderly currency and credit systems, and the government's limited market influence. During this period, bills mainly served for payment, settlement, and financing purposes.

Following the founding of the PRC, the country entered a planned economy era that limited commercial credit, thereby restricting bill development. The Third Plenary Session of the Eleventh Central Committee of the CPC in 1978 marked a shift, announcing the start of reform and opening up that gradually transitioned the country from a planned economy to a socialist market economy. This change paved the way for the development of the bill market in New China. The embryonic stage of the bill market spanned from 1978 to 1994. During this period, the PBC initiated bill business to tackle "chain debts" and manage corporate debt risks. It promoted commercial credit bills and issued management measures to encourage bill business growth. However, progress was slow due to the nascent market economy and inadequate regulations.

The 1995 introduction of *The Negotiable Instrument Law of the PRC* marked the beginning of a standardized and rapid development phase in China's bill market. During this period, the PBC built upon the early exploration and operation of commercial bills, continuing to refine market rules and regulations. The enactment of *The Negotiable Instrument Law of the PRC*, alongside *Measures for Payment and Settlement* and *Measures for the Administration of Acceptance, Discount, and Rediscount of Commercial Bills*, provided clear direction and established the legal framework for the development of China's bill market.

The establishment of ICBC's Bill Business Department, China's first specialized bill agency, led to more specialized bill operations and diversified market participants. During this period, the central bank's rediscount system improved, and rediscount tools started to play a crucial role. As the market economy grew rapidly and the bill market system continuously improved, China's bill market experienced swift development.

The period from 2009 to 2016 was a transformation and development stage in the bill market. In 2009, the PBC officially launched the milestone ECDS, marking the bill market's entry into the electronic era. This era saw rapid growth in electronic commercial draft, continuous market innovation, an increasing trend toward bill financialization, and the emergence of large-scale bill-related risk events.

On December 8, 2016, with the establishment of the Shanghai Commercial Paper Exchange Company Ltd., China's bill market entered a stage of standardized and innovative development. This platform serves as a crucial financial infrastructure, functioning as a registration and custody center, business trading hub, innovation incubator, risk management nexus, and data repository for the bill sector. Its creation has profoundly impacted China's bill market, heralding an era of centralized trading and ushering in a new phase of growth. In this environment, bill innovations are flourishing, institutional frameworks are being refined, and technological applications are advancing rapidly.

Today, bills have evolved into an essential financial instrument with multiple functions: exchange, payment, settlement, financing, regulation, credit, investment, and trading. They play an irreplaceable role in promoting the development of the real economy, advancing financial supply-side structural reform, and transmitting monetary policies.

II. Services for Economy and Finance

The evolution of bills in China has been driven by the needs of the commodity, monetary, credit, and financial sectors. This evolution, shaped by market exploration and government planning, has expanded bill functions to include exchange, payment, settlement, financing, credit, investment, trading, and regulation. As a result, bills have played an increasingly significant role in social and economic development. Experience demonstrates that bill development must align with economic, financial, and credit growth in scope, depth, and pace. The bill system should maximize the role of bills at each historical stage. A well-crafted system can effectively regulate market behaviors, clarify rights and obligations, reduce transaction uncertainties, and promote the growth of the commodity economy. Conversely, a system lagging behind industry development can hinder bill market innovation. Moreover, regulatory gaps or overlaps can impede the healthy growth of the bill market and undermine the role of bills in serving the real economy.

Serving the economy and finance is the foundation and goal of the bill system. A robust bill system must align with the economic, credit, and financial development of its time to effectively support the growth of both the economy and the bill market. A country's bill system at any given time is considered sound, advanced, and reasonable if it reflects the nation's economic and financial development level and fundamental conditions. At the macro level, it should represent the direction of advanced productive forces, promote the growth of the market economy, and keep pace with the times. At the micro level, it should facilitate the use of bills, minimize disputes among economic participants, and fully utilize bill functions. This principle is evident in the formulation of *The Negotiable Instrument Law*, the establishment of the acceptance and discount system, and the introduction of laws and regulations such as *The Negotiable Instrument Law of the PRC* after the founding of the PRC.

Bills play a crucial role in positively impacting the real economy, credit, money market, and capital market. For the real economy, bills offer two main advantages: First, they provide a convenient payment method. Bills eliminate the need for large cash transactions and enable easy transfers through endorsement. This promotes circulation, enhances efficiency, and makes transactions faster, more accurate, and safer. Buyers benefit from delayed payments, while sellers can receive preferential terms like commercial discounts. Moreover, bills can be endorsed and transferred for financing or payment purposes. Second, bills provide a convenient and low-cost financing channel. The expansion of bill business has created accessible financing options for the real economy, especially for SMEs. This facilitates the transfer of core enterprise credit to SMEs and reduces financing costs, supporting their growth and development. Commercial acceptance bills are user-friendly, involve simple processes, and can be issued independently by enterprises within their acceptance capacity. This bypasses bank loan approval constraints and broadens financing channels. Furthermore, issuing commercial acceptance bills doesn't require margin or acceptance fees. This helps curb payment arrears, improve liquidity, and reduce corporate financing costs. Bank acceptance bills, backed by bank credit, typically offer lower financing costs than ordinary loans, with simpler processes and shorter financing cycles. For SMEs with relatively low credit ratings, these bills provide unique advantages in addressing financing challenges, thanks to their bank credit backing and rapid lending speed.

Bills serve as key carriers of credit, with bank bills representing bank credit and commercial bills embodying commercial credit. By fostering bill development under controlled risk conditions, we can further harness social credit and reduce currency supply. Moreover, by deeply integrating bills into the supply chain, we can expand enterprises' financing capabilities beyond traditional bank credit. This approach enables businesses to fully utilize diverse financing channels, meeting their funding needs more effectively.

In finance, the bill business plays a significant role in driving the growth of the money market. Various bill products serve as key trading items, cementing the bill market's position as a vital component of the money market. Inter-financial institution interbank discounting accelerates short-term fund financing and reallocation, becoming an essential asset for banks and other financial entities. The central bank's rediscounting and repurchase operations, as monetary policy tools, significantly impact policy transmission, facilitate credit institution adjustments, and steer financing expansion for SMEs.

Second, bill business diversifies financial market products. Bills, with their multiple attributes of payment, funds, credit, and assets, coupled with the diverse bill-holding institutions, lead to derivative products that bridge the money and capital markets. These include bill asset securitization, bill discounting, interbank discount options, interest rate swaps, and term swaps. As a core carrier, bills leverage the money market's low risk, short-term nature, and high liquidity. The introduction of financial instruments can increase returns while controlling risks, making bills essential for financial investment product innovation. Banks and other financial institutions have introduced innovative bill appreciation services, including consultation, brokerage, instant discount tools, and comprehensive bill asset management and pool products. These new offerings not only enrich the financial market and meet business financing needs but also accelerate interest rate marketization. Bill transaction prices, highly sensitive to fund supply and demand, have established a relatively complete market price index and formation mechanism. Moreover, the competitive relationship between bill discounting and short-term working capital loans allows financial institutions to expand loan fluctuations and tiered pricing through customer segmentation, further guiding loan interest rate marketization.

SECTION 2

Insights from Bill Development and Future Prospects

I. Insights from Bill Development

Bills thrive on credit, originate from payment needs, evolve through financing mechanisms, flourish with innovation, and possess limitless potential in supporting the real economy.

1. Leveraging the Comparative Advantages of Bills to Serve the Real Economy

The bill market has played a crucial role in supporting real economic development for millennia. In ancient China, primitive bills like *fubie* and *zhiji* emerged as credit vouchers during the Zhou Dynasty. Financial instruments such as *feiqian*, *shutie*, and *jiaozi* further propelled economic advancement during the Tang and Song dynasties. The Qing Dynasty witnessed the proliferation of old-style bills from money houses and bill shops, significantly aiding enterprise trade growth.

In the 1930s, amid various economic and social upheavals, China's industrial and commercial sector faced significant challenges. To regulate market funds and stimulate industry development, acceptance bills and discount services were widely promoted as effective market remedies. During the War of Resistance Against Japan, measures were taken to maintain economic growth and support the stable operation of key industries such as agriculture, industry, and mining. These included the introduction of the joint discount and lending system by the Joint General Office of the Four Banks and the promotion of bill discounting business by the Nationalist Government. The Chongqing United Bill Acceptance Office was established to assist industry and commerce and promote production, with funds financed through bills primarily for production-related enterprises.

Other financial instruments such as promissory notes and checks were issued in revolutionary base areas in different periods to support production and aid the development of these areas. After the founding of the PRC, the PBC began to handle bill acceptance business to support private enterprises, maintain the national economy, and improve people's livelihood. After the start of the economic reform and opening up, the bill business was revived to tackle corporate "chain debts" and promote commercial credit.

The introduction of bills not only resolves debt issues between enterprises but also strongly supports the growth of the commodity economy and the undertaking of reform and opening up. Various systems were subsequently introduced to standardize bill business development and enhance the use of bill services in the real economy. The advent of electronic commercial draft prompted commercial banks to accelerate bill innovation, significantly bolstering real economic development. The establishment of the Shanghai Commercial Paper Exchange Company Ltd. further propelled this innovation, addressing enterprise development challenges with specific bill products. This expansion has broadened both the scope and depth of bill support for the real economy.

Bills, as credit instruments integrating payment, settlement, financing, investment, trading, and regulatory functions, offer distinct advantages over bonds, stocks, loans, accounts receivable, and letters of credit. These advantages include lower entry barriers, enhanced safety, convenience, efficiency, a solid legal foundation, robust infrastructure, and versatile functionality. Electronic commercial drafts, in particular, excel with their data-driven issuance, high security, electronic trading, transparency, efficiency, institutionalized protection, and broad applicability, all of which support real economic development more effectively. In bolstering the growth of the real economy, especially for SMEs, bills provide wider coverage, stronger support, and greater cost-effectiveness. This allows for full utilization of the comparative advantages of bills in fostering the development of the real economy.

2. Establishing Systems to Safeguard the Growth of the Bill Market

The development of bills and the construction of the bill system are mutually reinforcing, creating a synergy crucial for the bill market's healthy growth. In the early Republic of China period, the Beiyang Government's five-year legislation marked the beginning of the country's legal construction for the bill market. The introduction of *The Negotiable Instrument Law* transformed the historical situation where bill business had no legal support. The Anhui Bengbu Discount Office, China's first bill-specialized institution, significantly altered the bill market's operational model and prompted notable adjustments in its organizational system. In 1933, the Shanghai Commercial Paper Exchange Company Ltd. changed traditional bill clearing system, introducing centralized clearing, thereby improving efficiency.

During the War of Resistance Against Japan, the Nationalist Government further advanced the development of the bill market and consistently improved institutional regulations. The Central Bank assumed bill clearing functions, and rediscounting officially moved under its purview. During the War of Liberation, the Central Bank oversaw nationwide bill exchange.

The Shanghai Commercial Paper Exchange Company Ltd. actively promoted a transition from a mixed direct and agency exchange system to a direct exchange system.

After the founding of the PRC in 1949, a series of institutional regulations such as *Interim Measures for the Acceptance and Discount of Commercial Bills*, *Trial Measures for Rediscounting*, and *Measures for Bank Settlement* laid the groundwork for the use of bills and the promulgation of *The Negotiable Instrument Law of the PRC*. *The Negotiable Instrument Law of the PRC* of 1995 marked a new era in the development of China's bill market. This law, along with *Measures for Payment and Settlement* and *Measures for the Administration of Acceptance, Discount, and Rediscount of Commercial Bills*, shaped the legal structure of China's bill market. It was during this period that the PBC's rediscount system improved, with rediscounting starting to play a dominant role. In 2009, the central bank launched the ECDS. The *Measures for the Administration of Electronic Commercial Draft Business* and eight other normative systems provided institutional support for the development and circulation of electronic commercial draft in China. To manage frequent irregularities in the bill market, the China Banking and Insurance Regulatory Commission issued a series of institutional regulations to regulate financial institutions' interbank business operations, effectively preventing and controlling bill risks. The establishment of the Shanghai Commercial Paper Exchange Company Ltd. led to the introduction of various bill systems, causing significant changes in market development.

After a century of development, the bill market has continually enhanced and refined its institutional construction. However, some challenges remain in the construction of China's bill market system. The evolution of the bill legal system has lagged behind the rapid growth of the bill market. Moreover, the absence of a unified bill system and flaws in certain regulations impede the development of the bill market.

The bill system regulates the behavior of bill users and market participants. Experience shows that a country's bill system for a specific period reflects its economic development and basic national conditions at a macro level. It represents the development direction of advanced productive forces, stimulates the growth of the market economy, and keeps pace with the times. At a micro level, a scientific, advanced, and reasonable bill system facilitates the use of bills, minimizes conflicts between economic participants, and maximizes bill functionality. The future development of the bill market calls for improved institutional framework. Possible areas for breakthroughs include

- acknowledging the non-causation principle of bills and piloting financing bills;
- accelerating the revision of *The Negotiable Instrument Law of the PRC* to clarify the legal status of innovative bill products such as electronic commercial drafts, supply chain bills, and standardized bills, as well as bill derivatives;
- improving the bill market's coordination and supervision systems;
- refining the accrual rules for credit assets and risk assets;

- strengthening the information disclosure mechanism and promoting the establishment of bill rating, evaluation, and guarantee mechanisms; and
- implementing a bill brokerage system with standardized entry and exit protocols.

3. Enhancing Infrastructure Development for the Bill Market

The long-term growth of the bill market relies on essential infrastructure development. In 1933, the establishment of the Shanghai Commercial Paper Exchange Company Ltd. transformed the bill clearing pattern, previously dominated by a combination of money house bills and bund bank bills, enabling Chinese commercial banks to have their own clearing institution. The Shanghai Commercial Paper Exchange Company Ltd., an important infrastructure of the bill market, was the first clearing institution entirely established by commercial banks in China's financial history. It played a crucial role in supporting modern bill clearing and served as a model for other clearing institutions. In 1935, the Shanghai Bank Bill Acceptance Office was established as a mutual-aid organization to regulate interbank funds in an imperfect credit environment. It demonstrated the feasibility of using acceptance bills to stimulate economic growth in situations of scarce funds and difficult circulation. The Chongqing United Bill Acceptance Office, established during the War of Resistance Against Japan, improved the circulation of commercial bills, activated the use of funds, and promoted industrial and commercial production by enhancing the credit of commercial and enterprise bills.

Since the founding of the PRC, the most significant infrastructure developments in the bill market have been the launch of the ECDS and the establishment of the Shanghai Commercial Paper Exchange Company Ltd. In 2009, the PBC introduced the ECDS, giving rise to revolutionary electronic bills. Following the implementation of Yin Fa [2016] Document No. 224, electronic bills quickly became a hot product in the bill market, occupying over 95% of the market share. The completion of ECDS addressed fundamental issues of low efficiency, information asymmetry, and high risks in paper bill transactions. The Shanghai Commercial Paper Exchange Company Ltd. unified the bill market, creating a centralized trading, registration, custody, settlement, and monetary policy operation platform, transforming China's previously fragmented bill market.

The Shanghai Commercial Paper Exchange Company Ltd. has implemented large-scale projects, including

- constructing and promoting bill exchange clients,
- integrating with the ECDS system,
- merging paper and electronic bills,
- directly connecting bill trading systems,
- launching an online bill clearing system,
- implementing online discount and rediscount operations, and
- trialing a commercial bill information disclosure platform.

These efforts have created a safe and reliable platform for bill market development. To spur innovation and support micro, small, and medium-sized enterprises, supply chain businesses, and commercial acceptance bills, the Shanghai Commercial Paper Exchange Company Ltd. developed systems for innovative products like the Bill Payment Pass, the Discount Pass, and standardized bills. It also launched an electronic commercial draft information disclosure system, fostering bill market growth and supporting bill business development. All bill market participants have reformed and optimized their systems to integrate seamlessly with the Shanghai Commercial Paper Exchange Company Ltd. Meanwhile, the Beijing-Tianjin-Hebei Collaborative Bill Trading Center, Wuhan Bill Trading Center, Finance Company Bill Platform, and central enterprise Commercial Bill Pass Platform are hastening their launches, and private bill platforms are also moving toward standardization.

The growth of the bill market requires ongoing infrastructure development. This means keeping up with times while optimizing and enhancing the bill system. Steps should include promoting the creation of commercial acceptance bill platforms in the Yangtze River Delta region, establishing commercial credit bill platforms for state-owned enterprises and local governments on the basis of Enterprise Bill Pass, accelerating the construction of commercial bill information disclosure platforms, and promoting the development of international bill trading centers.

4. Enhancing Credit for the Development of Commercial Credit

The growth of the bill market relies hinges on strong credit, with a robust credit environment being crucial for bill operations. Acceptance bills, which convert static book credit into tradable face credit, are exceptional credit tools. Zhang Naiqi, a Chinese economist and financial scientist, introduced this concept during the 1930s acceptance bill boom. Financial scientist Yang Yinpu advocated for credit reports in bill acceptance and discounting to bolster bill credit and promote discounting. The acceptance bill surge led to the formation of an acceptance discount market, and discount business, a crucial financing channel, drew attention from all sectors. The bill's credit function became prominent. During the War of Resistance Against Japan, to ease the fiat currency shortage and boost credit chips, the Chongqing bill market issued promissory notes to replace the fiat currency issued by the KMT government from 1935 onwards. With the establishment of the Chongqing United Bill Acceptance Office in 1944, the affiliated United Credit Reporting Office was also initiated.

Revolutionary base areas saw the evolution of discounting business and promissory notes as currency substitutes, showcasing bills as credit tools. On September 29, 1943, the South Hebei Bank issued *A Notice on the Issuance of Promissory Notes*, clearly stating that the issuance of promissory notes could develop rural credit concepts and bill credit. In 1979, China's financial community began exploring bank and commercial credit integration, using bank credit to guide commercial credit. Bills from this era originated from the credit function to resolve "chain debt" issues and foster commercial credit.

Bills, rooted in commercial credit from commodity trade, have evolved over centuries, especially after more than 40 years of reform and opening up, to become significant credit tools with multiple functions: payment, settlement, financing, investment, trading, regulation, and exchange. However, the development of credit in China's bill market has always been imbalanced. Commercial acceptance bills lag behind bank acceptance bills in acceptance and discount credit businesses. The overall credit level of Chinese enterprises, particularly small and medium-sized ones, is low. Concerns about commercial bill circulation and redemption have led to low acceptance of electronic commercial draft in the market.

In recent years, China has been actively promoting the construction of a social credit system. The State Council's *Outline of the Social Credit System Construction Plan (2014–2020)* emphasizes the need to enhance business integrity and promote societal integrity comprehensively. On January 17, 2021, the PBC officially launched its second-generation credit reporting system, laying a foundation for the growth of commercial bills. The bill market's management has been continually improving with the introduction of the commercial bill information disclosure system. To foster bill credit development, efforts should be made to roll out evaluation and guarantee mechanisms. A robust credit rating system can enhance the market acceptance of bills, particularly commercial ones. The bill market should expedite the construction of a credit system, establish bill credit rating agencies, and offer comprehensive and dynamic bill credit rating and tracking services for acceptance and discounting entities. It should also improve the bill guarantee mechanism and promote the development of insurance credit and guarantee credit enhancement. Financial institutions like banks and insurance companies can collaborate with supply chain enterprises that have high credit ratings and stable production and sales relationships to provide confirmation, protection, guarantee, and other services for commercial bills, thereby boosting their market recognition. Commercial banks should intensify efforts to explore and improve credit and discount methods for commercial acceptance bills, thereby promoting their growth.

5. Taking Proactive Measures to Strengthen Bill-Related Risk Prevention and Control

Risk, the uncertainty of future losses, is an inevitable aspect of the bill business. Since ancient times, bill market participants have implemented measures to mitigate risks. Bill shops used special paper to prevent forgery in bills of exchange, while money houses enforced strict discounting requirements, refusing to handle discounts without guarantees for unfamiliar individuals. The Shanghai Bank Bill Acceptance Office required collateral from affiliated banks when issuing bills. Acceptance applications could only be signed after valuation by the acceptance office. During the War of Resistance Against Japan, the Joint General Office of the Four Banks issued the *Interim Measures for Promoting Bank Acceptance and Discount Business*, requiring goods and a complete set of documents like lading bills and insurance policies as collateral for acceptance bills. The Chongqing United Bill Acceptance Office also required necessary collateral when issuing acceptance bills. Promissory notes during that time were mainly issued to replace currency, but as inflation intensified, more promissory notes with larger denominations were issued, triggering market speculation and price increases. During the Liberation War, the call money market flourished unchecked, and distorted forms of the bill market, such as "posting bills," emerged, severely disrupting market order. Following the resumption of bill business after the start of reform and opening up, bill risk cases increased due to the growing prominence of bill payments in settlement structures. Commercial banks responded by reshaping business processes, establishing dedicated positions, and implementing dual-person cross-bill verification mechanisms to prevent fraud.

In the 21st century, some commercial banks engaged in illegal acceptance and irregular guarantee management, resulting in numerous fake and financing bills. The deep involvement of illegal bill intermediaries in bill business planted hidden dangers for risk cases in the bill market. With the introduction of electronic bills, market innovation flourished; however, bill product innovation often outpaced regulation. After numerous risk cases emerged in 2016, bill market participants began to reconsider their development models, and regulatory authorities started to reshape the market through infrastructure and regulatory improvements.

In recent years, regulatory authorities like the PBC and the China Banking and Insurance Regulatory Commission have issued a series of notices, including *A Notice on Issues Related to Improving Bill Business System*, *A Notice on Effectively Strengthening the Administration of Commercial Bill Acceptance, Discount, and Rediscount Business*, and *A Notice on Risk Warning for Bill Business*, to strengthen the supervision of commercial bill business and standardize the handling process. To prevent various financial risks, the Shanghai Commercial Paper Exchange Company Ltd. has proactively built a risk prevention system for the bill market. It has vigorously promoted electronic commercial draft businesses, increased the proportion of electronic bill transactions, and strengthened risk and market monitoring systems, tracking and analyzing market risk signs in a timely manner. The exchange has also improved prevention mechanisms and optimized trading processes. After years of development, the ecological environment of the bill market has greatly improved. There has been a substantial increase in the proportion of electronic bills, more standardized business rules, and enhanced transparency and security in transactions such as bill payment settlement, direct processing, and electronic platform trading. Secondary market trading on the exchange has reduced the space for non-standard bill intermediary activities. Proactive account management effectively prevents the risk of counterfeit bills. System optimization and technological empowerments have further improved risk control levels in the bill market, significantly reducing the number of malicious cases.

Despite improvements, bill-related risks still warrant attention. For electronic commercial drafts, we must vigilantly monitor operational, compliance, and credit risks. The payment process for electronic bills, facilitated by ECDS, does not necessitate the use of the DVP settlement method. This separation of funds and payment carries risks of bill funds embezzlement and non-payment from endorsees. For bank acceptance bills, the high proportion of acceptance margin deposits maintained by some small and medium-sized commercial banks requires serious consideration. Commercial acceptance bills warrant special attention to redemption risks stemming from excessive bill issuance by certain enterprises. As the bill market expands, diverse financial institutions, including banks, financial companies, securities firms, trusts, and insurance companies, will participate in market activities. The absence of uniform regulation may result in varying standards and policy scales for similar business operations across institutions. This regulatory and policy asynchrony could create institutional obstacles and policy barriers in bill business, introducing significant uncertainty to the growth of the bill market. Therefore, it is imperative for participating entities to continually reinforce their risk management.

6. Focusing on Innovation for the Prosperity of the Bill Market

The evolution of the bill market has consistently been marked by innovative practices. For instance, the establishment of the Shanghai Bank Bill Acceptance Office brought about innovations in credit tools and operating methods. It introduced financing bills such as acceptance bills, which required member banks to provide collateral before issuing bills. Bills could be transferred and discounted between member banks and if necessary, these bills could be rediscounted by the acceptance office. An acceptance fund was established to share the profits and losses. These innovative measures facilitated the acceptance office's bill operations and the turnover of interbank funds, providing valuable reference for the innovative development of the bill market.

In May 1949, on the eve of the victory of the Liberation War, Beihai Bank issued *Measures for Handling Discount of Public Enterprise Promissory Notes*. This move facilitated fund turnover for public enterprises to promote and restore production through bill exchange and discount business. The introduction of *The Negotiable Instrument Law of the PRC* in 1995 attracted more participants and stimulated market innovation capabilities, leading to advancements in bill functions, pricing mechanisms, and regional markets. As bill interest rates became more market-driven, competition in bill business heightened. Financial institutions started to develop new bill types to enhance competitiveness and expand markets. The China Bill Network was launched, and electronic bill products like CMB's "Bill Pass" online bill business and ICBC's "YeePay" electronic credit bills were introduced. Commercial banks started creating personalized bill service models and products based on customer needs. Special bill services for bill-bill exchange (bill splitting), guaranteed discounting, entrusted discounting, buyer interest payment discounting, and accounts receivable bill securitization were introduced.

With the flourishing of the bill market, breakthroughs were made in participant diversity, product innovation, and business innovation. Bill wealth management and bill asset management business started to thrive, and bill trading was continuously innovating. Commercial banks' bill business models had undergone a transformation, and the degree of market intensification was increasing. *A Notice on Regulating and Promoting the Development of Electronic Commercial Draft Business* expanded market participation, allowing non-bank financial institutions such as securities companies, fund companies, futures companies, insurance companies, trust companies, and asset management companies to directly participate in bill market transactions. During the 13th Five-Year Plan period, innovative bill products emerged one after another. The Shanghai Commercial Paper Exchange Company Ltd. launched a trial operation of a digital bill trading platform. The targeted launch of Bill Payment Pass and Discount Pass has effectively solved the problem of enterprise bill circulation and discounting.

They also introduced a commercial bill information disclosure platform, established a credit constraint mechanism for acceptors, and promoted the improvement of the credit environment in the bill market. Additionally, a supply chain bill platform was launched to achieve equal splitting of bills, opening new paths for the development of accounts receivable bills. Standardized bills were introduced, bridging the gap between the bill market and the bond market and expanding corporate financing options. To address low acceptance of commercial acceptance bills, 51 central enterprises jointly established "Enterprise Bill Pass," a mutual recognition platform. This platform enhanced central enterprise credit, reduced both accounts receivable and payable, and lowered financing costs for chain enterprises through the transmission of industrial chain credit. Commercial banks also launched innovative products like online rapid discounting, bill pools, blockchain bills, and green bills, further expanding bill services for the real economy.

7. Utilizing Technology to Unleash the Potential of Bill Business

Technology, encompassing both science and engineering, has transformed the bill market through traditional and financial innovations. *The Negotiable Instrument Law*, which incorporated both special and general rules for bills of exchange, promissory notes, and checks, had simplified the bill legal system, reflecting the progress of China's legislative technology. The transformation of China's modern bill exchange system had improved the efficiency of the bill exchange process, embodying technological thinking to some extent.

The first promissory note issued by a provincial government in 1934 for buying millet in Xiang-Gan Province of the Chinese Soviet Republic used a traditional vertical bill format. This note demonstrated technical expertise with its comprehensive information and thoughtful design. Huainan Bank's promissory notes, printed with handwritten steel plate oil, further exemplified this skill. In particular, because the people in the base areas were not very familiar with promissory notes, the Xiang-Gan Province of the Chinese Soviet Republic included detailed explanatory text on the promissory notes for buying millet, reflecting the wisdom of the printers.

In the 21st century, the ability to apply science and technology to the bill market has improved. The development of an internal management system for bills in the ICBC Bill Business Department has enhanced the security and operational efficiency of the bill business. The China Bill Network, through a unified electronic service system, has developed a nationwide bill trading and quotation platform, breaking down information blockages caused by market segmentation. Major banks like CMB, China Minsheng Bank, and ICBC have introduced electronic bill products based on their internal systems, expanding commercial bank bill innovation. With the advancement of information technology and the emergence of electronic bills, some financial institutions have started to integrate electronic and differentiated services, heralding the era of "Internet Plus Bills."

The boom in financial technology development has further deepened the role of technology in the bill market. For example, China Zheshang Bank launched a mobile digital bill platform based on blockchain technology and completed its first transaction in 2017, marking the application of blockchain technology in the bank's core business area. On March 15, 2017, Ganzhou Bank launched its first domestic blockchain bill business. In November 2017, Bank of Jiangsu successfully processed interbank bill discounting business based on blockchain technology. On January 25, 2018, the Shanghai Commercial Paper Exchange Company Ltd.'s digital bill trading platform was successfully launched and operated. This created a settlement method of "on-chain confirmation and off-line settlement," exploring the possibility of connecting blockchain systems with centralized systems. The supply chain bill platform, launched in 2020, has integrated bills into the supply chain through technological empowerment. This has enabled differentiated bill issuance and circulation, bill splitting, and bundled payments to meet diverse payment and financing needs of enterprises.

Bill market participants are leveraging technology to strengthen the bill system. ICBC is promoting the use of artificial intelligence technology and leveraging the machine learning capabilities of "ICBC Turing" to analyze enterprise discount willingness and enterprise relationship graphs. Enterprise Bill Pass integrates information technology with financial services, seamlessly connecting with information systems to provide comprehensive financial services. By utilizing financial technologies such as blockchain, big data, and artificial intelligence, it aims to promote safe and efficient circulation of commercial bills issued by central enterprises. JD Instant Discount, Tongcheng Bill Network, Deepbill Network, and other platforms have increased their use of financial technology to provide online bill financing matching services. Cloud Chain, Ouyeel, and JDH are also using technology to manage supply chain bill business.

While capitalizing on financial technology trends to develop the bill market, it's important to acknowledge the current shortcomings in the application of this technology. To develop the bill market, we need to consider improving the bill technology system, strengthen IT infrastructure, and promote the development of bill platforms. Leveraging technological advancements such as blockchain, big data, artificial intelligence, cloud computing, and the Internet of Things will invigorate the growth of the bill market.

8. Strengthening Research for Bill Development

The growth of the bill market is intricately linked with theoretical research. Starting from 1928, *The Bankers Weekly* took the lead to publish articles on acceptance bills and discount business from countries like the United States. Inspired by these articles, a group of excellent experts and scholars in China began advocating for acceptance bills and promoting the development of the discount business. *The Negotiable Instrument Law*, enacted in 1929, was established through the efforts of many sociologists, based on China's national conditions and existing bill laws in other countries, reflecting the nation's wisdom.

In 1980, after the PBC approved pilot bill business in Shanghai, the SFS formed the Bill Discount Research Association, which focused on studying the application of bill business in a socialist market. In 2002, the ICBC's Bill Business Department initiated the establishment of the China Urban Finance Society Bill Research Association, and launched China's first professional journal on bills, the *Bill Research*.

In addition, professional personnel in bill financing have been trained through organized training courses and touring lectures. Nowadays, the theoretical study of China's bill market is becoming more robust, with various entities actively conducting research. Professional bill think tanks and the Shanghai Commercial Paper Exchange Company Ltd. have produced significant research results. The Shanghai Commercial Paper Exchange Company Ltd. has investigated market demand by conducting multi-level events like bill market symposiums, the China Bill Market Summit Forum, and trader salons. It has also organized experts from within and outside the organization to compile monographs on bills, and initiated essay solicitations and research projects. These efforts have enhanced the overall research level of the bill industry and started to shape the application research system of the bill market.

In recent years, several professional bill committees and research institutions have been established successively, including the China Urban Finance Society Bill Professional Committee, the CBA Bill Professional Committee, the Shanghai Finance Society Bill Professional Committee, and the Jiangxi Provincial Finance Society Bill Professional Committee, as well as Joint Institute for Commercial Paper of JUFE and BOJJ, the Cloud Bill Research Center of Central University of Finance and Economics, the China Bill Research Center, and the China Commercial Bill Research Center. These organizations have explored the development of the bill market, enhanced the research atmosphere, produced valuable research results, and provided advice for the growth of the bill market. Some bill market participants and service institutions have also actively carried out research activities of various forms. Institutions like BOCOM, Postal Savings Bank of China, CMB, SPD Bank, Bank of Jiujiang, Changshu Rural Commercial Bank, SPFS, Gotten Finance, and LX Digital Technology regularly analyze the bill market, further advancing overall industry research.

As we enter the 14th Five-Year Plan (2021–2025) and promote the new dual-circulation development pattern, the bill market faces numerous opportunities. We should strive to elevate our theoretical understanding of bill applications, transform application achievements, and provide intellectual support for the bill market's long-term, stable, innovative, standardized, and orderly growth. The China Financial Society should strengthen its role in promoting China's bill market and enhancing theoretical research. Universities should also contribute to cultivating talent, ensuring a steady influx of new contributors for sustainable development of the bill market. We eagerly await prosperous bill market evolution, reaching new heights in theoretical research, system building, and innovation fostering.

II. Future Prospects

The new era of economic development and the building of a dual-circulation new development pattern have necessitated high-quality financial services for the real economy. Amid macroeconomic stability and counter-cyclical and cross-cyclical adjustments of macroeconomic policies, the bill market has entered a new stage of development.

1. Bills as a Vital Tool for Serving the Real Economy, Especially SMEs and Private Enterprises

From a credit system building perspective, the bill market remains the most suitable short-term financing tool for corporate credit in the near future. China's real economy has long faced a significant funding gap. From 2017 to 2021, the demand index for small business loans ranged from 61% to 78%, showing improvement in recent years. The average loan demand index for medium-sized and large enterprises was 60% and 58%, respectively. However, the average loan approval index from banks was only 50%, indicating that bank loan approval rates fell short of meeting the real economy's loan demand. This funding shortage was even more acute for SMEs and private enterprises.

Bills, created to meet enterprise payment and settlement demands, have evolved into a low-cost financing channel for businesses after decades of development. In 2021, the weighted average interest rate for bill discounting was 2.85%, 95 basis points lower than the loan prime rate for the same period. This difference highlights the significant impact of bills on reducing financing costs for the real economy. As the bill market continues to grow, its capacity to serve the real economy has improved. In 2021, acceptance bills issued in the market amounted to 24.15 trillion yuan, a year-on-year increase of 9.32%. The proportion of bill acceptance balance to social financing amount was 4.77%. Discounted bills accumulated to 15.02 trillion yuan, a year-on-year increase of 11.93%, with the proportion of bill discount balance to renminbi loan balance standing at 5.16%.

The bill market offers unique advantages in serving SMEs as well as private enterprises. According to data from the Shanghai Commercial Paper Exchange Company Ltd., the proportion of bills used by SMEs in 2021 was 72.19%. With 98% of bill users being SMEs, bills have become a vital tool for addressing financing challenges for these businesses and private enterprises. In recent years, the government has implemented a series of policies to support the growth of the real economy. As a low-cost and easily accessible financial tool, bills will continue to play a significant role in serving the real economy, especially SMEs and private enterprises.

2. Fintech-Empowered Bills as an Important Payment Method for Enterprises

From a technological perspective, the widespread application of financial technology facilitates innovative development in the bill market. This enhances both the depth and breadth of bill business development while improving efficiency. Bill payment, empowered by financial technology, are poised to become a significant payment method for enterprises. Looking back, the payment and exchange functions are the roots of bill development and the foundation for the full life cycle of bill functionality. Unlike other payment methods such as cash, promissory notes, checks, and bills of exchange, commercial bills offer deferred payment, endorsement and transfer, and discounting before maturity. The issuance and circulation of electronic bills, which rely on the ECDS, can effectively constrain default behavior. This is particularly beneficial for enterprises, especially those in the supply chain.

However, in the early stages of the bill market's development, factors such as low market transparency and the decentralized development of regional bill markets led China to predominantly use off-line payment methods. The asynchronous payment of goods posed security risks to the bill market. Thanks to financial technology, traditional off-line payments have transitioned to online ones. Organizations such as the Shanghai Commercial Paper Exchange Company Ltd., commercial banks, third-party bill platforms, and enterprises have used technology to develop online bill payment products. This has enabled bill monetization, expanded the scope of bill payments, improved coverage, and enhanced efficiency and popularity. In the future, the launch of digital bills will further enhance the security and convenience of bill payments. As financial technology evolves, bill payments will become an increasingly important payment method for enterprises.

3. Bills as an Effective Tool for Currency Control, Monetary Policy Transmission, and Liquidity Regulation

China's financial market requires ongoing reform and development. The bill market will continue to play a crucial role in enhancing the functions of the short-term capital market. Bills, traditionally used for payment and settlement, offer unique advantages. Bill acceptance reduces enterprise operating fund usage through deferred payment, while bill endorsement meets short-term fund and payment needs between enterprises.

Electronic bills, unlike their paper counterparts, serve dual roles as credit and payment tools. Their internet-based nature enables payment monetization. Document Yin Fa [2016] No. 224 states that "financial institutions should focus on leading enterprises or group enterprises in close relationships with the upstream and downstream industrial chain, and promote the use of electronic bills by these enterprises." In supply chain finance, electronic bills effectively link enterprises, facilitate credit transmission from high-quality firms, and clear receivables and payables. This achieves the invoicing of accounts receivable.

Commercial bills, particularly commercial acceptance bills, support real economic development through credit mechanisms and payment monetization. They meet enterprise funding needs without actual currency release, serving as an effective tool for reducing currency issuance and transmitting monetary policy. The PBC can guide credit and fund allocation through rediscounting, achieving "precise drip irrigation" and providing financial support for SMEs. Additionally, it can regulate the liquidity of the financial system through open market operations in the bill market.

4. Bills as an Ideal Product for General Investors

From an investment supply perspective, standardized bills are likely to become publicly accessible in the future, making them an ideal product for general investors. From 2009 to 2012, the bill market saw rapid development. Bill wealth management, with its high returns, low risk, zero threshold, and short terms became a popular choice. As a result, businesses started to explore the investment function of bills through bill asset management and bill wealth management.

China's first bill yield right asset securitization product, launched in 2016, drew investor attention due to its high yield and low risk. In 2019, the Shanghai Commercial Paper Exchange Company Ltd. released four standardized bills. In February 2020, the PBC issued the *Measures for the Administration of Standardized Bills (Draft for Comments)*, supporting the investment of standardized bills in asset management products. In June of the same year, the PBC issued the *Measures for the Administration of Standardized Bills*, which defines standardized bills as equally divided beneficiary certificates and brought them closer to standardized debt assets. This development of standardized bills opened new avenues for the evolution of bill investment products. By the end of 2021, sixteen financial institutions had created and issued 58 standardized bills, totaling 61.73 billion yuan. Standardized bills, as part of the money market instruments, allow trading entities in the interbank bond market to invest by purchasing them, marking a significant step toward bill securitization.

As technology advances, bill business conducted through the internet and platforms will inevitably become the trend of the times. Bill investment products will also evolve through the internet and platforms. In the future, standardized bills and other bill investment products are expected to become accessible to the market, the public, and individuals. The bill market will continue to innovate investment products and develop derivative products like bill forward, swaps, options, and futures to cater to diverse investor preferences. As enterprises and individual investors increasingly engage with bill investment products, bills are set to solidify their position as an ideal investment vehicle for general investors.

5. Shanghai Commercial Paper Exchange Company Ltd.'s Potential as an International Platform

The development of the Shanghai Commercial Paper Exchange Company Ltd. has laid the infrastructure groundwork for the development and innovation of the bill market. The exchange is expected to become an international bill trading platform. Bills, as a product of economic exchange and commercial credit development, have the potential to boost international trade, a concept supported by the experiences of developed bill markets in countries like the United States, the United Kingdom, and Japan, and regions like Taiwan (China).

As China's bill market infrastructure, the Shanghai Commercial Paper Exchange Company Ltd. performs functions such as bill quotation trading, registration and custody, clearing and settlement, and information services. It also plays a role in monetary policy by conducting central bank rediscounting operations. The exchange acts as a multifaceted hub, serving as the registration and custody center, business transaction center, innovation and development center, risk prevention and control center, and data information center for China's bill market. With its progress, an international bill exchange can be established to integrate the global bill market, enhance bill trading and utilization, promote cross-border bill transactions, and improve the efficiency of offshore financial markets. The international bill exchange can also strengthen cross-border payment and settlement functions of bills, reduce corporate financing costs, introduce advanced international experiences, and open China's bill market to the world. It can diversify innovative bill products, promote the comprehensive opening of the financial industry, and deepen financial reform.

6. Establishing an Integrated Commercial Acceptance Bill Platform in the Yangtze River Delta Region

From a basic platform construction perspective, the bill business has broad development potential. The Yangtze River Delta region, one of the most active and open regions in China's economic landscape, comprises a third of the bill market and has always served as a demonstration area for this market. In 2018, the integrated development of the Yangtze River Delta region became a national strategy, charting a new course for the area. Yi Gang, President of the PBC, expressed his support for the Shanghai Commercial Paper Exchange Company Ltd. to promote accounts receivable securitization in the region at the 11th Lujiazui Forum in 2019. Consequently, the exchange started to build a supply chain bill platform and promote Discount Pass and Bill Payment Pass services in line with these requirements, yielding positive results.

The Yangtze River Delta region boasts a mature commercial credit environment, with commercial bill discounting across its four provinces representing over 40% of the total. In an environment that encourages supply chain finance development, commercial acceptance bills show significant growth potential. The region's strong commercial credit landscape facilitates further exploration of the role of commercial acceptance bills and the development of commercial bill financing. Establishing an integrated commercial acceptance bill platform in the Yangtze River Delta region will bolster regional enterprises' credit awareness, improve the business environment, optimize the area's economic structure, and create a solid foundation for promoting integrated development. Moreover, it will serve as a model for the growth of commercial bills across China.

7. Establishing a Commercial Credit Bill Platform: Building on Enterprise Bill Pass

Commercial bills are currently one of the most effective tools for enhancing corporate credit in China's economic development. On August 26, 2019, CRHC collaborated with 51 central enterprises to form the Central Enterprise Commercial Acceptance Bill Mutual Recognition Alliance. The alliance launched and operated Enterprise Bill Pass, a platform connecting central enterprises and commercial banks and linking to the ECDS of the PBC. This platform provides one-stop services such as commercial bill issuance, acceptance, endorsement, discounting, and payment. Its credit mutual recognition and credit enhancement mechanisms diversify the payment methods between enterprises, maximize the commercial credit value of central enterprises, and minimize their comprehensive financing costs in the industrial chain. Building on the success of Enterprise Bill Pass, state-owned enterprises and local governments are poised to create a commercial credit bill platform. This unified credit platform aims to encourage wider use of electronic commercial draft in production and operations. By facilitating the circulation of enterprise bills, it can establish a closed-loop operation for commercial acceptance bills, thereby improving supply chain efficiency. Such a platform promises multiple benefits: reduced financing costs for enterprises, accelerated fund generation, a more positive credit environment for commercial bills, enhanced corporate credit, and increased circulation of commercial acceptance bills.

8. Institutional and Technological Innovation: Stimulating the Bill Market's Potential

Innovation is a key driver for market development. In the bill market, innovation enhances vitality and stimulates growth. The establishment of the Shanghai Commercial Paper Exchange Company Ltd. has brought new opportunities, infusing the market with boundless vitality for innovation. Technological advancements have spurred major state-owned banks, including the ICBC, SPD Bank, China CITIC Bank, Bank of China, CMB, and China Guangfa Bank, to launch innovative products like fast and online discounting. Tech companies, such as JD.com, have introduced instant discount products. The emergence of third-party platforms for rapid discounts and bill matching has significantly improved the efficiency and experience of enterprise bill discounting financing.

Financial technology has greatly enhanced the intelligence level and risk prevention capabilities of the bill market. For instance, the ICBC uses machine learning to create "ICBC Turing," a tool for graph analysis of enterprise discount willingness and relationships. Pudong Development Bank employs technologies like knowledge graphs, artificial intelligence, and machine learning to improve bill payment, financing, and risk control. It utilizes big data analysis techniques such as knowledge graph inference, collaborative filtering, and social network analysis to identify potential customers and deliver precise services. The ABC analyzes customer profiles using bill transaction data, combined with external data on credit, ratings, industry, commerce, finance, and regulation. This helps assess customer risk status, providing valuable references for customer selection and risk prevention. The Shanghai Commercial Paper Exchange Company Ltd.'s Bill Payment Pass has widened online bill payment channels, while the Discount Pass has established a nationwide unified discounting service platform, addressing issues like scattered discounting markets and information asymmetry. The launch of the supply chain bill platform has made bills divisible and improved the convenience of bill financing. Standardized bills connect the money and capital markets, further expanding bill financing channels.

Looking forward, the bill market will continue to leverage its institutional and technological advantages to stimulate market development potential. It will utilize institutional innovation to enhance the front-end acceptance payment and financing circulation functions of bills, aiming for payment convenience and short-term bill finance. Simultaneously, it will rely on technological development to boost backend trading and investment functions, making bills more akin to bonds and securities.

9. Leveraging Technology and Enhancing Credit Environment to Reduce Bill Market Risks

Advancements in science and technology, along with improvements in the bill market's credit environment, can significantly mitigate overall risk. Financial technologies like big data, blockchain, and artificial intelligence offer innovative solutions for regulating and mitigating risks in the bill market. A real-time supervision platform can monitor and intercept suspicious transactions and quotations, shifting the bill risk control checkpoint forward. A bill market monitoring model allows for T+0 post-event analysis of potential operational risks related to violations. Smart contracts can establish unified rules and order in the bill market, while blockchain's immutable timestamps provide cost-free access to bill market information, addressing risk information asymmetry.

Improving the overall social credit environment is fundamental for reducing risks in the bill market. Measures to build a credit society can enhance overall social credit awareness and foster a favorable business environment. Stricter penalties for dishonesty should be implemented to increase the cost of social dishonesty and reduce the likelihood of credit default. Risk should be controlled and prevented. In the future, by harnessing technological capabilities and bolstering the credit environment, risk can be effectively controlled throughout the entire life cycle of bills, significantly reducing the overall risk in the bill market.

10. Digitalization of Bills and Development Direction of Digital Bills

From the perspective of integrating bills and technology, digitalization of bills and digital bills are the main development paths in the bill market. Bill digitization involves transforming, standardizing, legalizing, and trading bill and credit information through technological methods. Since the 18th National Congress of the CPC, the Central Committee has prioritized the development of the digital economy, elevating it to a national strategy. *The 14th Five-Year Plan for National Economic and Social Development of the PRC and the Long-Range Goals for 2035* further stress "accelerating digital development and building a digital China" as a key strategic goal during the 14th Five-Year Plan period. Digitalization of bills and digital bills, as crucial components of the digital economy, play a significant role in accelerating the development of the digital economy, advancing industrial digitization and digital industrialization, continually improving the bill market's infrastructure, and enhancing China's credit environment. The digital development of bills will aim for advancements in six key areas:

- Digitalization of bills. Technology drives the digitization of bills. Financial technologies, including artificial intelligence, big data, blockchain, and cloud computing, should be harnessed to enhance technological sophistication in the bill sector. These advancements can stimulate growth, foster innovation, and cultivate a more robust credit environment in the bill market.
- Informatization of bill digitalization. Informatization is an essential step toward digitizing bills. The development of electronic and online bills enhances bill informatization standards. To advance this process, we must improve our ability to extract bill information, expand data mining sources, refine the processing of both structured and unstructured data, enhance our capacity to analyze and apply bill data, and continue to promote the evolution of bill information systems.
- Regulation of bill digitalization. Regulation supports the digital development of bills. To enhance this, a multi-level bill market security governance system should be established. The diversity of bill market collaborative governance mechanisms should be improved, along with the establishment of a comprehensive bill market supervision system. Additionally, financial institutions should strengthen their management of bill compliance. The criteria for bill information disclosure should be further clarified, thereby improving the uniformity and standardization of information within the bill market.
- Standardization of bill digitalization. Standardization is crucial for the digital evolution of bill operations. Efforts should be made to expedite the development of a national standard system in this field, hasten the transformation of standardized infrastructure, and encourage the creation of standardized risk prevention and control standards. A standardized indicator system for the bill market should be developed to facilitate easy trading, investing, pricing, and rights confirmation for bills, while respecting the confidentiality needs of specific industries and bill-related businesses.
- Legalization of bill digitization. Legalization safeguards the digital development of commercial bills. Efforts should be made to revise *The Negotiable Instrument Law of the PRC* to clarify the legal status of electronic and digital bills, as well as related innovative products. This will ensure the commercial bill market's development is legally grounded, and provide economic revitalization support for commercial bills. Furthermore, the bill market's institutional system needs continuous improvement. A market system and regulatory framework aligning with the digital economy's development should be established to foster the digital transformation of the bill market.
- Tradability of digital bills. Tradability is a key objective in the development of digital bills, which encompasses both bill business trading and bill data trading. To facilitate bill trading, it's crucial to improve the bill business trading system, promote the development of bill data trading infrastructure, and accelerate research into innovative products in the bill market, such as bill funds and derivatives. This will improve the

product system of the bill market and increase its efficiency in supporting the growth of the real economy.

Advancements in these six key areas unlock vast potential for bill trading and innovation, particularly in serving the real economy, SMEs, and green finance. As technology empowers the development of digital bills, new mediums can be introduced promptly. The concept of bill digitization can guide the exploration of digital bill pathways. To promote digital bills in the future, we need to establish strategic thinking and build a sound market ecosystem. This involves developing a framework system, focusing on top-level design, enhancing market transparency through stronger information disclosure, and improving infrastructure via technological empowerment. By leveraging data, we can use digital bills to serve the real economy, innovate service models, and support SMEs. We need to intensify regulatory efforts to prevent market risks and ensure coordinated, step-by-step development. This approach will pave the way for an orderly progression in the digital bill landscape.

Summary

Before the start of reform and opening up in 1978, China's financial system underwent continuous changes and exploration. During the planned economy era, China implemented a highly centralized management system and lacked the basic conditions for the development of commercial bills. However, with the start of reform and opening up, bills were promoted as a payment and settlement tool to address the "chain debt" issue. The establishment of the rediscount monetary policy led to the initial development of the bill market. The enactment of *The Negotiable Instrument Law of the PRC* filled the legal void in bill development. The establishment of the Bill Business Department by the ICBC drove the market toward intensive management and gradually unleashed innovation potential. A market-oriented bill interest rate pricing mechanism was essentially formed, particularly with the launch of the China Bill Network, which enabled electronic queries of market information and significantly boosted bill market activity. During this period, bills played a vital role in economic and financial development. They effectively resolved the "chain debt" issue during the economic transformation period, clarifying debt problems and offering market-oriented funding channels. Moreover, bills strongly supported the development of the commodity economy and the undertaking of reform and opening up, paving the way for deeper subsequent reforms.

In the 21st century, the bill market's role in supporting the real economy has significantly increased. In 2008, bill acceptance and discount amounts were 5.54 and 7.73 times higher, respectively, than in 2001. In 2021, the acceptance amount reached 24.20 trillion yuan, an increase of 240.85% or 17.10 trillion yuan compared to that in 2008. The discount amount reached 45.90 trillion yuan, a 240% or 32.40 trillion yuan increase from 2008. Commercial bills have become a powerful tool for improving the operational conditions of enterprises. Bill financing has also evolved into an important short-term financing channel, promoting a rebalancing of the financing structure. Rediscounting has gradually become an essential tool for central bank regulation and played a unique role in guiding commercial bank credit lending. Simultaneously, the bill business has improved the asset quality of China's commercial banks.

Bills are a financial instrument with a rich history spanning millennia. As economies, finance, and credit systems evolved, the scope of bills expanded and their functions became more sophisticated. Reflecting on the development of the bill market, we recognize the importance of serving the real economy, refining bill regulations, and fortifying market infrastructure. It's crucial to enhance the credit environment, bolster risk management, and encourage market innovation. We must harness financial technology and advance bill market research. Looking ahead, bills are poised to become a vital tool for supporting the real economy, especially small and medium-sized private enterprises. Aided by financial technology, they could evolve into a primary business payment method and an effective instrument for managing currency issuance, transmitting monetary policy, and regulating liquidity. They may also gain popularity among retail investors. The Shanghai Commercial Paper Exchange Company Ltd. shows promise as an international platform, while an integrated commercial acceptance bill platform could emerge in the Yangtze River Delta region. State-owned enterprises and local governments are expected to establish commercial credit bills using the Enterprise Bill Pass system. Institutional and technological innovations are likely to unlock the bill market's potential further, leveraging technological advancements and an improved credit environment to mitigate overall bill-related risks. The future of the bill market lies in digitalization and the development of digital bills.

APPENDIX

Major Events in the Development of China's Negotiable Instruments

1. During the Zhou Dynasty, early forms of bills, such as *zhiji*, *fubie*, and *shuqi*, emerged.
2. During the Tang Dynasty, *feiqian*, China's earliest bill of exchange, and *shutie*, its first check, were introduced.
3. During the Song Dynasty, *jiaozi* and *huizi* emerged, expanding the circulation of bills.
4. The Ming and Qing dynasties marked the pinnacle of ancient Chinese bill usage with the advent of money houses and bill shops. Money houses issued money house bills, which were actually promissory notes. Bill shops, representing China's earliest specialized exchange institutions, significantly increased the prevalence of bills and effectively solved cross-regional exchange problems. This development profoundly influenced the evolution of China's financial system.
5. On March 19, 1923, the Anhui Bengbu Discount Office was established as China's first specialized institution for bills.
6. On October 30, 1929, *The Negotiable Instrument Law*, China's first official bill law, was officially promulgated.
7. On January 10, 1933, the Shanghai Commercial Paper Exchange Company Ltd. was established. It was a groundbreaking clearing institution in Chinese finance, established entirely by commercial banks.
8. On March 16, 1936, the Shanghai Bank Bill Acceptance Office was created. It was China's first specialized institution to offer both bill acceptance and discounting services.
9. On October 2, 1944, with government support, the Chongqing United Bill Acceptance Office began to operate, serving as a dedicated bill agency.
10. In 1979, the government introduced a planned and controlled policy to open up commercial credit, with the PBC authorizing select enterprises to issue commercial bills.
11. In February 1981, the Yangpu District and Huangpu District offices of the PBC in Shanghai pioneered the first local commercial acceptance bill discounting service.

12. In October 1981, the Xuhui District Office of the PBC in Shanghai collaborated with its Tianchang County Sub-Branch in Anhui Province to launch the first cross-provincial bank acceptance bill discounting business.
13. In 1982, the PBC implemented the "three bills and one card" policy, encouraging commercial banks to expand their bill operations.
14. In December 1984, the PBC issued the *Interim Measures for the Acceptance and Discount of Commercial Bills*. This allowed nationwide operation of acceptance and discounting business, though it stipulated that bills of exchange could not circulate or transfer except for discounting to banks.
15. In 1986, the PBC and the ICBC jointly issued the *Notice on Implementing the Commercial Bill Acceptance and Discount Method to Clean Up Late Payment*. This was in response to enterprises being in arrears with each other, seriously tying up funds. The "chain debt" issue had significantly affected social capital turnover and the normal operation of enterprise production. The notice was implemented in Beijing, Shanghai, and ten other cities, using commercial bill acceptance discounting to clear outstanding payments and expand discounting business.
16. In April 1986, the PBC issued the *Trial Measures for Rediscounting*, officially starting to handle rediscount business.
17. In December 1988, the PBC issued the *Measures for Bank Settlement*, which came into effect on April 1, 1989. This measure abolished the restriction that banks must determine the payee and paying bank when issuing bills of exchange. It allowed commercial bills to be endorsed and transferred, and processed for discount, interbank discount, and rediscount.
18. On May 10, 1995, the 13th session of the Standing Committee of the 8th National People's Congress deliberated and passed *The Negotiable Instrument Law of the PRC*, which came into effect on January 1, 1996. This law defines bill types, forms, and contents, clarifies the rights and obligations of parties involved, and legally regulates bill-related behavior.
19. In June 1996, the PBC issued the *General Provisions on Lending*, which listed bill discounting as a type of loan alongside credit loans and guaranteed loans. categorizing bill discounting as a loan type alongside credit and guaranteed loans. Bill discounting was subsequently included in loan caliber and credit scale management statistics.
20. In August 1997, the PBC issued the *Implementing Measures for the Administration of Negotiable Instruments*, which came into effect on October 1, 1997. Building on *The Negotiable Instrument Law of the PRC*, these measures further reinforced regulations on bill subjects, behaviors, rights and obligations, and illegal practices.
21. In March 1998, the PBC decided to improve the rediscount and discount interest rate formation mechanism. The rediscount rate became the legal benchmark interest rate, adjusted by the central bank based on market fund supply and demand. The discount rate was then derived by adding points to the rediscount rate.
22. In February 2000, the Judicial Committee of the Supreme People's Court passed the *Provisions of the Supreme People's Court on Several Issues Concerning the Trial of Negotiable*

Instruments Dispute Cases, which came into effect on November 21, 2000. This document provides judicial interpretations of *The Negotiable Instrument Law of the PRC*, focusing on bill preservation, endorsement, and legal liability.

23. On November 9, 2000, the Bill Business Department of ICBC was established, which was China's first specialized institution for bill business approved by the head office of the PBC.
24. In July 2001, the PBC issued *A Notice on Effectively Strengthening the Administration of Commercial Bill Acceptance, Discount, and Rediscount Business.* The notice clarified that "bill financing" would no longer be included in the deposit-loan ratio assessment of financial institutions. Commercial banks were required to establish separate accounting subjects for bill discount, interbank discount, and rediscount businesses. The notice highlighted value-added tax invoices as a criterion for evaluating trade backgrounds. It also suggested that central cities should centralize the operation and management of commercial bill business to improve efficiency, achieve economies of scale, and mitigate bill-related risks.
25. In November 2002, the PBC released *A Notice on Issues Related to Handling Bank Bills and Bank Bill Acceptance Business.* They decided to remove the acceptance risk control indicator, as stated in *A Notice of the People's Bank of China on Strengthening the Administration of Bank Acceptance Business.* This indicator had stipulated that "the total acceptance amount for bank acceptance bill business shall be controlled, and shall not exceed 5% of the balance of various deposits at the end of the previous year." The removal of this restriction was intended to foster the growth of the bill acceptance business.
26. In June 2003, the China Foreign Exchange Trading Center, a subsidiary of the PBC, established and launched the "China Bill Quotation System," also known as the China Bill Network. This system provides price matching and inquiry services for bill interbank discounting and repurchase businesses between financial institutions.
27. On January 4, 2007, the Shibor mechanism was officially launched. In April of the same year, the ICBC became the first to introduce Shibor-based bill interbank discount and repurchase quotation rates. By November, the bank had pegged discount rates to Shibor quotations, marking a significant shift from fixed to floating interest rates in the pricing of bill businesses.
28. In October 2009, the PBC launched the ECDS. On the system's inaugural day, CMB made history by issuing both the first national electronic bank acceptance bill and the first electronic commercial acceptance bill.
29. In July 2013, the PBC issued *A Notice on Further Promoting Interest Rate Marketization Reform*, abolishing the practice of determining discount rates by adding points to rediscount rates. Instead, financial institutions were granted the freedom to set discount rates independently, based on market supply and demand.
30. In February 2014, the China Banking Regulatory Commission and the National Development and Reform Commission jointly issued the *Measures for the Administration of Service Prices of Commercial Banks.* This document transformed the bank acceptance rate from a

fixed handling fee, previously set at 0.05% of the face value charged to the issuer under *Measures for Payment and Settlement*, to a "market adjustment price." Consequently, the bill acceptance fee transitioned to market-oriented pricing.

31. On January 24, 2014, the Bill Professional Committee of the China Urban Finance Society was established.
32. In April 2014, five Chinese regulatory bodies, including the PBC, the China Banking Regulatory Commission, the China Securities Regulatory Commission, the China Insurance Regulatory Commission, and the State Administration of Foreign Exchange, jointly issued the *Notice on Regulating the Interbank Business of Financial Institutions* (Yin Fa [2014] No. 127). This notice aimed to standardize interbank business development, curb non-standard practices, and promote the return of interbank business to liquidity management methods. It also clarified the attributes of financial assets under repurchase agreements, specifying that assets such as bank acceptance bills should have reasonable fair value and high liquidity.
33. In May 2014, the China Banking Regulatory Commission issued *A Notice on Standardizing the Governance of Interbank Business of Commercial Banks* (Banking Regulatory Office [2014] No. 140). The notice stipulated that, interbank activities, including bill buying and resale, be managed by a dedicated department. This approach would entail centralized authorization, credit granting, list management, approval, and accounting operations.
34. In 2014, the CBA established the Bill Professional Committee.
35. On January 15, 2015, the Bill Professional Committee of the SFS was established.
36. In April 2016, the PBC and the China Banking Regulatory Commission jointly issued *A Notice on Strengthening the Supervision of Bill Business to Promote the Healthy Development of the Bill Market*. The notice demanded strict inspection of the authenticity of trade backgrounds, rigorous standardization of interbank account management, and effective prevention and control of bill business risks.
37. On November 6, 2016, Joint Institute for Commercial Paper of JUFE and BOJJ was established, the country's first research institution specializing in bills.
38. On December 5, 2016, the PBC issued the *Measures for the Administration of Bill Trading* to regulate bill market behavior.
39. On December 8, 2016, the Shanghai Commercial Paper Exchange Company Ltd., spearheaded by the PBC, commenced operations. This launch marked the official inception of China's nationwide unified bill trading platform.
40. On March 27, 2017, the PBC issued *A Notice on Implementing the Transfer and Switching of the ECDS* (Yin Fa [2017] No. 73), deciding to transfer the ECDS to the Shanghai Commercial Paper Exchange Company Ltd. for operation.
41. On September 14, 2017, the Bill Professional Committee of Jiangxi Financial Society was established.
42. On December 8, 2017, the Shanghai Commercial Paper Exchange Company Ltd. hosted the Summit Forum on the Reform and Development of the Bill Market in Shanghai.

During this event, Shanghai University of Finance and Economics, Shanghai Commercial Paper Exchange Company Ltd., and China Bill Research Center jointly held an unveiling ceremony.

43. On January 25, 2018, the experimental production system of the digital bill trading platform was successfully launched and put into trial operation.
44. On April 27, 2018, the PBC, China Banking and Insurance Regulatory Commission, China Securities Regulatory Commission, and State Administration of Foreign Exchange jointly issued the *Guiding Opinions on Regulating the Asset Management Business of Financial Institutions.*
45. On May 2, 2018, the China Banking and Insurance Regulatory Commission issued *A Notice on Regulating Inter-Provincial Bill Business of Banking and Financial Institutions* (Banking and Insurance Regulatory Office [2018] No. 21). This notice regulated inter-provincial bill business for banking and financial institutions. It proposed regulatory requirements for inter-provincial transactions and credit businesses, mandating that institutions conduct inter-provincial bill transactions through bill market infrastructure. Additionally, the notice aimed to restrict high-risk inter-provincial paper bill transactions.
46. On May 9, 2018, the MOC and eight other departments jointly issued *A Notice on Launching Pilot Projects for Supply Chain Innovation and Application.*
47. On September 26, 2018, the PBC issued *A Notice of the General Office of the People's Bank of China on the Rediscount of Paper and Electronic Bills After the Integration of Transactions in Shanghai Commercial Paper Exchange Company Ltd.* (Yin Ban Fa [2018] No. 180). This notice marked the formal unification of paper and electronic bill rediscounting operations.
48. On December 6, 2018, the Shanghai Commercial Paper Exchange Company Ltd. released the first yield curve in the bill market.
49. On December 6, 2018, the Shanghai Commercial Paper Exchange Company Ltd. successfully held a press conference on the innovative supply chain product Bill Payment Pass in Shanghai.
50. On May 27, 2019, the Shanghai Commercial Paper Exchange Company Ltd. officially launched its Discount Pass service.
51. On August 15, 2019, with approval from the PBC, the Shanghai Commercial Paper Exchange Company Ltd. announced the establishment of standardized bills. This move aimed to enhance liquidity support for small and medium-sized financial institutions.
52. On August 20, 2019, with the approval of the PBC, the Shanghai Commercial Paper Exchange Company Ltd. successfully created its first standardized bills.
53. On December 6, 2019, the Shanghai Commercial Paper Exchange Company Ltd. released an interbank discount yield curve for urban commercial bank bills. This curve, covering credit types of "urban commercial acceptance" and "national bill discount," offered a pricing benchmark for bills accepted by small and medium-sized banks.
54. On January 16, 2020, the bill information disclosure platform was launched for trial operation.

55. On April 26, 2020, the supply chain bill platform was successfully put into trial operation.
56. On June 18, 2020, the first batch of supply chain bill discounting business was successfully launched.
57. On June 24, 2020, the PBC issued the *Measures for the Administration of Standardized Bills* to standardize the financing mechanism of standardized bills, was set to be implemented from July 28, 2020.
58. On July 28, 2020, the Shanghai Commercial Paper Exchange Company Ltd., in collaboration with the China Foreign Exchange Trading Center and the Interbank Market Clearing House, issued the *Rules for Information Disclosure of Standardized Bills* (Bill Exchange Announcement [2020] No. 2) and *Rules for Custody and Settlement of Standardized Bill Basic Assets* (Bill Exchange Announcement [2020] No. 3).
59. On July 30, 2020, the first batch of 14 standardized bills were successfully created after the official implementation of the *Measures for the Administration of Standardized Bills.*
60. On November 3, 2020, the cross-border renminbi trade financing transfer service platform was officially launched on the Shanghai Commercial Paper Exchange Company Ltd.
61. On December 23, 2020, the PBC issued Announcement No. 19 of 2020 to regulate the disclosure of information on commercial acceptance bills. This regulation was set to take effect on August 1, 2021.
62. On December 30, 2020, the Shanghai Commercial Paper Exchange Company Ltd. issued Announcement No. 4 of 2020, *Operating Rules for Information Disclosure of Commercial Acceptance Drafts*, set to take effect on August 1, 2021.
63. On May 26, 2021, Premier Li Keqiang presided over an executive meeting of the State Council to discuss shortening the acceptance period of commercial bills from one year to six months to alleviate the pressure on enterprises.
64. On August 1, 2021, the information disclosure of commercial acceptance bills was officially launched.
65. On January 14, 2022, the PBC issued *Measures for the Administration of Acceptance, Discount, and Rediscount of Commercial Drafts (Draft for Comments).*

Bibliography

"A Bouquet of Market News." *Xinhua Daily*, November 29, 1944.

Acceptance Bill Instructions (May 1936), collected by Shanghai Archives. Archives of the Joint Preparatory Commission: S177-1-72.

Bai, Xiaoping. "Research on Ancient Chinese Sales Contracts." Master diss., Lanzhou University, 2006.

Bank Treasures: Collection of Shanghai Bank Museum (Shanghai Bank Museum, 2003).

"Bill Exchange Report 1950." In *Shanghai Bank Association Archives: S172-4-34.*

Bu, Qixuan. "TCL: 'JDH' Is Not Simple." *Chinese Small and Medium Enterprises*, no. 6 (2020): 39–41.

"Business Brochure of Shandong Beihai Bank." In *Compilation of Chinese and Foreign Financial Regulations (Volume 3)*, edited by Financial Research Institute of the Head Office of the People's Bank of China, 1988.

"The central bank also handles the bill exchange industry." *Ta Kung Pao* (Chongqing Edition), June 3, 1942.

"The Central Bank's 1946 Annual Business Report." In *Compilation of Historical Archives of the Republic of China (Volume 5)*, edited by The Second Historical Archives of China. Nanjing: Jiangsu Ancient Books Publishing House, 2010.

Chen, Qitian. *A Tentative Study of Shanxi Bill Shops*. Beijing: The Commercial Press, 1937.

Cheng, Nianpeng. "Notice to Customers from Domestic Enamel Business Office for Issuing Commercial Acceptance Drafts." *The Bankers Weekly*, no. 42 (1932): 33–36.

China Financial Society, China Numismatic Museum, Photography Department of Xinhua News Agency, and Central Literature Publishing House, ed. *An Encyclopedia of Precious Cultural Relics Archives in Chinese Finance (Ancient Volume)*. Beijing: Central Literature Publishing House, 2002.

———, *An Encyclopedia of Precious Cultural Relics Archives in Chinese Finance (Modern Finance Volume 4)*. Beijing: Central Literature Publishing House, 2002.

———, ed. *An Encyclopedia of Precious Cultural Relics Archives in Chinese Finance (Modern Finance Volume 3)*. Beijing: Central Literature Publishing House, 2002.

———, ed. *An Encyclopedia of Precious Cultural Relics Archives in Chinese Finance (Revolutionary Finance Volume 1)*. Beijing: Central Literature Publishing House, 2002.

———, ed. *An Encyclopedia of Precious Cultural Relics Archives in Chinese Finance (Revolutionary Finance Volume 2).* Beijing: Central Literature Publishing House, 2002.

———, ed. *An Encyclopedia of Precious Cultural Relics Archives in Chinese Finance (Revolutionary Finance Volume 3).* Beijing: Central Literature Publishing House, 2002.

China Financial Yearbook Editorial Board. "Rediscount Business." In *China Financial Yearbook (1995).* Beijing: China Printing Corporation, 1996.

China Industrial and Commercial Bank Bill Business Department, and Financial Market Management Department of the Shanghai Headquarters of the People's Bank of China. *China Bill Market Development Report (2008).* Beijing: China Financial Publishing House, 2009.

———. *New Century China Bill Market Development Report (2000–2011).* Beijing: China Financial Publishing House, 2013.

Chongqing Archives and Financial Research Institute of the People's Bank of Chongqing. *Historical Materials of the Four Union General Office (Part 2).* Beijing: Archives Publishing House, 1993.

Chongqing Archives, ed. "Financial Research Institute of the People's Bank of Chongqing." In *Historical Materials of the Joint General Office of the Four Banks (Part 1).* Beijing: Archives Publishing House, 1993.

———, ed. "Financial Research Institute of the People's Bank of Chongqing." In *Historical Materials of the Joint General Office of the Four Banks (Part 2).* Beijing: Archives Publishing House, 1993.

Chongqing Financial Writing Group, ed. *Chongqing Finance (Volume 1).* Chongqing Publishing House, 1991.

"Commercial Banks Apply to the Central Bank for the Procedures of Rediscounting, Pledging, and Bill of Exchange Conversion." In *Selected Financial Regulations of the Republic of China*, edited by the Second Historical Archives of China, Jiangsu Branch of the People's Bank of China, et al. Beijing: Archives Publishing House, 1989.

Compilation Committee of *The Grand View of Xuzhou Paper Currency. The Grand View of Xuzhou Paper Currency.* Beijing: China Literature and History Publishing House, 2003.

Cui, Ning, and Jingshi Zhang. "Connecting the Two Major Financing Markets Brings Standardized Bills Closer." *Financial Market Research*, no. 3 (2020): 90–97.

Cui, Xiaocen. *Central Bank Theory.* Beijing: The Commercial Press, 1935.

Dai, Jianbing. "A Tentative Exploration of Modern Chinese Money Bills." *Journal of Hebei University of Economics and Trade*, no. 5 (1996): 73–78.

Dai, Zhiqiang. "Several Questions About *Jiaozi* in the Northern Song Dynasty." *Chinese Numismatics*, no. 3 (2006): 43–46, 95–96.

Deng, Chenxi. "The Government of the Shanxi-Hebei-Shandong-Henan Border Region Has Announced the Interim Measures for the Administration of Foreign Exchange in This Region." In *Financial and Economic Construction (Volume 1 and Volume 2).* Taiyuan: Shanxi People's Publishing House, 1987.

Detailed Rules for the Operations of Bank Bill Acceptance Office (March 13, 1936), collected by Shanghai Archives. Archives of the Joint Preparatory Commission: S177-1-72.

Di, Gang. "The Innovative Application of Blockchain Technology in the Digital Bill Scene." *Chinese Financiers*, no. 5 (2018): 69–71.

Ding, Haibin, and Lulu Yang. "Research on Commercial Documents in the Pre-Qin Period." *Archives*, no. 3 (2019): 4–11.

"The Discount Rate Announced by the Bank Bill Acceptance Office" (April 7, 1936). *The Bankers Weekly*, no. 20 (1936): 13.

"Draft Amendment to the *Central Bank Law*." In *Compilation of Chinese and Foreign Financial Regulations (Volume 3)*, edited by Financial Research Institute of the Head Office of the People's Bank of China, 1988.

Du, Lijuan. "The Human Resource Management of Shanxi Bill Shops and Its Implications for Modern Banks." *Oriental Enterprise Culture*, no. 20 (2011): 52.

Du, Deqing. "The Bill Law: Legal Assurance for the Development of Bills." *China Industry and Commerce*, no. 7 (1995).

Du, Wenyu, and Kexi Wang, "The Issuance, Recovery, Exchange, and Trading of Paper Currency in the Song Dynasty." *Journal of Historical Science*, no. 1 (1992): 24–30.

Du, Xuncheng. "The Evolution of China's Credit System in the 1920s and 1930s." *Chinese Social Sciences*, no. 4 (2002).

———. *The Common Law of Modern Chinese Money Industry: From the Perspective of Shanghai Money Industry*. Shanghai University of Finance and Economics Press, 2006.

Economic Research Office of the General Administration of Bank of China. *National Bank Yearbook 1936*. Shanghai: Hanwen Zhengkai Printing Company, 1936.

Fan, Xiaozhong. "The Investigation and Inspiration of Resolving 'Chain Debt' in the Early 1990s." *Journal of Hubei University of Economics*, no. 11 (2019): 29–31.

Financial History Research Office of the Financial Research Institute of the Head Office of the People's Bank of China, ed. *The Financial Market of Modern China*. Beijing: China Financial Publishing House, 1987.

Financial Research Editorial Department, ed. *Acceptance and Discount of Bills*. Shanghai Financial Society, 1983.

Financial Research Institute of the People's Bank of China and Financial Science Research Institute of the Ministry of Finance. *Currency of Chinese Revolutionary Base Areas (Part 2)*. Beijing: Cultural Relics Publishing House, 1982.

Financial Research Institute of the People's Bank of China, Shandong Branch and Financial Research Institute of the People's Bank of China. *Historical Materials of Beihai Bank in China's Revolutionary Base Areas*. Jinan: Shandong People's Publishing House, 1986.

"The First Conference of the Bank Bill Acceptance Office" (March 31, 1936). *The Bankers Weekly*, no. 20 (1936): 12.

First Meeting of Members of the Bill Acceptance Office, collected by Shanghai Archives. Archives of the Joint Preparatory Commission: S177-1-21.

Fu, Weiqun. *Jiufu Yumin: A Illustrated History of Shanghai Money House Bills*. Shanghai Bookstore Publishing House, 2002.

Fu, Yuanhong. "Research on Innovative Models of Internet Supply Chain Finance." PhD diss., Zhejiang University, 2019.

Gao, Guancheng. *Selected Historical Materials of the Central China Bank*. Beijing: China Radio and Television Publishing House, 2003.

"General Rules for Handling Shanghai Commercial Bank Discount and Lending Business by the Central Bank Discount and Lending Committee." In *Complete Collection of Financial Regulations (Continued)*, edited by Economic Research Department of the Central Bank. Taipei: Taiwan Student Bookstore, 1971.

Guo, Rongsheng. *A Chronicle of Mr. Kung Hsiang-hsi's Life in the Republic of China Period*. Taipei: Taiwan Commercial Press, 1981.

Hebei Provincial Financial Research Institute. *Bank of the Jin-Cha-Ji Border Region*. Beijing: China Financial Publishing House, 1988.

Heilongjiang Financial Research Institute. *Historical Materials on Financial Activities in the Heilongjiang Base Region (1945–1959)*. 1984.

Hong, Jiaguan, and Jifeng Zhang. *Financial Market in Modern Shanghai*. Shanghai People's Publishing House, 1989.

Hong, Jiaguan. *Historical Materials about Central Banks*. Beijing: China Financial Publishing House, 2005.

———. *Shanghai Finance in the 20th Century*. Shanghai People's Publishing House, 2004.

Hong, Rongchang. "Promissory Notes During the Red Army Period." *Chinese Numismatics*, no. 2 (2009): 39–40.

Hou, Guangqing, and Xueqin Zhao. "On the Origin and Nature of Feiqian." *Journal of Shanxi University of Finance and Economics*, no. 4 (1997): 72–73, 84.

Hou, Lin. "Tracing the Development Path of Commercial Bills: Improving the Construction of Credit System." *Financial Market Research*, no. 9 (2021): 60–67.

Hu, Mengjia. "Advice to the Research Committee on the Negotiable Instrument Law." In *Research on the Negotiable Instrument Law*, edited by The Bankers Weekly Editorial Office. Shanghai: The Bankers Weekly, 1922.

Huang, Jia, and Hongjuan Ming. "The Application of Blockchain Technology in Digital Bill Trading Platforms." *Journal of Hubei University of Technology* (Humanities and Social Sciences Edition) 35, no. 6 (2018): 41–44.

"Interim Measures for Promoting Bank Acceptance and Discount Business." In *Historical Materials of the Joint General Office of the Four Banks (Part 3)*, collected by Chongqing Archives and Chongqing Financial Research Institute of the People's Bank of China. Beijing: Archives Publishing House, 1993.

"Issues Regarding the Revitalization of the Shanghai Market." *The Bankers Weekly*, no. 19 (1935): 9.

Jia, Daquan. "The Emergence of *Jiaozi*." *Sichuan Finance*, no. 1 (1994): 5–29.

Jia, Zhangwang. *New Democratic Revolution Currency Chart*. Beijing: Communist Party History Publishing House, 2018.

Jiang, Jianqing. *Harvest of Time: A Collection of Boutique Appreciations at the Bank Museum*. Shanghai People's Fine Arts Publishing House, 2013.

Jin-Cha-Ji Border Region Bank Jidong Sub-Branch. "Provisional Regulations on Promissory Notes Issued by the Jidong Branch." In *Selected Historical Materials on the Fiscal and Economic History of the North China Liberated Area (Volume 2)*, edited by the Editorial Group for the Fiscal and Economic History of the North China Liberated Area. Beijing: China Financial and Economic Publishing House, 1996.

Jin, Guobao. "Causes and Measures for Creating a Discount Market." In *Bill-Related Issues and Banking Legislation*, edited by Jin Baoguo. Beijing: Zhonghua Book Company, 1947.

———. "The Bill-Related Issues in the Banking Law." In *Bill-Related Issues and Banking Legislation*, edited by Jin Baoguo. Beijing: Zhonghua Book Company, 1947.

———. "A Brief Discussion on Acceptance Bills." In *Bill-Related Issues and Banking Legislation*, edited by Jin Baoguo. Beijing: Zhonghua Book Company, 1947.

———. "Discussion with Guests on Acceptance Bills." In *Bill-Related Issues and Banking Legislation*, edited by Jin Baoguo. Beijing: Zhonghua Book Company, 1947.

———. "Issues Related to the Promotion of Commercial Acceptance Bills." In *Bill-Related Issues and Banking Legislation*, edited by Jin Baoguo. Beijing: Zhonghua Book Company, 1947.

———. "Speech at the 7th Star Five Dinner Party of the China Association for Domestic Production and Marketing Cooperation on May 6, 2021." In *A Collection of Insightful Quotes at Dinner Tables*.

———. "The Significance and Promotion of Commercial Acceptance Bills." In *Bill-Related Issues and Banking Legislation*, edited by Jin Baoguo. Beijing: Zhonghua Book Company, 1947.

———. "Why and How to Create a Discount Market." *The Bankers Weekly 15*, no. 16 (1931).

Jing, Hailong. "Empirical Analysis of the Effect of Interest Rate Policy Regulation in Qinghai Province in 2009." *Qinghai Finance*, no. 8 (2010): 14.

Jingshi Xueyi Society, ed. *Modern Economic Dynamics*. Beijing: World Book Company, 1939.

Joint Institute for Commercial Paper of JUFE and BOJJ, ed. *A History of Negotiable Instruments*. Beijing: China Financial Publishing House, 2020.

Kong, Xiangyi. *Historical Materials on Finance in Shanxi During the Republic of China*. Beijing: China Financial Publishing House, 2013.

Kong, Yan. "Deepen the Application of Bills in Supply Chain Finance." *Financial Market Research*, no. 11 (2020): 2–7.

"The Letter of the General Management Office of the Bank of China on the Acceptance and Discount Methods for Bills During Special Period." In *Historical Materials of the Joint General Office of the Four Banks (Part 3)*, collected by Chongqing Archives and Chongqing Financial Research Institute of the People's Bank of China. Beijing: Archives Publishing House, 1993.

"Letter on Implementing Discount Rate Management Policy and Signing Opinions by the Central Business Bureau (October 27, 1938)." Unpublished archives in the Chongqing Branch of the Joint General Office of the Central Bank, Bank of China, BOCOM, and China Rural Bank: 02920001380000147000.

Letter to the Bank of China, the Central Bank, and Bank of Communications (March 19, 1936), collected by Shanghai Archives. Archives of the Joint Preparatory Commission: S177-2-606.

Li, Jun. "Steadily Building a Unified Chinese Bill Market." *China Money Market*, no. 9 (2003).

Li, Pengjie. "The Rise and Fall of Shanxi Bill Shops and the Development of Accounting in China." *China Market*, no. 27 (2016): 137–138, 155.

Li, Wei. "The Inspiration of Shanxi Bill Shops' Bill System on Modern Enterprises." *China Economist*, no. 9 (2017): 59–60.

Li, Xia. "Exploration of the Causes for the Failure of Shanxi Bill Shop Transformation." *Economic Outlook of Bohai Rim*, no. 11 (2018): 75–76.

Li, Yang. *Six Decades of Finance in New China*. Beijing: China Finance and Economics Publishing House, 2009.

Liang, Hongzhi. *Bills: A Mirror of Social Change*. Beijing: Science Press, 2016.

Lin, Yin. *Rites of Zhou: An Annotated and Translated Version*. Beijing: Bibliographic Literature Publishing House, 1988.

Lin, Yuli. "Establish A Modern Electronic Service System for the Bill Market." *China Finance*, no. 18 (2003): 19.

Liu, Fang. "On the Development of Commerce in the Western Zhou Dynasty." *Journal of Baoji Normal University* (Philosophy and Social Sciences Edition), no. 2 (1989): 52.

Liu, Huiyu. *Research on the Central Bank of China (1928–1949)*. Beijing: China Economic Publishing House, 1999.

Liu, Qiugen, and Xiuli Xie. "The Initial Development of Commercial Credit Documents in the Ming and Qing Dynasties: A Focus on Bills of Exchange and Acceptance." *Chinese Numismatics*, no. 1 (2006): 3–11, 79.

"Loan Policy for Production Enterprises." In *Selected Financial Regulations of the Republic of China*, edited by The Second Historical Archives of China, Jiangsu Branch of the People's Bank of China, et al. Beijing: Archives Publishing House, 1989.

Lu, Baojiang. "On Bill-Related Risks and Prevention." *Research on Rural Finance in Guangxi (Semi-Monthly)*, no. 3 (2001): 63.

Lu, Yangyuan, and Qingqiu Fang. *A Social and Economic History of the Republic of China*. Beijing: China Economic Publishing House, 1991.

Luo, Yong. "Knowing, Understanding, Abiding By, and Using the Law to Ensure the 'Two Laws.'" *Finance and Economy*, no. 6 (1995).

Ma, Linghe. "Research on the Pioneering Modern Bengbu Discount Office." *Journal of Bengbu University 3*, no. 2 (2014): 181–184.

Ma, Yinchu. *On China's Banks*. Beijing: The Commercial Press, 1929.

———. *The Complete Works of Ma Yinchu (Vol. 4)*. Hangzhou: Zhejiang People's Publishing House, 1999.

Materials on the Remittance, Acceptance and Discount Services by the China State Bank (1931). *The China State Bank Archive Q278-1-109-85*.

"Measures for Handling Bill Exchange at Beihai Bank." *Shandong Political Daily*, no. 1 (1949): 62–63.

Meng, Xin, 'The Inspiration of Shanxi Bill Shops on Modern Bank Management." *Modern Economic Information*, no. 16 (2014): 300, 307.

Ministry of Finance. "The Ministry of Finance Has Formulated an Outline of Measures to Improve Local Financial Institutions." *Commercial Monthly Report 18*, no. 5 (1938): 57.

Minutes of the Seventh Meeting of the Clearing House Committee (February 22, 1933). The Joint Preparatory Commission Archives: S177-1-18.

"Monthly Report of the Clearing House in 1950." In *Archives of Shanghai Commercial Paper Exchange Company Ltd.: Q52-2-22.*

"The Negotiable Instrument Law of the Republic of China." In *Compilation of Chinese and Foreign Financial Regulations (Volume 3)*, edited by Financial Research Institute of the Head Office of the People's Bank of China, 1988.

"Observations on Bengbu Discount Office." *The Bankers Weekly*, no. 27 (1923): 24–42.

"Opening of Bank Bill Acceptance Office." *The Bankers Weekly*, no. 20 (1936): 10.

"Organizational Regulations of the Committee of the Bank Bill Acceptance Office and the Convention on Members Banks." *The Bankers Weekly*, no. 20 (1936): 11.

"Outline of Measures for Improving Local Financial Institutions Issued by the Ministry of Finance" (April 28, 1938). In *Selected Financial Regulations of the Republic of China*, edited by the Second Historical Archives of China, Jiangsu Branch of the People's Bank of China, et al. Beijing: Archives Publishing House, 1989.

PBC Shanghai Branch. *Historical Materials of Shanghai Money Houses*. Shanghai People's Publishing House, 1960.

People's Bank of China, and Industrial and Commercial Bank of China Liaoning Branch. "Several Practices for Organizing the Acceptance and Discounting of Commercial Bills." *China Finance*, no. 5 (1987).

"Provisional Regulations of the State Bank of the Chinese Soviet Republic." In *Currency of Chinese Revolutionary Base Areas (Part 2)*, edited by The Financial Research Institute of the People's Bank of China and the Financial Science Research Institute of the Ministry of Finance. Beijing: Cultural Relics Publishing House, 1982.

Qiao, Jianwei. "Research on Risk Management of Shanxi Bill Shops and Its Inspiration for Modern Banks in China." PhD diss., Hebei University of Economics and Trade, 2013.

Que, Fangping. *The Institutional Evolution in China's Bill Market*. Beijing: China Financial Publishing House, 2005.

"Regulations on the Handling of Interbank Placement by the Central Bank Placement Committee." *Financial Weekly*, no. 2 (1948).

"Relief for Industrial, Commercial, and Financial Issues." *Industrial and Commercial Semi-Monthly*, no. 7 (1935): 8.

"Resolution of the Council on the Approval of the 1948 Loan Policy for Production Enterprises." In *Historical Materials of the Joint General Office of the Four Banks (Part 2)*, edited by Chongqing Archives and Chongqing Financial Research Institute of the People's Bank of China. Beijing: Archives Publishing House, 1993.

"Resolution of the Joint General Office of the Four Banks on the Proposed Use of Bill Discounting Method for Working Capital Loans." In *Historical Materials of the Joint General Office of the Four Banks (Part 3)*, collected by Chongqing Archives and Chongqing Financial Research Institute of the People's Bank of China. Beijing: Archives Publishing House, 1993.

"Revisions to the Shanghai Banking Industry Regulations." In *An Economic History of the Republic of China: The Bankers Weekly 30th Anniversary Commemorative Issue*, edited by Zhu Sihuang. Shanghai: The Bankers Weekly, 1948.

Shaan-Gan-Ning Border Region Bank. "Bank Regulations (Draft)." In *Collected Works Commemorating Zhu Lizhi*, edited by the Party History Research Office of the Henan Provincial Party Committee of the Communist Party of China. Beijing: Party History Publishing House, 2007.

"Shandong Beihai Bank Qinghe Branch Group Stock Brochure and Organizational Draft." In *Compilation of Chinese and Foreign Financial Regulations (Volume 3)*, edited by Financial Research Institute of the Head Office of the People's Bank of China, 1988.

"Shanghai Bank's Articles of Association." In *Principles of the Negotiable Instrument Law*, edited by Wang Dunchang. Beijing: The Commercial Press, 2016.

"Shanghai Commercial Paper Exchange Company Ltd. Monthly Report Issue 12." In *Shanghai Bill Coking Archive, 1949: Q52-2-21*.

Shang, Ming, Wenqing Bai, et al. *The Financial Dictionary*. Chengdu: Sichuan People's Publishing House, 1992.

Shangguan Yongqing. *The Past, Present, and Future of Shanxi Merchant Banks*. Taiyuan: Shanxi Economic Publishing House, 2009.

Sheng, Mujie. "On the Discount and Lending Policy of the Central Bank." *Economic Review* 1, no. 5 (1947).

Shi, Ruomin. *Bill Merchants and Modern China*. Beijing: China Yanshi Press, 2014.

Shi, Tao. "An Analysis of the Evolution of the Bill Exchange System in Modern China." *Journal of Harbin University of Commerce* (Social Sciences Edition), no. 1 (2012): 69–77.

———. *History of Modern Chinese Central Banks*. Beijing: Commercial Press, 2021, 141–142.

Shu, Xiong. "The Current Situation, Restrictive Factors, and Development Path of China's Electronic Bill Market." *Guangxi Financial Research*, no. 6 (2008): 37.

Song, Hanguang. "Driving New Momentum in Financial Technology and Embarking on a New Journey in the Bill Market: Practice and Prospects of Financial Technology Application in Bill Exchanges." *Financial World*, no. 12 (2020): 22–24.

———. "The Application of Blockchain in Digital Bills." *China Finance*, no. 10 (2018): 42–43.

"Supplementary Measures to the Policy on Loans for Production Enterprises." In *Selected Financial Regulations of the Republic of China*, edited by The Second Historical Archives of China, Jiangsu Branch of the People's Bank of China, et al. Beijing: Archives Publishing House, 1989.

Sun, Jianhua. *Financial Development and Institutional Changes in Modern China (1840–1945)*. Beijing: China Financial and Economic Publishing House, 2008.

Sun, Rong. "Building a New Highland in the Bill Market: Interview with Song Hanguang, Chairman of the Shanghai Commercial Paper Exchange Company Ltd." *Chinese Financiers*, no. 5 (2018): 29–33.

The People's Bank of China. *A Brief History of Financial Development Under the Leadership of the CPC*. Beijing: China Financial Publishing House, 2021.

The Second Historical Archives of China, Jiangsu Branch of the People's Bank of China, et al. *Selected Financial Regulations of the Republic of China*. Beijing: Archives Publishing House, 1989.

The Second Historical Archives of China. *Compilation of Historical Archives of the Republic of China*. Nanjing: Phoenix Publishing House, 2010.

Wakayama Prefecture. "Created by Our Own Country." Trans. Tao Yue. *Research on the Posting System in Ningbo (1)*. *The Bankers Weekly* 15, no. 35 (1931).

Wan, Liming. "Bengbu Discount Office." *China Finance*, no. 17 (2015): 98–99.

———. "Institutional Innovation of Modern Chinese Bill Intermediary Institutions and Its Implications: Taking Shanghai Bank Bill Acceptance Office as an Example." *Journal of Shanghai University of Administration*, no. 2 (2008): 59–67.

———. "On the Institutional Changes of Shanghai Commercial Paper Exchange Company Ltd. After World War II." In *Research on the Changes of China's Financial System*, edited by Fudan University Center for the Study of Chinese Financial History. Shanghai: Fudan University Press, 2008.

———. "The Shanghai Bank Association and Bill Legislation in the 1920s and 1930s." *Social Science Research*, no. 5 (2007): 169–174.

———. *A Study on the Institutional Changes of the Modern Chinese Bill Market*. Shanghai Far East Publishing House, 2014.

———. *Research on Shanghai Commercial Paper Exchange Company Ltd. (1933–1951)*. China Book Publishing House, 2019.

Wang, Guitang, and Yinghui Li. "From the Perspective of a Financial Institution's Bill Business, We Can See the Development Orientation of China's Bill Market." *Financial Theory and Practice*, no. 5 (2000): 11–15.

Wang, Hanqiang. *Commercial Credit and Commercial Bills of Exchange*. Beijing: China Finance and Economics Publishing House, 1986.

Wang, Hongman. *The Joint General Office of the Four Banks and the Economy of the Southwest Region During the War*. Fudan University Press, 2011.

Wang, Jijie. "Research on Several Issues of Feiqian in the Tang Dynasty." *Hubei Numismatics*, no. 14 (2015): 40–42.

Wang, Xiaoneng. *Tutorial on the Negotiable Instrument Law*. Beijing: Peking University Press, 2001.

Wang, Xu. "A Study on the Origin and Evolution of *Zhiji* as a Traditional Chinese Contract." *Journal of Liaoning University (Philosophy and Social Sciences Edition)* 43, no.5 (2015): 137–145.

Wang, Xugang. "Research on the Impact of Commercial Bill Information Disclosure on the Bill Market." *National Circulation Economy*, no. 25 (2021): 163–165.

Wang, Yaying. "The Internal Control Mechanism of Shanxi Bill Shops and Its Implications for Modern Enterprises." *Commercial Accounting*, no. 10 (2014): 98–100.

Wang, Yidian. *A Century's Journey of Rishengchang Bill Shop*. Taiyuan: Shanxi Economic Publishing House, 2013.

Wei, Xiaoxiao. "The Causes and Lessons of the Failure of Shanxi Bill Shops' Modernization Transformation." *Journal of Qiqihar University (Philosophy and Social Sciences Edition)*, no. 2 (2017): 98–100.

"Work Report of the Joint General Office of the Four Banks 1941." In *Compilation of Historical Archives of the Republic of China (Volume 5, Part 2, Finance and Economy 4)*, edited by the Second Historical Archives of China. Nanjing: Phoenix Publishing House, 2010.

Wu, Jiayu, and Xiaozheng Wang. "Analysis of the Background, Impact, and Measures of Shanghai Commercial Paper Exchange Company Ltd." *Journal of Hangzhou Financial Training Institute*, no. 2 (2017): 19–22.

Xiao, Xiaohe. "Ideas and Suggestions for Promoting the Development of Green Bills." *Contemporary Financiers*, no. 4 (2019): 93–95.

———. "Standardizing Bill Brokerage Behavior for the Bill Market's Development." *Shanghai Securities Journal*, November 25, 2016.

Xiao, Xiaohe, and Bei Yu. "On Accelerating the Establishment of a Nationwide Unified and Standardized Bill Information Platform." *Shanghai Securities Journal*, April 11, 2015.

Xiao, Xiaohe, and Jia Zi. "Exploration of the Development of Digital Bill." February 22, 2022. https://m.yicai.com/news/101324853.html.

Xiao, Xiaohe, and Rui Jin. "Actively Developing Green Bills and Striving to Serve the High-Quality Development of the Green Economy." *China Urban Finance*, no. 6 (2019): 53–56.

Xiao, Xiaohe, and Shen You. "New Thoughts on Developing Digital Bills." March 21, 2022. https://mp.weixin.qq.com/s/NxElWi5u0_6yQhbnzSqING.

Xu, Wentao, Xiaoqing Tang, and Wangshu Cheng. "The Development and Implementation of Standardized Bill Business." *Financial Accounting*, no. 9 (2020): 30–34.

Xiao, Xiaohe, and Ziwei Li. "Research on the Development Trends of China's Bill Market: A Historical Perspective." *Journal of Shanghai Lixin Institute of Accounting and Finance* 33, no. 1 (2021): 45–56.

———. "Review and Inspirations of China's Bill Market since the Founding of the CPC." *Credit Report* 39, no. 9 (2021): 7–17.

Xu, Cangshui and Zhongba Yao. *Suggestions on Research Regarding the Negotiable Instrument Law*. Shanghai: The Bankers Weekly, 1922.

Xue, Pingshuan. "On the Financial Industry of Chang'an, the Capital of the Tang Dynasty," in *Collection of Tang History Essays*, edited by Du Wenyu (Xi'an: Sanqin Publishing House, 2006), 296–321.

Yan, Hongzhong. *A History of Chinese Finance*. Shanghai University of Finance and Economics Press, 2020.

Yang, Jie, and Xiaoshan Cheng. "Shanxi Bill Shops: The Embryonic Form of China's Modern Financial Industry (III): The Business Operation of Shanxi Bill Shops." *Rural Credit Cooperative of China*, no. 2 (2015): 111–112.

Yang, Yinpu. *A Glimpse of Shanghai Financial Organizations*. Beijing: The Commercial Press, 1930.

———. *On China Finance*. Beijing: The Commercial Press, 1930.

———. *Yang Zhu's Theory on Chinese Finance*. Shanghai: Dawn Book Company, 1932.

Yao, Chengyang, Guanlin Huang, Wenxuan Qiu, Yunzhu Gu, and Yu Hong. "The Application of Blockchain Technology in the Industry Finance Internet Field: Taking Chinese Enterprise Cloud Chain as an Example." *Heilongjiang Science* 12, no. 12 (2021): 156–157.

Yao, Sui. *History of Chinese Finance*. Beijing: Higher Education Press, 2007.

Yu, Xuepeng. "Research on the Concentrated and Differentiated Competitive Strategy of Industrial Bank's Bill Business." Master's thesis, Fudan University, 2009.

Yuan, Yuanfu, and Mingyang Miao. *A Brief History of Chinese Finance*. Beijing: China Financial Publishing House, 2001.

Zhang, Du. "The Evolution of the Central Bank in the Past 20 Years." Collection of China's Second Historical Archives.

Zhang, Ge. "Research on Chongqing's Financial Market during the War of Resistance Against Japanese Aggression (1937–1945)." PhD diss., Southwest University, 2019.

Zhang, Guiping. "A Study on the Management System of Shanxi Bill Shop Operations." PhD diss., Capital Normal University, 2005.

———. *A Study on the Management System of Shanxi Bill Shop Operations*. Beijing: China Economic Publishing House, 2005.

Zhang, Guohui. *A Study on Late Qing Money Houses and Bill Shops*. Social Science Literature Publishing House, 1989.

Zhang, Junli. *History of Currency in the Revolutionary Base Areas of Eastern Zhejiang*. Ningbo: Ningbo Publishing House, 2002.

Zhang, Lizhou. *Bill Revolution*. Beijing: CITIC Publishing Group, 2019.

Zhang, Naiqi. "China's Bill Market." *Central Bank Monthly*, no. 1 (1936).

Zhang, Shufan. *History of Currency in Huainan Resistance Base Area*. Beijing: China Financial Publishing House, 2004.

Zhang, Xueying, and Zipei Zhang. "The Causes for the Decline of Shanxi Bill Shops." *Chinese and Foreign Entrepreneurs*, no. 14 (2015): 257.

Zhang, Yalan. "Why Shanxi Bill Shops Failed to Transform into Modern Banks: From the Perspective of Social Fault Development." *Journal of Taiyuan University (Social Sciences Edition)* 20, no. 5 (2019): 36–45.

Zhang, Yingxue, Yun Xiao, and Yongshen Jia. "It is necessary to promote the method of bill settlement." *Economic Work Communication*, no. 6 (1992).

Zhang, Zhuanfang. *History of Currency in the Shanxi-Hebei-Shandong-Henan Border Region (Volume 1): History of Currency in the Revolutionary Base Areas of Southeast Shanxi*. Beijing: China Financial Publishing House, 1996.

Zhao, Baofu. *Research on Bill Shop Credit and Brands*. Beijing: China Financial Publishing House, 2010.

Zhao, Xuejun. *The Development and Evolution of Commercial Credit in China*. Beijing: Fangzhi Publishing House, 2008.

Zheng, Chenglin. "From Bidirectional Bridges to Multilateral Networks: Shanghai Bank Association and Banking Industry (1918–1936)." PhD diss., Central China Normal University, 2003.

Zhejiang East Bank. "Bank Regulations." In *Selected Historical Materials on Currency in the Revolutionary Base Areas of China (Volume II)*, edited by the People's Bank of China Financial Research Institute and the Ministry of Finance Fiscal Science Research Institute. Beijing: Cultural Relics Publishing House, 1982.

Zhou, Weijun. "What Is a Standardized Bill? Product Analysis and Outlook Suggestions." *Financial Market Research*, no. 12 (2019): 101–108.

Zhu, Boquan. "Shanghai Commercial Paper Exchange Company Ltd." In *20th Century Shanghai Cultural and Historical Data Library (Volume 5)*, edited by Lu Jianxin and Wanyan Shaoyuan. Shanghai Bookstore Publishing House, 1999.

Zhu, Ruigen. "Feiqian in the Tang Dynasty." *China Numismatics*, no. 2 (1992): 78.

Zhu, Sihuang. *An Economic History of the Republic of China: The Bankers Weekly 30th Anniversary Commemorative Issue*. The Banking Society, Bankers Weekly, 1948.

Zhuo, Hanping. *A Brief History of Modern Chinese Monetary Banks*. Nanjing University Press, 1992.

Zuo, Zhifang, Chengtao Wang, and Jun Zhong. "Revision of the Negotiable Instrument Law: Logic and Suggestions." *Financial Horizons*, no. 11 (2015): 56.

Index

C

ABOUT THE EDITORS

Xiao Xiaohe is an economist and senior researcher with over 40 years of experience in China's financial and banking sectors. He served as Deputy General Manager of the Bill Dealing Center at the Industrial and Commercial Bank of China, founding President of the Bill Professional Committee at the Shanghai Financial Association, and Chief Expert at the Jiangxi Financial Association. Xiao is currently the Executive Dean and Chair of the Academic Committee at the Joint Institute for Commercial Paper of JUFE and BOJJ.

As a guest professor and mentor at multiple universities, Xiao pioneered courses on negotiable instruments and has guided over 40 graduate students. His expertise spans macroeconomics, financial markets, bill markets, and commercial bank management. Xiao has authored more than 200 research articles in prominent publications such as the *Financial Times and China Monetary Market* and has written or contributed to over 30 books. His recent works focus on foundational studies of bill markets and banking operations, earning him significant recognition in the field.

A trailblazer in financial reform, Xiao introduced centralized fund management practices in state-owned banks, laying the groundwork for domestic FTP management systems and influencing China's modern financial landscape.

Dr. Zhao Weizhe is a Research Fellow at the Jiuyin Bill Research Institute, Jiangxi University of Finance and Economics; a Special Research Fellow at the Supply Chain Finance Branch of the China Federation of Logistics & Purchasing; a Member of the Currency and Financial Instruments Committee of the Shanghai Lawyers Association; and a Senior Partner at Beijing Yingke (Shanghai) Law Firm. His work focuses on legal practice and theoretical research in the field of negotiable instruments, with extensive experience in their application within supply chains, inter-financial institution transfers, and the resolution of criminal and civil cases involving such instruments. He also conducts in-depth research on risk control measures for electronic commercial bills.